AMERICAN APOCRYPHA

ESSAYS ON THE BOOK OF MORMON

ESSAYS ON MORMONISM SERIES

Line Upon Line:
Essays on Mormon Doctrine
Gary James Bergera, ed.

The Word of God:
Essays on Mormon Scripture
Dan Vogel, ed.

The Wilderness of Faith:
Essays on Contemporary Mormon Thought
John Sillito, ed.

The New Mormon History:
Revisionist Essays on the Past
D. Michael Quinn, ed.

Faithful History:
Essays on Writing Mormon History
George D. Smith, ed.

The Search for Harmony:
Essays on Science and Mormonism
Gene A. Sessions and *Craig J. Oberg, eds.*

Multiply and Replenish:
Mormon Essays on Sex and Family
Brent Corcoran, ed.

Tending the Garden:
Essays on Mormon Literature
Eugene England and Lavina Fielding Anderson, eds.

The Prophet Puzzle:
Interpretive Essays on Joseph Smith
Bryan Waterman, ed.

Mormon Mavericks:
Essays on Dissenters
John Sillito and Susan Staker, eds.

AMERICAN APOCRYPHA

ESSAYS ON THE BOOK OF MORMON

Edited by

Dan Vogel and *Brent Lee Metcalfe*

Signature Books Salt Lake City

To Marge, for her love and support

Dan Vogel

For Tara, my sanctuary of hope and serenity
and for our children, my life mentors
Brenton, Courtney, Michala, Alisha, and Jen

in memory of
Fr. Raymond E. Brown and Rev. William Barclay
who opened exhilarating interpretive vistas

Brent Lee Metcalfe

COVER ILLUSTRATION: UNTITLED, BY JIM WARD MORRIS, 2002, COLLAGE ILLUSTRATION, 8" X 8"

COVER DESIGN: JULIE EASTON

∞*American Apocrypha: Essays on the Book of Mormon* was printed on acid-free paper and composed, printed, and bound in the United States of America.

www.signaturebooks.com

08 07 06 05 04 7 6 5 4 3 2

Library of Congress Cataloging-in-Publication Data
American Apocrypha : essays on the Book of Mormon / edited by Dan Vogel and Brent Lee Metcalfe.
p. cm.
Includes bibliographical references.
ISBN 1-56085-151-1 (pbk.)
1. Book of Mormon. 2. Smith, Joseph, 1805-1844.
I. Vogel, Dan II. Metcalfe, Brent Lee.

BX8627 .A64 2001
289.3'22–dc21

2001049512

CONTENTS

EDITORS' INTRODUCTION

IN 1833 JOSEPH SMITH WROTE TO ROCHESTER, NEW YORK, NEWS-paper editor N. C. Saxton that "[t]he Book of Mormon is a record of the forefathers of our western Tribes of Indians ... By it we learn that our western tribes of Indians are des[c]endants from that Joseph that was sold into Egypt, and that the land of America is a promised land unto them, and unto it all the tribes of Israel will come." When Saxton failed to print the letter in its entirety, Smith wrote to him again: "I was somewhat disappointed on receiving my paper with only a part of my letter inserted in it. The letter which I wrote you for publication I wrote by the commandment of God, and I am quite anxious to have it all laid before the public for it is of *importance* to them."[1]

Two years later, in conversation with an itinerant minister, Smith reconfirmed that the angel who revealed the gold plates to him "said the Indians were the *literal descendants* of Abraham."[2] Published revelations also repeatedly affirmed that Native Americans are Lamanites—Israelite descendants of Book of Mormon peoples.[3]

Had the Book of Mormon been what Joseph Smith said—not an allegory with spiritual import but a literal history of Hebrew immigrants to America—this should have been verified by now. Instead, the varied inhabitants and exotic locales in the Book of Mormon remain elusive; what some would term "Book of Mormon archaeology" is non-existent. The more we learn, the more inconceivable the Book of Mormon version of ancient America becomes. For instance, the deciphering of Mayan hieroglyphs has not produced the name of a Nephite or a Book of Mormon worldview. In the absence of confirming evidence, one should probably not be surprised to see that in recent years, apologists have redoubled their efforts to defend the book's historicity.

Once largely unorganized, defenders of Book of Mormon historicity rallied around the 1979 organization of the Foundation for Ancient Research and Mormon Studies (FARMS), now affiliated with Brigham Young University and sponsored by the LDS church. Despite FARMS's official status, an examination of its voluminous literary output discloses a clear willingness to utilize unorthodox approaches to defend orthodoxy. Their sometimes less-than-civil manner of responding to naysayers also suggests an undercurrent of insecurity, if not desperation.

In defending the Book of Mormon's antiquity, these neo-traditionalists found it necessary to revise the view that the book's Jaredite, Nephite, and Lamanite lands encompassed the entire western hemisphere and that all Native Americans descend from these peoples. When problems involving Book of Mormon distances and population growth were pointed out,[4] defenders of the book's antiquity hesitated to abandon long-standing assumptions about its geography—especially since they were supported by a straightforward reading of the text and by Joseph Smith's revelations—but eventually advanced a new, more localized geography. Instead of identifying the "small" or "narrow neck of land" with the Isthmus of Panama, the "land northward" with North America, and the "land southward" with South America as the traditional geography held, they began to assert that the book's events took place in the limited region of Mesoamerica (i.e., the area immediately surrounding the Isthmus of Tehuantepec in southern Mexico) and that most indigenous peoples do not descend from the Lamanites.[5]

Although unable himself to make the transition, Elder B. H. Roberts of the First Council of Seventy recognized the apologetic value of a limited geography. On 22 January 1921, at a meeting of a specially appointed "Book of Mormon Committee," he said that if it were possible to set aside one of Joseph Smith's uncanonized revelations designating the coast of Chile in South America as the place of Lehi's landing, "it would be easier to reply to adverse critics of the Book of Mormon." Otherwise, "[t]he enormous distances to travel present a serious difficulty."[6]

In reality, the Limited Tehuantepec Theory and those who champion it represent a last gasp of Book of Mormon apologetics. The theory is supported by pseudoscientific studies and specialized interpretations that cannot bear rigorous scrutiny. Still, the new apologists embrace their theory like an article of faith despite the violence it does to the Book of Mormon text, early Mormon history, Joseph Smith's divine edicts, and Mesoamerican archaeology.[7] Regardless, the Tehuantepec theory should be seen for what it is: an apologetic device. Specifically, it is an *ad hoc* hypothesis designed to shield a central hypothesis from adverse evidence—in this case, the Book of Mormon's historicity.[8] Rather than accept negative evidence, apologists often invent *ad hoc* hypotheses to protect and maintain a crumbling central hypothesis. This tactic violates what is called the principle of parsimony, or Occam's Razor, which posits that the best hypothesis is the simplest or the one that makes the fewest assumptions. Needless to say, the Book of Mormon's revisionist geographers ask that we make numerous unsupported assumptions. Because their theory does not fit comfortably with the many geographic and directional cues in the Book of Mormon, it requires elaborate explanations and additional *ad hoc* hypothesizing.

To highlight some of the problems of such an approach, let us consider some of the intricacies of the new theory. In what follows, we will illustrate the difficulty in matching the Book of Mormon to any specific time and place. This is not to address the book's interesting and impressive literary, theological, psychological, and spiritual qualities that have had such a profound impact on people. Is the Book of Mormon pseudonymous? We think so. Apocryphal? Yes. Is it therefore less able to touch people's hearts? No. Our position is that the scriptural tradition includes fiction—parables, poetry, hyperbole, psalms, historical verisimilitude, and other genres—and that such writing can be as powerful in providing people with spiritual guidance as non-fiction. To acknowledge the obvious fictional quality of the Book of Mormon is not to detract from the beauty and brilliance of the sermons, visions, and other imagery.

To weigh the new geography, one should look at the Isthmus of Tehuantepec and ask whether it could reasonably be called a "narrow" or "small neck of land," which the Book of Mormon describes as being "only the distance of a day and a half's journey for a Nephite" (Alma 22:32). BYU archaeologist Ross T. Christensen suggested that the isthmus must have grown wider since Nephite times, arguing that "the Coatzacoalcos and other rivers of this Isthmus must have unloaded enormous deposits of silt over the past 1,500 years."[9] Because there is no scientific support for this speculation, most new Book of Mormon geographers have since rejected it. Accepting Tehuantepec's present dimensions, BYU anthropologist John L. Sorenson proposed that its 120 miles of difficult terrain could be crossed in a day and a half by a good runner.[10] Yet, despite its identification as an isthmus, Tehuantepec as a cartographic feature is not even recognizable from the ground. It provides nothing of the bottleneck between the southern and northern lands that the Book of Mormon describes.

This has led to highly specialized and convoluted interpretations of several Book of Mormon passages. For instance, entrance into the "land northward" was made through a "narrow pass" or "passage" (Morm. 2:29; 3:5), a feature that was nothing more than the place where the "neck of land" connects the land northward with the land southward. This is indicated by two Book of Mormon passages. First, Alma 63:5 uses "narrow neck" as a synonym for "narrow passage" when it says that Hagoth launched his ship into the "west sea, by the narrow neck which led into the land northward." Second, Alma 50:34 describes the "narrow pass" much as Alma 22:32 describes the "small neck" as being flanked by east and west seas. Attempting to prevent the Lamanites from getting into the "land northward," Moroni's army met them "by the narrow pass which led by the sea into the land northward, yea, by the sea, on the west and on the east." Obviously, there is trouble in the fact that the Isthmus of Tehuantepec is neither a "narrow passage" leading through or between two nearby seas, nor is it militarily a strategic location.

Rather than seeing the "narrow pass" as simply the contact point between the northern and southern lands, John Sorenson speculates that it refers to a two-mile-wide, twenty-mile-long, east-to-west ridge of gravel in the northern section of the Isthmus of Tehuantepec that travelers in that region utilized to pass over swampy, sometimes flooded land. "At times during that [rainy] season," Sorenson argued, "the ridge would indeed lead 'by the sea, on the west and on the east' (Alma 50:34), for the water in the flooded basins would be on both sides of the ridge and would have barred travel as effectively as the sea."[11] To accept this interpretation, one must believe that the Nephites considered these marshlands or lagoons "seas." In addition, it is hard to imagine why the ridge would be strategic enough to head off the Lamanites in view of the wider, more accessible route frequented by traders along the southern coast. This situation led new geographer David Palmer to postulate two "narrow passes" on the "neck of land," one on the north and another on the south.[12]

An even more difficult problem facing new geographers is the orientation of the isthmus because the seas are not on the east and west but rather on the north and south. Sorenson and others therefore theorize, without support from the Book of Mormon, that the Nephite directional system was unique, being tilted "45 degrees or more" to the west, that Nephite north corresponded to present northwest.[13] Only by shifting the Mesoamerican map in this manner can they place the Gulf of Mexico and Pacific Ocean on the east and west of the isthmus. It seemingly escapes them that the primary directional cue for an assumed ancient American Jewish-temple culture would be, in a Mesoamerican setting, southeast towards the sun, whereas Sorenson's proposed shift is to the northeast away from the sun.[14]

Aside from distance problems, traditional geography fits the Book of Mormon's description with far less struggle, manipulation, and assumptions. Early Mormons, like many of their contemporaries, viewed Panama as just one portion of a longer neck which ran from southern Mexico to South America—in other words, the Isthmus of Tehuantepec to the Isthmus of Panama and everything in between. This is what the editor of the church's *Times and Seasons* meant when he wrote in 1842 that the Nephites "lived about the narrow neck of land, which now embraces Central America."[15] A straightforward reading of Alma 22:32 fits well with the thirty-mile-wide Isthmus of Panama. In fact, this key geographical passage tells of a boundary "line" on the southernmost portion of the isthmus running "from the east to the west sea." Sorenson accepts that this "line" runs from sea to sea and thinks that Tehuantepec's 120 miles of rough terrain could be crossed in a day and a half by a good runner. Others have suggested different solutions.

Paul M. Hanson of the Reorganized LDS church, for instance, attempted to defend the Tehuantepec designation by arguing that the line in Alma 22:32 does not seem to stretch completely across the isthmus, observing that "the text does not state that the 'line' extended from the east *sea* to the west sea, but 'from the east to the west sea.'"[16] Although this is true, the context seems to imply that the line traverses the entire "neck of land."

Alma 22:32 adds that the "land southward" ("the land of Nephi and the land of Zarahemla") would be entirely surrounded by water if not for the "small neck of land" which took a Nephite a day and a half to cross. Put simply, the "line" dividing the lands of Bountiful and Desolation must cut completely across the neck, leaving the southern landmass isolated, "nearly surrounded by water." Consequently, the Nephite occupation of "the land of Bountiful, even from the east unto the west sea ... had *hemmed in* the Lamanites on the south," blockading the sole access route to the land northward (Alma 22: 33[-34], emphasis added). The new geography's land southward is not surrounded by water except where it connects with Tehuantepec.[17] Neither can the new geography draw an east-to-west boundary line without tilting the map.

On the other hand, even within Hanson's strict interpretation, an east-to-west line can be drawn completely across the Isthmus of Panama that touches the "west sea" but not the "east sea." Seventeenth-century traveler Lionel Wafer, when describing the southern region of Panama, drew such a line as Alma 22:32 suggests, stating: "I should draw a Line also from ... the South part of the Gulf of St. Michael, directly East, to the nearest part of the great River Darien."[18] The River of Darien mentioned by Wafer is today's Gulfo de Uraba, situated on the east side of the Isthmus of Panama, which allows one to draw an east-to-west line across the isthmus at precisely the location described by Mormon. Thus, traditional geography best fulfills the requirements of Alma 22:32.

The origin of the Book of Mormon's geography is apparent to anyone familiar with the mound builder myth current in Joseph Smith's day. According to this once-popular view, the monuments of North, Central, and South America were constructed by a single race of white-skinned, Christian agriculturalists who were eventually destroyed by the ancestors of the current American Indians in the Great Lakes Region.[19] No wonder the Book of Mormon was immediately seen as a history of the mound builders by Mormon missionary and convert alike. Unitarian Jason Whitman, for example, reported in 1834 that the Mormons "suppose the mounds throughout the western states, which have heretofore excited so much curiosity, are the remains of the cities of the Nephites and Lamanites."[20] The Book of Mormon not only tapped into the mound builder myth for its history but also for its prophetic message (see Ether 2:10). Should Smith's contemporaries fail to repent, the Book of Mormon declared, God would unleash the Indians on them.[21] With a burial mound in nearly every corn field, or so it appeared, the Book of Mormon's jeremiad seemed more than plausible to many in Jacksonian America.

Long distances and rapid population growth are not the only problems the new apologists have to address. Historical anachronisms are plentiful. For instance, such things as steel, horses, and wheat were first imported to the Americas by the Spaniards.[22] Apologists counter with *ad hoc* hypotheses: steel is actually iron; horses are deer; wheat is amaranth; goats are brockets; cows are deer, brockets, camelidae, or bison; and tents are makeshift huts. In short, things are not what they appear. Never mind that Mesoamerica had no metallurgy to speak of until after Book of Mormon times, that the Nephites used the horse to pull chariots in battle and over long distances, or that tents are described as being "pitched," portable, and reusable.[23] Only with increasing difficulty do apologists accept the Book of Mormon at face value.

Again, the nature of faith is not what is at question here, but rather the structure of reason and theory. Some people would like to erect a closed system that admits only "positive" evidence. If apologists had their way, there would be no means to refute their theory and hence no method by which to fairly evaluate the Book of Mormon's historical claims. However, this brief discussion already points to the danger in that. Embraced by the vast majority of Latter-day Saints since 1830, the hemispheric geography emerged from an astute—albeit pre-critical—reading of the Book of Mormon text, buttressed by Joseph Smith's revelations. The hemispheric reach of the Book of Mormon may be embarrassing to revisionist Book of Mormon geographers, but the fact remains that it made perfect sense to those steeped in the mound builder myth.

The essays in this collection question apologetic views of Book of Mormon historicity or respond to its proponents. While it is impossible to answer every argument and issue, our contributors cut a deep and wide furrow through this ever-growing apologetic. Edwin Firmage, Jr., provides several reasons why the Book of Mormon is not ancient. He finds, for instance, that ideas develop in the order of Joseph

Smith's dictation of the book instead of in historical sequence, as one might otherwise expect.

For those who consider the Book of Mormon to be unique because of the supernatural manner in which it was dictated, Scott C. Dunn's essay stands as a caution. He provides examples of what is known as "automatic writing," the alleged supernatural means by which some of the canons of modern literature, as well as other religious texts, were produced. One might ask upon what grounds we accept the Book of Mormon and reject similar productions?

Surveying the on-going research in population genetics, Thomas W. Murphy challenges the long-held belief about Native Americans being of Jewish descent. Evidence gathered thus far confirms what scientists have long suspected: the vast majority of Amerindians are of Asiatic origin. The fact that not even a lingering Hebrew genetic marker has been found among Native Americans has lead to some wild *ad hoc* hypothesizing, some of which Murphy reviews.

In the first of two essays, Dan Vogel explores the experiences of the Book of Mormon witnesses, finding that they saw the plates only in vision and never actually handled them. In a second essay, he reviews and responds to those who deny that Book of Mormon bands of "secret combinations" were inspired by early-nineteenth-century anti-Masonic rhetoric.

George D. Smith discusses Mormon general authority B. H. Roberts's mixed response to Book of Mormon problems. In two works, both unpublished during his lifetime, Roberts outlined the internal and external difficulties surrounding the Book of Mormon's historical claims. The general authority was unable to resolve many of these issues himself, and some of them continue to occupy Book of Mormon scholars.

David P. Wright examines the Isaiah passages in the Book of Mormon to show their modern rather than ancient source, which is the King James version of the Bible. Responding to those who would like to explain away the errors in these passages, Wright demonstrates that the variants in the Book of Mormon are in fact responses to the 1611 English text and are often disruptive to the underlying Hebrew.

Susan Staker traces the development of the seer's role in the Book of Mormon and related revelations and notes its similarity to Joseph Smith's own evolving self-image.

Finally, Robert M. Price explores Joseph Smith's motives and methods in composing the Book of Mormon, comparing Joseph Smith to the pseudepigraphists. Price is particularly interested in Smith's method of using well-known Bible stories and texts to create new scripture. He concludes that Smith–like the pseudepigraphists–was trying to give to new ideas the authority of the old prophets and to rewrite the past in order to give meaning to the present.

Versions of Edwin Firmage Jr.'s and Scott C. Dunn's essays appeared previously in *Sunstone* magazine (see Firmage, "Historical Criticism and the Book of Mormon: A Personal Encounter," *Sunstone* 16 [July 1993]: 58-64; Dunn, "Spirit Writing: Another Look at the Book of Mormon," *Sunstone* 10 [June 1985]: 17-26); a version of Thomas W. Murphy's essay previously appeared on *Mormon Scripture Studies: An E-Journal of Critical Thought* (*http://mormonscripturestudies.com*). The remaining articles are published here for the first time.

NOTES

1. Joseph Smith to N. C. Saxton, 4 Jan., 12 Feb. 1833, in Dean C. Jessee, comp. and ed., *The Personal Writings of Joseph Smith* (Salt Lake City: Deseret Book, 1984), 273, 275. For more on the claimed Israelite origin of Native Americans, see Kenneth W. Godfrey, "Joseph Smith, the Hill Cumorah, and Book of Mormon Geography: A Historical Study, 1823-1844," delivered at the 1989 Mormon History Association Meeting; Brent Lee Metcalfe, "A Documentary Analysis of the Zelph Episode," delivered at the 1989 Sunstone Symposium; Brent Lee Metcalfe, "Disinterring Zelph," *Mormon Scripture Studies: An E-Journal of Critical Thought* (*http://mormonscripturestudies.com*).

2. Joseph Smith, journal, 9 Nov. 1835, emphasis added. See Scott H. Faulring, ed., *An American Prophet's Record: The Diaries and Journals of Joseph Smith* (Salt Lake City: Signature Books and Smith Research Associates, 1987), 51; Dean C. Jessee, ed., *The Papers of Joseph Smith* (Salt Lake City: Deseret Book, 1989-), 2:70; Dan Vogel, ed., *Early Mormon Documents* (Salt Lake City: Signature Books, 1996-), 1:44.

3. Doctrine and Covenants 28:8-9, 14; 30:6; 32:2; 3:18-20; 10:48; 19:27; 49:24; 54:8; 57:4; 109:65-66.

4. Among the first publications to do so was M. T. Lamb, *Book of Mormon: Is It from God?* (Salt Lake City: Salt Lake Herald, 1885).

5. For a discussion of the history and development of the Limited Tehuantepec Theory, see John L. Sorenson, *The Geography of Book of Mormon Events* (Provo, UT: FARMS, 1992), 7-206. The best presentation of the

Limited Tehuantepec Theory to date is John L. Sorenson, *An Ancient American Setting for the Book of Mormon* (Salt Lake City: Deseret Book; and Provo, UT: FARMS, 1985).

6. Janne M. Sjodahl, diary, archives, Historical Department, Church of Jesus Christ of Latter-day Saints, Salt Lake City, Utah. See also B. H. Roberts, *New Witnesses for God,* 3 vols. (Salt Lake City: Deseret News, 1909), 3:503. For more on Chile as the place where Lehi and his entourage disembarked, see Dan Vogel, "Lehi's Chilean Landing: Early Sources and Lingering Traditions," *Mormon Scripture Studies: An E-Journal of Critical Thought* (*http://mormonscriputrestudies.com/bomor/dv/lehitrav.asp*).

7. For a critique of the new theory, see Deanne G. Matheny, "Does the Shoe Fit? A Critique of the Limited Tehuantepec Geography," in *New Approaches to the Book of Mormon: Explorations in Critical Methodology,* ed. Brent Lee Metcalfe (Salt Lake City: Signature Books, 1993), 269-328. See also Glenna Nielsen, "The Material Culture of the Book of Mormon," delivered as the May 1992 Sunstone Book of Mormon Lecture; Hampton Sides, "This Is Not the Place," *DoubleTake* 5 (Spring 1999): 46-55. For an incomplete and evasive response to Matheny, see John L. Sorenson's review in *Review of Books on the Book of Mormon* 6 (1994): 297-361.

8. A hypothesis is considered *ad hoc* in a fallacious sense when it "accounts only for the particular fact or facts it was invented to explain and has no other explanatory power, that is, no other testable consequences" (Irving M. Copi and Keith Burgess-Jackson, *Informal Logic* [Upper Saddle River, NJ: Prentice Hall, 1996], 264). Unlike other auxiliary hypotheses that support or validate a central theory, an *ad hoc* hypothesis serves to explain away problems with the larger theory. For example, when it was discovered that many people do not fit the predicted patterns of biorhythm theory, advocates concocted a new category of people: the arhythmic. Similarly, when water dowsers fail to locate water in controlled experiments, they often blame their lack of success on psychic interference, including negative vibrations from skeptical researchers. The late-seventeenth-century phlogiston theory of heat is another such hypothesis, as are any of a number of since-disproven "scientific" theories. See entry for "*ad hoc* hypothesis" in Robert Todd Carroll, *The Skeptic's Dictionary* (*http://skepdic.com/adhoc.html*); Theodore Schick Jr. and Lewis Vaughn, *How to Think about Weird Things: Critical Thinking for a New Age,* 2nd ed. (Mountain View, CA: Mayfield Publishing Co., 1999), 155-165.

9. *University Archaeological Society Newsletter,* No. 67 (7 July 1960): 3.

10. Sorenson, *An Ancient American Setting,* 17.

11. Ibid., 43.

12. See David A. Palmer, *In Search of Cumorah: New Evidences for the Book of Mormon from Ancient Mexico* (Bountiful, UT: Horizon Publishers, 1981), 31-34.

13. Sorenson, *An Ancient American Setting,* 39-42; and Palmer, *In Search of Cumorah,* 34-36. See also Sorenson's review of Matheny, *Review of Books,* 305-314; Sorenson, *The Geography of Book of Mormon Events,* 401-415.

14. Sorenson's misuse of Hebrew orientation has been criticized by colleague John A. Tvedtnes who has urged that the new geographers discard their weak theory of orientation and "begin a search for a more reasonable explanation for the Book of Mormon description of the narrow neck of land and the placement of the seas" (*Newsletter and Proceedings of the Society for Early Historic Archaeology,* No. 149 [1982]: 9). Brevard S. Childs, professor of Old Testament at Yale's divinity school and author of the article on "Orientation" in *The Interpreter's Dictionary of the Bible* ([Nashville, 1962], 3:608) told Dan Vogel some years ago that Sorenson's theory about directional points in ancient America was "wild" and "without foundation" (personal communication).

15. *Times and Seasons* 3 (15 Sept. 1842): 915.

16. Paul M. Hanson, "Book of Mormon," *Saints' Herald* (8 Jan. 1951).

17. Sorenson, *An Ancient American Setting,* 6.

18. Lionel Wafer, *A New Voyage and Description of the Isthmus of America* (London, 1699), 70. Our citation of Wafer is illustrative only; we are not suggesting that Smith read Wafer.

19. See Dan Vogel, *Indian Origins and the Book of Mormon: Religious Solutions from Columbus to Joseph Smith* (Salt Lake City: Signature Books, 1986).

20. Jason Whitman, "The Book of Mormon," *Unitarian* (Boston; 1 Jan. 1834): 43, cited in Vogel, *Indian Origins,* 32.

21. 3 Ne. 16:14-15; 20:15-20; 21:11-13; Morm. 5:20-24. See also Doctrine and Covenants 87:5; 109:65-66.

22. See Book of Mormon references to steel: 2 Ne. 5:15; Jarom 1:8; Ether 7:9; horses: 1 Ne. 18:25; Enos 1:21; Alma 18:9-12; 20:6; 3 Ne. 3:22; 4:4; 6:1; Ether 9:19; and wheat: Mosiah 9:9.

23. For references to horse-drawn chariots, see Alma 18:9-12; 20:6; 3 Ne. 3:22; and for portable tents, see: 1 Ne. 18:23; 2 Ne. 5:7; Enos 1:20; Mosiah 2:5-6; 7:5; 9:4; 18:34; 22:2; 23:5; 24:20; Alma 2:20, 26; 22:28; 27:25; 46:31; 47:9; 51:32, 34; 52:1; 58:13, 17, 25; 62:18; Hel. 3:9; Morm. 6:4; Ether 9:3; 14:28; 15:8-11.

1.

Historical Criticism and the Book of Mormon: A Personal Encounter

Edwin Firmage, Jr.

NEARLY TWENTY YEARS AGO, AS A FIRST-YEAR GRADUATE STUDENT AT the University of California, Berkeley, my ambition was to become another Hugh Nibley, whose writings I had loved since I was twelve. As a young admirer, I did not understand everything I read. On my first encounter, I was not quite sure, for example, what the difference was between Sethe and Seth; it was all German to me. But Nibley was my mystagogue. Through him, I had my first vision of a strange and exciting antiquity. Even now, despite a very different scholarly outlook, I cannot help but admire him; he remains to my mind the most original thinker and social critic Mormonism has known. Still a neophyte, but armed with German and a little Arabic, Greek, and Hebrew, and intent on acquiring the requisite apologetic tools, I came to Berkeley to study ancient Near Eastern languages, particularly Egyptian, the language of mysteries par excellence.

Not long after my arrival, I was asked to teach the Book of Mormon in the Gospel Doctrine class in my Berkeley ward. I welcomed the opportunity, as it would give me a chance to delve deeper into the book. By any standard, my wife and I were faithful Mormons who attended church, visited the temple, and prayed together. I expected my study of the Book of Mormon to result in an increase of faith as it had on my mission. But within six months, I no longer believed the Book of Mormon to be an ancient text.

To this day, I am not sure how it happened, although I can isolate several issues that played a role in my change of mind. Still, none of them individually should have been sufficient to have caused such a turn of mind. Indeed, even taken together, they seem inadequate to the task of breaking down the wall of faith. I have often thought that what happened to me in Berkeley was fundamentally a conversion or, if you like, an anti-conversion. The process had all of the inscrutable suddenness that characterized some of the conversions I had witnessed as a missionary. Like a conversion to faith, the effects of my change of mind propagated with amazing speed. Almost overnight my whole outlook on life was different. The particular problems that I encountered as I re-read the Book of Mormon were catalysts, not the active agents of my reform. Something else far more powerful was ultimately the force behind the conversion. I do not know why that something had the effect it did any more than I know why missionary-guided conversions seem, on occasion, to radically alter newcomers to the faith. One thing is certain: it was a close reading of the Book of Mormon that provoked this change. How ironic, I thought, that after doing precisely what Elder Ezra Taft Benson had been admonishing us to do—study the Book of Mormon—I now found myself regarding it as a work of historical fiction.

My study began to take a different direction since I had given up on the Book of Mormon's historicity. How was I now to explain it? Thus began an intensive period of thoughtful study. It culminated in a hastily written document on Book of Mormon origins which I completed in the summer of 1984. Producing this document was an exercise in catharsis; for a time I did little else. Once it was done, I felt little inclination to return to the Book of Mormon as an object of serious study. Perhaps coincidentally, my interest in Egyptian also waned. But my interest in ancient history, if anything, increased. More and more I was drawn into the world of ancient Israel and particularly to its cult. I was now free to enter into biblical study without feeling as though I had to perform mental gymnastics to make the Bible conform to a Mormon world view. Once again I was fortunate to have a guide. But this time the guide was not a mystagogue but a rabbi and teacher. For the next three years, under Jacob Milgrom, I read the book of Leviticus, and in good Jewish tradition, our study was painstaking, methodical, down-to-earth, and always rooted in the text. By the end of my third year, our graduate seminar in biblical Hebrew had covered, I think, eight chapters in all. After years of looking at Nibley's big picture, I could now see its finer details.

The remaining pages of this essay will present a few of what, for me in 1984, were discoveries of some importance. These do not by any means constitute a comprehensive explanation of the Book of Mormon. Nor are they offered as proofs of my thesis that the book is modern, but as examples of how the assumption that it is modern resolves otherwise significant difficulties.

THE EGYPTIAN CONNECTION

Like many pseudepigraphic works before it, the Book of Mormon announces itself as a translation from an ancient source that was miraculously preserved by divine providence. In this respect, it is not particularly noteworthy. It is, however, rather less like its apocryphal congeners in that it also lays claim to an Egyptian genealogy—a genealogy that has attracted authors of sapiential, magical, and alchemical works since Greco-Roman times but which seems out of place in a work of Christian apologetics. One might be inclined to seek an explanation of the book's syncretic blend of Judaism and Egyptian genealogy in Joseph Smith's involvement in popular magic, but its Egyptian connection has a simpler explanation.

Nephi, the first and most important of the putative writers whose compositions make up the Book of Mormon, tells us that his work was written "in the language of my father, which consists of the learning of the Jews and the language of the Egyptians" (1 Ne. 1:2).[1] The plain sense of this statement is that the Book of Mormon was written in Egyptian while its theology derived from Judaism.[2] That Lehi's family read and wrote Egyptian is also evident in the fact that the "plates of brass," which had been kept by Lehi's kin, are also said to have been written in Egyptian (Mos. 1:4). Lehi is at pains to preserve this linguistic heritage (and anyone who has ever had to learn Egyptian can sympathize). Soon after leaving Jerusalem, Lehi asks his sons to return and get the plates of brass from Laban "to preserve unto our children *the language of our fathers*; and also that we may preserve unto them the words which have been spoken by the mouth of all the holy prophets

... since the world began, even down unto this present time" (1 Ne. 3:19; emphasis added). Both the brass plates and the Book of Mormon were written, according to Lehi, in the Egyptian language and not just Egyptian characters.

Despite Hugh Nibley's efforts to make this extraordinary notion palatable, it is wildly improbable. Is one seriously to believe that for several generations Lehi's family was at home in the Egyptian language? Moreover, are we to believe that centuries before the Old Testament was translated into Greek (Septuagint), Lehi's kin had privately sponsored the translation of the entire Hebrew canon into Egyptian? This, of course, presupposes that a sacred canon of scripture existed in the sixth century CE, which few biblical scholars believe. Nevertheless, besides Nibley, no serious historian of the ancient Near East would credit the idea that a Jewish family had gone to the trouble and expense of translating or having others translate the canon into Egyptian and of engraving this enormous translation on brass plates.

How, then, is one to explain the Book of Mormon's Egyptian connection? The answer lies in an incident in the early history of the translation. In February 1828 Joseph Smith had permitted Martin Harris, his scribe, to take a transcription of some characters and their "translation" to have their accuracy verified. Harris chose to take the transcription to Professor Charles Anthon, a noted classicist at Columbia University. In Smith's 1838 history, the professor is reported to have identified the characters as "Egyptian, Chaldaic, Assyriac, and Arabic" (JS-H 2:64).[3] According to this account, Anthon also certified the correctness of the translation. While we may well doubt this latter claim, Anthon may have ventured to identify the nature of the characters.[4] The Book of Mormon itself, in an interesting case of prophecy after the fact, suggests that Anthon ventured no translation (2 Ne. 27:9-20). Harris, perhaps willfully, seems to have taken Anthon's remarks on the transcription as a vindication of Smith's translation. In any event, what Anthon may have said off-the-cuff, Harris took as gospel truth. A leading scholar had identified these characters as Egyptian, and therefore, that is what they had to be. Smith, though he probably knew better, undoubtedly found this identification useful. Perhaps already wondering what he should call his Book of Mormon language, he now had a credible response for the curious. Henceforth, if anyone should ask what language the Book of Mormon had been translated from, Smith could say Egyptian and could cite Anthon's expert testimony to that effect. Indeed, he could parry all such questions by having the Book of Mormon itself proclaim its Egyptian origin. It is no accident that at each of the two beginning points in the translation (1 Nephi and Mosiah, explained later), the Book of Mormon advertises itself as a translation from Egyptian. The Egyptian connection, born in an off-hand remark by Charles Anthon, thus proves to be explainable by reference to Smith's experience as author.

The Egyptian connection is of course incidental to the basic story of the Book of Mormon, which Joseph Smith already knew by the time Harris visited Anthon. Still, it has important implications for our assessment of the authenticity of the book and also for our understanding of what was involved in Smith's "translation." At the very least, the Egyptian angle illustrates that the translation was susceptible to suggestion, even of the most extravagant kind. More importantly, it indicates that Book of Mormon problems can reasonably be explained by reference to Joseph Smith's own experience.

PROPHECY AND THE ORDER OF TRANSLATION

The Book of Mormon is a collection of three distinct compositions: the so-called "small plates" of Nephi (1 Nephi-Words of Mormon), Mormon's abridged history of the Nephites (Mosiah-Mormon), and the history of the Jaredites (Ether). It is from the second of these that the Book of Mormon gets its name. Mormon, we are told, chose to include Nephi's record with his abridgment in order to preserve Nephi's extensive prophecies about the coming of Christ (Words of Mormon 4). In 1 Nephi 11ff., for example, Nephi foretells Jesus' birth to a virgin in Nazareth, his miracles, the appearance of John the Baptist, Jesus' baptism, and Jesus' death. Nephi reveals that the Messiah's name will be Jesus Christ (2 Ne. 25:19), that he will be crucified and rise after three days (v. 13). He predicts the natural disasters preceding the coming of the resurrected Christ to America, as described in 3 Nephi. He sees Jesus' visit to the survivors of the cataclysms in America and to the twelve new-world apostles whom Jesus selects (1 Ne. 12; 2 Ne. 26). These last prophecies are of special importance. There could be no doubt for anyone who read Nephi's record that the resurrected Jesus would appear in America.

It is therefore surprising that in the early part of Mormon's abridged history, prophecies about the coming of Jesus say nothing about the latter's coming to America (see Mos. 3:5ff.; 7:27; 15; Al. 4:13; 5:50; 6:8; 7:7ff.). Not until Alma 16:20 is it clearly stated that Christ would appear there. "Many of the people did inquire concerning the place where the Son of God should come; and they were taught that he would appear *unto them* after his resurrection" (italics mine).[5] The people's uncertainty, shared significantly by Alma himself (7:8), implies that nothing was known about Christ's promise to visit America, as described in such detail by Nephi. The discrepancy between the prophetic material in 1-2 Nephi and that in Mosiah-Alma 16 calls for explanation.

As in the case of the Egyptian connection, the explanation is found in the story of how the Book of Mormon was translated. In June 1828 some 116 pages of translation, virtually everything that had been completed up to that point, mysteriously disappeared after being lent to Martin Harris. For some time thereafter, Joseph Smith was forbidden to translate, and though perfunctory efforts began again in the autumn, nothing substantial was produced until the arrival of Oliver Cowdery in April 1829. When translation began again in earnest, instead of re-doing what had been lost, Smith continued from the point where the 1828 translation had stopped—with Mosiah—and then translated 1 Nephi to Words of Mormon last of all. This reconstruction of the order of translation is confirmed by the handwriting analysis carried out by Dean Jessee.[6] Jessee tentatively identified the handwriting of John Whitmer and of an additional unknown scribe in the first fifteen chapters of 1 Nephi where, had Smith and his scribe at the time (Oliver Cowdery) begun there, we should have expected to find Cowdery's handwriting. However, we know that towards the end of the translation in June 1829, John Whitmer briefly acted as scribe. Mosiah and Alma, then, antedate 1-2 Nephi in order of dictation.

With this in mind, it is not difficult to explain why prophecies of Jesus in Mosiah and Alma 1-16 evidence no awareness of Nephi's prophecies of Jesus' American ministry. The explanation is simply that during the initial stages of the new 1829 translation (Mosiah to Alma 16), Joseph Smith himself had not yet conceived the notion of Christ's visit to America. The ignorance of Nephi's prophecies manifested by the characters in Mosiah and Alma 1-16 reflects the fact that

Smith, the creator-translator, did not yet himself know the turn his narrative was to take. Nephi's unambiguous prophecies reflect the fact that they were translated, or as I would now prefer to say, composed, after the events they claimed to foretell.

This is not the only instance where the order of translation affected the content. One striking aspect of 1 and 2 Nephi is the relative dearth of prophecies relating to the immediate history of the Nephites and Lamanites. Thus, for example, 1 and 2 Nephi predict the European discovery of America, the persecution of the American Indians, the translation of the Book of Mormon itself, the loss of the 116 pages, the Charles Anthon incident, and the three witnesses of the divinity of the Book of Mormon. From the perspective of subject matter, therefore, 1 and 2 Nephi continue the narrative left off in Mormon. The disproportionate attention these books bestow on prophecy, and especially on prophecy relating to modern events, contrasts with their disinterest in more immediate issues and suggests that the purpose of 1 and 2 Nephi was to outline God's continuing influence in American history after the close of the Book of Mormon era. In other words, having finished the story of the Book of Mormon as he had originally conceived it, Smith decided to address topics of subsequent modern history when he faced the gap left in the book by the loss of the 116 pages. The resulting text was necessarily prophetic rather than historical in nature.

LDS readers who have noticed the two different genres that characterize 1 Nephi-Words of Mormon and Mosiah-Ether will perhaps observe that one need not resort to historical criticism to explain the difference; the Book of Mormon itself tells us that the so-called "small plates" of Nephi were deliberately written to preserve prophetic rather than historical detail (cf. 1 Ne. 9:1ff.). But this only indicates that the early Book of Mormon's turn to prophecy was intentional. The existence of a separate set of plates devoted to matters prophetic is, I think, demonstrably a fictional explanation of how new source material turned up to replace the lost 116 pages and why this new material focused on prophecy at the expense of history. The Book of Mormon itself provides the strongest reason for regarding the small plates as a fiction: nowhere in Mosiah to Mormon is reference ever made to a separate set of small plates. What the record keepers pass from generation to generation is called simply the plates of Nephi without ever a hint of a separate prophetic collection. There is a single set of plates called the plates of Nephi which is maintained to the end of Book of Mormon history (e.g., Mos. 28:11, 20; Al. 37:2; 44:24; 3 Ne. 5:10; 26:11; 4 Ne. 19, 21; Morm. 1:4; 2:17,18) and which is valued for its sacred as well as historical content (Mos. 1:2 with vv. 6-7; Al. 37:2; 3 Ne. 26:7,11).

Another reason for regarding the existence of the small plates as literary fiction is the peculiar way in which they are linked via the Words of Mormon to the rest of the Book of Mormon. The most striking thing about the Words of Mormon is that it is supposed to be Mormon's *last* words: "And now I, Mormon, being about to deliver up the record which I have been making into the hands of my son Moroni ... wherefore, I chose these things to finish my record upon them. ... And now I, Mormon, proceed to finish out my record ..." (1, 5, 9). What, then, is this editorial intrusion doing in the middle of the Book of Mormon? If, indeed, the Words of Mormon is a valedictory, then it belongs at the end of Mormon's abridgment and not in the plates of Nephi. If, as Mormon says, his own abridgement had already been completed, what need was there for these transitional verses since they link not his abridgment of Lehi's record but Nephi's self-contained account to the beginning of Mosiah? In my opinion, there seems little choice but to accept the "Words of Mormon" as Smith's attempt to knit two parts of his translation together while explaining how he providentially happened to have something like a duplicate of the lost portion.

Joseph Smith's sensitivity to the problems connected with the lost pages is apparent in the preface to the 1830 (first) edition, which explains that he has substituted Nephi's record for the lost material and implicitly therefore that no one should expect the translations to match exactly. He thus protects himself from the charge of fraud should the two translations ever be compared. (This fear is made explicit in Doctrine and Covenants 10:10ff.) Despite this caveat, one is entitled to suspect its motive. If Smith were ever confronted with the lost material and it failed to match up with the new translation, he could simply assert that it had been altered. Does he save face any better by coming up with an altogether different production? Is he not just as vulnerable to a charge of fraud on this account–that is, that he has deliberately avoided this test of his prophetic ability by translating a different work? It would be more logical for Smith's critics to have left the manuscript untouched in order to see just how well he would do. These questions in themselves do not constitute an indictment, but it nevertheless seems only fair to admit that Smith's reticence to retranslate is suspicious. It appears to me, at least, as if he feared he could not.

So, 1 Nephi-Words of Mormon proves to be an epilogue to the Book of Mormon proper not only in terms of order of composition but also in terms of subject matter. It is implicitly recognized as such by the fact that a new set of records had to be created to explain its appearance.

Much more could be said about the effect of the order of translation on the development of the Book of Mormon narrative, but I will limit myself to just one last example. The key to this case is the fact that nowhere in the Book of Mormon's many detailed prophecies of the last days is anything ever said about the establishment of a new church. The nature of God's work subsequent to the appearance of the Book of Mormon is very vague, particularly so after the detailed prophecies pertaining to Smith's involvement in the translation.[7]

Not surprisingly then, while Nephi foresees the rise of a "great and abominable" church following the apostolic era, he says nothing of the Apostasy as Mormons understand that term today–that is, the utter elimination of the legitimate church of God. By the same token, nothing is said of the Restoration, as understood by Latter-day Saints today. The Book of Mormon portrays cases of apostasy and restorations in every era, but these are localized events. Joseph Smith, as he portrays himself in the Book of Mormon, is not the prophet of the Restoration but the translator of the Book of Mormon. He is a seer rather than the first elder. Smith's calling, as described in the Book of Mormon, is connected solely with the Book of Mormon. He will be a "Moses" (2 Ne. 3:6ff) in that his book will play an important role in the gathering of Israel. The powers promised to Smith are those necessary for the book's production (v. 11). Smith, in fact, used a seer stone during parts of the translation, thus the term seer. He is promised "judgment in writing" (v. 17). The "great and marvelous work and a wonder" (2 Ne. 27:26) to come about in the last days is the Book of Mormon–nothing more or less. The phrase has this same meaning in the early sections of the Doctrine and Covenants that preceded publication of the Book of Mormon (D&C 4:1; 6:1; 11:1; 12:1; 14:1). After that, and still almost a year before the church is founded, references to a "marvelous work" cease.

Accordingly, it appeared that concrete plans to found a church occurred either after the translation of the Book of Mormon or during its last stages when the incorporation of additional prophecies may have proved too difficult. Perhaps the thought surfaced during Smith's intense involvement in prophesying of his own role in the Lord's latter-day work. While one has to use arguments from silence with caution, the unusual detail of Book of Mormon prophecies concerning Smith's life, foretelling as they do his name (2 Ne. 3:15) as well as every major event in the coming forth of the Book of Mormon, is the surest reason for regarding the silence as significant. On reflection, the silence makes sense. Little if anything in Smith's experience up to 1829 would have led him to think about founding a church. One looks in vain, for example, in his 1832 and 1835 diaries for evidence that his first vision or interviews with Moroni led him to anticipate a subsequent role as a church leader. The same is true even of Smith's 1838 manuscript history.

Given the Book of Mormon's silence on the possibility of a new church, how can one explain what I like to call the handbook of church government found in Moroni 1-6 and 8? These chapters are the epitome of church government that tell how one is initiated as a member, how the eucharist is administered, who governs the church, etc.–all basic issues of church administration conveniently gathered together as if to instruct would-be church builders. If, as suggested by the manuscript evidence, 1 and 2 Nephi were composed after the remainder of the Book of Mormon (including Moroni), why is nothing more said about the appearance of a new church, such as appears to be adumbrated in Moroni?

One possibility is that while Moroni 1-6 and 8 do indeed look like a handbook, they were intended not as the basis for a new church but as a guide for reforming an existing institution. If so, it was to have been the Book of Mormon, itself as much as anything else, that would have contributed to the reform. The Book of Mormon need not portray Joseph Smith as playing a pivotal role as a church reformer, much less a founder.

A more radical explanation would be that Smith in fact composed

Moroni after 1 and 2 Nephi. While I do not necessarily favor this explanation, I offer the following pieces of evidence in its defense. First, it was toward the end of the translation (June 1829) that Oliver Cowdery began working on what we now call Section 20 of the Doctrine and Covenants, known to have been begun in 1829.[8] This suggests that indeed the idea of a new church was beginning to exercise Smith's mind. If this is what motivated the collection of materials in Moroni, and if Moroni had been composed before 1 and 2 Nephi, then we should expect some "foretelling" of the idea. Second, if we exclude from the Book of Mormon 1 Nephi through Words of Mormon and also Moroni, and if we restore the 116 pages of Mormon's abridgement, the resulting book is in fact a book by Mormon—that is, the book as it was perhaps originally conceived in Smith's mind—the work of a single author. The loss of the 116 pages dealt this conception and Smith's vision a blow. While Smith was eventually able to recover his gift of translation, the structure of the Book of Mormon changed—above all, the 116 pages had to be replaced. The fact that Smith did not immediately move to provide a substitute suggests that he may have needed time to consider its ramifications. Best perhaps to finish the story as he had already conceived it and worry about the replacement later. All of the additions (Ether, 1 Nephi-Omni/Words of Mormon, and Moroni) in this scenario come toward the end of the translation process. The complex story of large and small plates and multiple authorship are thus explained as the consequence of an accident on the one hand and a theological development in Smith's mind on the other. The succession of insignificant record keepers from Jacob down to the time of Mosiah is required only in order to fill up the chronological gap between the end of the founding family's story and that of Mosiah, the two Almas, and the Nephite wars.

Permit me a few more comments on the subject of Moroni's church handbook. In saying that it is unique, I am not claiming that the concerns it treats are not addressed elsewhere in the Book of Mormon; some are, some are not. What is unique is the fact that the resulting guidelines are assembled in one location as an instruction manual. Each of the topics taken up were matters of debate in Smith's time, which explains why they are treated at all.

Many readers of this essay may recall Alexander Campbell's dictum that the Book of Mormon includes "every error and almost every truth discussed in New York for the last ten years."[9] "He [Joseph Smith]," according to Campbell, "decides all the great controversies–infant baptism, ordination, the trinity, regeneration, repentance, justification, the fall of man, the atonement, transubstantiation, fasting, penance, church government, religious experience, the call to the ministry, the general resurrection, eternal punishment, who may baptize, and even the question of freemasonry, republican government, and the rights of man."

The matter of infant baptism, which heads up Campbell's list, is broached for the first and only time in Moroni 8:4ff–part of what I have called the handbook. This is puzzling since the Nephites have been practicing baptism at least since Alma the Elder's time (Mos. 18:10ff). How is it that only at the end of the history does the question arise? By way of comparison, although there is no trace of it in the New Testament, infant baptism was nevertheless an established practice by the late second century when Tertullian advised against baptising children for fear they would sin before they could be reasonably expected to act differently (*On Baptism,* xviii). Infant baptism is mentioned by Irenaeus and is an apparently normative albeit localized practice (II:xxii). The issue can scarcely have been avoided by the Nephite church.

Nevertheless, Moroni 8 implies that the issue is new: Mormon and Moroni are initially at a loss for a response. Even with his thorough knowledge of Nephite history, Mormon has to go to God himself for an answer (v. 7). Mormon's justification (v. 8) is a pastiche of New Testament sentiments taken out of context in a manner not uncharacteristic of the rest of the Book of Mormon. His quotation of Jesus to the effect that "the law of circumcision is done away in me" is the most peculiar. This Pauline sentiment makes sense in its original social setting: the struggle to establish the independence of the gentile church from Jewish ritual. But what relevance does it have to Moroni's practical difficulty? In fact, the problem faced by Paul could scarcely have arisen among Nephite leaders who all along had championed the rejection of Jewish "Law" in terms that could be called anti-Jewish. The problem of infant baptism cannot realistically be located in the sort of world which the Book of Mormon itself would lead us to expect. But in Joseph Smith's world, the issue was very much alive. Presbyterians, the most popular group around Palmyra, New York, held with Calvinism that baptism as a sign of conversion was not necessary as a means to salvation. It was not administered to infants. Methodists, the next largest group in the area, required infant baptism. Baptists, also well represented, who felt that only believers should be baptized, excluded children from the rite. Universalists allowed baptism in any number of forms but held that it was not mandatory. The Friends did away with sacraments altogether. One could therefore find among major religious movements in the area just about every possible attitude toward baptism. The key to understanding Moroni 8, and many of the other passages discussed below, is the reference to Ancient American "disputations" (vv. 4-5), which these revelations are meant to quell. This is, in fact, the only hint of such disputations in the Book of Mormon. Reference to theological conflict makes great sense in the context of New York revivalism.

How one sees infants is not the only controversial point about baptism, and we should therefore expect that if Smith set out to settle matters of controversy once and for all, he would address himself to other points of debate. The passage in 3 Nephi 11:22ff. does just that. It too is introduced by the key word "disputations" (v. 22, also 28ff.), which are again unanticipated. We often hear of political dissension in the Nephite camp, but nowhere previously is anything said about disagreements among the faithful about how baptism should be done. Nothing is left to speculation in 3 Nephi. Every word and action is specified in detail. Christ himself—what better authority—makes clear its necessity and scope. This is important since the New Testament lacks such explicit divine instruction. The uncertainty which this issue evoked in the minds of nineteenth-century seekers after the "primitive church" could only thus be completely dispelled—with explicit instruction to fill the gap in the New Testament picture of the church.

Similarly missing from the New Testament are details about how to administer the eucharist (the Mormon "sacrament"), which are obligingly supplied by 3 Nephi 18. Verse 34 explains that this is, again, because of disputations. In this case, we should expect no disputes at all since the eucharist only comes into being with Jesus' advent. Nevertheless, the exact significance of each act is, as in the earlier cases, carefully spelled out (vv. 7, 11).

Having chosen twelve disciples to govern his American church, Jesus gives the disciples power to bestow the Holy Ghost (v. 37). This almost completes the rudimentary framework for church organization. All the church lacks is a name, which is providentially supplied in Chapter 27. Once more the motivation is "disputations" (vv. 4ff.), but again, mention of these squabbles comes out of nowhere. One wonders why, if there were debates, the church leader did not simply solicit a revelation on the matter and put an end to it as the Book of Mormon prophetic tradition would suggest. Coming from Jesus' mouth, the statement claims more authority and provides, in a New Testament tradition, what the New Testament does not: explicit details from Jesus himself for the organization of a church. The reader may have noticed that these items–the ordination of the twelve, the mode of baptism, the eucharist, and the authority to bestow the Holy Ghost–constitute what we earlier called the handbook of the church in Moroni 1-6 and 8, which epitomizes the lengthier treatment in 3 Nephi. Unlike 3 Nephi, however, Moroni's handbook is explicitly designed for "some future day." With such perfect instruction, the primitive American church operates without any disputes at all (4 Ne. 2). This is an extreme form of what Robert Wilken calls the "myth of Christian beginnings."[10] Eusebius expresses it concisely:

> Until then [the early second century] the church had remained a virgin, pure and uncorrupted, since those who were trying to corrupt the wholesome standard of the saving message ... lurked somewhere under cover of darkness. But when the sacred band of the apostles had in various ways reached the end of their life, and the generation of those privileged to listen with their own ears to the divine wisdom had passed on, then godless error began to take shape through the deceit of false teachers, who now that none of the apostles was left threw off the mask [and] attempted to counter the preaching of the truth by knowledge falsely so called. (*Ecclesiastical History*, 3.32.7-8)

"Eusebius wrote a history," writes Wilken, "in which there is no real history, for there is no place for change in his portrait of Christianity. The true church always remains the same from generation to generation. ... There is no genuine history, for there *can be* no history ... The history of the church is a history of an eternal conflict between the truth of God and its opponents."[11] Although they make different uses of it, this myth is basic to Protestants and Catholics alike; needless to say, it is important to Mormons. It is precisely this image of pristine

Christianity under the apostles that underlies 4 Nephi. It is also the prototype for the primitivist model described in 3 Nephi and explicitly recommended for later implementation in Moroni 1-6, 8.

One consequence of this notion is the idea that diversity cannot be tolerated. In other words, the only way to explain differences is to say that divergent views contradict or oppose the true faith. If there can be only *one* way of doing things, then "disputations" are necessarily a sign of trouble. By attributing his handbook for church administration to Jesus, Joseph Smith established a form that should be beyond dispute. The solution to sectarian squabbles, the one ultimately chosen by Joseph Smith, was to establish a church based on the unambiguous constitution of ancient American Christianity. As Eusebius demonstrates, the notion of a post-apostolic crisis need not lead to what Mormons would call the Apostasy. It is possible that Smith's handbook of church government, while ultimately providing the basis for the new Church of Christ (Latter-day Saints), was initially intended as an epitome for emulation by existing institutions.

CONCLUSION

In the preceding pages, I have tried to show how a historical-critical view of the Book of Mormon illuminates some of its more interesting problems. Many questions remain, and many problems have yet to be discovered and analyzed. I myself have questions about the Book of Mormon's origins that I cannot yet answer. However, that fact does not diminish the certainty of my conclusion that the Book of Mormon is a modern text.

NOTES

1. Note that only in Mormon 9:32 is the Egyptian said to be "reformed." Otherwise, the Book of Mormon's designation is simply "Egyptian."

2. The anachronistic reference to "Jews" is worth noting but remains tangential to the present discussion.

3. According to W. W. Phelps, probably quoting Harris in his 15 Jan. 1831 letter to Eber D. Howe (*Mormonism Unvailed* [Painesville, OH: the Author, 1836], 273), Anthon is said to have described the transcription as "short hand Egyptian."

4. In the preface to his *Classical Dictionary* (1825), Anthon shows some

acquaintance with Champollion's treatise on Egyptian. Even so, his ability to translate anything must have been minimal, to say the least. It is doubtful that Anthon ventured a translation. Anthon himself denied having authenticated Smith's translation. His two versions of the interview, occasionally at odds with each other, are discussed in Richard Bushman, *Joseph Smith and the Beginnings of Mormonism* (Urbana: University of Illinois Press, 1984), 88, where additional literature on the topic is also given. However, Anthon may have ventured to identify the provenance of the characters. The reason for thinking so is that Harris's description of the figures as "short hand Egyptian" reflects a knowledge of current Egyptological terminology, of which Harris could not have been aware. Champollion (*Précis du Système Hiéroglyphique* 1:18, 20, 355) describes hieratic as "tachygraphie," which is rendered "short hand" in the American review of Champollion's work (*American Quarterly Review*, June 1827, 450). The references to Champollion's *Précis* and to Anthon's reviews of this work derive from a helpful article published by FARMS ("What Did Charles Anthon Really Say," *FARMS Update*, May 1985). Anthon is known to have been familiar with this work (*Classical Dictionary* [4th ed., 1845], 45) and is the only known source from which Harris could have learned this usage.

5. A general designation of the Nephite people is intended.

6. "The Original Book of Mormon Manuscript," *BYU Studies* 10 (1970): 259-78.

7. The one post-translation event that does appear prominently is the gathering of Israel. But the gathering of Israel is seen not as the response to an institutionalized church but as the effect of the Book of Mormon gospel which was to prepare people for an imminent second coming. Cf. John A. Clark: "[Martin] said he verily believed that an important epoch had arrived–that a great flood of light was about to burst upon the world ... that a golden Bible had recently been dug from the earth ... and that this would ... settle all religious controversies and speedily bring on the glorious millennium" (*Gleanings by the Way* [Philadelphia, 1842], 223). Harris's statement does not, of course, necessarily represent Smith's point of view. But it is entirely consonant with the stated purpose of the Book of Mormon (cf. e.g., 1 Ne. 14:7; 2 Ne. 27:26ff.; 28; 29; 30).

8. Lyndon Cook, *The Revelations of the Prophet Joseph Smith* (Provo, UT: Seventy's Mission Bookstore, 1981), 126n3.

9. *Delusions: An Analysis of the Book of Mormon* (Boston, 1832), 13.

10. Robert Wilken, *The Myth of Christian Beginnings* (South Bend, IN: University of Notre Dame Press, 1980).

11. Ibid., 73.

2.
Automaticity and the Dictation of the Book of Mormon

Scott C. Dunn

"THIS IS A COURSE IN MIRACLES. PLEASE TAKE NOTES." WITH THESE words, Helen Cohn Schucman, a Columbia University medical psychologist and self-described atheist, was introduced to an inner voice that identified itself as Jesus Christ. Despite great reluctance, Schucman obediently began dictating the words of the voice to a colleague. The result after ten years was a 1,500-page manuscript that was published in 1976 as a three-volume work, *A Course in Miracles.*[1] In the years that followed, thousands of people in dozens of states and fifteen countries began to study, individually or in groups, the words of this massive work which promises to bring the miracles of love and inner harmony into their lives.[2]

Two years before this voice made itself known to Schucman, another woman, Jane Roberts, began to experience psychic forces in her life. A novelist with no particular interest in the occult, Roberts conducted experiments in this new domain, which soon led her into contact with "Seth," a discarnate personality who spoke through the medium of Roberts's mind and voice. In these sessions, Roberts lapsed into a trance while Seth lectured on complex philosophical and metaphysical subjects beyond the educational experience of Jane Roberts herself. By recording Seth's dictation, Roberts and her husband produced over a dozen books which have acquired considerable popularity.[3]

Equally curious is the case of Levi H. Dowling, a man born just a month before the martyrdom of Joseph Smith. Dowling, who pursued careers as a pastor, medical doctor, and writer, experienced visions from childhood and was eventually commissioned by "Visel the Goddess of Wisdom" to record *The Aquarian Gospel of Jesus the Christ.* This scripture-like production purports to be a "transcription from the Akashic Records," recounting a heretofore unknown ministry of the Savior. Still available in bookstores today, this work comments on the natures of God and man, prophesies its own coming forth, and contains other teachings familiar to Bible-reading Christians.[4]

In spite of their disparate backgrounds, Schucman, Roberts, and Dowling are all part of a phenomenon known as "channeling" or "automatic writing." In this essay, the term *automatic writing* refers to the ability to write or dictate text in a relatively rapid, seemingly effortless and fluent manner with no sense of control over the content. Indeed, except for sometimes knowing a word or two moments in advance of writing or speaking, the individual is typically not consciously aware of what the content of the writing will be.[5] Channeling is a form of the same phenomenon that allegedly involves a spirit being (or entity) transmitting information through a living medium.[6]

Channeling attracted widespread public attention in the 1980s when author-actress Shirley MacLaine disclosed that she had experimented with the phenomenon.[7] MacLaine's books introduced a number of people to J. Z. Knight who claims to channel "Ramtha, the Enlightened One," said to have lived in fabled Lemuria some 35,000 years ago.[8] Knight's popularity soared, just as it has for Kevin Ryerson, Jach Pursel, and other modern-day mediums who ply their gifts through books and high-priced seminars.[9]

But even before this, automatic writing was by no means an obscure or rare occurrence. For decades, similar works by Chelsea Quinn Yarbro, Alice A. Bailey, Ruth Montgomery, and others have captured a following among the reading public.[10]

A consideration of this phenomenon is important for Mormons since a number of authors have asserted that this was the method through which Joseph Smith produced the Book of Mormon.[11] Such a claim, if correct, can have important implications for the way Latter-day Saints approach their scriptures. Before exploring the validity of this contention, however, it will be helpful to acquire a greater understanding of the various forms, techniques, and sources of automatic writing.

I

Many people who produce such writing attribute its composition to an outside intelligence. In some instances this external consciousness may have a name and personality all its own. These so-called "channeled texts" frequently revolve around some religious theme. For example, the *Oahspe* claims to be a "New Bible in the Words of Jehovih [sic] and His Angel Ambassadors." *Oahspe* was published in 1882 by dentist John Newbrough who claimed that the book's angelic spirit authors controlled his hands on the typewriter each morning for fifty weeks. Like the conventional Bible, this volume consists of various "books" and includes an account of the creation and early history of the earth as well as doctrinal and prophetic discourses. Interestingly, this production also contains several lines of unusual characters or "hieroglyphics" which are translated in the book's glossary. Although a number of *Oahspe* doctrines are reminiscent of Mormon teachings (including the plurality of gods and the potential godhood of humanity), it specifically rejects Mormonism and many other religions as creations of "false Gods in the lower heavens" (Es. 18:1-2, 7-8).[12]

Probably better known is the *Urantia Book*, a "2,100-page 'library' of cosmology, philosophy, and religion," published in 1955. Disciples of this work consider it to be a "divine revelation," a work that "will change you." It is said to answer "the three Most Vital Questions being asked ... on earth today," namely "Who Am I? What am I doing here? [and] Where am I going?"[13]

Such familiar promises notwithstanding, the average reader is likely to find this massive volume a bit bizarre. The first fourth of the book claims to have been "sponsored by a Uversa Corps of Superuniverse Personalities acting by authority of the Orvonton Ancient of Days." Among the authors listed for the separate sections are "Perfector of Wisdom," "Mighty Messenger," "One High in Authority," "Melchizedek," "Brilliant Evening Star," "Chief of Seraphim," "Chief of Midwayers," and other unusual characters. Other sections of this book include "The Local Universe," "The History of Urantia [Earth]," and "The Life and Teachings of Jesus."[14]

However, not all channeled texts are so strongly reminiscent of biblical format and teachings as these. For instance, Aleister Crowley, one of the twentieth century's most prominent occult figures, is said to have transcribed a book of esoteric poetry and meditations entitled *The Holy Books of Thelema,* supposedly dictated by an invisible "praeterhuman intelligence" who turns out to be Crowley's Holy Guardian Angel. Like many books in this genre, these revelations were later edited for punctuation and versification.[15]

Crowley himself denied that his work constituted automatic writing even though it was produced "with the utmost rapidity." He countered that the prose "is wholly different from anything that I have written myself. It is characterized by a sustained sublimity of which I am totally incapable and it overrides all the intellectual objectives which I should myself have raised. It does not admit the need to explain itself to anyone, even to me. I cannot doubt that these books are the work of an intelligence independent of my own."[16] Far from disqualifying his works as automatic writing, Crowley's description is indeed typical for this phenomenon.

Not all automatic texts claim a connection to the supernatural. Indeed, a number of well-known literary works came into being through this method without further attribution. Charlotte Brontë is said to have written her masterpieces *Villette* and *Jane Eyre* at a constant rate with her eyes shut. Calling her a "trance-writer," critics Sandra M. Gilbert and Susan Gubar quote entries from the author's journal that describe her visionary experiences and moments of "divine leisure" in which "the stream of thought ... came flowing free & calm along its channel."[17] Similarly, the English poet A. E. Housman once noted that entire stanzas of poetry would come into his mind all at once.[18] More on the mystical side is the visionary William Blake, who claimed that his lengthy poem *Jerusalem* was "dictated" to him. Though it is not clear if Blake meant this as an allusion to his many communications with disembodied spirits, it at least suggests the spontaneous and effortless production of literature characteristic of automatic writing.[19]

Still another well-known poet to compose material in this fashion is Robert Graves, who once related that while working on a historical novel, "a sudden overwhelming obsession interrupted me. It took the form of an unsolicited enlightenment on a subject I knew almost nothing of. ... My mind worked at such a furious rate all night, as well as all the next day, that my pen found it difficult to keep pace with the flow of thought. ... within three weeks, I had written a 70,000-word book about [an] ancient Mediterranean Moon-Goddess," later published as *The White Goddess*.

Like so many of its practitioners, Graves denied that this was automatic writing. "I studiously avoid witchcraft, spiritualism, fortune-telling, automatic writing and so on. ... I beg [people] not to mistake me for a Joseph Smith junior, a Mary Baker Eddy, or that sort of person."[20] Yet Graves's experience exactly fits the definition of automatic writing. This illustrates two important points: First, this phenomenon is not connected to spiritualism per se and can occur in both religious and secular contexts. Second, whether or not a scribe attributes his work to an outside source is irrelevant to the definition of automatic writing. No doubt the reason such literary works are seldom connected with the supernatural is that, unlike channeled texts, the authors seldom attribute their composition to anyone other than themselves.[21]

II

A similar variety is evident in the manner in which automatic writing may be obtained. Some individuals experience words or thoughts in their minds which they then write down or dictate. This is what happened to Lilian D. Johnson, who believed she was in psychic contact with a group of departed spirits. She would sit at a typewriter, ask questions, and receive the answers in her mind. The discourses prompted by this method were published in a book entitled *Spray from an Inland Sea*.[22] Similarly, Jane Roberts records that when in mental contact with the spirit personality Seth, "the words tumbled through my head and out my mouth."[23]

Many individuals are able to produce automatic writing with no mental involvement whatever. In these instances, the person usually holds a pen or pencil and writes freely without knowing what he or she is writing and may simultaneously carry on a conversation on an entirely unrelated subject.[24] Indeed, some people must be distracted before their hand can produce involuntary writing. Others require complete silence.[25]

Some people generate works through the medium of the ouija board, whose pointer spells out the individual letters of each word. A number of purveyors of automatic writing, including the prolific Jane Roberts, began with this technique.[26]

Stone- or crystal-gazing (scrying) are still other well-documented methods of producing automatic writing. In such instances, the individual may experience some sort of vision while the hand writes. Typically, the text reports what was seen in the vision, but in some cases, the stone-gazer sees written words. One woman relates: "I had been trying to obtain automatic writing while looking in the crystal. I was also wondering who had put a pair of lost scissors in a very conspicuous place, where I had just found them. I saw a name written, and found that my right hand had written the same name."[27] Other dictations describe something seen inside the crystal. One psychologist reports that a young boy dictated a fantastic adventure story, which he saw enacted in the crystal while his hand wrote automatically at the same time.[28]

A number of people, Jane Roberts for example, create involuntary script while in a trance.[29] Nevertheless, others produce their works while fully awake and alert. This was the case with Helen Schucman, the woman through whom *A Course in Miracles* was composed. One writer reported that if the "telephone rang during a dictation session, she could interrupt to answer it; the voice [that dictated the work] waited patiently for her return and then resumed, in mid-sentence if necessary, exactly where she had broken off."[30]

As with technique, the quality of material obtained through automatic writing varies widely. Much of it is, as one author observes, "taken up with platitudinous moralising, or verbosely expressed spiritual philosophy, most of it on a level inferior to what the writer could produce in a normal fashion."[31]

However, this is not always the case. Some works seem to exhibit awareness of facts and writing skills far beyond what the individual normally possesses. In speaking through Jane Roberts, for example, the personality of Seth once carried on a conversation with a professor of psychology using appropriate terminology and making references to esoteric philosophical theories of which Jane herself had no apparent knowledge. The psychologist later wrote that he "chose topics of conversation which were clearly of tolerable interest to Seth and considerable interest to me, and which by that time I had every reason to believe were largely foreign territory to Jane. Also ... I chose to pursue these topics at a level of sophistication which I felt, at least, made it exceedingly improbable that Jane could fool me on." He was so impressed by the results that he affirmed, "I do not believe that Jane Roberts and Seth are the same person, or the same personality, or different facets of the same personality."[32]

III

Some have suggested that the varying quality and different methods employed in obtaining automatic writing–ouija boards, dictation, crystal-gazing, and others–indicate that this is not one but an entire collection of qualitatively different phenomena.[33] This allows believers in a particular channeled text to label one such work "inspired" while dismissing others as mere psychological phenomena. Such a claim might be plausible if it could be shown, for example, that ouija boards always produce drivel while crystal-gazing produces impressive literature. However, this is simply not the case. Individuals who produce high-quality writing often use the same method as those who produce clearly inferior works.[34] Some use a variety of methods with no apparent difference in the fluency or quality of the writing. At least one automatic writer received various texts through a ouija board, handwriting, dictation, and visions and maintained the same apparent style and quality throughout.[35] It would appear that the use of crystals, ouija boards, dictation, or manual writing are only different techniques or expressions of the same underlying process.[36]

Of course, one could attempt to make a case for multiple phenomena based on varying quality alone. However, our inability to objectively measure depth of thought and quality of expression renders this a difficult claim to substantiate. Moreover, the fact that the quality of some individuals' automatic writing improves over time casts doubt on the validity of using varying quality to identify different phenomena.[37]

IV

There is much to suggest a connection between automatic writing and certain forms of creative inspiration. For instance, a number of novelists who have outlined their plots and planned their characters and settings nevertheless find themselves typing hurriedly away, anxiously waiting to see what twist their story will take next. In some instances, they find the effortless flow of ideas so pronounced that they speak of its source as their own personal muse. Seen this way, automatic writing becomes a fairly ordinary occurrence that emerges in varying degrees depending on the talent and training of the practitioner.[38]

But such an observation, while helpful, still leaves questions about the most extreme forms of this occurrence. This is especially so in the case of channeled texts, which appear to be authored by totally independent and invisible beings. Where do these unusual works come from?

The most immediate explanation would be to accept the claims of their purveyors. In other words, it may indeed be the case that a frequently reincarnated spirit named Seth speaks through Jane Roberts or that Jesus Christ communicated *A Course in Miracles* to a psychologist named Helen Schucman. Not surprisingly, followers of these works have occasionally produced evidence to support their claims.[39]

Yet while intriguing and even miraculous circumstances surround some of this material, there is also good reason not to accept it at face value. This is especially true in the case of channeled texts that purport to be the new works of long-dead authors dictating material from the spirit world. For example, several years ago a woman published a book that she claimed was authored by the ghost of the noted American psychologist William James. Unfortunately, the vapid writing of this work bears no resemblance to James's own literary style. If we are to accept these claims as correct, we can only wonder at the devastating effect that death had on James's personal abilities.[40]

Partly for this reason, students of automatic writing have sought other explanations for its origins. Many available studies suggest that both the content of automatic writing and its spirit authors are the creation of the unconscious mind. Indeed, information found in automatic writing can often be traced to events, facts, or ideas to which the automatic writer was exposed during his or her lifetime.

Consider the case of a woman who claimed that the writing she produced was dictated by her deceased mother, a spirit who referred to herself as "My Dearest." Under the questioning of a psychologist, "My Dearest" (i.e., the mind or entity that composed the writing) revealed that she was not the woman's mother at all but was merely a personality that emerged to comfort the woman when her mother died. Further questioning revealed details apparently drawn from the woman's memories. "My Dearest" expressed a fondness for "yellow steps" and, when asked why, explained that the steps to her house had been painted yellow when she was young. The woman through whom the writing was "transmitted" did not remember this at all. Later on, the psychologist was able to verify that the steps to the woman's childhood home had been painted yellow when she was three years old.[41]

Similar results were realized by Dr. P. L. Harriman, who employed a group of students to experiment with automatic writing: "Under hypnosis they were made to live through in imagination some difficult situation. They were told they would forget all about it on waking. The subjects had previously been trained in automatic writing, and after being brought out of their hypnotic state they were given paper and pencil and encouraged to write while at the same time engaging in desultory conversation. The automatic writings so obtained were frequently concerned with the anxieties and conflicts set up by the imaginary difficult situations. One student, who had been told by the hypnotist that he was summoned to the Dean's office, produced a screed containing a list of minor offenses and neglected duties. He had in fact been guilty of them all."[42]

Experiments of this sort have also been performed with crystal-gazing. One psychologist reported working with an individual who, through this means, was able to recall forgotten events that occurred as far back as the age of fifteen months. The accuracy of this recall was confirmed by the subject's mother.[43]

In some instances individuals may weave details from their memories into a work of fiction. Psychologist Ernest Hilgard tells of a subject "whose story telling was of a high order whether he was hypnotized or not. ... Under hypnosis he had told a story of early nineteenth century England with such clarity and verisimilitude that he convinced those who heard him—himself as well—that it must have been a case of regression to a prior experience. Only careful depth interviewing proved that he had forgotten memories sufficient to supply the details he had recounted so that the reincarnation concept was not necessary."[44]

None of this is to suggest deliberate deception on the part of the automatic writer. On the contrary, the best-known practitioners appear to be sincere individuals who are unfamiliar with the latent abilities of the human mind. When they discover that they can rapidly produce writing of a quality superior to their natural powers, they understandably infer that such works must come from an outside source. Psychologists refer to this phenomenon as *dissociation*—a general term that covers mental activities concealed from conscious awareness. Dissociative states may involve automatic writing, spontaneous creativity, spirit possession, multiple personality, or combinations of these.[45]

V

But what, if anything, does all this have to do with the Book of Mormon? In fact, a number of parallels exist between Joseph Smith's production of scripture and instances of automatic writing. These parallels can best be illustrated by a detailed recounting of one of the most extensively documented examples of the latter: the case of Patience Worth. This unusual story began one hot summer evening when Pearl Curran, a St. Louis housewife, was persuaded by some friends to experiment with a ouija board. After some false starts, the pointer began spelling out words. Pearl's mother dutifully took down the letters as they were called out. Through the ouija board came the curious declaration: "Many moons ago I lived. Again I come—Patience Worth my name."[46]

The group began carrying on conversations with "Patience" who, though reticent to talk about herself, indicated that she was an English woman who had lived in the seventeenth century. Using what appeared to be an archaic form of English, she carried on saucy discussions filled with pungent metaphors and sarcastic retorts. More interesting, Worth dictated numerous poems and epigrams which eventually attracted a great deal of attention.

Unlike many instances of automatic writing, these works exhibited impressive literary quality. One of the preeminent literary critics of his day, William Marion Reedy, though not believing Patience Worth to be a spirit, referred to her poems as "extraordinary" and "near great." A professor of English from Virginia found some of them superior to the verse of Chaucer, Spenser, and even Shakespeare. While many critics were not as enthusiastic, even the most unbelieving admitted that there were occasional passages of "undeniable simplicity and beauty" or that it was "all good literature and deserves reading on that account alone." In 1916 and again in 1918, Patience Worth was listed in a highly respected and authoritative anthology of poetry. The same volume that included ten poems by Amy Lowell and five by Edna St. Vincent Millay listed some eighty-eight by Patience Worth, several of them marked as "poems of distinction."[47]

In time the entity who identified herself simply as a wench dictated a number of novels and plays. These, too, received substantial critical acclaim. The most popular was *The Sorry Tale*, a massive historical novel relating to the life of Jesus Christ. The work generally received favorable reviews and earned Patience Worth a place among the outstanding authors of 1918 as judged by the Joint Committee of Literary Arts of New York. A reviewer for the *New York Times* called *The Sorry Tale* "a wonderful, a beautiful, and a noble book," one "constructed with the precision and the accuracy of a master hand." Another scholar and critic wrote that the segment "describing the crucifixion–a chapter of five thousand words ... dictated in a single evening–is a composition of appalling force and vividness, and an interpretation upon a high and sincere plane." Still another critic, also noting the book's spiritual and emotional impact, referred to it as a "fifth gospel," a term Mormons sometimes apply to 3 Nephi.[48]

Like believers in the Book of Mormon, followers of Patience Worth adduced linguistic evidence to show that the writing dictated through Pearl Curran did indeed belong to antiquity. Although some of the language was more ungrammatical than archaic, there appear to be occasional uses of genuinely obsolete English words which Curran would probably not have known.[49] More striking still is the high incidence of Anglo-Saxon words in Patience Worth's vocabulary. Though modern English descends from Anglo-Saxon, it currently uses a rather high percentage of words borrowed from other languages. The Declaration of Independence uses only 42 percent Anglo-Saxon words, the King James Bible 77 percent, and Chaucer 64 percent. However, Worth's language, as measured in one of her novels, consists of an amazing 90 percent Anglo-Saxon words.[50] In light of the fact that one must go back to writings of the thirteenth century to find a comparable percentage, it becomes apparent that her productions are, as one scholar put it, nothing less than a "philological miracle."[51]

Another startling thing about the works attributed to Patience

Worth is their accuracy on factual details that Curran apparently could not have known, a defense often applied to writings given through Joseph Smith.[52] Regarding *The Sorry Tale,* one author notes that "scholars and literary critics agreed that even a lifetime of reading all available knowledge of the Holy Land (reading that apparently never took place, but even if it had) still would not have given [Curran] the information to produce a book with such verisimilitude."[53] Similarly, after publication of *Hope Trueblood,* Patience's novel of English life, the *London Times* asserted that the book "reveals a familiarity with nature as it is found in England, and with the manners of English life of the older time." Another British paper commented that sections of the work appeared "to show an uncanny knowledge of English social life in the 17th century and before."[54]

Like Joseph Smith, Pearl Curran appears to have lacked the education necessary to produce such works. Individuals close to her were quick to point out that while she was an intelligent woman, she was clearly unacquainted with early English literature and "never had read anything archaic."[55] This curious situation prompted one observer to note that "if Patience Worth be an invention, the inventor is a genius of no mean order."[56]

While for many years Curran received communications from Worth through a ouija board, this was not her only method. Just as Joseph Smith eventually began to dictate revelations without the aid of a seer stone, so Curran began to dictate the words of Patience Worth without any physical object. Curran "simply saw the pictures and the words in her head and called them out, as coming from the hand of Patience Worth."[57]

As with other such writers, Curran was not in a state of trance but was fully alert while dictating Worth's words. She would look over at a friend, wave, or even write a letter while dictating. Her dictation was effortless, fluent, and could be performed for hours without stopping. She was known to have dictated nearly 6,000 words in a single sitting and was once timed at producing 110 words per minute. In contrast, when Curran composed her own writing, the process was slower, sometimes requiring most of an afternoon to write a single letter.[58]

One respected journalist made an intriguing observation about the composition process: "Each time the story was picked up at the point where work stopped at the previous sitting, without a break in the continuity of the narrative, without the slightest hesitation, and without the necessity of a reference to the closing words of the last preceding instalment."[59] Compare this with the observation made by Emma Smith concerning the production of the Book of Mormon: "[Joseph] would dictate to me hour after hour; and when returning after meals, or after interruptions, he would at once begin where he had left off, without either seeing the manuscript or having any portion of it read to him. This was a usual thing for him to do."[60]

Pearl Curran is like Joseph Smith in still another way: for both, available evidence militates against the likelihood of conscious fraud. In the case of Curran, there was little motive for deception, since publication of Patience Worth's writings ended up costing the Currans and their friends a great deal of money. And if Curran were interested in fame, it would have been much more to her advantage to put her own name to the material she dictated because the association with the occult actually hindered the acceptance of her work in the literary world. Furthermore, Curran and her immediate associates were known by all as individuals of unimpeachable honesty.

Perhaps the most compelling evidence in favor of Curran's sincerity is the fact that much of the writing was produced in settings that seem to exclude the possibility of deliberate deception. For example, Walter Franklin Prince, a professional researcher of psychic phenomena who carefully and skeptically analyzed the case, reported the following: "A poem of 25 lines was demanded, the lines beginning with the letters of the alphabet, except X, in due order. It was instantly dictated. I asked for a conversation between a lout and a maid at a country fair to be couched in archaic prose, and a poem in modern English on 'The Folly of Atheism'—first a passage of one and then a passage of the other, thus alternating to the end. This seemed to me an impossible mental feat. But it was done so rapidly as to tax the recorder—four passages of humorous prose abounding in archaic locutions, alternating with four parts of a poem in modern English of lofty and spiritual tenor; and when assembled each factor made a perfectly articulated little piece of literature."[61] In such a situation, there was clearly no opportunity for Curran to work out the poetry and memorize it in advance.

Prince compared Patience Worth's writings with known works of literature but discovered no indication of plagiarism. He did, however, find some linguistic similarities with poetry from Dorset, a community in the part of England said to be the home of Patience Worth.[62]

Interestingly, this same Walter Prince conducted an extensive study of the Book of Mormon. In an article entitled "Psychological Tests for the Authorship of the Book of Mormon," he concluded that it reflected events and ideas common to nineteenth-century New England. It is not surprising, then, to discover that Prince was far more impressed with the supernatural aspects of the Patience Worth case than he was with the Book of Mormon, which he considered to be the product of Joseph Smith's unconscious mind.[63]

VI

But beyond these general parallels to the experience of automatic writers, what is the evidence that Joseph Smith's translation is an example of this phenomenon? To begin with, the content of automatic texts is often similar to that of the Book of Mormon: Examples include multiple authorship, use of archaic language, accounts of bygone historical figures, accurate descriptions of times and places apparently unfamiliar to the writer, narratives with well-developed characters and plot, accounts of various ministries of Jesus Christ, poetics, occasionally impressive literary quality, doctrinal, theological, and cosmological discussions, and even discourses by deity.

More importantly, the manner in which Joseph Smith produced the Book of Mormon, and apparently many revelations and other scriptures as well, bears strong resemblance to the process of automatic writing. For example, there is no indication that Smith used notes or outlines or conducted major reworkings of his materials prior to their initial publication. While such conditions are characteristic of a relatively simple translation task, they are also typical of automatic writing.

In addition, the bulk of the Book of Mormon, dictated after Oliver Cowdery became Smith's scribe, was completed in approximately ninety days.[64] This represents fairly rapid work for a book of this length–588 typeset pages in the first edition–even if the translation progressed well every day. Again, the speed and ease with which Smith worked is characteristic of automatic writing.

Even more significant are the statements by Martin Harris, David Whitmer, Emma Smith, Joseph Knight Sr., Elizabeth Ann Whitmer

Cowdery, Isaac Hale, and others, which report that Smith pronounced the words of the text with his face buried in a hat, looking at a seer stone or possibly the spectacle-like pair of transparent stones known as the "interpreters" or urim and thummim. Emma Smith and Elizabeth Whitmer Cowdery report that he would perform this operation for hours on end. Most of these accounts, some of them by eyewitnesses, indicate that he was reading words or sentences that he saw in the sacred instruments. This certainly implies a relatively effortless or automatic process.[65] Moreover, this use of a crystal or stone is a well-known method of producing automatic writing.

Some have suggested that the Book of Mormon was produced not by effortless dictation but rather represents a conceptual translation in which Smith had to work out the meanings of passages in his head. This supposition is often based on analysis of the book's grammatical errors which seem to reflect Smith's idiom.[66] However, to make inferences about translation based on a study of content is valid if, and only if, it is certain that the text is truly a translation in the ordinary sense of that term. This has not been shown. Moreover, as automatic writing demonstrates, the presence of one's own language or memories in a text by no means indicates that it was produced through extensive mental effort or conscious planning.

Proponents of a "free" or conceptual translation frequently cite a passage in Doctrine and Covenants 9, which informs Oliver Cowdery that in order to interpret an ancient record, he must "study it out in [his] mind" (vv. 7-8). However, Oliver was using an entirely different approach than Joseph. Section 8 reminds Oliver of his "gift of working with the rod," which had already "told [him] many things." It was apparently through this rod that he was promised the ability to "translate all those ancient records which have been hid up, [that] are sacred."[67] It is quite natural for this method to require some mental study since such rods gave yes-or-no answers by moving in one direction or the other to confirm or reject propositions.[68] On the other hand, there is no reason to believe that these instructions had anything to do with Joseph's method of translating with the seer stone or urim and thummim. On the contrary, neither the eye-witness accounts of Smith's scrying nor the literature on stone-gazing in general indicates that such stones gave the user "spiritual impressions" or required mental deliberation.[69] Instead, these objects produced clear visions and allowed virtually effortless dictation. That this is the way the Book of Mormon was translated is further suggested by a revelation reminding Smith of the manuscript "which God had given thee sight and power to translate" (D&C 3:12).[70]

Although a few details of the Book of Mormon translation seem to conflict with the classic automatic writing model, these differences are not as significant as may first appear. For example, some sources indicate Smith knew a fair amount about the content of the Book of Mormon before he began translating.[71] Nevertheless, while these sources relate his general awareness of events in the book, they do not reveal the degree to which he was able to anticipate particular passages. At least one account suggests that occasionally he was surprised by details that emerged while he was dictating.[72]

Furthermore, a period of anticipation or preparation prior to automatic writing is not unknown. Before producing *Oahspe,* John Newbrough was visited by its angelic authors, asked if he would "perform a mission for Jehovih," and was told to prepare for this experience. This preparation consisted of a special diet, charity work, and a series of interviews in which the angels asked this dentist "questions relative to heaven and earth, which no mortal could answer intelligently." Finally, ten years after the first visitation, the angels told him how to proceed with the automatic typing of their work.[73] Similarly, Joseph Smith's earliest knowledge of Book of Mormon contents resulted from interviews with the angel identified as Moroni, one of the book's authors.

Such a preparatory or incubation period is evident in instances of sudden insight and other unconscious mental processes. One researcher characterizes spontaneous creativity as consisting of "preparation-incubation-illumination." Attempts to remember someone's name are a good example. Many people experience a process in which they try to remember, fail, and then have the name suddenly come to mind later while thinking on an unrelated subject. Such instances demonstrate the mind's ability to think and plan without conscious awareness of these processes.[74]

Another seeming contrast between the Book of Mormon and automatic writing is the assertion that Smith sometimes had portions of the manuscript read back to him before continuing.[75] However, these sources do not indicate that Smith did so to keep track of the story line or to maintain his place in the narrative. Indeed, remarks by Emma Smith and Parley P. Pratt indicate that this was, in fact, not necessary.[76] Furthermore, an examination of the Book of Mormon manuscripts suggests that comparatively little editing or revising was done as it was recorded. This is precisely what we would expect from a text produced through automatic writing.[77]

Published criticisms of an automatic writing model of the Book of Mormon have been similarly weak. One author, Klaus Hansen, stated that "the length of the work, requiring a consistent and sustained effort over three months, diminishes the plausibility of the automatic writing hypothesis."[78] This indicates ignorance of the fact that the best examples of channeled or automatic writing, e.g., the Patience Worth novels or *A Course in Miracles,* were longer and required a greater amount of sustained participation than the Book of Mormon.

Blake Ostler has put forth what is essentially an automatic writing model, though he is reluctant to call it that.[79] He states that Smith's "state of consciousness differs from ... most reports of automatic writing in that he did not lose consciousness of his surroundings or become dispossessed of his personal identity," apparently unaware that the same is true of *A Course in Miracles* and all of the Patience Worth literature. "Further," Ostler continues, "there is no evidence that [Smith] claimed to hear a voice or take dictation from another personality, unlike cases of spirit writing or channeled text."[80] But this also applies to such dramatic instances of automatic writing as *The Aquarian Gospel of Jesus Christ* and *The White Goddess.* In spite of his attempts to distance Smith from these works, nothing in Ostler's characterization of the translation process is inconsistent with the best-documented instances of this phenomenon.

In spite of seeming conflicts, then, it is clear that Smith's translation experience fits comfortably within the larger world of scrying, channeling, and automatic writing. Indeed, the automatic processes discussed here provide the best model for understanding the translation of the Book of Mormon.

VII

In addition to clarifying the translation process, an automatic writing model of the Book of Mormon helps illuminate issues that never have been adequately explained. Such is the case with the extensive use of the Bible in the Book of Mormon. In addition to the lengthy passages from Isaiah, the Book of Mormon is replete with allusions, expressions, and quotations from the King James translation of the Old and New Testaments.[81] Since many of these quotations occur in settings hundreds of years before the biblical manuscripts were composed, it seems unlikely that these verbatim extractions were engraved on the Nephite plates. Some people have attempted to resolve this problem by speculating that when Smith came to a passage in the ancient record that paralleled biblical ideas, he used the King James Bible to assist in the translation.[82] Unfortunately, this explanation is not supported by the known accounts of the translation process, none of which mentions Smith using a Bible or, for that matter, even having one present.

Automatic writing, on the other hand, provides a simple explanation of these circumstances. Just as individuals under hypnosis have been able to quote lengthy passages in foreign languages which they heard at the age of three, so have automatic writers produced detailed information from books that they have read but in some cases cannot remember reading.[83] Thus, if Smith's scriptural productions borrowed material from the Bible, this is entirely consistent with other instances of automatic writing. This quirk of memory, known as cryptomnesia, may also explain the presence of styles and literary patterns that are found both in the Book of Mormon and the Bible.[84]

Because such feats of recall occur in automatic writing, this helps us understand the inclusion in the Book of Mormon of so many concepts that seem to belong to nineteenth-century New England. A number of Mormon writers have pointed out that the Book of Mormon incorporates theological concepts and addresses religious debates common to Smith's environment. The book also capitalizes and expands on theories of the origin of the American Indian that were circulating in that part of the country at that time but have been rejected by anthropologists and ethnologists today.[85] The existence of these parallels has caused believers and skeptics alike to assign an inordinate degree of significance to the question of whether Smith had direct access to and studied books whose ideas are echoed in the Mormon scriptures.[86]

But automatic writing renders such a question irrelevant. Automatic texts often contain information available to the writer in the most obscure manner imaginable. One researcher described a woman who, with a ouija board, produced automatic writing that recounted "almost exactly" the death notices in an available newspaper. Although the woman apparently had not read these obituaries, she had done the crossword puzzle found on the same page in the newspaper. It seems that her mind had picked up and stored material that was in her field of vision as she worked the crossword puzzle; she had unconsciously read and unconsciously written information of which her conscious mind was entirely unaware. Interestingly, the researcher further reported that the writing contained information to which the woman had no access whatsoever.[87] It should not be surprising, therefore, to find Smith's scriptural productions repeating things he may have heard or overheard in conversation, camp meetings, or other settings without any concerted study of the issues.

An understanding of automatic writing also reveals a number of problems with certain Book of Mormon apologetics. For example, an oft-repeated defense of the Book of Mormon asserts that Smith was too ignorant and uneducated to create a book of such complex construction and profound teachings.[88] But this is exactly what other producers of automatic texts have accomplished, most notably the unlettered Pearl Curran, whose moving religious novel won the praises of historians and literary critics alike.[89] If the Book of Mormon is to be defended as a uniquely inspired ancient text, it must be done on stronger ground than this.

Similarly, some apologists have claimed that evidence for the Book of Mormon's ancient character "proves" or validates its doctrinal teachings.[90] Such claims are clearly made in ignorance of automatic texts, many of which evidence historical and philosophical knowledge beyond that of the writer. Since the theologies of these other writings clash with the Book of Mormon and with each other, it is fallacious to suggest a connection between doctrinal claims of a book and the miraculous aspects of its contents.

This last point in particular raises a much larger question: On what basis do we designate a book as scripture? Believers say the Book of Mormon is a holy book, but why? Because its language or content are miraculously beyond the knowledge of the writer? This is true of other books. Because it was brought forth by supernatural means? This is also true of other books. Because it teaches Christian principles? This is true of other books. Because it changes lives for the better? This, too, is true of other books. Because people feel they have received a spiritual witness of its divinity? Even this is true of other books.[91] In fact, there does not appear to be anything of a historical, theological, philosophical, or literary quality in the scriptural writings of Joseph Smith that has not been matched by those well outside the Mormon tradition. While Latter-day Saints who take issue with this statement may point to masses of evidence that they feel support the claims of their scriptures, this disparity in evidence probably results from the disproportionate attention they devote to their own book to the exclusion of similar works produced by nearly identical means.

Of course, there are many ways of understanding the parallels to automatic works. It may be argued that automatic writing is God's true means of giving revelations and translations (in the case of Joseph Smith) which has been counterfeited by Satan (in the cases of Jane Roberts, Pearl Curran, and others). But this raises the difficult question of why Satan would assist in the production of such fine literary works as *Jane Eyre,* such moving religious novels as *The Sorry Tale,* or such uplifting instructional works like *A Course in Miracles.*

An alternative view that circumvents this difficulty might be that not only did God use automatic writing to help his prophets produce latter-day scripture, but he also used it to inspire great literature as with Pearl Curran and Charlotte Brontë. In this view, Mormons might consider Patience Worth to be a real seventeenth-century woman whom God permitted to pierce the veil and communicate with a twentieth-century American housewife. But this explanation may bother more traditional Latter-day Saints, especially since the teachings of so many automatic texts run counter to LDS theology.[92]

Still another possibility is that some or all of these books are wholly or partially the result of psychological processes. Unfortunately, this does not resolve the central problem: How does one distinguish inspired books from psychological phenomena? It is easy enough to say that the Book of Mormon is inspired while other books are not. But without more evidence of clear differences, such an assertion will not be convincing to outsiders who are acquainted with automatic writing. If Mormons are to interpret the evidence consistently, we must either revise our understanding of the role of the standard works or adopt a more pluralistic attitude about the validity of other forms of spiritual phenomena such as automatic writing.

NOTES

1. *A Course in Miracles*, 3 vols. ([New York]: The Foundation for Inner Peace, 1975).

2. For accounts of this book's origins, see Robert Skutch, *Journey without Distance: The Story behind A Course in Miracles* (1984; Mill Valley, CA: Foundation for Inner Peace, 1996); Kenneth Wapnick, *Absence from Felicity: The Story of Helen Schucman and Her Scribing of A Course in Miracles* (Roscoe, NY: Foundation for "A Course in Miracles," 1991); John Koffend, "The Gospel According to Helen," *Psychology Today*, Sept. 1980, 74-90; Brian Van der Horst, "Simple, Dumb, Boring Truths–and A Course in Miracles," *New Realities* 1 ([1977]): 8-15, 24-25; and Brian Van der Horst, "Miracles Come of Age: An Update on A Course in Miracles," *New Realities* 3 ([1979]): 48-55.

3. Jane Roberts, *The Coming of Seth* (New York: Simon and Schuster, Pocket Books, 1966); idem.; *The Seth Material* (Englewood Cliffs, NJ: Prentice-Hall, 1970). The words "A Seth Book" adorn each volume dictated by Roberts's trance personality. These works sell at least well enough for the well-known publisher Prentice-Hall to continue publishing this material.

4. *The Aquarian Gospel of Jesus the Christ* (London: L. N. Fowler & Co., [1964]), 11-17. Although this book contains some doctrines that Mormons would find familiar ("What I have done all men can do, and what I am all men shall be"), it nevertheless denies that Jesus was the Christ in any sense normally understood by Mormons or Christians in general (13-14).

5. In the main I follow Dr. Ian Stevenson of the University of Virginia who defines automatic writing as "writing that is done without the writer being conscious of what he is writing, or even (occasionally) the act of writing. Perhaps I should say 'fully conscious' because automatic writers may have some awareness of what they are writing as they write. The activity appears to occur, however, without the subject's ordinary voluntary control and for this reason is called 'automatic.' ... Usually the writing proceeds rapidly, sometimes far more so than the subject's normal writing does" ("Some Comments on Automatic Writing," *Journal of the American Society for Psychical Research* 72 [Oct. 1978]: 316.) This agrees with the definition given by psychologist and hypnotherapist Milton H. Erickson (*Hypnotic Investigation of Psychodynamic Processes*, vol. 3 of *The Collected Papers of Milton H. Erickson on Hypnosis*, ed. Ernest L. Rossi, 4 vols. [New York: Irvington Publishers, 1980], 17) and psychologist Ernest R. Hilgard. Although some writers use the term to refer only to manual handwriting, this essay follows those authors who apply it to both writing and dictation since they appear to be expressions of the same underlying process. As Hilgard notes, "The 'pure case' [of automatic writing] is an activity carried

out with no awareness whatever that it is going on. An activity may be carried out in awareness, however, without any sense of control over it" (*Divided Consciousness: Multiple Controls in Human Thought and Action*, Wiley Series in Behavior, ed. Kenneth MacCorquodale [New York: John Wiley & Sons, 1977], 131).

6. Arthur C. Hastings, "Channeling and Spiritual Teachings," in Charles T. Tart, ed., *BodyMind Spirit: Exploring the Parapsychology of Spirituality* (Charlottesville, VA: Hampton Roads Publishing Company, 1997), 198. This agrees with the definition of Jon Klimo, *Channeling: Investigations on Receiving Information from Paranormal Sources* (2nd ed.; Berkeley, CA: North Atlantic Books, 1998). Although this definition is widely used, Klimo's book addresses the fact that the precise meaning of the term *channeling* is a matter of debate among "true believers" of various stripes.

7. Shirley MacLaine, *Out on a Limb* (New York: Bantam Books, 1983). This became a national bestseller and the source for a television miniseries starring MacLaine.

8. Shirley MacLaine, *Dancing in the Light* (New York: Bantam Books, 1985).

9. Jon Klimo, "The Psychology of Channeling," *New Age Journal*, Nov.-Dec. 1987, 36-38; Klimo, *Channeling*, 1; Hastings, "Channeling and Spiritual Teachings," 198, 201-202.

10. A good bibliography of these works and related studies before 1980 can be found in Stevenson, "Some Comments on Automatic Writing," 329-32.

11. This idea has been asserted, though not carefully analyzed, by Lawrence Foster (*Religion and Sexuality: Three American Communal Experiments of the Nineteenth Century* [New York: Oxford University Press, 1981], 296-97n15) and David Techter ("Who Wrote the Book of Mormon? Part Two," *Fate* 30 [Apr. 1977]: 77). Isaac Woodbridge Riley also mentions the possibility of automatic writing in producing the so-called Anthon transcript (see *The Founder of Mormonism: A Psychological Study of Joseph Smith, Jr.* [New York: Dodd, Mead & Co., 1902], 84-85). Among the first authors to suggest an automatic-writing origin of the Book of Mormon was the noted psychologist William James (*The Varieties of Religious Experience: A Study in Human Nature* [1902; reprint, New York: Collier Books, 1961]). James observed that the inspired writings of many noted religious leaders, including St. Paul, Jeremiah, and Ezekiel, exhibit automatic or semi-automatic production (371-76). Even a few Latter-day Saints have suggested this possibility. BYU professor Nels Nelson theorized that Smith was the "channel" for the angel Moroni who spiritually communicated the meaning of the ancient inscriptions to the young prophet ("The Human Side of the Book of Mormon," *The Mormon Point of View*, Apr. 1904, 124-37). J. C. Homans, under the alias of Robert C. Webb, cited Nelson and advanced a more secular automatic-writing interpretation (*The Real Mormonism* [New York: Sturgis & Walton Company, 1916], 25-36).

12. *Oahspe: A New Bible in the Words of Jehovih [sic] and His Angel Ambassa-*

dors (New York: Oahspe Publishing Association, 1882; reprint ed., [Amherst, WI: Palmer Publications, 1972]). See Laura Horst, *A Condensed Version of Oahspe* (Np: published by author, 1977), 18-21, 11.

13. Clyde Bedell, *Clyde Bedell's Concordex of the Urantia Book* (2nd ed. enl.; Laguna Hills, CA: published by author, 1974), 19, 16, 12, 11.

14. *The Urantia Book* (Chicago, IL: Urantia Foundation, 1955).

15. Grady Louis McMurty, "Preface," in Aleister Crowley, *The Holy Books of Thelema* (York Beach, ME: Samuel Weiser, 1983), vii-viii, ix-x. Crowley did most of his work around the turn of the twentieth century, but various supporters keep it in print.

16. Ibid., xviii.

17. Sandra M. Gilbert and Susan Gubar, *The Madwoman in the Attic: The Woman Writer and the Nineteenth-Century Literary Imagination* (New Haven, CT: Yale University Press, 1979), 311-13.

18. A. E. Housman, *The Name and Nature of Poetry* (Cambridge: Cambridge University Press, 1933), as cited in Stevenson, "Some Comments on Automatic Writing," 318.

19. Geoffrey Keynes, ed., *Blake: Complete Writings* (London: Oxford University Press, 1966), 621. Blake makes this claim in his preface to Book I of Jerusalem. For a critical analysis of this claim, see Northrop Frye, *Fearful Symmetry: A Study of William Blake* (Princeton, NJ: Princeton University Press, 1947), 38; or Kathleen Raine, "A Note on Blake's 'Unfettered Verse,'" in Alvin H. Rosenfeld, ed., *William Blake: Essays for S. Foster Damond* (Providence, RI: Brown University Press, 1969), 383. Although such commentaries sometimes reinterpret Blake's sayings in a less mystical way, an awareness of automatic writing explains the poet's method without twisting his own claims.

20. Robert Graves, *Five Pens in Hand* (1958; reprint ed., Freeport, NY: Books for Libraries Press, 1970), 54-55, 58, 63, 64; see also Michael Kirkham, *The Poetry of Robert Graves* (New York: Oxford University Press, 1969), 197-98.

21. An exception to this is James Merrill's *The Changing Light at Sandover* (New York: Atheneum Publications, 1982), which won the 1984 American Book Award for poetry and contains lengthy passages purportedly dictated by disembodied spirits.

22. Lilian D. Johnson, *Spray from an Inland Sea* (Boston: Branden Press, 1974), 7. Like Graves, Johnson denies that her work represents automatic writing. However, this appears to be due to her unfamiliarity with its various manifestations. Many automatic writers have employed methods which exactly parallel Johnson's.

23. Roberts, *The Seth Material,* 31. This comment echoes a statement of Helen Schucman, scribe for *A Course in Miracles,* who described the process like this: "There's no actual sound, and the words come mentally but very clearly. It's a kind of inner dictation you might say" (as recorded in Skutch, *Journey without Distance,* 56).

24. This appears to be similar to Pearl Curran's ability to dictate a poem

composed by a disembodied spirit while Curran wrote a letter to a friend. This is the reverse of conversing-while-writing, but the two appear to be essentially the same phenomenon (Irving Litvag, *Singer in the Shadows: The Strange Story of Patience Worth* [New York: The Macmillan Co., 1972], 213-14).

25. Anita M. Mühl, *Automatic Writing* (Dresden and Leipzig: Theodor Steinkopff, 1930), 21-22.

26. Roberts, *The Seth Material,* 16-24. This was also the case with Pearl Curran; see Litvag, *Singer in the Shadows,* 212-13.

27. Theodore Besterman, *Crystal-Gazing: A Study in the History, Distribution, Theory and Practice of Scrying* (2nd ed.; New Hyde Park, NY: University Books, 1965), 126-27.

28. This psychologist also used crystal-gazing with automatic writing to elicit early memories from patients. See Mühl, *Automatic Writing,* 111-26.

29. Roberts, *The Seth Material,* 1. Roberts reports that while her husband could see and hear her as Seth, she couldn't; she was unable to "be Jane and Seth at once" (60). Cf. Mühl, *Automatic Writing,* 22.

30. Koffend, "The Gospel According to Helen," 84. See also Mühl, *Automatic Writing,* 2; Litvag, *Singer in the Shadows,* 107, 213-14. When asked if this was an automatic process, Schucman replied, "Oh, no. It's not automatic at all. I'm perfectly aware of what I'm doing" (qtd. in Skutch, *Journey without Distance,* 56). In other words, she was not in a trance and was aware of the content, although her dictation was effortless and unplanned.

31. D. J. West, *Psychical Research Today* (London: Gerald Duckworth & Co., 1954), 58.

32. Roberts, *The Seth Material,* 107-108.

33. Telephone conversation with psychologist Joyce Sohler, Feb. 1984.

34. Robert Skutch ("Messages from the Higher Self ..." *New Realities* 4 [July 1982]: 18-19) describes experiences that essentially parallel those of Curran (see n24) and Johnson (n22). Skutch wrote down words that came into his mind, but like Johnson, he felt that this was unrelated to automatic writing. Skutch admitted that his earliest efforts produced nonsense, although he considered his later writing to be surprisingly insightful. The experiences of all three individuals exhibit the same qualities of effortlessness and unanticipated and uncontrolled content.

35. The example is that of Pearl Curran (Litvag, *Singer in the Shadows,* 212-14). This is not to say that all of her literary productions were of equal value or identical style. Yet, the difference is no greater than one would expect from any accomplished author and certainly not enough to attribute different sources or authorship.

36. This phenomenon seems to operate in other areas besides writing. Rosemary Brown claimed that her music compositions were dictated by the spirits of Brahms, Chopin, Liszt, and others. At least some of her music displays an impressive level of quality. Her story was related on the CBS television program *Sixty Minutes,* 14 Apr. 1970, and in *Time* magazine ("Voices of Si-

lence," *Time* [6 July 1970]: 68, cited in Litvag, *Singer in the Shadows,* 294-95). A phenomenon that might be called "automatic drawing" has also been documented and studied (Mühl, *Automatic Writing,* 100-106).

37. As an example of evolving quality, see Skutch, "Messages from the Higher Self," 18-19. As predicted, after an earlier version of this essay appeared in print, some critics seized upon the issue of quality to vindicate the uniqueness of LDS scriptures. Richard Lloyd Anderson ("Imitation Gospels and Christ's Book of Mormon Ministry," in *Apocryphal Writings and the Latter-day Saints,* ed. C. Wilfred Griggs [Provo, UT: Brigham Young University Religious Studies Center, 1986], 53-107) discusses spiritualist works about Jesus Christ and makes judgments about their authenticity. His chief criteria are (1) consistency with Mormon interpretations of the Bible and (2) his personal opinion of each work's literary merit. Not surprisingly, the Book of Mormon wins. Such an approach is likely to have little impact on those whose lives have been touched by the works Anderson either disparages or ignores.

38. Robert Graves distinguished between poetry that is written "by those who rely on inspiration, checked by commonsense, and those who rely on intellectual verse decorated by the artificial flowers of fancy." He labels the former "Muse poetry" and adds that the ultimate "source of creative power in poetry is not scientific intelligence, but inspiration" (Graves, *Five Pens in Hand,* 58, 64; see also Kirkham, *The Poetry of Robert Graves,* 197-98.) Creative inspiration also occurs in other disciplines, including physics, chemistry, and mathematics. A good overview of the phenomenon of sudden insight can be found in Harold A. Larrabee, *Reliable Knowledge* (Washington, DC: University Press of America, 1981), 130-42. For a list of related sources and a discussion of spontaneous creativity linked to dissociated mental processes, see Hilgard, *Divided Consciousness,* 195-96, 203.

39. A variation of this approach attributes the writer's abilities to a merging with other minds (called a "transpersonal state") resulting from altered states of consciousness. See Adrian Parker, *States of Mind: ESP and Altered States of Consciousness* (London: Malaby Press, 1975), 54-74, 120-24. See also John C. Gowan, *Trance, Art, and Creativity* (Westlake Village, CA: Published by author, 1975), 56-70.

40. Stevenson, "Some Comments on Automatic Writing," 322-24; Litvag, *Singer in the Shadows,* 165-68. Stevenson notes that where style comparisons are equivocal, computerized wordprint studies may be helpful to compare the new work with that of the author.

41. The identity of the subconscious personality was not suggested by the psychologist's questions but was volunteered by "My Dearest" only when asked why she had emerged (Mühl, *Automatic Writing,* 43-47).

42. The summary here is that of West, *Psychical Research Today,* 58. The research was first reported in Philip Lawrence Harriman, "The Experimental Production of Some Phenomena Related to the Multiple Personality," *Journal of Abnormal and Social Psychology* 37 (1942): 244-55.

43. Mühl, *Automatic Writing,* 112-19. (This experiment is also mentioned by Eve Juster, "Introduction," in Besterman, *Crystal-Gazing,* xvii.) Milton Erickson has noted that both crystal-gazing and automatic writing ("somewhat comparable phenomena") are valuable psychotherapeutic tools for eliciting long-forgotten information (*Innovative Hypnotherapy,* vol. 4 of *The Collected Papers of Milton H. Erickson on Hypnosis,* 21; *Hypnotic Investigation,* 17). This is not to say that all information obtained through automatic writing or hypnosis is factual. On this point, see Milton V. Kline, *Forensic Hypnosis: Clinical Tactics in the Courtroom* (Springfield, IL: Charles C. Thomas, Publisher, 1983), 113-23; and Martin T. Orne, "The Potential Uses of Hypnosis in Interrogation," in *The Manipulation of Human Behavior,* ed. Albert D. Biderman and Herbert Zimmer (New York: John Wiley & Sons, 1961), 169-96.

44. Hilgard, *Divided Consciousness,* 196.

45. For a comprehensive theory of dissociation, see Hilgard, *Divided Consciousness.*

46. Litvag, *Singer in the Shadows,* 1-2, 27-28.

47. These critics are quoted in Litvag, *Singer in the Shadows,* 62, 161, 124, 180-81. The poetry collection was the *Anthology of Magazine Verse and Year Book of American Poetry,* edited by William Stanley Braithwaite.

48. Litvag, *Singer in the Shadows,* 180, 152, 160, 155-56.

49. Ibid., 161, 117.

50. Ibid., 89-90.

51. West, *Psychical Research Today,* 62. There is, of course, a discrepancy in Patience's thirteenth-century English and her alleged seventeenth-century existence. But as with the apologetics of many religions, believers have explanations for such problems that they deem entirely plausible.

52. This is the principal line of defense in several of the essays in Noel B. Reynolds, ed., *Book of Mormon Authorship: New Light on Ancient Origins* (Provo, UT: Brigham Young University Religious Studies Center, 1982).

53. Litvag, *Singer in the Shadows,* 160.

54. Ibid., 189-90.

55. Ibid., 160, 76-77. See also 125, 281, 293.

56. This was William Marion Reedy, cited in ibid., 81.

57. Ibid., 212-13.

58. Ibid., 107, 213-14, 116, 133, 212, 281-82, 146.

59. Casper S. Yost, "Preface," in Patience Worth, *The Sorry Tale: A Story of the Time of Christ,* ed. Casper S. Yost (New York: Henry Holt and Co., 1917), iv; Litvag, *Singer in the Shadows,* 94.

60. Joseph Smith [III], "Last Testimony of Sister Emma," *Saints' Herald* 26 (1 Oct. 1879): 290; reprinted in Dan Vogel, *Early Mormon Documents,* 3+ vols. (Salt Lake City: Signature Books, 1986-), 1:542. Similarly, Parley P. Pratt noted that in dictating revelations, "there was never any hesitation, reviewing, or reading back, in order to keep the run of the subject" (*The Autobiography of Parley Parker Pratt* [5th ed.; Salt Lake City: Deseret Book Co., 1961], 62).

61. Walter Franklin Prince, "The Riddle of Patience Worth," *Scientific American* 134 (July 1926): 22; see also Litvag, *Singer in the Shadows,* 250, 273.

62. Walter Franklin Prince, *The Case of Patience Worth* (1927; reprint ed., New Hyde Park, NY: University Books, 1964), 80ff., 271. Prince was founder of the Boston Society for Psychical Research and the research officer for the American Society for Psychical Research. He had a reputation for being careful, studious, and demanding.

63. Walter Franklin Prince, "Psychological Tests for the Authorship of the Book of Mormon," *American Journal of Psychology* 28 (1917): 373-89; and Prince, "A Footnote: Authorship of the Book of Mormon," *American Journal of Psychology* 30 (1919): 427-28. See also the detailed discussion of Book of Mormon problems in Prince's correspondence with Brigham Young University professor M. Wilford Poulson, M. Wilford Poulson Collection, Special Collections, Harold B. Lee Library, Brigham Young University, Provo, Utah (hereafter referred to as BYU Special Collections).

64. This was accomplished between the beginning of April and the end of June 1829. See Stan Larson, "'A Most Sacred Possession': The Original Manuscript of the Book of Mormon," *Ensign* 7 (Sept. 1977): 87-88.

65. Richard Van Wagoner and Steven C. Walker, "Joseph Smith: 'The Gift of Seeing,'" *Dialogue: A Journal of Mormon Thought* 15 (Summer 1982): 50-53; James E. Lancaster, "The Translation of the Book of Mormon," in *The Word of God: Essays on Mormon Scripture* (Salt Lake City: Signature Books, 1990), 97-112. That the translation would proceed "hour after hour" is indicated by Emma Smith and Elizabeth Ann Whitney Cowdery (ibid).

66. B. H. Roberts, "Translation of the Book of Mormon," *Improvement Era* 9 (Apr. 1906): 428-29; B. H. Boberts, *A Comprehensive History of the Church,* 6 vols. (1930; reprint ed., Provo, UT: Brigham Young University Press, 1965), 1:127-33; Sidney B. Sperry, *Answers to Book of Mormon Questions* (Salt Lake City: Bookcraft, 1967), 184-86; Paul R. Cheesman, *The Keystone of Mormonism: Little Known Truths about the Book of Mormon* (Salt Lake City: Deseret Book Co., 1973), 44-46; Edward H. Ashment, "The Book of Mormon–A Literal Translation?" *Sunstone* 5 (Mar.-Apr. 1980): 10-14.

67. The phrase "gift of working with the rod," which appeared in the Book of Commandments, has been changed to "gift of Aaron" in the current Doctrine and Covenants (D&C 8:6). See Robert J. Woodford, "The Historical Development of the Doctrine and Covenants," 3 vols. (Ph.D. diss., Brigham Young University, 1974), 1:190-92.

68. See, for example, the Reverend Laban Clark's account of an encounter with the Vermont "rod-men" in Barnes Frisbie, *The History of Middletown, Vermont* (Poultney, VT, 1867), 54-55 (also Vogel, *Early Mormon Documents,* 1:611-12).

69. The expression "spiritual impressions" belongs to D. Michael Quinn, who asserted that "it was actually the impressions of the Holy Ghost ... which provided the translation." This seems to be an unjustified interpretation of

Diedrich Willers's observation that "by using these spectacles [the urim and thummim], he (Smith) would be in a position to read these ancient languages, which he had never studied, and that the Holy Ghost would reveal to him the translation in the English language." This statement is far too general to be considered a description of the translation process. Indeed, if anything, the statement that the translation was revealed "in the English language" suggests a minimum of mental study (see D. Michael Quinn, ed. and trans., "The First Months of Mormonism: A Contemporary View by Rev. Diedrich Willers," *New York History* 54 [July 1973]: 320-21, 326).

70. That the urim and thummim operated like the seer stone is suggested by Joseph Knight Sr., who commented that when Smith "put the urim and thummim into his hat and Darkened his Eyes[,] then he would take a sentance and it would apper in Brite Roman Letters[,] then he would tell the writer" (Dean Jessee, "Joseph Knight's Recollection of Early Mormon History," *BYU Studies* 17 [Autumn 1976]: 35). Of course, a number of difficulties exist in distinguishing between the operations of these two implements, since many sources use the terms "Urim and Thummim" and "seer stone" interchangeably (Van Wagoner and Walker, "The Gift of Seeing," 53).

71. Lucy Mack Smith, *Biographical Sketches of Joseph Smith the Prophet and His Progenitors for Many Generations* (1912; reprint ed., Independence, MO: Herald Publishing House, 1969), 92; Joseph Smith to John Wentworth, 1 Mar. 1842, in Dean C. Jessee, comp. and ed., *The Personal Writings of Joseph Smith* (Salt Lake City: Deseret Book Co., 1984), 214.

72. David Whitmer, reporting on the translation of 1 Nephi at the Whitmer home, states that when Smith "first came to where Jerusalem was spoken of as a 'Walled City' [1 Ne. 4:4], he stopped until they got a Bible and showed him where the fact was recorded–Smith not believing it was a walled city" (M. J. Hubble interview with David Whitmer, 13 Nov. 1886, qtd. in Stanley B. Kimball, "Missouri Mormon Manuscripts: Sources in Selected Societies," *BYU Studies* 14 [Summer 1974]: 486). For a critical analysis of Whitmer's report, see Brent Metcalfe, "The Priority of Mosiah: A Prelude to Book of Mormon Exegesis," in *New Approaches to the Book of Mormon: Explorations in Critical Methodology*, ed. Brent Lee Metcalfe (Salt Lake City: Signature Books, 1993), 395-444.

73. Horst, *A Condensed Version of Oahspe*, 26-29, 20. The case of Patience Worth provides another example: Early in July 1915, "Patience Worth" hinted that "something momentous was going to take place, something that she was approaching with trepidation." Approximately two weeks later, Patience began dictating her most famous work, *The Sorry Tale* (Litvag, *Singer in the Shadows*, 91-92).

74. Larrabee, *Reliable Knowledge*, 140-42. See also Hilgard, *Divided Consciousness*, 195-96. Jerald and Sandra Tanner point out that after losing the first 116 manuscript pages of the Book of Mormon, Joseph Smith generated additional material rather than retranslate the lost portion. To the Tanners, this indicates conscious plotting ("A Black Hole in the Book of Mormon," *Salt Lake*

City Messenger, No. 72 [July 1989]: 1-15). Unfortunately, the Tanners have not produced any documentary evidence (outlines, rough drafts, or telling comments in letters or diaries) to substantiate such planning. But as this discussion shows, conscious awareness of a problem does not preclude an unconscious solution. The fact that the arrangement was announced by divine revelation (D&C 10:1-45) and commented on by a Book of Mormon character (1 Ne. 9:2-6) suggests just such a phenomenon.

75. David Whitmer stated that each line of the translation was read back to Smith to ensure its correct transcription (David Whitmer, *An Address to All Believers in Christ* [Richmond, MO: published by author, 1887], 12).

76. Joseph Smith [III], "Last Testimony of Sister Emma," 290; Pratt, *Autobiography,* 62. Pratt notes that none of the revelations underwent "revisions, interlinings, or corrections," presumably meaning during the dictations that he witnessed, for the revelations were clearly corrected and even enlarged from time to time. See Woodford, "Historical Development of the Doctrine and Covenants."

77. Larson, "A Most Sacred Possession," 89-90.

78. Klaus Hansen, *Mormonism and the American Experience,* Chicago History of American Religion series, ed. Martin E. Marty (Chicago: University of Chicago Press, 1981), 16.

79. Blake Ostler, "The Book of Mormon as a Modern Expansion of an Ancient Source," *Dialogue: A Journal of Mormon Thought* 20 (Spring 1987): 66-123.

80. Ibid., 105. Like many believers in a particular text, Ostler focuses on peripheral issues rather than the automaticity that is at the core of this phenomenon.

81. See Walter F. Prince to M. Wilford Poulson, 5 Sept. 1933, Poulson Collection, BYU Special Collections; H. Michael Marquardt, "The Use of the Bible in the Book of Mormon," *Journal of Pastoral Practice* 2 (1978): 95-136.

82. B. H. Roberts, *New Witness for God,* 3 vols. (Salt Lake City: Deseret News, 1909), 3:440-45; Sperry, *Answers to Book of Mormon Questions,* 206.

83. Litvag, *Singer in the Shadows,* 293-94; Stevenson, "Some Comments on Automatic Writing," 319-20.

84. Among the many works noting such literary parallels, two are John W. Welch, "Chiasmus in the Book of Mormon," and Noel B. Reynolds, "Nephi's Outline," both in *Book of Mormon Authorship,* 33-74.

85. Dan Vogel, *Indian Origins and the Book of Mormon* (Salt Lake City: Signature Books, 1986); Van Hale, "Defining the Contemporary Mormon Concept of God," in *Line upon Line: Essays on Mormon Doctrine,* ed. Gary James Bergera (Salt Lake City: Signature Books, 1989), 7-15; Dan Vogel, "The Earliest Mormon Concept of God," in ibid., 17-52; Mark Thomas, "Revival Language in the Book of Mormon," *Sunstone* 8 (May-June 1983): 19-25; George D. Smith Jr., "Defending the Keystone," *Sunstone* 6 (May-June 1981): 45-50; Madison U. Sowell, "Defending the Keystone: The Comparative Method Reexamined," *Sunstone* 6 (May-June 1981): 44, 50-53; Robert Wauchope, *Lost Tribes and*

Sunken Continents: Myth and Method in the Study of American Indians (Chicago: University of Chicago Press, [ca. 1962]).

86. Madison U. Sowell gives a good overview of the debates over *View of the Hebrews* in "The Comparative Method Reexamined," although he himself asserts that "no proof exists at present to show that Joseph Smith had a *direct* knowledge of Ethan Smith's work" (53; emphasis added). Others who seem concerned with this question are Robert N. Hullinger (*Mormon Answer to Skepticism* [St. Louis: Clayton Publishing House, 1980], 36, 39, 44-47, 57) and Hugh Nibley ("A Strange Thing in the Land: The Return of the Book of Enoch, Part 2," *Ensign* 5 [Dec. 1975]: 72-76). Robert Paul also seems to feel it is important that Joseph Smith did not read much as a youngster ("Joseph Smith and the Manchester [New York] Library," *BYU Studies* 22 [Summer 1982]: 341-42).

87. Stevenson, "Some Comments on Automatic Writing," 324-25. Stevenson says "there was no question of dishonesty, so far as I could tell."

88. The LDS church *Ensign* publishes faith-promoting stories that express amazement over "an uneducated farm boy [writing] an epic book, this complex and incredible" (Joseph Giacalone, "Growing into the Church," *Ensign* 14 [June 1984]: 64). This argument is also implicit in the question that missionaries sometimes ask their investigators: "Could any man have written this book?" (*The Uniform System for Teaching Families* [Salt Lake City: The Church of Jesus Christ of Latter-day Saints, 1973], C-27).

89. Litvag puts it this way: "It doesn't seem possible that a relatively uneducated woman, no matter how ambitious (or tireless) or innately talented, could force-feed herself enough information to so skillfully write a life of Christ that a professional historian of high standing would call it the greatest since the Gospels" (*Singer in the Shadows,* 290).

90. An articulation of this assumption can be found in the introduction to Reynolds, *Book of Mormon Authorship,* 1-3.

91. One area where the Book of Mormon may differ from other automatic texts is in religious doctrine. But to say that the Book of Mormon is scripture because its doctrine is true and that its doctrine is true because it is scripture is hopelessly circular. A bigger problem with the doctrinal criterion is the fact that Book of Mormon teachings sometimes contradict current Mormon theology (see Hale, "Defining the Contemporary Mormon Concept of God"; and Vogel, "The Earliest Mormon Concept of God").

92. For example, both Jane Roberts's and Pearl Curran's works embrace the notion of reincarnation; *A Course in Miracles* expresses a clear disdain for the physical body; the God of *The Urantia Book* is spiritual rather than embodied.

3.

Lamanite Genesis, Genealogy, and Genetics

Thomas W. Murphy

IN MARCH 2000 SCOTT WOODWARD, A PROFESSOR OF MICROBIOLOGY at Brigham Young University, launched a multi-million dollar study funded by philanthropists Ira Fulton and James Sorenson.[1] Their Molecular Genealogy Research Group (MGRG) is compiling a database of DNA and genealogical records that can be used to identify connections between present and past human beings. Applying data from DNA to trace family histories and linkages between populations offers considerable promise to Latter-day Saint genealogists.[2] It also constitutes a boost to broader scientific research into the history and geography of genes, as well as to global migration and world population histories.[3] While the embrace of molecular research at an LDS-owned university may be a welcome development for many well-educated Mormons, this burgeoning interest may also provoke reconsideration of assumptions that have been long held by many, if not most, Mormons.

Some optimism was expressed by church members that such research would vindicate the Book of Mormon as an ancient document. The hope was that DNA would link Native Americans to ancient Israelites, buttressing LDS beliefs in a way that has not been forthcoming from archaeological, linguistic, historical, or morphological research. For those who held such an expectation, the data collected by MGRG and results of similar research projects have been disappointing.[4] So far, DNA has lent no support to the traditional Mormon beliefs about the origins of Native Americans. Instead, genetic data have confirmed that migrations from Asia are the primary source of American Indian origins. This research has substantiated already-existing archaeological, cultural, linguistic, and biological evidence. While DNA shows that ultimately all human populations are closely related, to date no intimate genetic link has been found between ancient Israelites and indigenous Americans, much less within the time frame suggested by the Book of Mormon.[5] Therefore, after considering the research in molecular anthropology summarized here, I have concluded that Latter-day Saints should not realistically expect to find validation for the ancient historicity of the Book of Mormon in genetics. My assessment echoes that of geneticist and former LDS bishop Simon Southerton whose survey of the literature "failed to find anything that supported migration of Jewish people before Columbus" and "no reliable scientific evidence supporting migrations from the Middle East to the New World."[6]

This essay outlines two insights into the geography and history of human genes and their implications for Mormon thought. If the embrace of DNA research has an impact on Mormon views, it will likely propel new approaches to scripture and history already underway in intellectual circles. First, genealogical data inscribed in genes suggest to current researchers that humans and chimpanzees share a common ancestor that lived in Africa between 5 and 7 million years ago. This adds to an abundance of archaeological and other data pointing to the same conclusion and adds to the challenges one encounters in trying to uphold scriptural literalism. Second, new genetic clues are being discovered that confirm scientific views about ancient migration patterns. Ancestors of Native Americans seem to have separated from their Asian neighbors about 40,000-50,000 years ago and from each other in what may have been three or more separate waves of migration 7,000-15,000 years ago. No link between American Indians and ancient Israelites is evident in the data.

DNA AND HUMAN ORIGINS

As readers may know, deoxyribonucleic acid (DNA) consists of a double-stranded molecule containing the genetic code—the major component of human chromosomes that links human beings to all other forms of life on earth. Because of a common evolutionary past, the cells of living organisms share fundamental similarities. Beginning about 1.2 billion years ago, structurally complex eukaryotic cells appeared, containing a variety of structures within the cell membrane. DNA is among the most important of those structures: nuclear DNA, found in the nucleus of the cells, and the more abundant mitochondrial DNA (mtDNA), found outside the nucleus and inherited directly from mothers. Both nuclear and mtDNA share a similar structure but are organized differently.[7] Through comparisons of DNA and mtDNA in populations and across the spectrum of living organisms, scientists have discovered a veritable genealogical record. Often labeled molecular anthropologists, these scientists have begun using genetic markers to chart evolution and migration.[8]

The Third Chimpanzee

Jared Diamond, a professor of physiology at UCLA's medical school, draws upon DNA evidence to support the argument that humans ought to be classified as the third chimpanzee. Scientists have long pointed to anatomical similarities with monkeys and apes for the classification of humans as primates, but analysis of DNA helps us realize just how closely related we are. Monkeys share an impressive 93 percent of their genetic code with humans, while apes and humans share at least 95 percent; humans and chimpanzees share an astounding 98.4 percent. The genetic difference between us and chimpanzees (pygmy and common) is less than between common gibbons and siamang gibbons. It is also less than between closely-related North American bird species such as the red-eyed vireos and white-eyed vireos. Diamond concludes that "we are just a third species of chimpanzee" and that "our important visible distinctions from the other chimps–our upright posture, large brains, ability to speak, sparse body hair, and peculiar sexual lives–must be concentrated in a mere 1.6 percent of our genetic program."[9]

African Origins

DNA not only confirms our genetic relationship with chimpanzees and gorillas but points to Africa as the birthplace of humanity, supporting the fossil record. Analysis of protein immunological data suggests that humans and chimpanzees shared a common African ancestor 5-7 million years ago.[10] Fossils from the genera *Australopithecus* and *Ardipithecus* show that multiple species of ancient hominids with chimp-like brains walked on two feet between 6 million and 1 million years ago.[11] The emergence of a larger-brained hominid *Homo habilis* around 2 million years ago is followed by that of *Homo erectus* and archaic *Homo sapiens* around 1.7 million and 500,000 years ago, respectively. These species spread from Africa throughout much of Europe and Asia. The first fully modern human fossils date from Africa at about 100,000 years ago and from Europe, Asia, and Australia at about 40,000 years ago. Scientists vigorously debate whether the evolution to *Homo sapiens sapiens* was a gradual multiregional transition throughout the Old World or whether fully modern *Homo sapiens*, emerged from its place of origin to displace regional archaic species like the Neanderthals found in Europe and western Asia.[12]

In fact, the biggest impact that molecular anthropologists have made occurred in the rivalry between the multiregional view and that of a modern emergence out of Africa. Allan C. Wilson, Rebecca L. Cann, and colleagues utilized mtDNA of living humans to construct a genealogy that indicated a common female ancestor in Africa less than 200,000 years ago.[13] This provoked a discussion about the applicability of mtDNA data to issues of evolution. Paleoanthropologists Robert Corruccini and Glenn Conroy criticized the assumptions and simplifications in this approach.[14] However, the early findings have been substantiated by more thorough analyses of mitochondrial genome variation and by several population studies of nuclear DNA which show more genetic variation in Africa than elsewhere, indicating an African origin for all humans.[15] The recent extraction of DNA from Neanderthal fossils lends further weight to the out-of-Africa hypothesis. These studies found that the mtDNA of Neanderthals falls outside the range of variation found in modern humans and that Neanderthal and human lineages split about 600,000 years ago.[16] Further analysis of mtDNA and nuclear DNA by Alan R. Templeton of Washington University confirmed a recent migration from Africa (ca. 80,000-150,000 years ago) but indicated that it was characterized by some interbreeding and not complete replacement of at least one earlier human expansion out of Africa (ca. 420,000-840,000 years ago).[17]

Stanford geneticist Luigi Luca Cavalli-Sforza has synthesized data from blood groups and protein polymorphisms (proteins occurring in different forms) to calculate genetic distances between populations. By comparing genetic dates to those derived from archaeology and linguistics, he was able to prepare a model of global human colonization. According to his calculations, modern humans first entered Asia approximately 100,000 years ago. They spread from Asia to Australia approximately 55,000 years ago and to Europe approximately 43,000 years ago. The data are less conclusive about the exact timing of the migration from Asia to the Americas, but an Asian origin is clearly indicated and the possible time frame stretches from 15,000 to 50,000 years ago. A closer comparison of Amerindians and East Asians, as opposed to all Asians, suggests a possible date for the first settlement of America approximately 32,000 years ago.[18]

The Mormon Context

Biblical historicity was central to Mormon theology from its inception. When the Book of Mormon was published in 1830, early America was embroiled in debates about the role of scripture in an age of skepticism and reason. The existence of two New World continents with people who were unaccounted for in the Bible caused a theological crisis in Christianity beginning in the early sixteenth century.[19] Questions about the historicity of the Bible were rampant both in European and early American intellectual circles. In 1794-95 Thomas Paine wrote an influential series of pamphlets entitled *The Age of Reason* that defended the reasonableness of belief in God but portrayed the Bible as mythology and hearsay.[20] The Joseph Smith family, like others, found themselves embroiled in this controversy. Asael Smith confronted his son Joseph Smith Sr. with a copy of Paine's book when he heard that his son was attending Methodist services. Lutheran minister Robert N. Hullinger has sympathetically written a portrait of this debate and its impact on the Smith family and Mormon theology. He believes that the Book of Mormon and parts of the Pearl of Great Price and the Doctrine and Covenants constituted Joseph Smith Jr.'s response to this skepticism.[21] In an 1842 letter, the Mormon founder stated his position on these issues when he declared "the bible to be the word of God as far as it is translated correctly" while claiming a higher status for the Book of Mormon as "the word of God."[22] But Smith's tendency to read the Bible in literal terms is also evident in his designation of Independence, Missouri, as the site of the original Garden of Eden.[23] In the context of this debate, the Book of Mormon defended literal readings of the Bible against the onslaught of rationalism while validating some of the concerns of skeptics about inaccuracies in the Bible.

Internal debate on the Bible and human origins, fueled by Charles Darwin's publication of *On the Origin of Species* in 1859, has generally shown LDS scholars and some church authorities to be in support of science.[24] Brigham H. Roberts, an LDS authority who supported pre-Adamic life and the antiquity of the earth, stood out as an early spokesperson for the harmonization of science and theology.[25] His approach found sympathy and support from such LDS authorities as Apostle John A. Widtsoe, President David O. McKay, and First Presidency counselor Hugh B. Brown. More recently, such leaders as Apostles Mark E. Peterson and Bruce R. McConkie and church presidents Harold B. Lee and Ezra Taft Benson have taken a stand against what they see as the dangers of science and of evolution in particular.[26] LDS sociologist Armand L. Mauss has noted a trend among Mormons towards Protestant fundamentalism in the latter part of the twentieth century.[27] Despite this trend, the LDS First Presidency has not taken a definitive stand for or against evolution.[28] This is encouraging for the many young Mormons embarking on careers in science and seeking ways to resolve tensions between their academic careers and personal spirituality. Attempts by Latter-day Saints to balance these perspectives can be found in such publications as *Brigham Young University Studies*, *Dialogue: A Journal of Mormon Thought*, the *FARMS Review of Books*, and *Sunstone*.[29] Perhaps the new genealogical data extracted from genomes may propel the LDS leadership to acknowledge the possibility of God's hand in science and evolution, as the Catholic leadership has done.[30] This would imply a more liberal interpretation of not only the Bible but also of the revelatory texts that defend biblical literalism.

MOLECULAR ANTHROPOLOGY AND NATIVE AMERICAN ORIGINS

To date, molecular anthropology has not provided support for the Book of Mormon as a history of ancient America. Non-LDS scientists have long considered the book's view to be inconsistent with the archaeological record.[31] In 1973 Michael Coe, an archaeologist at Yale University, pointed to Joseph Smith's inability to "read 'Reformed Egyptian' or any other kind of hieroglyphs," observing:

> There is an inherent improbability in specific items that are mentioned in the Book of Mormon as having been brought to the New World by Jaredites and/or Nephites. Among these are the horse (extinct in the New World since about 7,000 B.C.), the chariot, wheat, barley, and metallurgy (true metallurgy based upon smelting and casting being no earlier in Mesoamerica than about 800 A.D.). The picture of this hemisphere between 2,000 B.C. and A.D. 421 presented in the book has little to do with the early Indian cultures as we know them, in spite of much wishful thinking.[32]

For similar reasons, LDS archaeologists Dee F. Green and Deanne G. Matheny have been critical of naïve attempts to link the Book of Mormon to archaeological sites.[33] Life-long efforts by Brigham H. Roberts and Thomas S. Ferguson to use archaeological evidence to corroborate the Book of Mormon ended in personal disillusionment.[34] Genetic evidence poses similar difficulties. When asked about DNA evidence, Michael Crawford, a biological anthropologist at the University of Kansas, stated: "I don't think there is one iota of evidence that suggests a lost tribe from Israel made it all the way to the New World. It is a great story, slain by ugly fact."[35] Oxford geneticist Bryan Sykes and Russian geneticist Miroslava Derenko have both substantiated Crawford's conclusion through agreement that "the Indian gene pool is Siberian, not Middle Eastern."[36]

Crawford's conclusions in *The Origins of Native Americans: Evidence from Anthropological Genetics* show why he rejects Mormon claims. Genetic similarities, morphological resemblance, craniometric affinities, and cultural similarities between Asians and New World populations led him to conclude, "This evidence indicates extremely strong biological and cultural affinities between New World and Asian populations and leaves no doubt that the first migrants into the Americas were Asians, possibly from Siberia."[37]

Following this statement, he acknowledges that "[t]his evidence does not preclude the possibility of some small-scale cultural contacts between Amerindian societies and Asian or Oceanic seafarers." Despite this cautious qualification, his work shows that Amerisraelite Lamanites could not possibly have been the "principal ancestors of the American Indians," as claimed in the current introduction to the Book of Mormon.[38] If there was contact with other people, he has yet to see evidence of this, although the evidence has not ruled out the possibility of limited encounters.

As Crawford indicates, the current data showing an affinity between Native American and Asian populations are abundant. For instance, he lists more than a dozen alleles for blood proteins unique to New World and Asian populations and identifies additional genetic systems which are not exclusive to them but occur at different frequencies elsewhere. These include "the human leukocyte antigen (HLA) system, the various blood groups, and even the mitochondrial DNA (mtDNA) Asian haplotypes." Amerindian and Siberian populations seem to "share a genetic predisposition to otitis media," a middle ear infection.[39] Such findings substantiate the archaeological, linguistic, anatomical, and physiological studies that show an Asian origin for America's first inhabitants.

Mitochondrial DNA (mtDNA)

Native Americans were among the first humans studied for mtDNA variation. In fact, some of the most revealing research into Indian origins comes from these data. Begun in 1985, the research identified a frequent (40 percent) polymorphic genetic marker in Pima-Papago of southern Arizona, also uniquely present, though in low frequency, among East Asians. A second study of mtDNA variation in 1990 found that the Pima-Papago, Yucatan Maya, and the Ticuna from Brazil all shared high frequencies of the same genetic marker. Researchers identified four unique mtDNA families in these three populations and concluded that despite their distance from each other, they were closely related and most likely all came from the same founding population.[40] In the following years, research has confirmed that "almost all Native American mtDNAs (about 98 percent) were defined by one of four sets of specific mutations and clustered in four well-defined groups of haplotypes which were termed 'haplogroups.' The four haplogroups were termed A, B, C and D."[41]

Stanford linguist Joseph Greenberg entered the discussion in 1987 with a study of Native American languages. Initially his findings appeared alongside, but are now deeply imbedded in, the study of Native American genetics. Greenberg proposed that Native American languages could be divided into three families: Amerindian (comprising most languages of North and South America), Na-Dene (comprising Navajo, Apache, and languages spoken in the Pacific Northwest), and Eskimo-Aleut.[42] Cavalli-Sforza added that a significant correlation can be found between the dendrograms (family tree classifications) of genetic and linguistic evidence.[43] Other linguists generally accepted Greenberg's classifications of Eskimo-Aleut and Na-Dene language families but objected to lumping the remaining languages into a single Amerindian family.[44] Yet a recent publication by Cavalli-Sforza showed correlations between Greenberg's linguistic classifications and his own genetic ones. He found that "Amerindians are genetically extremely variable and the [traditional] linguistic subgroupings within the Amerindian family do not correspond terribly well with the genetic results."[45] This indicated an Amerindian migration, or possibly multiple migrations, at least 30,000 years ago, older and more complex than those of later Na-Dene and Eskimo-Aleut speakers.[46]

Data subsequently gathered from more than six dozen Native communities and thousands of individuals from North, Central, and South America demonstrate that Amerindian populations generally contain all four mtDNA haplogroups. Important exceptions include the populations of lower Central America where only haplogroups A and B are present. Speakers of Na-Dene languages, likely products of a later migration, tend to have only haplogroup A. Haplogroup B, common among East Asians, Polynesians, and Amerindians, is found in low frequencies among Siberians, Eskimos, and Na-Dene speakers. This anomaly initially suggested the possibility of multiple migrations. The first would have been a population with haplogroups A, C, and D, the second may have carried haplogroup B, and the third would have been Na-Dene speakers. Oxford geneticist Bryan Sykes has suggested that the peculiar distribution of haplogroup B may be "the genetic echo of a second seaborne colonization that took the coastal route north up the coast of Asia and down the Pacific coast of North America" approximately 12,000-13,000 years ago. This wave of migration may have been prompted by the same post-Ice-Age environmental changes which launched a distinct branch of the same haplogroup from coastal China or Taiwan to colonize the Polynesian islands.[47] Italian geneticist Antonio Torroni estimates that the first migration occurred between 34,000 and 26,000 years ago, the second between 15,000 and 12,000 years ago, and the third 10,000 to 7,000 years ago. More recent analysis of the control region of mtDNA found support for an early arrival of all haplogroups. It is possible that "all Native

Americans derive from a single source population which colonized Beringia [now occupied by the Bering Sea] possibly around 30,000 years ago." The first migrants from Beringia would have given rise to Amerindians and subsequent migrations to the Na-Dene and Eskimo.[48] While researchers dispute the exact timing, number, and origin of migrations, there is virtual consensus that they began in Asia.

Haplogroup X

The mtDNA evidence initially appeared to leave room for a more complex picture of migrations. While about 98 percent of Native Americans are descended from one of the four haplogroups A-D, approximately 1 percent carry markers from a haplogroup, now designated X, that does not belong to the A-D categories. Prior to understanding European mtDNA, researchers speculated that this fifth haplogroup may have originated from recent admixture from Europeans. On the results of recent research, Torroni observes:

> Among Native Americans, haplogroup X appears to be essentially restricted to northern Amerind groups, including the Ojibwa (25 percent), the Nuu-Chah-Nulth (12 percent), the Sioux (15 percent), and the Yakima (5 percent), although it was also observed in the Na-Dene-speaking Navajo (6 percent). Substantial sequence differences exist between the Native American and European mtDNAs. Median network analysis showed that European and Native American haplogroup X mtDNAs are related yet (nearly) disjoint from each other, and that considerable genetic substructure exists within both groups. Thus, the presence of this haplogroup in North America cannot be attributed to recent admixture with Europeans. Estimates of the coalescence time of these mtDNAs in the Americas range between 12,000 and 36,000 years ago, indicating that haplogroup X represents an additional founding mtDNA lineage in Native Americans.[49]

Haplogroup X can be found in low frequencies in Europe, the Near East (including Israelis), and North America. Until recently, it was thought to be absent from living eastern-central Asian, Siberian, Central, and South American populations.[50] Summarizing research to date in 2000, Torroni proposed "that some Native American founders could have been of Caucasoid ancestry and haplogroup X might have been brought, directly or indirectly, to Beringia/America by the eastward migration of a 'Caucasoid' population which apparently did not contribute to the maternally derived gene pool of modern Siberian/East Asian populations."[51] Geneticist Theodore Schurr reported the presence of haplogroup X not only in "two Pre-Columbian North American populations" but also in "a few ancient Brazilian samples."[52] Because of variations within the Native American haplogroup that distinguish it from the European types, Michael D. Brown and colleagues dated its arrival in North America to 12,000-36,000 years ago.[53] Sykes's research echoes this timing and interpretation, tracing X's origin to the borders of Europe and Asia approximately 25,000 years ago, with an early separation into distinctive branches, one of which gave rise to the European and the other to the Asian/Native American matrilineages.[54]

The discovery of a rare haplogroup apparently linked to the Near East sparked the interest of some Latter-day Saints, even though it posed considerable difficulty for the chronology and geography of the Book of Mormon. The timing of its entry predates Book of Mormon events by thousands of years, and its distribution challenges both the traditional hemispheric Book of Mormon geography and the more recent limited geography in Central America posited by Foundation for Ancient Research and Mormon Studies (FARMS) researchers. The X variant neither appears spread across the American continents nor is it limited to a select Central American region.[55] A FARMS editorial noting the "European-like" characteristics associated with X suggested that it "may not be the last new haplogroup to be winnowed from the residual 'other' category." The editorial pointed to the possibility of haplogroup H (common among Europeans) among Maya Indians as an example of the complexity of the data and a caution against simplistic interpretations.[56] While the warning is a worthy one, most geneticists attribute the occasional presence of European haplogroups H and J and African haplogroup L to intermarriage with recent immigrant populations.[57] The identification of haplogroup X among Altaians from South Siberia in 2001 by Miroslava V. Derenko and colleagues invalidated Torroni's earlier speculations of a Caucasoid ancestry of haplogroup X because of its apparent absence, at that time, from Siberian/East Asian populations.[58] This new research confirms an ancient route of an X matrilineage branch across Asia, through Siberia, to the New World. Ultimately, as Derenko told a reporter from the *Financial Times*, the existence of haplogroup X does not constitute a linkage between ancient Israelites and American Indians much less within the time frame or geography suggested by the Book of Mormon.[59]

Y-Chromosomes

Mitochondrial DNA, inherited from a maternal lineage, provides only one method of investigating human genealogy. On the chromosomal level, men and women differ in that women possess two X-chromosomes and men have both X- and Y-chromosomes.[60] Because the Y-chromosome is inherited paternally, this offers an alternative investigative tool.

The Y-chromosome substantiates many conclusions already drawn from mtDNA, archaeology, and linguistics.[61] Its worldwide distribution and frequency provide support for an African origin for all humans[62] and for an Asian origin for Native Americans, probably a central Siberian origin. The earliest studies identified one major haplotype (defined as the DYS199 T allele) in southern and central Amerindians in frequencies above 90 percent, indicating a strong genetic homogeneity and common foundational population. It was found in lower frequencies among Eskimo and Na-Dene speakers and in far northeastern Siberians, possibly the result of back migration across the Bering Strait. Intermediate Y haplotypes of the kind that may have given rise to this major Native American marker have been found in Siberia.[63] Another recent study identified a second major founder haplotype in North, Central, and South American populations. Geneticists T. M. Karafet and colleagues labeled the earlier discovery (DYS199 T) haplotype 1G and the new one haplotype 1C. While 1C is found among Native Americans, Asians, and Europeans (2.3 percent), it reaches its highest frequencies outside of the Americas in Siberia. Another possible founder haplotype, 1F, appears most frequently in Siberia and Mongolia but not in Europe.[64] While the investigation of Y-chromosome lineages is not as far along as that of mtDNA, early results continue to substantiate much of what is already known from the other genetic markers and from archaeology, morphology, and linguistics.

Ancient DNA (aDNA)

Most studies in molecular anthropology have been conducted on living populations. While they are valuable in helping to identify the migration patterns of our ancestors, they only tell part of the story. Recent developments, including the invention of Polymerase Chain Reaction (PCR) in the mid-1980s, have made it possible to extract and analyze DNA from ancient fossil remains.[65] One of the most exciting results of this emerging field was the recent extraction of DNA from three Neanderthal skeletons. Another recent study linked the prehistoric Anasazi of the southwest United States to the modern populations of Pueblo Indians.[66] Studies of Anasazi, Fremont, and Oneota all show continuity between ancient and modern populations and continue to support Asian origins.[67]

Of most interest to Latter-day Saints might be the study of ancient Maya skeletons from Copán, Honduras. A team of geneticists led by D. Andrew Merriwether from the University of Michigan extracted DNA from nine skeletons and compared the results with living populations. They found that all nine individuals had belonged to mtDNA haplogroups C or D, thus indicating connections to living native populations. Yet, living Yucatec Maya are predominately from haplogroups A and B. Despite the apparent differences between these two Maya populations, which are widely separated by geography and time, the authors caution against reading too much into this small sample. Preliminary data indicated that several additional individuals who could not be fully typed were neither C nor D. Despite the additional clues about genetic patterns that this technology offers, it is as yet hampered by low extraction rates and the low frequency of most population-specific polymorphisms that would permit closer identification with modern populations.[68]

Israelite DNA

Population-based studies of Asians and Native Americans show statistically clustered, shared genetic markers between Native Americans and Asians.[69] Markers on the Y-chromosome, nuclear DNA polymorphisms and various types of mtDNA have also been used to cluster and chart relationships among Jews in Europe, Asia, and Africa. For instance, they have provided evidence of Jewish connections among probable Spanish-American descendants of *conversos*, the Spanish Jews forcefully converted to Christianity in the fifteenth century.[70] Studies using global databases examining a multitude of different markers have consistently failed to show a statistically significant clustering of indigenous Americans with Near Eastern, Israelite, or Jewish groups. However, LDS anthropologist John L. Sorenson, proponent of a limited geography of the Book of Mormon in Central America, has previously speculated that one should find as much or as little interaction, culturally and genetically, between Israel and ancient America as could be found among Israelites and the peoples of Eurasia.[71] If Sorenson is correct, then we can contrast the lack of evidence of an Israelite genetic presence in the Americas with actual clustering of genetic markers in Old World populations claiming a Jewish ancestry.

Researchers have uncovered distinctive genetic markers on the Y-chromosome that are useful in establishing linkages between ancient and contemporary Hebrew populations. Within the modern Jewish religion, there are three patrilineal castes that genetic anthropologists Neil Bradman and colleagues describe thus: "The Priests (Cohanim, singular Cohen), non-Cohen members of the priestly tribe (Levites), and Israelites (non Cohanim and non-Levites)." Notice that the term Israelite, as they use it, constitutes a subgroup "who are neither Cohanim nor Levites." While the priestly castes are present in most Jewish communities, one becomes a Jew through matrilineal heritage–that is, by being born to a Jewess–or through conversion. Thus "Israelite" haplotypes are diverse, with only the Cohen modal haplotype, out of genetic markers analyzed in this study, appearing in "Israelites" more frequently than 0.1 (14 out of 119). The Cohen haplotype is much more frequent in both Ashkenazic and Sephardic Cohanim (0.509, n = 54) than in Levites (0.037). Despite different understandings of the terms Jew and Israelite than Mormons hold, Bradman and colleagues date the origin of the Cohen haplotype to 2,100 to 3,250 years ago, putting it within the historical range of the alleged Lehite and Mulekite migrations to the New World. He concludes that it can "be useful for testing hypotheses regarding the relationship between specific contemporary communities and the ancient Hebrew population."[72]

Neil Bradman and Mark Thomas have used the Cohen haplotype to link ancient Hebrews to the modern population of the Lemba, a black, southern African, Bantu-speaking population with oral traditions asserting a Jewish ancestry. The researchers note that "claiming Jewish origins is not an unusual phenomenon: the myth of the lost tribes is a powerful story and many groups have claimed to be descendants of one or other of the tribes or have been put forward for that honor."[73] Claims regarding an Israelite ancestry for Native Americans would fit into this category, but DNA tests of the Lemba yielded a strikingly different outcome than for Native Americans. Two studies to date have demonstrated that one of the Lemba clans carries a high frequency of "a particular Y-chromosome termed the 'Cohen modal haplotype,' which is known to be characteristic of the paternally inherited Jewish priesthood and is thought, more generally, to be a potential signature haplotype of Judaic origin."[74] An additional study by Michael F. Hammer of the University of Arizona and colleagues in Europe and Africa has found considerable genetic continuity and a common pool of markers on the Y-chromosone shared by Middle Eastern Arabs and descendants of the Jewish Diaspora despite long-term residence in various parts of Europe, Asia, and Africa. At these markers, the Lemba showed more intermarriage with local populations than other members of the Jewish Diaspora but still clustered halfway between sub-Saharan Africans and others Jews.[75] Both Bradman and Tudor Parfitt have also publicly noted the lack of a comparable link between Native Americans and ancient Israelites.[76]

SHIFTING FOUNDATIONS

Evolution presents a minor challenge to popular Mormon beliefs in comparison to the problems posed by the scientific view of ancient America. New genetic evidence adds to an already impressive amount of linguistic, archaeological, cultural, biological, anatomical, and psychoanalytic data that challenge the traditional Book of Mormon view. That view includes the belief that the Lamanites described in the text are the "principal ancestors of the American Indians."[77] Remarkably, most Latter-day Saints are unaware of the many reasons why the scientific community rejects that claim.

The Book of Mormon's antiquity has been questioned since its publication in 1830. Among LDS scholars today, one can find individuals on either side of the issue, some of whom think that it is time to separate acceptance of the book as scripture from belief in its ancient origin. Others doubt that the book accounts for all or even most Native Americans and therefore propose a limited geography in Central America. Both groups reject a literal reading and agree that Nephites and Lamanites never actually rode horses, traveled in chariots, used steel swords, raised cattle, or ate wheat and oats.[78] FARMS has played a role in offering revisionist interpretations that seek to reconcile faith with science. But the DNA research may make this effort more difficult as the views of intellectuals and those of traditional Mormons continue to diverge.

Limited Geography

The difficulties in trying to link the Book of Mormon to ancient populations have prompted some LDS scholars, especially those associated with FARMS, to reinterpret Lamanite identity in the latter part of the twentieth century. Rejecting the hemispheric views of previous generations and of most contemporary Mormons, Sorenson proposed a limited geography around the Isthmus of Tehuantepec in Central America. He interpreted the Book of Mormon as a lineage history comparable to the *Popol Vuh* of the Quiché Maya rather than a hemispheric history as most Mormons have understood it, explaining that "the Book of Mormon is a partial record of events, emphasizing what happened to one group of people, put in their own ethnocentric terms, in the midst of other peoples each with its own version of events."[79]

If the events described in the Book of Mormon took place in a small setting in Central America, then where would an investigator look for genetic evidence of Israelites? FARMS scholar William Hamblin believes that "Lamanite" simply means "non-Nephite," a cultural rather than a biological designation: "Lamanite is not a genetic designator requiring us to insist that all inhabitants of the New World are genetically descended only from the Lehite colony." In this respect, he declares, "all modern Native Americans can be accurately described as cultural or political Lamanites, since they are non-Nephites."[80] By this logic, Hamblin himself, a non-Nephite, would be a Lamanite. So, one needs more specific criteria for distinguishing genetic Lamanites from cultural non-Nephites. Sorenson, too, is comfortable with the idea that "all native peoples of the New World may be appropriately classified 'Lamanites.'" He quickly clarifies that this says nothing about "'literal' descent." Like Hamblin, he expresses optimism that Lehite genes and ideas may eventually be found, but he cautions that the impact on the surrounding culture as Lehites spread out from Central America would have been "minor, culturally or biologically." Yet he identifies several places where significant movements of Mesoamerican peoples and ideas took place. These include northern Mexico, Arizona, New Mexico, and the southeastern United States: "Ecuador in the time of the Jaredites, and Peru, Ecuador, and Colombia at several later times, also felt the impress of Mesoamerican life and probably of the genes of its peoples."[81]

The social and historical variability of meanings for ethnic labels demands that one pay careful attention to the differences between biology and culture, as evident in the studies of the Lemba, the African tribe with established linkages to ancient Hebrews. The meaning of the term Israelite, like that of Lamanite, is variable over time and place.[82] Bradman and Thomas exercised considerable caution in their attempts to tie cultural categories to biological markers. Ultimately, they identified the Lemba's heritage through a paternal priestly lineage with a distinctive genetic marker on the Y-chromosome substantiated later by other researchers using additional Y-chromosome markers. Quests for Lamanite DNA are hampered by the absence of ancient historical sources that might substantiate or clarify the cultural classifications made in the Book of Mormon.

While FARMS researchers are careful to note the importance of cultural influences on the construction of categories, they express confidence in an Israelite genetic presence in Central America and perhaps as far away as Arizona to the north and Colombia to the south. As we have seen, genetic studies of indigenous peoples throughout North, Central, and South America have failed to link Native Americans from these locations to ancient Hebrews. At the same time, careful genetic studies in the Old World have proven capable of linking the Lemba of southern Africa to ancient Hebrews.

A Galileo Event

Recently an anonymous editorial addressing the "Problematic Role of DNA Testing in Unraveling Human History" appeared in the *Journal of Book of Mormon Studies.*[83] The editorialist urged against simplistic identification of Israelites with skin color and physical features. Accompanying the column was a set of photographs that illustrated the physical variation among modern "Jews." Readers were encouraged to approach "new light" from DNA with a skeptical eye and reminded that meanings applied to molecular data come from scientists, not from the DNA. While such critical thinking is a part of scientific inquiry, the anonymous author disparaged the value of molecular research, calling it a "new toy in human biology and anthropology," and dismissed molecular reconstructions of human history as "temporary, even faddish." In doing so, the writer exaggerated the impact of criticisms Rebecca Cann and colleagues received following their analysis of variation of mtDNA in living populations. Subsequent studies supported Cann's interpretation and confirmed a recent migration of modern humans out of Africa; this was not acknowledged in the editorial. Despite the general skepticism regarding DNA research that was urged in the editorial, the writer noted that "the DNA data has decisively confirmed" the Lemba traditions of Jewish ancestry, followed by a favorable report on speculations about low levels of gene flow between American Indians and Polynesians by Dr. Rebecca Cann–the very person whose more substantiated work on African origins the editorial cast doubt upon. This selected attention to a few instances of gene flow from South America to Polynesia misled readers by avoiding Sykes's "crystal clear" conclusion of Polynesian mtDNA of an ancestral origin in coastal China or Taiwan approximately 20,000-30,000 years ago.[84]

Perhaps the most troubling aspect of the article was its failure to provide a summary of the status of current research or to address the ethics of the research it proposed. It raised a question that will linger in many readers' minds: "So is there evidence from DNA studies of populations in America having Near Eastern/Jewish characteristics?" The author avoided answering by shifting to a hypothetical discussion between a philanthropist wanting to fund DNA research and a molecular expert. In this speculative encounter, the scientist discourages interest by raising questions about the efficacy of such studies. These include the likelihood of biological change in America and the Near East over 2,600 years from the time of Lehi, the possibility that Lehi's party was not genetically typical of Jews in Jerusalem at the time, problematic linkages between ethnicity and biology, the impact of intermarriage between Lehi's descendants and indigenous Americans, difficulty identifying direct descendants of Lehi, and only a "distant chance that someday we might know enough to identify [even] one group in Central America" through cultural and linguistic ties to the Near East. In an echo of the kind of ambivalence evident in the first half of the article, the author then ends by recommending the study of a mysterious group of Mexican Indians of purported Jewish origin identified by Raphael Patai in the 1930s but apparently unknown to any other researcher.

In a web-based article on "DNA and the Book of Mormon," Cooper Johnson from the Foundation for Apologetic Information and Research (FAIR) similarly dismisses the relevance of genetic research for interpreting the Book of Mormon.[85] Based on an oral presentation by BYU geneticist Scott Woodward at the 2001 FAIR Conference, Johnson concludes that current data from mtDNA "gives us absolutely nothing with which to base our conclusions as to the validity of the Book of Mormon." Like the FARMS editorialist, Johnson fails to summarize the data uncovered to date while nonetheless emphasizing its incompleteness and urging caution against jumping to hasty conclusions. He minimizes the importance of mtDNA and the Y-chromosome in one's genetic makeup relative to autosomal (non-sex linked genes or markers on the nuclear DNA) and emphasizes current difficulties involved in the extraction of ancient DNA. He accepts the "overwhelming" evidence that the Americas were occupied well before Lehi's reported arrival, and he uses the limited geographic framework to stress the small impact that Lehi's party would have had on a much larger population. He then incorrectly suggests that if a mother bears no daughters, her mtDNA "effectively comes to a screeching halt." This scenario would be true only if all the mother's sisters, cousins, and others who shared copies of the same mtDNA failed to have children. Most importantly, Johnson insists that attempts to test the validity of the Book of Mormon using only mtDNA are based on "an unsound and unacceptable hypothesis" because they beg the question of Lehi's genetic make-up. He fails to note that only the women in Lehi's party would have passed their mtDNA to succeeding generations. Regardless of this oversight, the critical point that Johnson is making is that a test of the validity of the Book of Mormon using genetic data needs to begin with some conception of the genetic makeup of Lehi's party, a task he sees as impossible.

After publication of the FAIR summary in 2002, Scott Woodward, founder of BYU's MGRG, clarified his view with respect to Johnson's article. Despite noting that much work on population genetics of the Americas is yet to be done, it would not surprise Woodward if geneticists ultimately failed to find any traces of mtDNA from Lehi's party, Jaredites, or Mulekites. He confirmed my critique of Johnson's claims by noting that if a woman without children had sisters, the copy of the grandmother's mtDNA would still be in the population. Woodward expressed his belief that people from the Book of Mormon would have made a "very small" contribution to the gene pool "compared to the pre-existing mtDNA in the Americas." Woodward advocates testing the Book of Mormon "on internal evidences" and believes that the presence or absence of genetic linkages to the Near East in the Americas is neither proof nor disproof of the Book of Mormon.[86]

The methodological concerns raised at FARMS, FAIR, and MGRG are comparable to those addressed and surmounted by Bradman, Thomas, and colleagues in their study of the Lemba and whose success offers hope to the anonymous editorialist that FARMS, or perhaps MGRG, can likewise identify a group in Central America with cultural and linguistic parallels that could be tested. The FARMS and FAIR authors exaggerate the likelihood of biological change in the Americas over the past 2,600 years. They are apparently unaware of research by Dennis O'Rourke of the University of Utah that revealed the tendency of ancient American mtDNA to reflect the same patterns of distribution evident in contemporary indigenous populations.[87] Furthermore, both articles fail to acknowledge the common pool of markers on the Y-chromosome shared by Jewish and non-Jewish populations in the Middle East and their continuity in widespread communities of the Jewish Diaspora.[88] Contrary to the views expressed by these authors, it is not necessary to know the exact genotype of Lehi, Sariah, or other members of their party, only to reasonably conclude that they would have been more like Jews and non-Jews in the Middle East than like Siberian populations in Asia.

In their welcome but unsatisfying attempts to provide plausible explanations for the lack of genetic evidence for Israelites in the Americas, both authors and BYU's leading geneticist implicitly reject long-standing popular Mormon beliefs, including those held by Joseph Smith, about Lamanites being the ancestors of today's American Indians. This shift in the foundations of Mormon beliefs about Indians, termed a "Galileo event" by Brent Metcalfe, may prove to be the most important historical result of wrestling with genetic data.[89]

Ethics of Genetic Research

The organization of the Human Genome Diversity Project (HGDP) in mid-September 1993 led to an outcry that it was being organized without the consultation of indigenous peoples. The HGDP sought the collection of molecular data to chart the history and geography of the human species. The dissent was aired in a public statement on 20 October 1993 from the South and Mesoamerican Indian Information Center (SAIIC) which questioned the ethics of research without oversight from the peoples whose genes would be subject to collection and study. This resulted in limited public research funds for the HGDP. Although SAIIC recognized the potential health benefits of genetic investigations, it also saw potential abuses.[90] With its large private endowment, the MGRG is less dependent upon public funding and oversight than the HGDP. Even though it is subject to the Human Subjects Institutional Review Board at BYU, the MGRG has been criticized for circumventing local ethics review in New Zealand.[91]

Prominent Native American scholars have raised ethical concerns related to the Book of Mormon and genetic research at BYU. Cherokee Jace Weaver at Yale University objects to the Book of Mormon as a perpetuation "of the old slur that Native Americans were descendants of the Ten Lost Tribes of Israel, a belief perpetuated by those who could not accept that indigenous peoples could develop any degree of 'civilization' without fertilization from the Old World."[92] In an article from *Financial Times* reprinted on the front page of *Indian Country Today*, Tom Goldtooth of the Indigenous Environmental Network referred to Mormon evangelism and plans by FARMS to pursue evidence of a genetic link between American Indians and ancient Israel as "ethnocidal indoctrination"; he promised to take appropriate action should such efforts continue.[93] While current research indicates the unlikelihood that FARMS will push such a claim, the potential use of genetic data to advance a view that many Native people find invasive and racist is a concern that will need to be addressed more thoroughly in the future at BYU.[94]

CONCLUSION

Before the emergence of molecular anthropology, John L. Sorenson anticipated the utility and futility of the types of molecular tests that are now available:

> Should some investigator find new methods to pursue research on the "blood lines" of a particular individual, family, or people, he or she might

> find that some native Americans are directly descended from Nephites of ancient times, that some are descended in part from others in Lehi's or Mulek's parties, that some are of Jaredite origin, and that still others have no discernible connection to any of those. Scientific, genealogical, or historical methods are not available; but more important, the scriptures indicate that the results would not matter as far as the Church and the gospel are concerned.[95]

Now that quantitative scientific methods can indeed test for an Israelite genetic presence in ancient America, we learn instead that virtually all Native Americans can trace their lineages to the Asian migrations between 7,000 and 50,000 years ago. While molecular anthropologists have the technological capability to identify descendants of ancient Hebrews, no traces of such DNA markers have appeared in Central America or elsewhere among Native Americans. Ultimately, as Sorenson noted, these findings may not matter to Latter-day Saints, who have a spiritual witness of the truth of the Book of Mormon. Yet, the discoveries caution against confusing a spiritual witness with scientific evidence. Spiritual witnesses may reach beyond science, but they should not be confused with it.

From a scientific perspective, the Book of Mormon's origin is best situated in early nineteenth-century America, and Lamanite genesis can only be traced historically to ca. 1828.[96] The term Lamanite is a modern social and political designation that lacks a verifiable biological or historical underpinning linking it to ancient American Indians.[97] The Book of Mormon emerged from an antebellum perspective, out of a frontier American people's struggle with their god, and not from an authentic American Indian perspective. As Mormons, we have a moral and ethical obligation to discontinue this view of Native American origins and publicly disavow the offensive teaching that a dark skin is a physical trait of God's malediction.

In 1973, after weighing the archaeological evidence against the antiquity of the Book of Mormon, Michael Coe implored Latter-day Saints:

> Forget the so-far fruitless quest for Jaredites, Nephites, Mulekites, and the lands of Zarahemla and Bountiful; there is no more chance of finding them than of discovering the ruins of the bottomless pit described in the book of Revelations. ... Continue the praiseworthy excavations in Mexico, remembering that little or nothing pertaining to the Book of Mor-

mon will ever result from them. And start digging into the archaeological remains of the Saints themselves.[98]

As we enter the twenty-first century, I would like to offer similar advice. We can continue our impressive genealogical research, and we should utilize the latest genetic technologies to enhance the precision and accuracy of our findings. But I believe that we should avoid a fruitless quest to tie Native American origins to the Middle East. There is as much chance of finding genetic proof of a Lehite civilization in the Americas as there would be of finding the Book of Mormon gold plates.

NOTES

I would like to thank the following for their helpful correspondence, comments and suggestions: Edward Ashment, Bryan Bean, Sterling Fluharty, Armand Mauss, Jenny McFarland, Jeffrey Meldrum, Brent Metcalfe, Tara Metcalfe, Kerrie Murphy, Simon Southerton, Trent Stephens, Dan Vogel, Scott Woodward, and David Wright. All conclusions, judgments, and potential errors in this essay are my own.

1. Jeffrey P. Haney, "Y. Researcher Curious about Your Bloodlines," *Deseret News*, 15 Aug. 2000; Lindsay Palmer and Roger Bryner, "Ethical Issues Surround DNA Research," *newsnet@BYU*, 28 Mar. 2000; Carolyn Peterson, "BYU's Genealogy-through-DNA Research Getting Boost from New DNA Research," *newsnet@BYU*, 28 June 2000; Allison Jones, "Y Molecular Group Works on Worldwide Family Tree," *newsnet@BYU*, 18 Nov. 2000. See also *http://molecular-genealogy.byu.edu*.

2. DNA analysis ignited public curiosity over whether Thomas Jefferson sired children with his slave Sally Hemings. See the online resources supplied by the Thomas Jefferson Foundation ("Jefferson-Hemings DNA Testing: An On-Line Resource" at *www.monticello.org*) and Philip W. Hendrick, *Genetics of Populations* (Sudbury, MA: Jones and Bartlett Publishers, 2000), 389-90.

3. The extent to which DNA analysis provides a portal to the past is illustrated in Bryan Sykes, *The Seven Daughters of Eve: The Science That Reveals Our Genetic Ancestry* (New York: W. W. Norton & Company, 2001).

4. Dan Egan, "BYU Gene Data May Shed Light on Origin of Book of Mormon's Lamanites," *Salt Lake Tribune*, 30 Nov. 2000; also Simon Southerton, "DNA Genealogies of American Indians and the Book of Mormon," 17 Mar. 2000, retrieved 20 Dec. 2000 from *www.exmormon.org*; Jonathan Higbee, "Where Is the Lamanite DNA?" retrieved 27 July 2000 from *www.geocities.com/Athens/Aegean/9636/tract/dna_additional.htm*. Despite a general lack of supporting evidence, at least one researcher at the Foundation for Ancient

Research and Mormon Studies (FARMS) has found reason for optimism in linguistic research. See Brian D. Stubbs, "Hebrew and Uto-Aztecan: Possible Linguistic Connections," *Reexploring the Book of Mormon*, ed. John W. Welch (Salt Lake City: Deseret Book and FARMS, 1992), 279-81.

5. While it is possible to find chance similarities at single loci, these have to be viewed within the larger picture. Kenneth K. Kidd et al., for example, report preliminary frequencies for three allele systems, observing that "[t]hese data make it clear that attempting to reach conclusions on population relationships from single loci is very risky. Roman Jews are most like Amazon Basin tribes in APOB and SST, but most like Cambodians at D20S5. Obviously, these gene frequency similarities cannot indicate close population affinities." Kenneth K. Kidd et al., "Nuclear DNA Polymorphism and Population Relationships," in *Genetic Diversity among Jews: Diseases and Markers at the DNA Level*, eds. Batsheva Bonné-Tamir and Avinoam Adam (New York: Oxford University Press, 1992), 37.

6. Southerton, "DNA Genealogies."

7. Robert Jurmain et al., *Introduction to Physical Anthropology* (8th ed.; Belmont, CA: Wadsworth, 2000), 44-45. Mitochondria are independent organisms living symbiotically in the human body within each and every human cell, although outside the nucleus. Since sperm consist only of nucleic material, mitochondria are transferred to the next human generation through the mother's egg cell.

8. Douglas Steinberg, "Genetic Variation Illuminates Murky Human History: Molecular Anthropologists Use DNA Markers to Chart Evolution and Migration," *The Scientist* 14[15] (July 2000): 10.

9. Jared Diamond, *The Third Chimpanzee: The Evolution and Future of the Human Animal* (New York: HarperCollins, 1992), 25.

10. See A. C. Wilson and V. M. Sarich, "A Molecular Time Scale for Human Evolution," *Proceedings of the National Academy of Sciences, USA* 63 (1969): 1088-93; and C. G. Sibley and J. E. Ahlquist, "The Phylogeny of the Hominid Primates as Indicated by DNA-DNA Hybridization," *Journal of Molecular Evolution* 20 (1984): 2-15, cited in Luigi Luca Cavalli-Sforza et al., *The History and Geography of Human Genes* (abridged ed.; Princeton, NJ: Princeton University Press, 1994), 86.

11. Michael D. Lemonick and Andrea Dorfman, "One Giant Step for Mankind: Meet Your Newfound Ancestor, a Chimplike Forest Creature That Stood Up and Walked 5.8 Million Years Ago," *Time*, 23 July 2001, 54-61.

12. Jurmain et al., *Introduction to Physical Anthropology*; Roger Lewin, *The Origin of Modern Humans* (New York: Scientific American Library, 1998). For an incisive new media presentation on human evolution, see the website "Becoming Human," *www.becominghuman.org*.

13. Allan C. Wilson and Rebecca L. Cann, "The Recent African Genesis of Humans: Genetic Studies Reveal That an African Woman of 200,000 Years Ago Was Our Common Ancestor," *Scientific American* (Apr. 1992), 68-73. For

an alternative point of view, see Alan G. Thorne and Milford H. Wolpoff, "The Multiregional Evolution of Humans: Both Fossil and Genetic Evidence Argue that Various Human Groups Arose Where They Are Found Today," *Scientific American* (Apr. 1992), 76-83. See also Christopher B. Stringer, "The Emergence of Modern Humans," *Scientific American* (Dec. 1990), 98-104.

14. Robert S. Corruccini, "Reaganomics and the Fate of the Progressive Neanderthals," *Integrative Paths to the Past: Paleoanthropological Advances in Honor of F. Clark Howell*, eds. R. S. Corruccini and R. L. Ciochon (Englewood Cliffs, NJ: Prentice Hall, 1994), 697-708; Glenn C. Conroy, *Reconstructing Human Origins: A Modern Synthesis* (New York: Norton, 1997).

15. Max Ingham et al., "Mitochondrial Genome Variation and the Origin of Modern Humans," *Nature,* 7 Dec. 2000, 708-713; Cavalli-Sforza et al., *History and Geography of Human Genes*, 89.

16. Matthias Krings et al., "Neanderthal DNA Sequences and the Origin of Modern Humans," *Cell* 90 (1997): 19-30; Ryk Ward and Chris Stringer, "A Molecular Handle on the Neanderthals," *Nature,* 17 July 1997, 225-26; Igor V. Ovchinnikov et al., "Molecular Analysis of Neanderthal DNA from the Northern Caucasus," *Nature,* 30 Mar. 2000, 490-93.

17. Alan R. Templeton, "Out of Africa Again and Again," *Nature,* 7 March 2002, 45-51.

18. Luigi Luca Cavalli-Sforza, *Genes, Peoples, and Languages* (New York: North Point Press, 2000), 61-63. For a discussion that dates the first migration as early as 15,000 years ago, see Ryk Ward, "Language and Genes in the Americas," *The Human Inheritance: Genes, Language, and Evolution*, ed. Bryan Sykes (Oxford: Oxford University Press, 1999), 135-57.

19. Anthony Pagden, *European Encounters with the New World* (New Haven, CT: Yale University Press, 1993); Stephen Greenblatt, *Marvelous Possessions: The Wonder of the New World* (Chicago: University of Chicago Press, 1991); Fernando Cervantes, *The Devil in the New World* (New Haven, CT: Yale University Press, 1994); Elsa Cecilia Frost, "Indians and Theologians: Sixteenth-Century Spanish Theologians and Their Concept of the Indigenous Soul," *South and Meso-American Native Spirituality: From the Cult of the Feathered Serpent to the Theology of Liberation*, ed. Gary H. Gossen (New York: Crossroad Publishing Company, 1993), 119-39.

20. Thomas Paine, *The Age of Reason*, Part I (New York: Macmillan Publishing Company, 1957 [1794]).

21. Robert N. Hullinger, *Joseph Smith's Response to Skepticism* (Salt Lake City: Signature Books, 1992). As Ed Ashment kindly reminded me, the Book of Mormon is far more than a response to skepticism; it is also "a condemnation of Masonry; a theory of the origin of the Amerindians, all of them; a condemnation of biblical polygamy; an assertion that Christianity always was, that it did not evolve out of Judaism; a declaration of a homousian trinity; an advocate of predestination (cloaked as 'foreknowledge'); etc." (private communication).

22. Joseph Smith, "Church History," *Times and Seasons* 3 (Mar. 1842): 706-710, in Dean C. Jessee, ed., *The Papers of Joseph Smith, Volume 1: Autobiographical and Historical Writings* (Salt Lake City: Deseret Book, 1989), 437.

23. John L. Brooke, *The Refiner's Fire: The Making of the Mormon Cosmology* (New York: Cambridge University Press, 1994), 198. For a more sustained argument for Joseph Smith's literalism and its implications, see William D. Russell, "Beyond Literalism," in *The Word of God: Essays on Mormon Scripture*, ed. Dan Vogel (Salt Lake City: Signature, 1990), 43-54.

24. David H. Bailey, "Science and Mormonism: Past, Present, Future," *Dialogue: A Journal of Mormon Thought* 29 (Spring 1996): 80-96.

25. Although not published until well after his death, the best example of Roberts's apologia in this regard is Brigham H. Roberts, *The Truth, the Way, the Life: An Elementary Treatise on Theology* (San Francisco: Smith Research Associates, 1994).

26. Bailey, "Science and Mormonism," 82-83.

27. Armand L. Mauss, *The Angel and the Beehive: The Mormon Struggle with Assimilation* (Urbana: University of Illinois Press, 1994).

28. Bailey, "Science and Mormonism," 85.

29. The personal struggles of two LDS professors at Idaho State University are outlined in a new book; see Trent D. Stephens and D. Jeffrey Meldrum, *Evolution and Mormonism: A Quest for Understanding* (Salt Lake City: Signature Books, 2001). They participated with me on a panel discussion, "DNA and Lamanite Identity: A Galileo Event," moderated by Brent Metcalfe at the 2001 Salt Lake City Sunstone Symposium.

30. Pope John Paul II, "Message to the Pontifical Academy of Sciences," cited in Stephens and Meldrum, who themselves use the pope's embrace of evolution to illustrate the need to "change our thinking and world views" in light of "new and accumulating scientific data" (Stephens and Meldrum, *op. cit.*, 79-80).

31. Overviews of some of the latest archaeological research into Native American origins include Robson Bonnichsen and D. Gentry Steele, *Method and Theory for Investigating the Peopling of the Americas* (Corvallis, OR: Center for the Study of the First Americans, 1994); Robson Bonnichsen and Karen L. Turnmire, *Ice Age Peoples of North America: Environments, Origins, and Adaptations of the First Americans* (Corvallis, OR: Oregon State University Press, 1999); Thomas D. Dillehay, *The Settlement of America: A New Prehistory* (New York: Basic Books, 2000). For a critique of archaeology from a Native American perspective, see Vine Deloria Jr., *Red Earth, White Lies: Native Americans and the Myth of Scientific Fact* (New York: Scribner, 1995).

32. Michael Coe, "Mormons and Archaeology: An Outside View," *Dialogue: A Journal of Mormon Thought* 8 (Summer 1973): 40-48. See also Edward H. Ashment, "'In the Language of My Father': Evidence of Ancient Egyptian and Hebrew in the Book of Mormon," in *New Approaches to the Book of Mormon:*

Explorations in Critical Methodology, ed. Brent Lee Metcalfe (Salt Lake City: Signature Books, 1993), 329-93.

33. Dee F. Green, "Book of Mormon Archaeology: The Myths and the Alternatives," *Dialogue: A Journal of Mormon Thought* 4 (Summer 1969): 71-80; Deanne G. Matheny, "Does the Shoe Fit? A Critique of the Limited Tehuantepec Geography," in *New Approaches to the Book of Mormon*, 269-328. See also Hampton Sides, "This Is Not the Place," *DoubleTake* 5 (Spring 1999): 46-55.

34. B. H. Roberts, *Studies of the Book of Mormon*, ed. Brigham D. Madsen (Salt Lake City: Signature Books, 1992); Stan Larson, *Quest for the Gold Plates: Thomas Stuart Ferguson's Archaeological Search for the Book of Mormon* (Salt Lake City: Freethinker Press and Smith Research Associates, 1996). On the other hand, organizations such as FARMS regularly publicize works they believe validate ancient claims.

35. Egan, "BYU Gene Data."

36. Suzan Mazur, "Mormons in the Olympic Spotlight: Polygamy and Scripture Threaten to Steal Some of the Thunder from the Winter Games in Utah," *Financial Times*, 9 Feb. 2002, retrieved 10 Feb. 2002 from *http://globalarchive.ft.com*.

37. Michael Crawford, *The Origins of Native Americans: Evidence from Anthropological Genetics* (New York: Cambridge University Press, 1998), 3-4. He provides an incisive perspective, though he omits some recent research and focuses primarily on North American native populations.

38. "Introduction," *The Book of Mormon: Another Testament of Jesus Christ* (Salt Lake City: The Church of Jesus Christ of Latter-day Saints, 1981).

39. Crawford, *The Origins of Native Americans*, 4-7.

40. See D. C. Wallace et al., "Dramatic Founder Effects in Amerindian Mitochrondrial DNAs," *American Journal of Physical Anthropology* 68 (1985): 149-55; and T. G. Schurr et al., "Amerindian Mitochrondrial DNAs Have Rare Asian Mutations at High Frequencies Suggesting a Limited Number of Founders," *American Journal of Human Genetics* 46 (1990): 613-23, cited in Antonio Torroni, "Mitochrondrial DNA and the Origin of Native Americans," *America Past, America Present: Genes and Languages in the Americas and Beyond*, ed. Colin Renfrew (Cambridge, UK: McDonald Institute for Archaeological Research, 2000), 77-87.

41. Torroni, "Mitochrondrial DNA," 79.

42. Joseph Greenberg, *Language in the Americas* (Stanford, CA: Stanford University Press, 1987).

43. See Cavalli-Sforza et al., *History and Geography of Human Genes*; Cavalli-Sforza, *Genes, Peoples, and Languages*.

44. See Renfrew, *America Past, America Present*.

45. Cavalli-Sforza, *Genes, Peoples, and Languages*, 136.

46. Ibid.

47. Sykes, *Seven Daughters of Eve*, 281-83.

48. Torroni, "Mitochrondrial DNA," 81-83.

49. Ibid., 85.

50. Michael D. Brown et al., "mtDNA Haplogroup X: An Ancient Link between Europe/Western Asia and North America?" *American Journal of Human Genetics* 63 (Dec. 1998): 1852-61.

51. Torroni, "Mitochrondrial DNA," 81-83.

52. Theodore G. Schurr, "Mitochondrial DNA and the Peopling of the New World," *American Scientist* 88/3 (2000): 246-53.

53. Brown et al., "mtDNA Haplogroup X," 1852.

54. Sykes, *Seven Daughters of Eve*, 213-20, 274, 281.

55. See John L. Sorenson, *An Ancient American Setting for the Book of Mormon* (Salt Lake City: Desert Book Company, 1996), for an argument for a limited geography and summary of the hemispheric view. For an example of LDS interest in haplogroup X, see Jeff Lindsay, "Genes Linking Eurasians and Native Americans," retrieved 20 Dec. 2000 from *www.jefflindsay.com.*

56. "Problematic Role of DNA Testing in Unraveling Human History," *Journal of Book of Mormon Studies* 9/2 (2000): 69-70.

57. See Schurr, "Mitochondrial DNA," 246.

58. Miroslava V. Derenko et al., "The Presence of Mitochondrial Haplogroup X in Altaians from South Siberia," *American Journal of Human Genetics* 69 (July 2001): 237.

59. Mazur, "Mormons in the Olympic Spotlight."

60. Genetic inheritance can actually be more complex than simply XX or XY, and many intersexed individuals inherit different variations of up to four X and Y chromosomes. For an interesting commentary on the U.S. medical response to such ambiguity, see Martha Coventry, "Making the Cut: It's a Girl! ... Or Is It? When There's Doubt, Why Are Surgeons Calling the Shots?" *Ms Magazine*, Oct./Nov. 2000, retrieved 20 Dec. 2000 from *www.msmagazine.com.*

61. E. S. Poloni et al., "Human Genetic Affinities for Y-Chromosome P49a,f/Taq I Haplotypes Show Strong Correspondence with Linguistics," *American Journal of Human Genetics* 61 (Nov. 1997): 1015-35.

62. L. B. Jorde et al., "The Distribution of Human Genetic Diversity: A Comparison of Mitochrondrial, Autosomal, and Y-Chromosome Data," *American Journal of Human Genetics* 66 (Mar. 2000): 979-88.

63. Fabrício Santos et al., "The Central Siberian Origin for Native American Y Chromosomes," *American Journal of Human Genetics* 64 (Feb. 1999): 619-28; Nestor Bianchi et al., "Origin of Amerindian Y-Chromosomes as Inferred by the Analysis of Six Polymorphic Markers," *American Journal of Physical Anthropology* 102 (Jan. 1997): 79-89.

64. T. M. Karafet et al., "Ancestral Asian Source(s) of New World Y-Chromosome Founder Haplotypes," *American Journal of Human Genetics* 64 (Mar. 1999): 817-31.

65. Bernd Herrmann and Susanne Hummel, eds., *Ancient DNA* (New York: Springer, 1994).

66. Shawn W. Carlyle et al., "Context of Maternal Lineages in the Greater

Southwest," *American Journal of Physical Anthropology* 113 (Sept. 2000): 85-101; Dennis H. O'Rourke et al., "Ancient DNA: Methods, Progress, and Perspectives," *American Journal of Human Biology* 8/5 (1996): 557-71.

67. Carlyle et al., *op. cit.*; O'Rourke et al., "Ancient DNA," 557-71; Ryan L. Parr et al., "Ancient DNA Analysis of Fremont Amerindians of the Great Salt Lake Wetlands," *American Journal of Physical Anthropology* 99 (Apr. 1996): 507-518; Anne C. Stone and Mark Stoneking, "mtDNA Analysis of a Prehistoric Oneota Population: Implications for the Peopling of the New World," *American Journal of Human Genetics* 62 (Apr. 1998): 1153-70.

68. D. Andrew Merriwether et al., "Ancient and Contemporary Mitochrondrial DNA Variation in the Maya," in *Bones of the Maya: Studies of Ancient Skeletons*, eds. Stephen L. Whittington and David M. Reed (Washington: Smithsonian Institution Press, 1997), 208-217.

69. Cavalli-Sforza, *Genes, Peoples, and Languages*; Cavalli-Sforza et al., *History and Geography of Human Genes*; Sykes, *Seven Daughters of Eve*; Templeton, "Out of Africa."

70. Nathan A. Ellis, "The Ashkenazic Jewish Bloom Syndrome Mutation blmAsh Is Present in Non-Jewish Americans of Spanish Ancestry," *American Journal of Human Genetics* 63 (Dec. 1998): 1685-93; Luis Carvajal-Carmona et al., "Strong Amerind/White Sex Bias and a Possible Sephardic Contribution among the Founders of a Population in Northwest Colombia," *American Journal of Human Genetics* 67 (Nov. 2000): 1287-95. For an intriguing account of the Castilian Christian attempts to expel Jewish and Muslim heterogeneity from the Iberian peninsula and their tendency to treat indigenous Americans as Jews and Moors (with implications for the quest for Amerisraelites), see Tzetvan Todorov, *The Conquest of America* (New York: HarperPerennial, 1984). See Bonné-Tamir and Adam, eds., *Genetic Diversity among Jews*.

71. Sorenson, *An Ancient American Setting*, 93. See also Connie Kolman and Noreen Tuross, "Ancient DNA Analysis of Human Populations," *American Journal of Physical Anthropology* 111 (Jan. 2000): 5-23.

72. Neil Bradman et al., "The Genetic Origins of Old Testament Priests," *America Past, America Present*, 31-44.

73. See Neil Bradman and Mark Thomas, "Why Y? The Y Chromosome in the Study of Human Evolution, Migration, and Prehistory," *Science Spectra* 14 (1998).

74. Bradman and Thomas, "Why Y?"; Mark G. Thomas et al., "Y Chromosomes Traveling South: The Cohen Modal Haplotype and the Origins of the Lemba, the 'Black Jews of Southern Africa,'" *American Journal of Human Genetics* 66 (Feb. 2000): 674-86.

75. Michael F. Hammer et al., "Jewish and Middle Eastern Non-Jewish Populations Share a Common Pool of Y-chromosome Biallelic Haplotypes," *Proceedings of the National Academy of Sciences USA*, 97 (June 2000): 6769-6774.

76. Mazur, "Mormons in the Olympic Spotlight."

77. See "Introduction," *The Book of Mormon*.

78. Interested Latter-day Saints can follow the debate in *Brigham Young University Studies, Dialogue: A Journal of Mormon Thought, FARMS Review of Books, Journal of Book of Mormon Studies*, and *Sunstone*. Online resources can be found at *farmsresearch.com, mormoncentral.com, mormonscripturestudies.com*, and *religioustolerance.org/lds_migr.htm*. Key examples of the debate among LDS scholars are Metcalfe, ed., *New Approaches to the Book of Mormon;* Roberts, *Studies of the Book of Mormon*; Sorenson, *An Ancient American Setting*; Vogel, ed., *The Word of God*; Noel B. Reynolds, ed., *Book of Mormon Authorship Revisited: The Evidence for Ancient Origins* (Provo, UT: FARMS, 1997); and Mark D. Thomas, *Digging in Cumorah: Reclaiming Book of Mormon Narratives* (Salt Lake City: Signature Books, 1999).

79. Sorenson, *An Ancient American Setting*, 55. For an archaeological critique of this perspective, see Matheny, "Does the Shoe Fit? A Critique of the Limited Tehuantepec Geography," in *New Approaches to the Book of Mormon*, 269-328. See also Dennis Tedlock, trans., *Popol Vuh* (New York: Touchstone, 1996). For discussions of Mormon Maya and Ladino interpretations of the Popol Vuh and Book of Mormon, see Thomas W. Murphy, "Reinventing Mormonism: Guatemala as a Harbinger of the Future?" *Dialogue: A Journal of Mormon Thought* 29 (Spring 1996): 177-92.

80. William J. Hamblin, "An Apologist for the Critics: Brent Lee Metcalfe's Assumptions and Methodologies," *Review of Books on the Book of Mormon* 6/1 (1994): 476.

81. Sorenson, *An Ancient American Setting*, 93-94.

82. See Shaye J. D. Cohen, *The Beginnings of Jewishness: Boundaries, Varieties, Uncertainties* (Berkeley: University of California Press, 1999); E. Theodore Mullen Jr., *Ethnic Myths and Pentateuchal Foundations: A New Approach to the Formation of the Pentateuch* (Atlanta, GA: Scholar's Press and the Society of Biblical Literature, 1997); E. Theodore Mullen Jr., *Narrative History and Ethnic Boundaries: The Deutoronomistic Historian and the Creation of Israelite National Identity* (Atlanta, GA: Scholars Press and the Society of Biblical Literature, 1993).

83. "The Problematic Role of DNA Testing in Unraveling Human History," *Journal of Book of Mormon Studies* 9/2 (2000): 66-74.

84. Sykes, *The Seven Daughters of Eve*, 101. The anonymous FARMS writer seems unaware of recent advancements on the question of whether Native Americans migrated to Polynesia. Matthew E. Hurles and colleagues, including Bryan Sykes, whom the FARMS author cites with approval, note that their study of Polynesian Y-chromosomes provided "no evidence for a Native American contribution to the Polynesian Y-chromosomal pool" (M. E. Hurles et al., "European Y-Chromosomal Lineages in Polynesians: A Contrast to the Population Structure Revealed by mtDNA," *American Journal of Human Genetics* 63 [Dec. 1998]: 1793-1806). See also Martin Richards et al., "mtDNA Suggests Polynesian Origins in Eastern Indonesia," *American Journal of Human Genetics* 63 (Oct. 1998): 1234-37. Of course, even if such evidence did exist, the common Polynesian and Amerindian genetic markers are still of Asiatic origin.

85. Cooper Johnson, "DNA and the Book of Mormon," retrieved 3 April 2002, *www.fair-lds.org/apol/bom/bom01.html.*

86. Scott Woodward to Tom Murphy, "Re: Clarification of FAIR Article," personal email, 9 Apr. 2002.

87. D. H. O'Rourke et al., "Spatial and Temporal Stability of mtDNA Haplogroup Frequencies in Native North America," *Human Biology* 72/1 (2000): 15-34.

88. Hammer et al., "Jewish and Middle Eastern Non-Jewish Populations."

89. A panel of LDS biologists and anthropologists, Trent D. Stephens, D. Jeffrey Meldrum, and myself, more explicitly emphasized the need to jettison the Lamanite ancestry claim for American Indians at the 2001 Salt Lake City Sunstone Symposium ("DNA and Lamanite Identity: A Galileo Event").

90. Copies of statements from the SAIIC as well as responses from participants in HGDP can be found at "Native Net, Human Genome Diversity Project Articles from Native-L, "retrieved 5 Sept. 2000 from *http://nativenet.uthsca.edu/nl/hgdp.html.* See also Morrison Institute for Population and Resource Studies, "Human Genome Diversity Project Frequently Asked Questions," retrieved 8 Sept. 2000 from *www.Stanford.edu/group/morrinst/ hgdp/faq.html.*

91. Martin Johnston, "Mormons Trigger NZ Ethical Concern over DNA," *The New Zealand Herald,* 17 May 2001, retrieved 19 May 2001 from *www.nzherald.com*; Kent Larsen, "BYU Molecular Genealogy Research Project Accused of Ethical Lapse in New Zealand," *Mormon News,* 18 May 2001, retrieved 19 May 2001 from *www.mormonstoday.com.*

92. Jace Weaver, "Missions and Missionaries," in Mary B. Davis, ed., *Native America in the Twentieth Century: An Encyclopedia* (New York: Garland Publishing, 1994), 348.

93. Suzan Mazur, "Mormon Scriptures on Indians Show Objectionable Side of Olympic Hosts," *Indian Country Today*, 21 Feb. 2002, retrieved 22 Feb. 2002 from *www.indiancountry.com.*

94. I have raised similar concerns in several publications. See my "Reinventing Mormonism," 177-92; "Laban's Ghost: On Writing and Transgression," *Dialogue: A Journal of Mormon Thought* 30 (Summer 1997), 105-126; "From Racist Stereotype to Ethnic Identity: Instrumental Uses of Mormon Racial Doctrine," *Ethnohistory* 46/3 (1999): 451-80; and "Other Mormon Histories: Lamanite Subjectivity in Mexico," *Journal of Mormon History* 26 (Fall 2000): 179-215.

95. Sorenson, *An Ancient American Setting*, 94.

96. See Doctrine and Covenants 3:18-20.

97. For examples of post-1828 historical and social uses of the label Lamanite, see my "Reinventing Mormonism," "Laban's Ghost," "From Racist Stereotype," and "Other Mormon Histories."

98. Coe, "Mormons and Archaeology," 48.

4.
The Validity of the Witnesses' Testimonies

Dan Vogel

APOLOGISTS HAVE LONG PUT FORTH THE IDEA THAT THE THREE and eight witnesses to the truthfulness of the Book of Mormon provide two kinds of testimony—one spiritual, the other physical—and that the two testimonies are complementary. The spiritual proves that Joseph Smith did not fabricate the plates, the physical that he did not delude the three witnesses.[1] This argument is designed more to persuade than to enlighten. For, in fact, the two events are not mutually exclusive and the true historical situation surrounding the experiences of the two groups is more complex than this implies.

In this essay I will examine the published testimonies of the witnesses, as well as other related historical sources, to try to determine more accurately the nature of their experiences. Hence, I will not explore the question of the witnesses' honesty and trustworthiness; this has been exploited at great length by those whose intent has been to present a false dichotomy: either the witnesses told the truth about their experiences, and therefore Joseph Smith's claims about the plates are true, or they lied and the plates never existed.[2] This either/or reduction misrepresents the situation facing those who wish to examine the historical nature of these events.

The important question is not whether the witnesses were trustworthy or if they continued to maintain their belief in the Book of Mormon throughout their lives. The central question—the question explored in this essay—concerns the nature of their experiences and if their statements are distinguishable from those claiming similar religious testimonies. In other words, are the statements by Book of Mormon witnesses different from other examples of religious testimony confronting historians? This essay will attempt to assess the nature of the vision of the three witnesses and investigate the assumption that the eight witnesses' experience was purely natural and physical.

PUBLISHED TESTIMONIES

Because the Testimony of Three Witnesses involves visionary experience, apologists place a great deal of weight on the Testimony of Eight Witnesses, which they assume was the result of a physical encounter with the gold plates. Without any reliable source describing the historical event behind the group statement,[3] some writers have relied solely on the published version for their reconstructions.

John Gee, for example, states as a matter of unquestionable fact that "the Eight Witnesses saw and handled [the plates] in broad daylight without any angels or anything extraordinary about the experience."[4] Similarly, William J. Hamblin asserts that "the Eight Witnesses ... claimed to have seen the plates in a completely nonvisionary setting."[5] Relying on the published testimony alone, Richard L. Anderson has attempted a reconstruction of the historical setting, stating that "Joseph Smith showed these eight men the metal plates, which they 'hefted' while turning the individual 'leaves' and examining the engravings of 'curious workmanship.'"[6] These writers reflect the commonly held assumption that only the three witnesses saw the plates "by the power of God," while the experience of the eight men was entirely this-worldly.

Indeed, the language of the Testimony of Eight Witnesses seems to imply a natural and physical experience. It declares:

> Be it known unto all nations, kindreds, tongues, and people, unto whom this work shall come: That Joseph Smith, Jun., ... has shown unto us the plates ... which have the appearance of gold; and as many of the leaves as the said Smith has translated we did handle with our hands; and we also saw the engravings thereon, all of which has the appearance of ancient work, and of curious workmanship. And this we bear record with words of soberness, that the said Smith has shown unto us, for we have

> seen and hefted, and know of a surety that the said Smith has got the plates of which we have spoken.[7]

The apparent materialism of this testimony reflects our assumptions about the physical limitations of visionary experiences.

I disagree with Anderson's assertion that the "printed testimonies must be taken at face value."[8] Instead, I argue that the testimonies by themselves cannot be used in recreating the historical setting for either group. In fact, both testimonies fail to provide historical details such as time, place, and date, while offering only the most minimal information about the historical events behind them.

The Testimony of Three Witnesses, for example, simply states that the three signatories, collectively, were shown the plates by an angel:

> Be it known unto all nations, kindreds, tongues, and people, unto whom this work shall come: That we ... have seen the plates which contain this record. ... And we also know that they have been translated by the gift and power of God, for his voice hath declared it unto us; wherefore we know of a surety that the work is true. And we also testify that we have seen the engravings which are upon the plates; and they have been shown unto us by the power of God, and not of man. And we declare with words of soberness, that an angel of God came down from heaven, and he brought and laid before our eyes, that we beheld and saw the plates, and the engravings thereon. ... And it is marvelous in our eyes. Nevertheless, the voice of the Lord commanded us that we should bear record of it.[9]

Fortunately, additional information is available regarding this experience, which provides historians with an opportunity to more fully assess the nuances of the testimony. In comparing the testimony against subsequent statements about the event, it becomes clear that the relationship is tenuous and superficial.

The testimony states that the witnesses were shown the plates by an angel. But in subsequent comments by the witnesses themselves, we learn, for example, that the three men did not experience the vision together, that Martin Harris's vision occurred separately. Both Harris and David Whitmer later testified that they also saw in their visions a table upon which rested a breastplate, the urim and thummim, the liahona, the sword of Laban, and brass plates—an interesting detail missing from the official testimony. The statement also fails to mention that the angel spoke, although it does refer to the voice of God.

The subsequent statements by Whitmer and Harris indicate that their experiences were much more subjective than implied by the naturalistic language of the testimony which does not mention the angel's glory, for instance. Clearly, without the subsequent details, our understanding of the experience would be faulty. Even this brief examination should stand as a caution against reconstructing the events based solely on the published testimonies. Yet, this is exactly what some religious enthusiasts and historians have done.

Without the subsequent statements of the participants, we would not know that the Testimony of Three Witnesses was a composite document reporting more than one event or that those events were more visionary than implied by the published document. Thus, similar errors are probably made when one attempts to reconstruct the historical event behind the Testimony of Eight Witnesses based on the published statement alone. Before tackling the problems associated with the eight witnesses, there is more to be gleaned from a closer look at the experience of the three witnesses.

TESTIMONY OF THREE WITNESSES

If the printed testimony were all that was available, one would assume that the three witnesses saw the angel and the plates together in a single vision. For more than a decade after the event, this is all the information many Mormons and non-Mormons had. However, subsequent statements by Joseph Smith and the witnesses challenge this view of a unified event.

Joseph Smith's history, written in 1838-39 and published in 1842, was the first to detail the experience. It not only revealed that Smith was present during the vision but that the event took place in the woods near the Peter Whitmer Sr. farm in Fayette, New York, following a revelation in June 1829 that promised Whitmer, Harris, and Oliver Cowdery a view of the sacred objects (Doctrine and Covenants 17; hereafter D&C). "According to previous arrangement," Smith said, "I commenced by vocal prayer to our Heavenly Father and was followed by each of the rest in succession." This process was repeated twice without receiving the desired manifestation. Since the revelation had stipulated that "it is by your faith that you shall obtain a view of them" (17:2), Harris withdrew, believing he was the cause of their failure. In Harris's absence, an angel appeared and showed the remaining men the plates. According to Smith's history:

> we knelt down again, and had not been many minutes engaged in prayer when presently we beheld a light above us in the air of exceeding brightness, and behold, an angel stood before us; in his hands he held the plates which we had been praying for these to have a view of: he turned over the leaves one by one, so that we could see them, and discern the engravings thereon distinctly: He addressed himself to David Whitmer, and said, "David, blessed is the Lord, and he that keeps all his commandments:" when immediately afterwards we heard a voice from out of the bright light above us, saying "These plates have been revealed by the power of God, and they have been translated by the power of God; the translation of them which you have seen is correct, and I command you to bear record of what you now see and hear."

After this vision, Smith joined Harris who was praying some distance away, and together, according to Smith, they experienced the same vision. Of this experience, Smith's history reports:

> I found [Harris] at a Considerable distance fervently engaged in prayer; he soon told me however that he had not yet prevailed with the Lord, And earnestly requested me, to join him in prayer, that he also might realize the same blessings which we had just recieved: we accordingly joined in prayer, and ultimately obtained our desires, for before we had yet finished, the same vision was opened to our view; at least it was again to me, and I once more beheld, and seen, and heard the same things; whilst at the same moment, Martin Harris cried out, apparently in an ecstasy of Joy "'Tis enough, 'tis enough; mine eyes have beheld, mine eyes have beheld", And jumping up he shouted, Hosanna, blessing God; and–otherwise rejoiced exceedingly.[10]

Subsequent statements by Harris and Whitmer confirm that Harris viewed the plates separately.[11] Thus, the implied unity of the published testimony is an imprecise implication.

Other Objects Seen

The June 1829 revelation promised not only "a view of the plates" but also "of the breastplate, the sword of Laban, the Urim and

Thummim, ... and the miraculous directors which were given to Lehi" (D&C 17:1). Both the testimony and Smith's history mention only the plates, but Whitmer and Harris confirm that they saw the other objects.

In 1884, for instance, Whitmer told E. C. Briggs of the RLDS church: "Between us and the angel there appeared a table, and there lay upon it the sword of Laban, the Ball of Directors, the record, and Interpreters. The angel took the Record, and turned the leaves, and showed it to us by the power of God."[12] During an 1877 interview with Edward Stevenson of the LDS church, Whitmer said: "A Light appeared & it Grew Brighter until an Angle Stood before us and on the appearance of A table Was laid the Plates[,] Urim & Thumin[,] Ball or Director[,] Sword of Laban &c & A voice Declared & Bore record of the truth of the Translation turning the Leaves over & thus the vision ended."[13]

Harris similarly testified that he had seen a table with several objects on it. In 1886 Stevenson recorded: "Brother Harris said that the angel stood on the opposite side of the table on which were the plates, the interpreters, &c., and took the plates in his hands and turned them over."[14] William Pilkington reported: "[Harris] bore his dying Testimony that he with the Prophet Joseph Smith did stand in the presence of an angel of God ... and that he saw the Engravings on the Plates, he also saw the Urim and Thummin, the Breast Plate and the Sword of Laban."[15]

The Angel Speaks

The testimony states that "the voice of the Lord commanded us that we should bear record of it." But Smith's history adds that the angel made a brief statement to David Whitmer, while the voice of God delivered the remainder of the message. Whitmer's and Harris's subsequent accounts imply that the angel spoke at some length, showing again that the published testimony is a limited document.

Harris repeatedly testified that he heard the angel speak. On one occasion he told Edward Stevenson, "The angel declared that the Book of Mormon was correctly translated by the power of God and not of man, and that it contained the fullness of the Gospel of Jesus Christ to the Nephites, who were a branch of the lost sheep of the House of Israel, and had come from the land of Jerusalem to America."[16] Pilkington reported that Harris said, "[A]fter the angel assended into Heaven[,] the Heavens were opened and he heard the voice of God declare that all that the angel had told him was verily true and that the Book of Mormon which contains the Everlasting gospel was translated correctly."[17]

Whitmer's individual circumstance is more complex, however. In his 1877 interview with Stevenson, he not only failed to mention the angel's speech but gave an account that significantly varied from Smith's history. While he was plowing on the morning prior to his vision of the plates, Whitmer recalled, "I he[a]rd a voice & Saw a personage Who Said [']Blessed is the Lord & he that keepeth his Commandments['] & the very next Round Bro. Joseph & Oliver Came along & Said [']Come David & be one of the witnesses of the Book of Mormon.[']"[18] Whitmer repeated the story to Stevenson during two additional interviews in 1886 and 1887.[19] In 1881 Whitmer also told Jesse R. Badham of the RLDS church about his pre-group vision, although Badham failed to record its message.[20] It appears that Whitmer's personal vision may have been incorporated into Smith's account of the group's experience, leading one contemporary scholar to wonder if the angel spoke to the witnesses at all.[21]

However, this scholar's assertion that the angel "did not ... apparently speak to the witnesses" was challenged by Richard Anderson, who pointed out that Whitmer himself mentioned the angel speaking in his 1887 pamphlet, *An Address to All Believers in Christ,* as well as in other reports.[22] In his *Address,* for example, Whitmer said that "[t]he angel who declared unto us that the Book of Mormon was true, also declared unto us that the Bible was true." He also heard God's "own voice and an angel from heaven declare the truth of it unto me."[23] Thomas W. Smith of the RLDS church remembered that Whitmer said the angel "turned over leaf by leaf, explaining the contents, here and there."[24] Following his 1861 interview with Whitmer, David H. Cannon of the LDS church similarly reported: "[Whitmer] also testified that an angel turned the leaves of the plates from which the Book of Mormon was translated, and as he turned them, testified that they contained a history of the ancient inhabitants of this continent, and that they had been translated by the gift and power of God."[25] Even if Smith's history meshed the two visions, it does not necessarily follow that the angel remained silent while showing the plates.

Yet there are contradictions among the various accounts of

Whitmer's testimony. While several interviewers report him saying that the angel spoke, though without detailing what was said,[26] many followed Smith's history by having the angel speak the words Whitmer heard in his pre-group vision.[27] Other interviews, in addition to those conducted by Stevenson, fail to mention the angel's speech at all.[28] William H. Kelley of the RLDS church went so far as to quote Whitmer: "[T]he angel stood before us. He was dressed in white, and spoke and called me by name and said 'Blessed is he that keepeth His commandments.' This is all that I heard the angel say."[29] Concerning what the angel said, Whitmer's interviews are perhaps irreconcilable. If the angel did speak during Whitmer's and Cowdery's vision, it should be regarded as further indication of the fragmentary nature of both the published testimony and Smith's history.

Nature of the Experience

Despite the use of naturalistic language in the Testimony of Three Witnesses–particularly the emphasis on seeing the plates with their "eyes" as well as the failure to mention the angel's glory–subsequent statements by Harris and Whitmer point to the visionary aspects of their experience. In other words, the event was internal and subjective and in the fullest sense a vision. Indeed, both men spoke repeatedly, although sometimes reluctantly, about this aspect of the event.

Harris, for example, told several residents of Palmyra, New York, that he had seen the plates with his "spiritual eyes." John H. Gilbert, who set the type for the Book of Mormon, recalled: "Martin was in the office when I finished setting up the testimony of the three witnesses. ... I said to him,–'Martin, did you see those plates with your naked eyes?' Martin looked down for an instant, raised his eyes up, and said, 'No, I saw them with a spir[i]tual eye.'"[30] When pressed about his vision, Harris also told John A. Clark: "I saw them with the eye of faith."[31]

According to Stephen Burnett, Harris told an Ohio congregation in 1838 that "he never saw the plates with his natural eyes only in vision or imagination," adding that the witnesses had seen the plates "spiritually or in vision with their eyes shut."[32] Reuben P. Harmon, a neighbor of Harris in Kirtland, Ohio, said that Harris "never claimed to have seen [the plates] with his natural eyes, only spiritual vision."[33] While living in Utah, Harris told Anthony Metcalf that he saw the angel and the plates in a "visionary or entranced state."[34]

Known as "the most interviewed witness" of the three, David Whitmer's accounts, like those of Harris, are clearly inward and subjective. John Murphy's recital of his interview with him in June 1880 focused on the inward nature of Whitmer's experience, comparing it to "impressions as the quaker when the spirit moves, or as a good Methodist in giving happy experience, a feeling."[35] Following publication of Murphy's account, Whitmer responded with a written "Proclamation" in which he reaffirmed his testimony and attached an affidavit attesting to his honesty and respectability in the community. Significantly, however, he did not dispute any specific statement in Murphy's version of the interview.[36]

The subjective aspect of Whitmer's experience was further detailed in an 1885 interview conducted by James Henry Moyle: "Mr D. Whitmer Sen did not handle the plates. Only saw them. ... Says he did see them and the angel and heard him speak. But that it was indiscribable that it was through the power of God. ... he then spoke of Paul hearing and seeing Christ but his associates did not. Because it is only seen in the Spirit." Moyle "asked if the atmosphere about them was normal." In other words, did the angel appear in normal surroundings or had the vision entirely obscured the natural world? According to Whitmer, "[I]t was indescribable, but the light was bright and clear, yet apparently a different kind of light, something of a soft haze." Moyle, a Mormon and recent law school graduate, noted his disappointment: "I was not fully satisfied with the explanation. It was more spiritual than I anticipated."[37]

Harris and Whitmer were merely stating what Smith's revelations had promised. Should Harris succeed in viewing the plates spiritually, a March 1829 revelation instructed, he should restrict his discussion of this to a simple declaration: "I have seen [the plates], for they have been shown unto me by the power of God and not of man" (D&C 5:25). The revelation Smith dictated three months later repeated the promise that the three men would see the plates "by the power of God" (D&C 17:2-3; also Eth. 5:3). Thus, drawing on the March 1829 revelation, the witnesses declared in their testimony that the plates "have been shown unto us by the power of God, and not of man."

Where Harris and Whitmer acknowledged the metaphysical nature of their experience, they stated it in terms commonly understood to describe a vision. Eighteenth-century mystic Emanuel Swedenborg said about his view of the spirits on the planet Mercury: "[W]hat I saw on that earth, was not seen with the eyes of my body, but with the eyes of my spirit."[38] This was also the language of the early American revivalists. Deeply affected by the revivals that swept through New England in the eighteenth century, Nathan Cole fell into a spiritual state in which "[i]t seemed as if I really saw the gate of heaven by an Eye of faith ... as plain as ever I saw any thing with my bodily eyes in my life."[39] In narrating his religious experience, the Reverend Charles Giles said, "I thought that I saw the glorious angel" as he "passed before the eye of my mind."[40] Joseph Smith reflected this custom, describing a vision he shared with Sidney Rigdon in February 1832 in the following words: "[T]he Lord touched the eyes of our understandings and they were opened, and the glory of the Lord shone round about. And we beheld the glory of the Son, on the right hand of the Father" (D&C 76:19-20; see also v. 12; 58:3; 110:1; Moses 1:11; 6:36).[41]

In later years, perhaps sensitive to the anti-Mormon emphasis on the nature of the witnesses' experience, or perhaps unintentionally, some believers began subtly introducing a physical emphasis into their accounts of what Harris and others saw. Simon Smith wrote in 1880 that Harris, on his deathbed, "did truly testify to me that he both saw and handled the plates that the Book of Mormon was translated from and that an angel of god did lay them before him and the other two witness's as recorded in the Book of Mormon."[42] In an affidavit written in 1921, George Godfrey reported, "[Harris] saw and handled the gold plates from which the said records were taken."[43] In 1922 William Harrison Homer quoted Harris as saying, "I saw and handled the plates upon which the Book of Mormon was written."[44]

The claim that Harris handled the plates in vision or handled them uncovered on a subsequent occasion seems incorrect. In addition to seeing the plates in vision, Harris frequently testified that he had more than once held or lifted the plates when they were in a box or covered with a cloth.[45] Thus, he apparently sometimes later shortened his narrative to the simple statement that he had both seen and handled the plates. This evidently confused some interviewers who may have assumed that Harris had handled the plates in his famous vision or that he had handled them uncovered on another occasion.

Theodore Farley, who heard Harris's testimony several times, tried to correct an unnamed woman who "testified that Martin Harris told her ... that he handled the plates of the Book of Mormon when the angel came down from Heaven and showed them." Farley responded, "Martin Harris never made that statement in our house that I heard of, but he did say that he saw in broad day light the angel come down from Heaven with those records, and he stood beside him. ... What Martin Harris had seen is what has been testified to in the Book [of Mormon]."[46]

Similar confusion surrounded Whitmer's testimony. In 1882 J. W. Chapburn and others asked him about his statement, and Whitmer replied: "These hands handled the plates, these eyes saw the angel, and these ears heard his voice; and I know it was of God."[47] Without further explication, Whitmer's interviewers assumed that he had handled the plates during his vision. Three years later, however, Zenas H. Gurley explicitly asked: "Do you know that the plates seen with the Angel (on the table) were real metal, did you touch them?" Whitmer answered, "We did not touch nor handle the plates."[48] Later that same year, James Moyle pressed Whitmer on this issue and recorded that he denied handling the plates.[49] Yet, Whitmer continued to be misrepresented. The *Omaha Herald* reported in October 1886 that Whitmer "insists that he handled and scrutinized the plates."[50] Of course, like Harris, Whitmer could have handled the plates while covered on an occasion separate from his vision.

Oliver Cowdery also probably intended to refer to separate occasions when he told a group in Council Bluffs, Iowa, according to Reuben Miller, "I beheld with my eyes. And handled with my hands the gold plates."[51] Remember, Cowdery had seen the angel and plates with Whitmer, and Whitmer said they "did not touch nor handle the plates." Like Harris and Whitmer, Cowdery probably handled the plates, covered by a cloth, sometime during his residence in Pennsylvania and then simply amalgamated the two experiences.

Despite the naturalistic sound of the printed testimony and the introduction of physical elements into later accounts, both Whitmer and Harris provide ample evidence that their vision was internal and subjective. In view of this evidence, Richard Anderson's description of "the natural-supernatural appearance of the angel with the plates" cannot be maintained.[52] Whitmer somehow knew, as Moyle reported, that his experience was comparable to the apostle Paul's "hearing and seeing Christ but his associates did not."[53]

Vision or Hallucination?

Since the vision of the three witnesses can be properly classified as a mystical experience, the subject of hallucination cannot be ignored. In their 1975 book, *Apparitions,* Celia Green and Charles McCreery of the Institute of Psychophysical Research in Oxford, England, described three types of apparitional experience: (1) that which is superimposed onto one's otherwise normal environment; (2) that which temporally replaces one's entire field of perception (sometimes referred to as a "waking dream"); and (3) that which partially obscures one's environment. Green and McCreery warn that what might appear to the viewer as the normal environment may be part of the hallucination. "[I]n cases in which the illumination differs from the normal," becoming lighter or darker during the experience, they argue, "[t]here seems to be a strong case for regarding the entire environment as hallucinatory." They elaborate further: "Now if the subject's surroundings appear illuminated, as well as the figure of the apparition itself, we seem driven to the conclusion that ... the whole environment the subject is seeing is hallucinatory."[54]

Whitmer's description caused James Moyle to conclude that the witnesses' surroundings had been replaced by a "different kind of light" and that the whole experience was "more spiritual" than he had been taught to believe. In 1878 Whitmer explained to Orson Pratt and Joseph F. Smith: "[W]e were overshadowed by a light. It was not like the light of the sun[,] nor like that of a fire, but more glorious and beautiful. It extended away round us, I cannot tell how far."[55] William H. Kelley reported Whitmer saying, "[A] light came down from above us and encircled us for quite a little distance around; and the angel stood before us."[56] Whitmer told a reporter for the *Omaha Herald* that "he beheld a dazzlingly brilliant light that surpassed in brightness even [of] the sun at noon day and which seemed to envelope the woods for a considerable distance around."[57]

From the preceding accounts, it appears, at least in Whitmer's case, that his experience was similar to a waking dream wherein the entire field of perception is hallucinatory. Unfortunately, no one asked Harris the type of questions that would have enabled us to make the same assessment of his experience, although one late reminiscence reported him saying that the "Angel of the Lord descended in a dazzling light of glory."[58]

In the context of the experiences of the three witnesses, the subject of hallucination cannot be satisfactorily explored without also examining Joseph Smith's role as a possible facilitator.

Hypnotism

The role Joseph Smith played is central. It was by his permission that the three men sought to become the promised witnesses; they followed him into the woods; they obeyed his instructions regarding the order of prayer; they had the vision because he was with them. Even Harris had no vision until Smith joined him. One wonders why Smith's presence was so important at an event not otherwise requiring it.

The possibility of some kind of trance state was explored by I. Woodbridge Riley in 1902 and Fawn Brodie in 1945.[59] Even Whitmer's grandson George W. Schweich suggested, "If that vision was not real it was *hypnotism*."[60] This possibility has never been adequately explored, let alone refuted. Of course, the question of the source—whether the vision was inspired by God or the result of some psychological state—can never be conclusively answered. But the case for hypnotism or some similar process is more compelling than one might at first presume.

That Smith was familiar with hypnotism, or at least with the concept that one person could cause another to hallucinate, comes from the Book of Mormon itself. Following the appearance of an angel who prevented Laman's and Lemuel's continued beating of Nephi, Laman declared that Nephi "worketh many things by his cunning arts, that he may deceive our eyes" (1 Ne. 16:38).

A glimpse into Smith's ability to evoke a vision in another person is provided by Philo Dibble who was present at Smith's and Sidney Rigdon's joint vision of three heavens on 16 February 1832 in Hiram, Ohio (see D&C 76). Dibble said that several people present in the room "saw the glory, and felt the power, but did not see the vision." He recalled:

> Joseph would, at intervals, say: "What do I see?" as one might say while looking out the window and beholding what all in the room could not see. Then he would relate what he had seen or what he was looking at. Then Sidney replied, "I see the same." Presently Sidney would say "what

> do I see?" and would repeat what he had seen or was seeing, and Joseph would reply, "I see the same." This manner of conversation was repeated at short intervals to the end of the vision. ...[61]

During the procedure, Dibble adds, Smith "sat firmly and calmly" while Rigdon "sat limp and pale, apparently as limber as a rag." Some might interpret Rigdon's condition as a hypnotic trance and conclude that Smith was leading him through a series of suggestions. Moreover, as the ultimate interpreter of the vision,[62] Smith could create the impression of a shared vision.

When objecting to Brodie's idea that Smith hypnotized the witnesses, Richard Anderson countered that "[t]hose hypnotized are normally aware of entering such a process."[63] This assumes that the witnesses were unaware of their changed mental state–which they were aware of–and did not voluntarily enter the revelation through fasting, prayer, and other such spiritual exercises–which they did.

Whitmer told one reporter, "A spirit of elevation seized him as of joy indescribable and a strange influence stole over him which so entranced him that he felt that he was chained to the spot."[64] Whitmer added to E. C. Briggs that "a light from heaven shone round us, and solemnity pervaded our minds."[65] To Anthony Metcalf, Harris said, "While praying I passed into a state of entrancement, and in that state I saw the angel and the plates."[66] Whitmer sometimes referred to this changed state as being "in the spirit."[67]

Their induction "in the spirit" was straightforward and was achieved just as spiritualists had done for millennia–through prayer. Smith reported that after kneeling, each man prayed in succession and that it was not "many minutes" before the angel appeared. Whitmer told Edward Stevenson that the vision came as he, Smith, and Cowdery "were sitting upon a log ... talking."[68] Whitmer does not report who spoke or the topic of their discussion, but if we recall Smith's later procedure with Rigdon, it is possible that Smith was continuing his induction of Whitmer.

Inducing visions is a function of charismatic religious leaders. Smith lived in a day when revival preachers moved their audiences to speak in tongues, fall into trances, and see visions of heaven, hell, the devil, or Jesus.[69] His followers expected no less from a man they called their prophet. If Smith sometimes induced visionary experiences, he had willing subjects to work with.

Witnesses as Fertile Ground

Another religious exercise not mentioned but integral to early Mormon practice is fasting. The Book of Mormon explains that the Nephite church met "together oft, to fast and to pray" (Moro. 6:5) and links fasting with prayer (Omni 1:26; Mos. 27:22; Al. 6:6; 17:3; 28:6; 45:1; Hel. 3:35; 3 Ne. 27:1). Six months after his vision, Cowdery assured Smith that he had not "taken my mind from meditating upon my mission ... nor of ... slacking my diligence in prayer and fasting."[70] Although not necessary to the creation of altered states of consciousness, prolonged fasting should not be overlooked, since hallucinations can occur through the lowering of one's blood sugar.[71] Regardless, the physical condition of the witnesses is perhaps less important than their emotional, psychological, and mental states.

Hallucinations occur in otherwise normal individuals–that is, people free from psychological impairment. At any given time, a segment of the population (anywhere from 1 percent to 8 percent) can be made to hallucinate either through hypnotic or non-hypnotic suggestion, sometimes called task-motivational instruction; in other words, hypnotism is not essential for the production of hallucination. Simple suggestion is often sufficient.[72] Moreover, Smith's claims would have attracted the kinds of people susceptible to visionary experiences; thus, the percentage of such people among Smith's early followers was probably much higher than a random sampling of the general population.

Significantly, each of the three witnesses had a history of visions before gathering to pray in the wilderness near the Whitmer farm in late June 1829. Such testimony must be considered if we are to fully understand the men who signed the testimony. This aspect of each man's background is certainly more relevant than that Oliver Cowdery was a school teacher and later a lawyer, that Harris was a respected businessman, or that Whitmer was later a good citizen of Richmond, Missouri.

Speaking of Harris's visionary experiences, Richard Anderson has written: "The reality of this experience and the honesty of Martin Harris are obviously harmonious. But if one rejects the supernatural event, he is left with the undisputed fact that the New York farmer was a man trusted implicitly by his community in business affairs."[73] An examination of Harris's business ethics reveals little about his religious propensities or the emotional or spiritual "reality" from which he would have evaluated Joseph Smith's claims. Those who knew Harris to be honest in business also described him as an unstable religious eccentric.

Lorenzo Saunders said Harris was "a good citizen ... a man that would do just as he agreed with you" but that he was also "a great man for seeing spooks."[74] William Hyde, who said he knew Harris well and that Harris once used him as a character witness, remarked that he could only "speak well of him," though he said that "on religious subjects I thought him slightly demented."[75] Jesse Townsend went so far as to call Harris a "visionary fanatic."[76] John A. Clark said Harris "had always been a firm believer in dreams, and visions, and supernatural appearances, such as apparitions and ghosts, and therefore was a fit subject for such men as Smith and his colleagues to operate upon."[77]

Harris told Joel Tiffany that he received revelations about Mormonism before his vision of the plates. He said Smith once expressed concern that he would not believe without seeing the plates, to which Harris responded: "Joseph, I know all about it. The Lord has showed to me ten times more about it than you know."[78] John A. Clark gave a specific example of Harris's early visionary claims: "[Harris] told a gentleman in Palmyra, after one of his excursions to Pennsylvania, while the translation of the Book of Mormon was going on, that on the way he met the Lord Jesus Christ, who walked along by the side of him in the shape of a deer for two or three miles, talking with him as familiarly as one man talks with another."[79] Albert Chandler, who helped bind the Book of Mormon, said Harris told him "he saw the devil, in all his hideousness, on the road, just before dark, near his farm, a little north of Palmyra."[80] While expressing skepticism about these specific reports, Mormon historian Ronald W. Walker admitted that Harris's "imagination was excitable and fecund."[81] Whether or not the specifics are accurate, Harris's propensity for visionary experience must be considered if we are to understand this Book of Mormon witness.

Furthermore, to describe Harris as a "skeptical witness"[82] distorts the truth. If Harris was at first skeptical, his actions quickly changed to those of a true believer. Following his hefting of the plates in a box in the fall of 1827, he gave money to help Smith move to Pennsylvania; he spent over two months in 1828 at Smith's residence in Harmony working as his scribe; and in early June 1829, he worked diligently to find a printer for the Book of Mormon, ultimately promising Egbert B. Grandin that he would mortgage his farm as security for the publication. By the time of his vision in late June 1829, Harris was certainly a believer.

Examining David Whitmer's activities prior to seeing the angel and the plates suggests that he too was in an emotional, suggestible state at the time of his vision. As he was returning to Fayette with Smith and Cowdery, he reported seeing a strange man, whom Smith later said was one of the Nephites transporting the plates to the Hill Cumorah. Upon arriving at his father's farm, Whitmer recalled, "they were impressed" that the same Nephite was under the Whitmers' "Shed."[83] Later, while milking cows in the shed, Whitmer's mother reported seeing the angel with the plates. While plowing in his fields on the morning prior to his group vision with the other two witnesses, Whitmer saw an apparition of a man and heard the words, "Blessed is the Lord & he that keepeth his Commandments." One should perhaps view his vision of the plates as the culmination of a highly charged period in his life. As Lyndon W. Cook has noted, Whitmer's accounts of "other supernatural experiences ... must be seen in connection with the more frequently printed evidence to fully appreciate this eyewitness's testimony [of the Book of Mormon]."[84]

Oliver Cowdery was perhaps the most significant individual connected with Mormon origins other than Joseph Smith. He has been described as follows:

> Oliver Cowdery was generally recognized by Mormon and non-Mormon alike as an astute and highly intelligent individual, and his mature life was spent in the practical vocation and avocation of law and politics. The fact that he considered the above experience [with the angel and plates] the most impressive and solemn event of his life must weigh heavily in favor of the objective reality of the vision. Above all, he had the emotional and intellectual capacity to know whether he was deceived. If this vision was real to him, there is a burden upon every informed person to face the great probability that the Latter-day Saints have indeed received modern revelation.[85]

Despite this sanguine appraisal, Cowdery was far from being the dispassionate teacher-lawyer described here, and at least during this early period of his life, he was known to be unstable and given to obsessive and morbid thoughts. Also, like Harris and Whitmer, he had a history of visions prior to late June 1829.

Shortly after meeting Cowdery in early April 1829, Joseph Smith dictated a revelation that described him as having already received revelations through the "Spirit of revelation" and the "rod of nature," or divining rod.[86] According to Smith's 1832 history, Cowdery came to Smith as a result of having received a vision of the plates: "[The] Lord appeared unto a young man by the name of Oliver Cowdry and shewed unto him the plates in a vision and also the truth of the work and what the Lord was about to do through me his unworthy servant therefore he was desirous to come and write for me."[87] In the months prior to Cowdery's meeting Joseph, Lucy Smith noticed that he became "entirely absorbed in the subject of the record that it seemed impossible for him to think or converse about anything else."[88]

Cowdery's writings from this period reflect his intense feelings about the subject. In a letter to Joseph Smith dated 6 November 1829, he said that "when I think of the goodness of christ I feel no desire to live or stay here upon the shores of this world of iniquity. ... This writing is to inform you of my prospects and hopes and my desires and my longing to be freed from sin and to rest in the Kingdom of my Savior."[89] On 28 December 1829, Cowdery again expressed his strong feelings: "Some times I feel almost as though I could quit time and fly away and be at rest in the bosom of my Redeemer for the many deep feelings of sorrow and the many long struglings in pray[er]s of sorrow for the Sins of my fellow beings ... almost as it were seperateth my spirit from my mortal body." He continued: "I would that you should understand [it] is my anxiety at some times to be at rest ... in the Paradice of my God."[90] About June 1829, Cowdery received a revelation concerning how the church would be built up, which concluded with the following statement from him: "I have written the things which [God] hath commanded me for behold his word was unto me as a burning fire shut up in my bones & I was weary with forbearing & I could forebear no longer."[91] Considering his state of mind and visionary predisposition, his obsessive thoughts may have carried him to the point of delusion; at least, this possibility should be taken into consideration when assessing his role as one of the three witnesses.

In defending the witnesses, Richard Anderson repeatedly exhibits an assumption that hallucinators are unstable and most likely uneducated. However, hallucinators are otherwise indistinguishable from other people and can function normally in society. To emphasize Harris's business ethics or Cowdery's intelligence or Whitmer's good citizenship is irrelevant to their potential to be inclined to see visions.

If the experience of the witnesses was some kind of hypnotism or the result of simple suggestion, the three men were willing subjects. As soon as Cowdery, Whitmer, and Harris learned that there were to be three special witnesses, they expressed a desire to volunteer and, as Smith records, "they became so very solicitious, and teazed me so much" that Smith received the revelation instructing them on how they would see the plates and other objects (D&C 17).[92] Thus, Smith may have taken three suggestible, willing subjects into the woods and used prayer as a method of induction. As Riley noted almost a century ago, "Repetition, steady attention, absence of mistrust, self-surrender to the will of the principal,—all the requisites are present, not as formulae but as facts."[93]

TESTIMONY OF EIGHT WITNESSES

Unlike their nineteenth-century counterparts, Mormon apologists today like to highlight the Testimony of Eight Witnesses which they assert describes a purely physical experience with the plates. Indeed, the language of the testimony implies a natural, physical experience. But despite the materialistic sound of the testimony, there is evidence that this experience was visionary as well.

Joseph Smith's history does not provide details about the testimony, only that the event occurred "soon after" the experience of the three witnesses.[94] According to David Whitmer, the three saw the plates in the "latter part" of June 1829 and the eight witnesses one or two days later.[95] Lucy Smith, whose husband and two sons were among the eight, said the event occurred in Manchester, New York, a "few days" after the experience of the three witnesses in Fayette. According to Lucy, Joseph Jr. chose eight men—his father (Joseph Sr.), two brothers (Hyrum and Samuel), the Whitmer brothers (Christian, Jacob, Peter, and John), and their brother-in-law (Hiram Page)—and "repaired to a little grove where it was customary for the family to offer up their secret prayers," where they then saw the plates.[96] Lucy added that "Joseph had been instructed that the plates would be carried" to the grove "by one of the ancient Nephites" and that "after the witnesses returned to the house the Angel again made his appearance to Joseph and received the plates from his hands."[97] Lucy's account provides details otherwise unavailable. Nevertheless, she does not describe the actual viewing of the plates.

The experience was probably spontaneous, perhaps inspired by the excitement of the three witnesses. Unlike the three (D&C 5:11; Eth. 5:2-4; 2 Ne. 27:12-14; D&C 17:1-9), no revelation preceded their experience. Indeed, the initial revelation outlining the need for witnesses, dated March 1829, seemed to limit their number, declaring: "[T]he testimony of three of my servants shall go forth with my word unto this Generation yea three shall know of A surety that these things are true for I will give them power that they may Behold & view these things as they are & to none else will I grant this power among this Generation."[98] This early revelation neither promised the appearance of an angel nor anticipated that the witnesses would hear the voice of God—only that three individuals would be given the exclusive privilege of seeing the plates "as they are," which could only be done through special "power." When this revelation was revised in 1835, the three witnesses were distinguished from the eight by the addition of the words—"for from heaven will I declare it unto them" (D&C 5:12), thus suggesting that the "power" to view the plates was no longer a difference between the groups.

A similar shift also seems to have occurred within the Book of Mormon itself.[99] In a passage dictated in Pennsylvania, Moroni gives the future translator permission to "show the plates unto those who shall assist to bring forth this work" (Eth. 5:2). Then, using similar language as in the March 1829 revelation, Moroni declares: "[U]nto three shall [the plates] be shown by the power of God; wherefore, they shall know of a surety that these things are true" (Eth. 5:3; cf. D&C 5:12-13). Again, one should not read one's own assumptions into this passage which was probably dictated in May 1829. Nothing in the text anticipates the appearance of an angel or the voice of God, only that the witnesses would be shown the plates "by the power of God."

Matthew Roper has argued that Ether 5:2-3 describes both sets of witnesses, claiming that those who "assist" are the eight, whereas those who are shown the plates "by the power of God" are the three.[100] This unwarranted application of hindsight fills an apologetic need to divide an obvious literary parallelism.[101] He feels that 2 Nephi 27:12-13 also describes the eight witnesses where Nephi predicts that "the eyes of none shall behold it save it be that three witnesses shall behold it, by the power of God, besides him to whom the book shall be delivered." Nephi qualifies his statement: "And there is none other which shall view it, save it be a few according to the will of God." Although the passage opened the door for additional testimony, one should take care not to read too much into it. For instance, it makes no qualitative distinction between the two groups, and there is nothing to specifically limit the "few" to eight–in fact, the passage is entirely open-ended.

More likely, the exclusivity of the three witnesses was relaxed when David Whitmer's mother, Mary Musselman, saw the angel and the plates shortly after Joseph Smith's arrival in early June 1829.[102] Her experience may have also helped shape the expectations of the three witnesses.

A Purely Physical Experience?

We have seen how important the statements of Whitmer and Harris were in more fully understanding their published testimony. The same is true for the eight witnesses, even though their statements are few. Christian Whitmer, Peter Whitmer Jr., Jacob Whitmer, and Joseph Smith Sr. left no commentary regarding their testimonies. Both Hyrum and Samuel Smith left brief accounts stating that they saw and handled the plates.[103] Hiram Page only testified that he saw the plates.[104] Of the eight, John Whitmer lived the longest and left the most detailed record, repeatedly testifying that he both saw and handled the plates.[105] Despite the lack of additional direct testimony, the best interpretation should consider all the available evidence.

Many learned more about the nature of the eight witnesses' experience following the failure of the church-sponsored Kirtland Safety Society Anti-Banking Company in 1837. Dissenters who soured on Joseph Smith's prophetic ability began to wonder if they should therefore reconsider the Book of Mormon's claims. A letter dated 15 April 1838 from Stephen Burnett to Lyman E. Johnson, who was a former member of the Quorum of Twelve Apostles living in Far West, Missouri, addressed this topic. According to Burnett, the dissenters differed in opinion about the status of the Book of Mormon. Warren Parrish, Luke S. Johnson, and John Boynton argued that it should be rejected, while Martin Harris, Cyrus Smalling, and Joseph Coe continued to believe in the book despite their rejection of Joseph Smith. Burnett said that Harris declared at a public meeting that he "never saw the plates with his natural eyes" and that "the eight witnesses [also] never saw them [with their natural eyes] & hesitated to sign that instrument for that reason, but were persuaded to do it." Upon hearing Harris's statement, Burnett concluded: "[I]f the witnesses whose names are attached to the Book of Mormon never saw the plates as Martin [Harris] admits, [then] there can be nothing brought to prove that any such thing ever existed."[106]

Burnett's account is supported by Warren Parrish, a fellow dissenter, who reported in August 1838 that "Harris, one of the subscribing witnesses, has come out at last, and says he never saw the plates, from which the book [of Mormon] purports to have been translated, except in vision, and he further says that any man who says he has seen them in any other way is a liar, Joseph [Smith] not excepted."[107] Parrish supplies the scriptural reference alluded to by Harris: the revelation dictated by Joseph Smith in June 1829 that promised the three hopeful witnesses that they would see the plates if their faith was strong and instructing them to testify to the world that they saw the plates "even as my servant Joseph Smith, Jun., has seen them; for it is by my power that he has seen them, and it is because he had faith" (D&C 17:5).

Harris's use of this revelation creates problems for those who wish to maintain that the experience of the eight witnesses was mundane. Indeed, considering the inclusive tone of the revelation, it seems unlikely that the eight witnesses would have been exempted from the conditions required by it, although the need for further witnesses had not been contemplated at the time of its reception. To maintain a purely physical experience for the eight witnesses, one must believe that Joseph Smith violated the logic of this revelation only days after its reception.

Although Harris rejected Smith's leadership, he continued to believe in the Book of Mormon and had little desire to impart information that could damage the book. At a subsequent meeting, according to Burnett, Harris expressed regret about revealing the true nature of the experience of the eight witnesses, stating that "he never should have told that the testimony of the eight was false, if it had not been picked out of h[im] but should have let it passed as it was." The fact that Harris's disclosure hurt his own position on the Book of Mormon argued in favor of its truth, at least in Harris's mind. His account is secondhand, but it cannot be dismissed for that reason alone. Harris was on intimate terms with the eight witnesses and was therefore in a position to know the details of their experience. Six of the eight were still alive at the time Harris made his statement (Christian Whitmer and Peter Whitmer Jr. had died in 1835 and 1836), and none of them contradicted him.

Hyrum Smith's response to the dissenters, reported by Sally Parker in August 1838, indirectly confirmed the impact of their statements. Parker wrote to "comfort" her relatives in Maine who were troubled about the developments in Kirtland. She offered two evidences that the plates were real. First, she heard Hyrum Smith, who recently visited her mid-Ohio town of Sunbury, declare that "he had but [two] hands and [two] eyes" and that "he had seene the plates with his eyes and handeled them with his hands." Next, she had lived near Lucy Smith and had heard her claim to have "hefted and handled" the plates while covered.[108] Both stories were obviously designed to counter the spiritualizing claims of the dissenters.

Hyrum's remark that "he had but ... [two] eyes" seems specially designed to counter claims that the eight witnesses saw the plates with their spiritual eyes. Hyrum's statement is not unlike the response of David Whitmer, who in 1886 told Nathan Tanner: "I have been asked if we saw those things with our natural eyes. Of course they were our natural eyes. There is no doubt that our eyes were prepared for the sight, but they were our natural eyes nevertheless."[109] Thus, Hyrum was not necessarily denying dissenter claims that he and the other witnesses had seen the plates in vision, only objecting to the implication that a vision was somehow inferior to a purely physical experience.

Is Hyrum's remark that "he had but [two] hands" also designed to counter claims that he had handled the plates in vision? Or should Hyrum's statement be understood as describing two or more separate events? We know that he handled the covered plates with other Smith family members at the time Joseph first brought them home. Perhaps, like Whitmer and Harris, he told of separate experiences in a single sentence.

Parker's account is unique because it also mentions that Hyrum saw the breastplate, which Hyrum described as concave and made of gold. Did Hyrum see the breastplate as part of his June 1829 experience? Or, like his mother, did he see the metallic object glisten through a thin cloth on a previous occasion shortly after Joseph brought the plates home in September 1827?[110] If Hyrum saw the breastplate as part of his experience as one of the eight witnesses, it might indicate that the experiences of the eight men varied and that their testimony, like that of the three witnesses, is fragmentary.

Similar events in Missouri presented another of the witnesses an opportunity to clarify his testimony. On 5 April 1839 Theodore Turley, who was then the church's business agent in Far West, publicly asked John Whitmer about his testimony. Whitmer had joined the dissenters and, unlike Harris, not only rejected Joseph Smith but also the Book of Mormon. Turley wanted to know how Whitmer's testimony about the plates could be true and yet the Book of Mormon be false. Before his anti-Mormon friends, Whitmer reaffirmed his testimony of the Book of Mormon, that he had both seen and handled the plates, but concluded by stating that the plates had been "shown to me by a supernatural power."[111] Given his experience, even if supernatural, how could he now reject the Book of Mormon, Turley wondered. Whitmer responded that he could not read the original script and therefore had no guarantee that Smith had translated it correctly.

Assuming that the experience of the eight witnesses was visionary, there are at least three possible scenarios to explain how they both saw and handled the plates. First, they saw and handled them in vision. Although instances of tangible apparitions are not unknown,[112] they are rare enough to render this possibility unsatisfactory.

Second, they saw them in vision but handled them in a box, or while covered, on some previous occasion. Both Hyrum Smith and John Whitmer testified that they handled the plates, but neither clearly placed the two events together. Whitmer reported publicly that "he had often handled the ... *golden plates.*"[113] Thus it is possible that the eight witnesses, or at least some of them, compressed separate experiences into a single statement, much like David Whitmer and Martin Harris. Thomas Ford's 1854 *History of Illinois,* which includes a detailed description of the witnesses' experiences, is consistent with this reconstruction. Ford claimed that his account came from "men who were once in the confidence of the prophet" but did not identify his sources. Nevertheless, his account is similar to the claims that dissident Mormons in Ohio and Missouri were making in 1838. According to Ford's informants:

> It is related that the prophet's early followers were anxious to see the plates; the prophet had always given out that they could not be seen by the carnal eye, but must be spiritually discerned; that the power to see them depended upon faith, and was the gift of God, to be obtained by fasting, prayer, mortification of the flesh, and exercises of the spirit; that so soon as he could see the evidences of a strong and lively faith in any of his followers, they should be gratified in their holy curiosity. He set them to continual prayer, and other spiritual exercises, to acquire this lively faith by means of which the hidden things of God could be spiritually discerned; and at last, when he could delay them no longer, he assembled them in a room, and produced a box, which he said contained the precious treasure. The lid opened; the witnesses peeped into it, but making no discovery, for the box was empty, they said, "Brother Joseph, we do not see the plates." The prophet answered them, "O ye of little faith! how long will God bear with this wicked and perverse generation? Down on your knees, brethren, every one of you, and pray God for the forgiveness of your sins, and for a holy and living faith which cometh down from heaven." The disciples dropped to their knees, and began to pray in the fervency of their spirit, supplicating God for more than two hours with fanatical earnestness; at the end of which time, looking again into the box, they were now persuaded that they saw the plates.[114]

Ford does not specify which set of witnesses his account describes, but it is obviously about the experience of the eight witnesses. Because the account has its own obvious historical weaknesses, most importantly Ford's failure to name his sources, Fawn Brodie was probably mistaken to place so much weight on this account alone. But in connection with the above discussion of the dissenters in 1838, Ford's narrative cannot be dismissed out of hand.[115] The details transmitted by Ford may be inaccurate, but the essence of the account contains an element of truth.

The suggestion that the witnesses handled the plates previously requires qualification. While the Smiths had ample opportunity to handle the plates on several occasions, the Whitmers and Page apparently did not have the same access. Smith moved from Manchester to Harmony in December 1827 and the plates were placed into a box and hidden in a barrel of dry beans;[116] several sources indicate that the plates were physically present in Harmony.[117] But when Smith and Cowdery moved to Fayette in early June 1829, Smith left the plates behind, presumably hidden somewhere in the hills of Pennsylvania. Rather than transport the plates himself, Smith explained to David Whitmer and his family, the angel would bring them to Fayette.[118] This change in approach was likely the result of Smith's concerns that they might be forcibly exposed to public view–fears that were reinforced when Martin Harris's traveling companion, a Mr. Rogers from Waterloo, attempted to cut open the sack containing the plates during a visit in March 1829.[119] Regardless, all contact with the plates in Fayette was strictly visionary. If the witnesses were shown an empty box or if their experience with the plates was purely visual and did not feature a box, it seems probable that at the signing of the testimony only some of the witnesses had handled them, that what was true for the group was not necessarily true for each man.

Third, Smith may have produced a box containing the plates or perhaps something of similar weight. The witnesses were permitted to lift the box, but their view of the plates was visionary. In other words, they may have seen the plates through the box. Thus, each man could claim that he had both seen and handled the artifact. This possibility is similar to Harris's experience prior to his June 1829 vision with Smith. Harris told John A. Clark in 1828 that he saw the plates "with the eye of faith ... just as distinctly as I see any thing around me,–though at the time they were covered over with a cloth."[120] He also told Stephen Burnett and others in 1838 that "he had hefted the plates repeatedly in a box [or] with only a tablecloth or a handkerchief over them, but he never saw them only as he saw a city through a mountain."[121]

Harris's claim should be understood, I believe, within the context of similar claims made by seers and clairvoyants in his day. People known as somnambulists claimed the ability to see concealed objects,[122] and it may have been the result of such a claim that former Palmyra resident William Hyde described Joseph Smith Sr. as a "somnambulist." When Hyde expressed a desire to see the plates, the senior Smith responded: "It will mean death for you to attempt to look at the plates. They are sewed in a silk sack and the first person who disbelieves the truth of my assertion will be obliterated." Hyde remarked,

"I began to think now that the man was demented and my belief was strengthened by the fact that Smith senior was a somnambulist."[123]

RELIABILITY OF MULTIPLE WITNESSES?

While one might feel confident about visions experienced by multiple witnesses, such a phenomenon does not automatically rule out the possibility of hallucination. Group hallucinations are known to have occurred outside Mormonism. Consider, for example, the many appearances of the Virgin Mary, often to multiple witnesses;[124] or visions of Shakers in Lebanon, New York, in the early 1840s. In one instance, eight Shakers signed an affidavit attesting that they saw, along with Emily Babcock, "the holy Angel standing upon the house-top ... holding the Roll and Book."[125] Group hallucinations have been observed by modern investigators of the paranormal. Green and McCreery, for example, state, "There are reports of groups numbering from two up to about eight people seeing the same apparition at the same time, but there are no well authenticated cases of groups much larger than this doing so."[126]

A detailed exploration of group psychology is beyond the scope of this investigation, but the fact that small groups can be hypnotized and experience the same imaginary phenomena should be sufficient to warn against the uncritical acceptance of group visionary experiences.[127] Generally, the illusion of group hallucination is achieved through the following mechanisms: expectation, anticipation, suggestion, and cross-infection that can begin prior to the hallucination, operate during the experience, and continue to modify the memories of the participants long afterwards.[128] Thus, expectation and anticipation might operate in producing similar experiences for various participants; communication between participants during the hallucination, ranging from verbal descriptions to subtle nuances in body language and facial expression, might facilitate similarity of experience (and if a leader-follower dynamic is operating, such as in hypnotist or spiritual guide situations, uniformity of experience is more easily achieved); and like any human experience, visions or hallucinations are not immune to reconstructive memory and subsequent communication between the participants which can contaminate their individual recollections rather than clarify them. Assuming that the experiences of the participants are similar but not identical, subsequent conversations may not bring out subtle differences. Although group hallucination is a documented fact and the dynamics of the phenomenon are more or less understood, it is not always easy to discover the principles operating in a given case since the subtleties of what operates largely on an unconscious level are not easily recovered from the participants themselves.

However, the existence of documented group hallucinations cautions against the reliability of multiple witnesses in the present discussion. The limited value of the published testimonies of the three and eight witnesses, and the fact that Cowdery and the eight witnesses gave little other information, leaves us unable to assess the strength or weakness of evidence that might have been derived from the simultaneous experience the testimonies seemingly present. Yet, even if we could compare the individual testimonies in detail, any presumed agreement between the accounts would not exclude the possibility of cross-infection.

In studying multiple hallucinators, Green and McCreery found that participants only apparently experience the same apparition. "[W]e do not know how precise the correspondence is between the images perceived by the various subjects," they explain. "Even in cases where the reports reveal no discrepancies, we cannot be sure that there were not some which did not emerge from the verbal statement. ... As a matter of fact, quite wide discrepancies could exist between the perceptions of one person and those of another without attracting any attention."[129] This means, theoretically, that the witnesses, in describing their experiences, would not have necessarily noticed discrepancies, even if their visions were similar but not identical.

Although Harris and Whitmer experienced their visions separately, it is generally assumed that their visions were identical. Harris's and Whitmer's accounts share common elements—the angel, the table, the plates and other objects, the angel speaking, and the voice of God—but one does not know if the two men saw the same angel, the same table, or the same plates, or if they heard the same voice or the same words or even if their experiences lasted the same length of time.

Moreover, similarities may be the result of preconditioning: the June 1829 revelation that promised what objects would be seen, their possible handling of the plates and feeling them through the cloth, their examination of characters Smith had transcribed from the plates, and Smith's own descriptions of the plates and other objects as well as his accounts of previous encounters with the angel. Joseph Smith reveals that the order in which each man prayed was "[a]ccording to previous arrangement." It is possible that prior discussions with the witnesses included other elements of preconditioning that were not recorded. Additionally, Smith's presence at both events and the possibility of transmitting information about Whitmer's experience may have been a contributing factor in Harris's further preparation.

Finally, differences in experiences may have blurred over time as details faded and general impressions remained. The publication of Smith's version of the experience in 1842 may have influenced Harris's and Whitmer's descriptions–Smith's account perhaps acting as a catalyst of uniformity. Indeed, the testimony itself was designed to unify multiple experiences.

Despite the general agreement between Harris's and Whitmer's stories, however, there is evidence that Harris's vision varied from that of the others. Whitmer, for example, told Orson Pratt and Joseph F. Smith in 1878: "I don't think [Harris] saw all that we did, but our testimony as recorded in the Book of Mormon is strictly and absolutely true just as it is written."[130] Palmyra resident Abner Cole claimed in 1831 that "there appears to be a great discrepancy, in the stories told by the famous three witnesses to the Gold bible," particularly between Harris's and Whitmer's description of what the plates looked like.[131]

It was perhaps this situation that forced Joseph Smith to distance himself from Harris's experience. Indeed, if the public noticed differences between Harris's and Whitmer's testimonies, Smith would have benefitted by emphasizing the fact that Harris received his vision separately from the other witnesses. In Smith's telling, the only link between what two men saw and what Harris experienced was his own claim that "the same vision was opened to our view." Smith's qualification that "at least it was again to me" opens the possibility that Harris's vision differed not only from Whitmer's and Cowdery's but also from Smith's.[132]

It seems that the potential difficulty with multiple subjective witnesses was anticipated in the revelation of March 1829 promising Harris a view of the plates but instructing that "he shall say no more unto them ['the people of this generation'] concerning these things, except he shall say: I have seen them, and they have been shown unto me by the power of God" (D&C 5:26).[133] As Abner Cole reported, the witnesses failed to strictly follow the revelation's instruction.

Significant to this issue is the portion of the Book of Mormon manuscript that Smith dictated in June 1829. It includes Nephi's commentary on what his father, Lehi, failed to notice in an identical vision. As Nephi explains to his brothers, "the water which my father saw was filthiness; and so much was his mind swallowed up in other things that he beheld not the filthiness of the water" (1 Ne. 15:27). Thus, the same vision was experienced differently by two people. Still, multiple attestations do not rule out the possibility of hallucination.

CONCLUSION

Given the fact that the three witnesses saw a vision and that the experience of the eight witnesses seems to have been similarly visionary, there is no compelling evidence that Joseph Smith actually possessed anciently constructed plates. To look at the issue critically, it would have been possible for him to make plates out of tin–which would be consistent with the reported weight of between forty and sixty pounds–and to allow the chosen few to feel them through a cloth.[134]

The real question is not the trustworthiness of the witnesses but whether testimony resulting from visions or hallucinations is reliable. Indeed, does the testimony of the Book of Mormon witnesses merit greater attention than that of other similar religious testimony? Or rather, is the nature of the witnesses' experiences different from the multitude of religious testimony confronting historians? Indeed, by what criteria do we accept the Book of Mormon witnesses while at the same time rejecting non-Mormon testimony? In the final analysis, nothing distinguishes the visions of the Book of Mormon witnesses from those of their contemporaries.

NOTES

1. B. H. Roberts, for example, argued: "Had the testimony of the three witnesses been the only kind given; that is, if the plates had been exhibited to the eight witnesses in the same manner as they had been revealed to the three, then perhaps, mental hallucination might have been urged with more show of reason. Or, if the three witnesses had seen the plates in the same manner as

the eight did, in a plain, matter-of-fact way, without display of the divine power, then the theory of pure fabrication, with collusion on the part of all those who assisted in bringing forth the work, would have more standing. But with the two kinds of testimony to deal with, it is extremely difficult for objectors to dispose of the matter" (B. H. Roberts, *A Comprehensive History of the Church of Jesus Christ of Latter-day Saints,* 6 vols. [Provo, UT: Brigham Young University, 1965], 1:150). More recently, Richard L. Anderson of Brigham Young University has similarly asserted: "Why are there two sets of witnesses? ... If you say, 'Well, Joseph Smith perhaps had made a set of plates so that people could examine something physical,' that doesn't explain the fact that the angel from God came with supernatural power and glory. ... There are those, especially in our day, who would say that Joseph Smith just got people emotionally excited. That's what this vision amounts to. If you say that, what about the physical evidence of the plates, which weighed between forty and sixty pounds and were described in detail? The physical and spiritual are complementary when you see the testimony of the Three and Eight Witnesses" (Richard L. Anderson, "Book of Mormon Witnesses" [Provo, UT: FARMS, 1994], 3-4).

2. See, for example, Richard Lloyd Anderson, *Investigating the Book of Mormon Witnesses* (Salt Lake City: Deseret Book Company, 1981).

3. The only possible exception comes from P. Wilhelm Poulson who interviewed John Whitmer in April 1878. However, Poulson's version of the interview is highly questionable. According to him, Whitmer said Joseph Smith simply handed the plates over "uncovered into our hands, and we turned the leaves sufficient to satisfy us" and they were "as material as anything can be" and "very heavy" (P. Wilhelm Poulson to Editors, 31 July 1878, *Deseret Evening News,* 6 Aug. 1878). But this is imbedded in a historical setting that is contradicted by more reliable sources. For example, Poulson represents Whitmer making the unique claim that the plates were shown to the eight witnesses "[i]n Joseph Smith's house" in Manchester, whereas Lucy Smith, the prophet's mother, said that they were shown to them in a nearby grove while she and others waited in the cabin for their return. Also suspicious is Poulson's unique claim that Whitmer said that "we were four persons, present in the room, and at another time [Smith] showed them to four persons more." Unfortunately, John Whitmer was dead when Poulson's account was published and could not challenge the accuracy of the reported interview. However, Poulson's subsequent publication of an interview with David Whitmer about the same time was challenged by the latter as containing invented conversation (P. Wilhelm Poulson to Editor, 13 Aug. 1878, *Deseret Evening News,* 16 Aug. 1878; reprinted in Lyndon W. Cook, *David Whitmer Interviews: A Restoration Witness* [Orem, UT: Grandin Book Co., 1991], 19-24; hereafter DWI).

An example of Poulson's inventiveness, and undoubtedly a part of the interview that provoked Whitmer's objection, is as follows: "[Harris] was not by us at all when we first saw the angel. First when we told him what we had seen, and were the second time in prayer all together, and when the angel appeared for a second time, we saw Martin Harris by us, and he saw, and we saw it, and our testimony, which we give to the world, is true exactly as you read it, we saw by the gift and power of God" (DWI, 21). This is contradicted not only by Joseph Smith's history but also by numerous statements of Martin Harris and David Whitmer. In this case, the invented statement reflects Poulson's concern to unify the experiences of the three witnesses and thus defend their printed testimony. In reporting his interview with John Whitmer, Poulson may have been similarly concerned about exaggerating the natural and physical in the experiences of the eight witnesses.

4. John Gee, Review of *New Approaches to the Book of Mormon: Explorations in Critical Methodology,* ed. Brent Lee Metcalfe (Salt Lake City: Signature Books, 1994), in *Review of Books on the Book of Mormon* 6 (1994): 111.

5. Ibid., 513; see also 507 and 509. Matthew Roper, in the same volume, makes similar statements (375).

6. Richard Lloyd Anderson, "Book of Mormon Witnesses," in Daniel H. Ludlow, ed., *Encyclopedia of Mormonism: The History, Scripture, Doctrine, and Procedure of the Church of Jesus Christ of Latter-day Saints,* 4 vols. (New York: Macmillan Publishing Co., 1992), 1:214. Anderson evidently believes the phrase in the testimony that "as many of the leaves as the said Smith has translated we did handle with our hands" implies that the witnesses actually turned each leaf in the unsealed portion of the plates. However, the wording is ambiguous enough to mean that they were handled as a group rather than individually. Accompanying Anderson's article is Harold T. Kilbourn's painting of Joseph Smith and the eight witnesses viewing the plates as they lay on the stump of a tree (215). Elsewhere Anderson represents Lucy Smith as saying that in preparation for viewing, the angel left the plates "on a tree stump" in the woods near the Smiths' Manchester cabin (Anderson, "Book of Mormon Witnesses" [FARMS], 9). However, Anderson has let an element from Kilbourn's artistic conceptualization of the event creep into his historical narrative since Lucy said nothing about a tree stump. See also Roberts, *Comprehensive History,* 1:148-49.

7. The first edition of the Book of Mormon included the testimonies at the end, whereas present editions have them in the front. The printer's manuscript of the Book of Mormon includes the earliest known copy of the Testimony of Eight Witnesses in Oliver Cowdery's handwriting (Testimony of Eight Witnesses, [June 1829], Printer's Manuscript of the Book of Mormon, 464, Restoration Scriptures, Library-Archives of The Reorganized Church of Jesus Christ of Latter Day Saints, Independence, Missouri; hereafter RLDS archives).

8. Anderson, *Investigating the Book of Mormon Witnesses,* xii.

9. The printer's manuscript of the Book of Mormon includes the earliest known copy of the Testimony of Three Witnesses in Oliver Cowdery's handwriting (see "The Testimony of Three Witnesses," [June 1829], Printer's

Manuscript of the Book of Mormon, 463-64). According to Joseph Smith's 1838-39 history, the testimony was not only signed by Oliver Cowdery, David Whitmer, and Martin Harris but authored by the witnesses themselves (see Joseph Smith, Manuscript History of the Church, Book A-1, 25, Joseph Smith Papers, archives, Historical Department, Church of Jesus Christ of Latter-day Saints, Salt Lake City, Utah (hereafter LDS archives); cited in Dan Vogel, *Early Mormon Documents,* 5 vols. [Salt Lake City: Signature Books, 1996-], 1:86; hereafter EMD).

Of the three witnesses, Oliver Cowdery is the most likely author. In an 1878 interview with Orson Pratt and Joseph F. Smith, Whitmer confirmed that each witness "signed his own name" ("Report of Elders Orson Pratt and Joseph F. Smith," *Deseret News,* 16 Nov. 1878 (DWI, 44); see also Joseph F. Smith to Samuel Russell, 19 Mar. 1901, Russell Collection, LDS archives (DWI, 258-59).

10. Smith, Manuscript History, 24-25 (EMD 1:84-85); cf. Joseph Smith Jr., *History of the Church of Jesus Christ of Latter-day Saints,* ed. B. H. Roberts, 7 vols. (2nd ed. rev.; Salt Lake City: Deseret Book, 1948 printing), 1:52-57; and "History of Joseph Smith," *Times and Seasons* 3 (1 Sept. 1842): 897-98.

11. For Martin Harris, see, e.g., A[nthony]. Metcalf, *Ten Years before the Mast. Shipwrecks and Adventures at Sea! Religious Customs of the People of India and Burmah's Empire. How I Became a Mormon and Why I Became an Infidel!* ([Malad City, ID]: n.p., [1888]), 71 (EMD 2:347); John E. Godfrey, Affidavit, 2 June [July] 1933, LDS archives (EMD 2:372); Ole A. Jensen, "Testimony of Martin Harris (One of the Witnesses of the Book of Mormon)," undated (ca. 1918), original in private possession, with photocopies at Utah State Historical Society, Salt Lake City; LDS archives; and Special Collections, Harold B. Lee Library, Provo, Utah, hereafter Lee Library (EMD 2:375). For David Whitmer, see, e.g., E. C. Briggs to Joseph Smith III, 4 June 1884, *Saints' Herald* 31 (21 June 1884): 396-97 (DWI, 127); "The Last Man," *Chicago Times,* 17 Oct. 1881 (DWI, 75-76); Edward Stevenson to Orson Pratt, 23 Dec. 1877, "Journal History," LDS archives (DWI, 15); George Q. Cannon, Journal, 27 Feb. 1884, LDS archives (DWI, 108-109); "Mormonism," *Kansas City Daily Journal,* 5 June 1881 (DWI, 63-64); Joseph F. Smith, Diary, 7-8 Sept. 1878, LDS archives (DWI, 25-26), with published version in "Report of Elders Orson Pratt and Joseph F. Smith" (DWI, 40).

12. Briggs to Joseph Smith III, 4 June 1884.

13. Edward Stevenson, Journal, 14:12, entry of 22-23 Dec. 1877, LDS archives (DWI, 11). Stevenson was told the same information in his January 1887 interview with Whitmer (Stevenson, Journal, 28:123-130, entry of 2 Jan. 1887 [DWI, 213]). For other instances where Whitmer mentioned seeing other ancient relics, see George Q. Cannon, Journal, 27 Feb. 1884; Joseph Smith III, Notes for Memoirs, 862-63, Smith Papers, RLDS archives, printed in *Saints' Herald* 83 (28 Jan. 1936): 114 (DWI, 135); William H. Kelley to *Saints' Herald,* 16 Jan. 1882, in *Saints' Herald* 29 (1 Mar. 1882): 68-69 (DWI, 86); "Mor-

monism," *Kansas City Daily Journal,* 5 June 1881; "Report of Elders Orson Pratt and Joseph F. Smith."

14. Edward Stevenson, "The Three Witnesses to the Book of Mormon. No. III," *Millennial Star* 48 (21 June 1886): 390 (EMD 2:325).

15. William Pilkington to Vern C. Poulter, 28 Feb. 1930, LDS archives (EMD 2:352); and William Pilkington, "Martin Harris' Dying Testimony Reported by Man at His Side," *Deseret News* (9 Apr. 1930): 6 (EMD 2:353).

16. Stevenson, "The Three Witnesses," 390.

17. Pilkington to Poulter, 28 Feb. 1930; see also Pilkington, "Martin Harris' Dying Testimony," 6. For other accounts where Harris mentions the angel speaking, see George Godfrey, Affidavit, 29 Oct. 1921, LDS archives (EMD 2:392); Alma L. Jensen, Statement, 1 June 1936, typescript, Lee Library (EMD 2:378); Ole A. Jensen, "Testimony of Martin Harris"; Simon Smith to Mark H. Forscutt, 11 Feb. 1881, Miscellaneous Letters and Papers, RLDS archives (EMD 2:381); William Harrison Homer, "Testimony given by Brother W. H. Homer, Jan. 3, 1922, 5:15 P.M., at 2522 No. Kodaio Blvd., Chicago, the home of his son-in-law and daughter, Mr. and Mrs. Merrill O. Maughan," LDS archives (EMD 2:314).

18. Edward Stevenson, Journal, 14:11-12 (22-23 Dec. 1877); see also Edward Stevenson to Editor, 21 Jan. 1878, *Salt Lake Herald* (2 Feb. 1878): 3 (DWI, 18-19). Lyndon Cook notes, "Reports are not clear if the voice was that of the personage or from some other source" (DWI, xiii).

19. See Edward Stevenson to Editor, 2 Mar. 1886, *Utah Journal* (Ogden, UT) (10 Mar. 1886): 3 (DWI, 186); Edward Stevenson, Journal, 28:127-28 (2 Jan. 1887).

20. "He bore a strong testamony–that An Angel Shewed him the book and the characters therein, and that the voice of God declaimed from the Heavens that it was translated by the gift and power of God. That this ministration was not the only one by any means–that [a] messenger had come to him in the fields and he was prepared for the coming testimony" (Jesse R. Badham, Journal, 20 Mar. 1881, RLDS archives [DWI, 57]).

21. See Cook, DWI, xiv.

22. Richard L. Anderson, Review of DWI, in *Journal of Mormon History* 20 (Spring 1994): 188.

23. David Whitmer, *An Address to All Believers in Christ* (Richmond, MO: David Whitmer, 1887), 29, 43.

24. *Fall River* (MA) *Herald,* 28 Mar. 1879 (DWI, 10).

25. Beatrice Cannon Evans and Janath Russell Cannon, *Cannon Family Historical Treasury* (Salt Lake City: George Cannon Family Association, 1967), 250.

26. See Metcalf, *Ten Years,* 73-74 (DWI, 247); Poulson to *Deseret Evening News,* 13, 16 Aug. 1878; James H. Hart to Editor, 23 Aug. 1883, *Deseret Evening News,* 4 Sept. 1883 (DWI, 98); and "Address Given by James H. Moyle at the Regular Sacrament Meeting, Fourth Ward, Pioneer Stake, 18 March 1945," in

Gene A. Sessions, ed., "Mormon Democrat: The Religious and Political Memoirs of James Henry Moyle" (Salt Lake City: Historical Department of the Church of Jesus Christ of Latter-day Saints, 1975), 444-47.

27. "The Last Man," *Chicago Times*; George Q. Cannon, Journal, 27 Feb. 1884; B. H. Roberts, *Conference Reports* (Oct. 1926): 126; "The True Book of Mormon," ca. July 1884, unidentified and undated newspaper clipping, William H. Samson, Scrapbook, 18:76-77, Rochester Public Library, Local History Room, Rochester, New York.

28. "Report of Elders Orson Pratt and Joseph F. Smith" (DWI, 35-46); Briggs to Joseph Smith III, 4 June 1884, 396-97; "Address by Elder James H. Moyle before the Ensign Stake Conference, in the Salt Lake Tabernacle, Sunday, March 22, 1908," in Gordon B. Hinckley, *James Henry Moyle: The Story of a Distinguished American and an Honored Churchman* (Salt Lake City: Deseret Book Co., 1951), 366-67.

29. Kelley to *Saints' Herald*, 1 Mar. 1882.

30. John H. Gilbert, "Memorandum, made by John H. Gilbert Esq, Sept. 8th, 1892[,] Palmyra, N.Y.," 5, Palmyra King's Daughters Free Library, Palmyra, NY (EMD 2:548). See also John H. Gilbert to James T. Cobb, 16 Mar. 1879, Theodore A. Schroeder Papers, Rare Books and Manuscripts Division, New York Public Library, New York City (EMD 2:526); "Mormon Leaders at Their Mecca," *New York Herald* (25 June 1893): 12 (EMD 2:551). Pomeroy Tucker, who was foreman in Grandin's printing office, said Harris "used to practice a good deal of his characteristic jargon about 'seeing with the spiritual eye,' and the like" (Pomeroy Tucker, *Origin, Rise, and Progress of Mormonism* [New York: D. Appleton and Co., 1867], 71). Palmyra Presbyterian minister Jesse Townsend reported that Harris claimed to have seen the plates with "spiritual eyes" (Jesse Townsend to Phineas Stiles, 24 Dec. 1833, in op. cit., 290).

31. John A. Clark to Dear Brethren, 31 Aug. 1840, *Episcopal Recorder* (Philadelphia) 18 (12 Sept. 1840): 98 (EMD 2:270).

32. Stephen Burnett to Lyman E. Johnson, 15 Apr. 1838, Joseph Smith Letterbook (1837-43), 2:64, 65, Smith Papers, LDS archives (EMD 2:291, 292-93).

33. Reuben P. Harmon, Statement to Arthur B. Deming, ca. 1885, *Naked Truths about Mormonism* 1 (Apr. 1888): 1 (EMD 2:385).

34. Metcalf, *Ten Years,* 70 (EMD 2:346).

35. John Murphy to Editor, undated, *Hamiltonian,* 21 Jan. 1881; rept. in *Kingston* (MO) *Times,* 16 Dec. 1887.

36. "A Proclamation," *Richmond* (MO) *Conservator,* 24 Mar. 1881; rept. in *Hamiltonian* (Hamilton, MO), 8 Apr. 1881; and Whitmer, *Address to All Believers,* 8-10; also published as a leaflet, "A Proclamation" (n.p., n.d.). The original proclamation is in LDS archives.

37. James Henry Moyle, Diary, 28 June 1885, LDS archives. Whitmer's account may be compared with reports of seeing apparitions within "a hazy col-

umn of light" or "misty light" (see, e.g., Celia Green and Charles McCreery, *Apparitions* [London: Hamish Hamilton, 1975]).

38. Emanuel Swedenborg, *Miscellaneous Theological Works of Emanuel Swedenborg* (New York: Swedenborg Foundation, 1951), 475.

39. Daniel B. Shea, *Spiritual Autobiography in Early America* (Princeton, NJ: Princeton University Press, 1968), 216.

40. George Peck, *Early Methodism within the Bounds of the Old Genesee Conference, from 1788 to 1828* (New York: Carlton and Porter, 1860), 186.

41. For an extended discussion of early-nineteenth-century visionary language, see Mark D. Thomas, *Digging in Cumorah: Reclaiming Book of Mormon Narratives* (Salt Lake City: Signature Books, 1999), 48-62.

42. Simon Smith to Joseph Smith III, 29 Dec. 1880 (EMD 2:380).

43. George Godfrey, Affidavit, 29 Oct. 1921.

44. Homer, "Testimony," 3 Jan. 1922.

45. See "Mormonism–No. II," *Tiffany's Monthly* 5 (Aug. 1859): 166 (EMD 2:306).

46. "Talk given by Theodore Farley, Sr., at Priesthood Session of Sharon Stake Quarterly Conference, March 25, 1940," 3, typescript, LDS archives (EMD 2:391).

47. *Saints' Herald* 29 (15 June 1882): 189 (DWI, 92).

48. "Copy–Questions asked of David Whitmer at his home in Richmond[,] Ray County[,] Mo–Jan 14–1885. relating to Book of Mormon, and the history of the Church of Jesus Christ of L.D.S. by Elder Z[enas] H. Gurley," 1, Zenas Gurley Collection, LDS archives (DWI, 152).

49. Moyle, Diary, 28 June 1885. Orson Pratt's 1859 claim that the angel had "laid his hands upon the head of David Whitmer" should likewise be dismissed ([Orson Pratt], "A Discourse by Elder Orson Pratt, delivered in the Tabernacle, Great Salt Lake City, January 2, 1859," *Journal of Discourses of the Church of Jesus Christ of Latter-day Saints,* 26 vols. [Liverpool: Albert Carrington [and others], 1853-86], 7:29).

50. *Omaha* (NE) *Herald,* 17 Oct. 1886 (DWI, 198). The reporter was D. C. Dunbar, who in a letter to James Henry Moyle dated Glendale, California, 15 February 1933, recalled that Whitmer told him "of his seeing the angel and handling the plates etc." (D. C. Dunbar, Correspondence, LDS archives [DWI, 207]).

51. Reuben Miller, Journal, 21 Oct. 1848, 1:[12] (EMD 2:494). Note that in the published version, Miller expanded his diary entry to say that Cowdery also handled the interpreters, although Cowdery had seen them in vision (Reuben Miller, "Last Days of Oliver Cowdery," *Deseret News* 9 [13 Apr. 1859] [EMD 2:495]).

52. Anderson, Review of DWI, 187.

53. James Henry Moyle, Diary, 28 June 1885. See also Acts 9:7; 22:9; and D&C 18:9.

54. Green and McCreery, *Apparitions,* 1-7, 8, 13.

55. "Report of Elders Orson Pratt and Joseph F. Smith."

56. Kelley to *Saints' Herald,* 16 Jan. 1882.

57. *Omaha Herald,* 17 Oct. 1886 (DWI, 197-98). For other times when Whitmer mentioned the enveloping spiritual light, see Metcalf, *Ten Years,* 73-74; Edward Stevenson, Journal, 24:30-37, entry of 9 Feb. 1886 (DWI, 181); George Q. Cannon, Journal, 27 Feb. 1884 (DWI, 108); and Nathan Tanner Jr., Journal, 13 May 1886, [55], LDS archives (DWI, 188).

58. William Pilkington, Address delivered in the Lewisville Ward, Rigby Stake, 23 Apr. 1939, typescript, LDS archives (EMD 2:367).

59. I. Woodbridge Riley, *The Founder of Mormonism* (2nd. ed.; New York: Dodd, Mead and Co., 1903), 218-31; Fawn M. Brodie, *No Man Knows My History* (2nd ed.; New York: Alfred A. Knopf, 1971), 77-78. For a discussion of the various attempts to explain Joseph Smith as a mesmerizer or hypnotist, see Gary L. Bunker and Davis Bitton, "Mesmerism and Mormonism," *BYU Studies* 15 (Winter 1975): 146-61.

60. George W. Schweich to I. Woodbridge Riley, 22 Sept. 1899, in Riley, *The Founder of Mormonism,* 219-20 (DWI, 256). On 26 November 1857, Isaac DeMill, then living in Saline (Michigan?), wrote his brother Freeborn DeMill and a sister living in Manti, Utah, mentioning a story he had heard about Joseph Smith's use of hypnosis or "magnetizing" in Broome and Onondaga Counties, New York, and that he had "learned the art of a German pedler" (Isaac DeMill to Brother and Sister, 26 Nov. 1857, 4, LDS Archives).

61. *Juvenile Instructor* 27 (15 May 1892): 303-304. That Rigdon was predisposed to visions is indicated by those he received during his visit to New York in December 1830 (Ezra Booth to Ira Eddy, 6 Dec. 1831, "Mormonism–Nos. VIII–IX" [Letter IX], *Ohio Star* [Ravenna, OH] 2 [8 Dec. 1831]: 1).

62. Dibble reports, "[A]nd many things were seen and related that are not written" (cf. D&C 76:115).

63. Anderson, *Investigating,* 188.

64. "The Last Witness Dead! David Whitmer, the Aged Patria[r]ch, Gone to His Rest. His Parting Injunction to His Family and Friends," *Richmond* (MO) *Democrat,* 26 Jan. 1888.

65. Briggs to Joseph Smith III, 4 June 1884.

66. Metcalf, *Ten Years,* 71.

67. Ibid., 73-74; Moyle, Diary, 28 June 1885; Briggs to Smith, 4 June 1884.

68. Edward Stevenson, Journal, 24:30-37 (9 Feb. 1886).

69. See, e.g., Brigham D. Madsen, *B. H. Roberts: Studies of the Book of Mormon* (Urbana and Chicago: University of Illinois Press, 1985), 298-316; and Thomas, *Digging in Cumorah,* 53.

70. Oliver Cowdery to Joseph Smith, 28 Dec. 1829, Joseph Smith Letterbook, 1:5 (EMD 2:408).

71. This calls to mind philosopher Bertrand Russell's statement: "From a scientific point of view we can make no distinction between the man who eats little and sees heaven and the man who drinks much and sees snakes. Each is

an abnormal physical condition, and therefore has abnormal perception." Russell, *Mysticism*, qtd. in Walter Kaufmann, *Critique of Philosophy and Religion* (Garden City, NY: Doubleday, 1961), 315.

72. Theodore X. Barber, Nicholas P. Spanos, and John F. Chaves, *Hypnosis, Imagination, and Human Potentialities* (New York: Pergamon Press, 1974), 74-77; Peter D. Slade and Richard P. Bentall, *Sensory Deception: A Scientific Analysis of Hallucination* (Baltimore: Johns Hopkins University Press, 1988), 68-76; and Martin T. Orme, "Hypnotically Abduced Hallucinations," in Louis Jolton West, ed., *Hallucinations* (New York: Greene and Stratton, 1962), 211-19. Roughly 5-10 percent of the population are very responsive to hypnotic suggestion, 25-30 percent are minimally responsive, while the rest fall somewhere in between.

73. Anderson, *Investigating*, 104.

74. Lorenzo Saunders, Interviewed by E. L. Kelley, 12 Nov. 1884, 4, E. L. Kelley Papers, "Miscellany," RLDS archives (EMD 2:149).

75. "'The Birth of Mormonism,'" *Deseret Evening News*, 10 Nov. 1888, 2.

76. Townsend to Stiles, 24 Dec. 1833, in Tucker, *Origin, Rise*, 289.

77. John A. Clark to *Episcopal Recorder*, 94 (EMD 2:262).

78. "Mormonism–No. II," 166.

79. Clark to *Episcopal Recorder*, 99 (EMD 2:271). See also *Guernsey Times*, 16 Apr. 1831; *American Friend and Marietta Gazette*, 30 Apr. 1831.

80. Albert Chandler to William Linn, 22 Dec. 1898, William Linn, *The Story of the Mormons* (New York: Macmillan Co., 1902), 49; see also Tucker, *Origin, Rise*, 45.

81. Ronald W. Walker, "Martin Harris: Mormonism's Early Convert," *Dialogue: A Journal of Mormon Thought* 19 (Winter 1986): 35.

82. See Anderson, *Investigating*, 107-118.

83. See Edward Stevenson, Journal, 14:10-18, entry of 22-23 Dec. 1877 (DWI, 13). That the Whitmers were excitable accords with Reverend Diedrich Willers's assessment. In June 1830 Willers, pastor of Zion's Church in Fayette, New York, where the Whitmers worshiped, wrote that the family was "gullible to the highest degree and even believed in witches" (Diedrich Willers to Reverend Brethren, 18 June 1830, Willers Collection, Carl A. Kroch Library, Cornell University, Ithaca, New York; for a translation of Willers's letter, originally in German, see D. Michael Quinn, "The First Months of Mormonism: A Contemporary View by Rev. Diedrich Willers," *New York History* 54 [July 1973]: 317-33).

84. Cook, DWI, x.

85. Anderson, *Investigating*, 53.

86. Book of Commandments 7:3, hereafter BofC. The revelation was altered to conceal the magical origins of Cowdery's "gift of working with the rod" (cf. D&C 8:6). For a discussion of Cowdery's divining rod, see D. Michael Quinn, *Early Mormonism and the Magic World View* (Salt Lake City: Signature Books, 1987), 31-35.

87. Joseph Smith, History, 1832, Joseph Smith Letterbook, 1:6 (EMD 1:31).

88. Lucy Smith, "Preliminary Manuscript," 91, LDS archives (EMD 1:376).

89. Oliver Cowdery to Joseph Smith, 6 Nov. 1829, Joseph Smith Letterbook, 1:7 (EMD 2:405).

90. Cowdery to Smith, 28 Dec. 1829, Joseph Smith Letterbook, 1:5.

91. Oliver Cowdery, "A commandment from God unto Oliver [Cowdery] how he should build up his church & the manner thereof," [ca. June 1829], Smith Papers, LDS archives (EMD 2:412).

92. Smith, Manuscript History, 1839, 23-24 (EMD 1:82-83).

93. Riley, *The Founder of Mormonism,* 228.

94. Smith, Manuscript History, 1839, 26 (EMD 1:86).

95. "Report of Elders Orson Pratt and Joseph F. Smith."

96. Smith, "Preliminary Manuscript," 102 (EMD 1:395); compare Lucy Smith, *Biographical Sketches of Joseph Smith the Prophet, and His Progenitors for Many Generations* (Liverpool: S. W. Richards, 1853), 140 (EMD 1:395).

97. Smith, "Preliminary Manuscript," 102, 104 (EMD 1:396).

98. Newel K. Whitney Collection, Special Collections, Lee Library; cited in H. Michael Marquardt, *The Joseph Smith Revelations: Text and Commentary* (Salt Lake City: Signature Books, 1999), 27. Cf. BofC 4:4//D&C 5:11-15.

99. See Brent Lee Metcalfe, "The Priority of Mosiah: A Prelude to Book of Mormon Exegesis," in Brent Lee Metcalfe, ed., *New Approaches to the Book of Mormon: Explorations in Critical Methodology* (Salt Lake City: Signature Books, 1993), 423-27.

100. See Roper's comments in *Review of Books on the Book of Mormon* 6/1 (1994): 373-75.

101. The same applies to the March 1829 revelation which instructs Smith that "he should not show [the plates] except I command him, and he has no power over [the plates] except I grant it unto him" (BofC 4:2//D&C 5:3) and promises the three witnesses special "power" to see the plates (BofC 4:4// D&C 5:13). The distinction between those to whom Smith shows the plates and those who see them by "power" is artificial.

102. "Report of Elders Orson Pratt and Joseph F. Smith" (DWI, 42); Stevenson, Journal, 24:36-37 (9 Feb. 1886); see also Andrew Jenson, "Still Another Witness," *Historical Record* 7 (Oct. 1888): 621; Edward Stevenson, "The Thirteenth Witness to the Plates of the Book of Mormon," *Juvenile Instructor* 24 (1 Jan. 1889): 23 (DWI, 217-18).

103. Hyrum reportedly said during a visit to Sunbury, Ohio, in 1838 that "he had seene the plates with his eyes and handeled them with his hands and he saw a bre[a]st plate and he told how it wass maid ... that [it] wass not so good gold as the plates for that was pure" (Sally Parker to John Kempton, 26 Aug. 1838, microfilm, Family History Library, Salt Lake City, Utah; a portion cited in Anderson, *Investigating,* 159). In December 1839 Hyrum evidently referred to his Book of Mormon testimony when he said: "I felt a determination to die,

rather than deny the things which my eyes had seen, which my hands had handled, and which I had borne testimony to" (*Times and Seasons* [Nauvoo, IL] 1 [Dec. 1839]: 23). Joseph Fielding, Hyrum's brother-in-law by his second marriage, said in 1841: "My sister [Mary Fielding Smith] bears testimony that her husband has seen and handled the plates, &c." (Joseph Fielding to Parley P. Pratt, 20 June 1841, in *Millennial Star* 2 [1841]: 52). Samuel Harrison Smith, who also died in 1844, is remembered to have testified in the spring of 1832 that he too had seen the plates and the "engravings thereon" and handled them (Daniel Tyler, "Incidents of Experience," in *Scraps of Biography* [Tenth Book of the Faith-promoting Series; Salt Lake City: Juvenile Instructor Office, 1883], 23).

104. In an 1847 statement, Page rejected the idea that he had forgotten his testimony, denying that his mind had become "so treacherous that I had forgotten what I saw" (Hiram Page to William E. McLellin, 30 May 1847, in *Ensign of Liberty* [Kirtland, OH] 1 [Jan. 1848]: 63). One of Page's sons told Andrew Jenson in 1888 that his father "seemed to rejoice exceedingly in having been privileged to see the plates" (*Historical Record* 7 [1888]: 614).

105. In 1836 Whitmer said he had "no hesitancy" about his testimony "but with confidence have signed my name to it. ... I have most assuredly seen the plates from whence the book of Mormon is translated, and that I have handled these plates" (John Whitmer, "Address," in *Latter Day Saints' Messenger and Advocate* 2 [Mar. 1836]: 286-87). Whitmer reportedly said to Theodore Turley in April 1839: "I handled those plates; there was fine engravings on both sides. I handled them. ... [T]hey were shown to me by a supernatural power" (Theodore Turley, "Memoranda," 1845, LDS archives. Turley's memorandum was used by Thomas Bullock when writing the history of the church in 1845; see Book C-1, 913; cf. Smith, *History of the Church,* 3:307-8.). Whitmer told Myron Bond in 1878 that he both "saw and handled" the plates (*Saints' Herald* 25 [1878]: 253).

106. Burnett to Johnson, 15 Apr. 1838.

107. *Evangelist* (Carthage, OH) 6 (1 Oct. 1838): 226.

108. Parker to Kempton, 26 Aug. 1838.

109. Nathan Tanner Jr. to Nathan A. Tanner, 17 Feb. 1909, typed copy, LDS archives (DWI, 192-93).

110. As reported only in the final version of Lucy's history, one day Joseph came to Lucy and showed her another artifact hidden under a cloth. She said Joseph handed her "the breast-plate spoken of in his history." It was wrapped in a "thin muslin handkerchief, so thin that I could see the glistening metal, and ascertain its proportions without any difficulty." Not only does she not identify the kind of metal she saw through the cloth, but her description of the breastplate's construction seems improbable. She said: "It was concave on one side, and convex on the other, and extended from the neck downwards, as far as the centre of the stomach of a man of extraordinary size." At each of the four corners of the plate were straps constructed "of the same material,"

which Lucy said were the width of two of her fingers. She could also discern that the straps had holes in the ends, much like a belt, for fastening the plate to the chest. Lucy estimated its worth to be about $500. Joseph placed it in the box with the plates and spectacles (Smith, *Biographical Sketches,* 107 [EMD 1:339-40]). As with the spectacles, Lucy's experience with the breastplate remains unconfirmed by corroborative testimony. Concerning her account of handling the breastplate, historian Dale Morgan stated: "She is the only one who ever claims to have handled this breastplate, and I am inclined to doubt that her memory is substantive" (John Philip Walker, ed., *Dale Morgan on Early Mormonism: Correspondence and a New History* [Salt Lake City: Signature Books, 1986], 384n53). After Lucy sees the breastplate and spectacles, they disappear from the record while the plates remain the only physical object occupying the box. When Harris later lifts the box, he is given to understand that only the plates occupy it. The same is true for Isaac Hale in Harmony, Pennsylvania. When Joseph moves to Pennsylvania, the plates are placed in an Ontario glass box measuring approximately 10 x 12 inches, which was then placed in a barrel of beans—much too small for the large breastplate Lucy described.

111. Theodore Turley, "Memoranda." Concerning this event, Richard Anderson commented: "From the strict point of view of evidence, this report is most impressive. With social pressure to deny and personal motivation to explain away his experience, John Whitmer insisted that he had in fact handled the plates" (Anderson, *Investigating,* 131). Anderson fails to consider Whitmer's statement in context, for his remark that the plates had been "shown to me by a supernatural power" tends to rule out a purely physical experience.

112. See, e.g., Barber, et al., *Hypnosis,* 74. Former Mormon and wife of T. B. H. Stenhouse, Fanny Stenhouse, reportedly claimed to have experienced "[a]n apparition seen, heard and felt" during her brief association with the Godbeites (see Boston Society for Psychic Research, *Noted Witnesses for Psychic Occurrences* [Boston: Boston Society for Psychic Research, 1928], 226-29; cited in Michael W. Homer, "Spiritualism and Mormonism: Some Thoughts on Similarities and Differences," *Dialogue: A Journal of Mormon Thought* 27 [Spring 1994]: 188).

113. "I. C. Funn," [John Whitmer Testimony], *Kingston* (MO) *Sentinel,* ca. Jan. 1878, reprinted in *Saints' Herald* 25 (15 Feb. 1878). 57.

114. Thomas Ford, *A History of Illinois, from Its Commencement as a State in 1818 to 1847* (Chicago: S. C. Griggs and Co., 1854), 258.

115. Brodie, *No Man Knows My History,* 79-80; see also Anderson, *Investigating,* 159-61.

116. E.g., "Mormonism—No. II," 170 (EMD 2:310).

117. E.g., Joseph Smith III, "Last Testimony of Sister Emma," *Saints' Herald* 26 (1 Oct. 1879): 290 (EMD 1:541).

118. E.g., Edward Stevenson, Journal, 14:18 (22-23 Dec. 1877).

119. "Testimony of Martin Harris Written by My Hand from the Mouth of

Martin Harris," dictated to Edward Stevenson, 4 Sept. 1870, Edward Stevenson Collection, Miscellaneous Papers, LDS archives (EMD 2:332-33).

120. John A. Clark to *Episcopal Recorder*, 99.

121. Burnett to Johnson, 15 Apr. 1838.

122. "Strange Case of Somnambulism," *Genesee Farmer and Gardener's Journal* 5 (3 Jan. 1835): 8; and 5 (17 Jan. 1835): 24.

123. "Birth of Mormonism. The Story of an Old Man Who Was There When the Tables of Stone Were Found," *Chicago Times*, 14 Oct. 1888.

124. See, e.g., Patrick Marnham, *Lourdes: A Modern Pilgrimage* (New York: Coward, McCann and Geoghegan, 1981); William A. Christian, *Apparitions in Late Medieval and Renaissance Spain* (Princeton, NJ: Princeton University Press, 1981); Michael Carroll, *The Cult of the Virgin Mary: Psychological Origins* (Princeton, NJ: Princeton University Press, 1986).

125. Philemon Stewart et al., *A Holy, Sacred and Divine Roll and Book; From the Lord God of Heaven, to the Inhabitants of Earth: Revealed in the United Society at New Lebanon, County of Columbia, State of New-York, United States of America* (Canterbury, NH: United Society, 1843), 303, 304.

126. Green and McCreery, *Apparitions*, 41. See also Leonard Zusne and Warren H. Jones, *Anomalistic Psychology: A Study of Magical Thinking* (Hillsdale, NJ: Lawrence Erlbaum Associates, 1989), 117-19, 135.

127. On hypnosis generally, see Barber, Spanos, and Chaves, *Hypnosis*.

128. See Zusne and Jones, *Anomalistic Psychology*, 135.

129. Green and McCreery, *Apparitions*, 41, 42.

130. Joseph F. Smith, Diary, 7-8 Sept. 1878. This portion of Whitmer's statement was omitted from the published version of the interview (see "Report of Elders Orson Pratt and Joseph F. Smith").

131. "Gold Bible, No. 6," *Palmyra Reflector* (19 Mar. 1831): 126 (EMD 2:249-50).

132. Significantly, Smith never qualified his visionary experience with Cowdery and Whitmer.

133. During an 1859 interview with spiritualist Joel Tiffany, Harris declined answering specific questions about his vision, stating that he was "forbidden to say anything how the Lord showed them to me, except that by the power of God I have seen them" ("Mormonism–No. II," 166). Harris was more forthcoming on other occasions.

134. William Smith said the plates "weighed about sixty pounds according to the best of my judgment" (William Smith, *William Smith on Mormonism* [Lamoni, IA: Herald Steam Book and Job Office, 1883], 12 [EMD 1:497]; see also "W[illia]m. B. Smith's Last Statement," [John W. Peterson to Editor], *Zion's Ensign* [Independence, MO] 5 [13 Jan. 1894]: 6 [EMD 1:511]). Martin Harris said he hefted the plates many times and estimated that they "weighed forty or fifty pounds" ("Mormonism–No. II," 166). A block of solid tin measuring 6 x 8 x 6 inches, the measurements Smith gave for the plates, or 288 cubic inches, would weigh 74.67 pounds. If one allows for a 30 percent reduc-

tion due to the unevenness and space between the plates, the package would then weigh about fifty pounds. Using the same calculations, plates of gold would weigh 140.5 pounds. Reed Putnam has suggested that the plates were made of copper with a 23-carat gilded surface–much like the ancient Mesoamerican alloy tumbaga. Reducing the weight of the plates by 50 percent, Putnam estimates that tumbaga plates would have weighed between 53 and 86 pounds (see Reed H. Putnam, "Were the Plates of Mormon of Tumbaga?" *Papers, 15th Annual Symposium on the Archaeology of the Scriptures* [Provo, UT: BYU Extension Publications, 1964; and "Were the Golden Plates Made of Tumbaga?" *Improvement Era* [Sept. 1966]: 788-89, 828-31). Following my own calculations, plates of copper would weigh sixty-five pounds, even without the gilding. The earliest tumbaga specimen–found in British Honduras and dating to the early classic period–has little to do with Nephi's supposed construction of plates a thousand years earlier. Metallurgy as such was not known in Central America until circa A.D. 900. Besides, with such a high copper content, the plates would have certainly corroded during their 1,400-year deposit in the moist soil of western New York, a fact that Putnam's theory cannot explain.

5.

B. H. Roberts: Book of Mormon Apologist and Skeptic

George D. Smith

BRIGHAM HENRY ROBERTS (1857-1933) DEVELOPED THE PRIMARY apologetic arguments used to defend the antiquity of the Book of Mormon, a book most Latter-day Saints believe narrates the story of the ancestors of the American Indian. While speaking to the church as a general authority, Roberts addressed the book as an ancient record; privately, however, he voiced doubts. In the last twelve years of his life, he encountered questions about Book of Mormon language, archeology, and geography that he could not answer. As he reexamined his earlier writings on the subject, he turned to his colleagues with two critical treatises that asked whether the prophet had created a "wonder tale" which, "I sorrowfully submit, points to Joseph Smith" as its author. He expressed his public faith and private doubts to the end of his life.

Roberts was no stranger to difficulty. He grew up without a father in working-class England, followed his seamstress mother to America to the Western towns of Bountiful and Centerville, Utah, apprenticed to a blacksmith, and worked in ranching and mining. Unable to read until age eleven, the self-educated immigrant attended the University of Deseret (later renamed the University of Utah) and became class valedictorian. He lived amidst the polygamy controversy and in 1889 went to jail for having more than one wife. Elected in 1898 to the U.S. House of Representatives, he was denied a seat because of his plural marriages despite support from Susan B. Anthony (even though he opposed women's suffrage) and from the *New York Times.*

Roberts defended the church's teachings through other ideological struggles. Darwin's theory of evolution, originally published in 1859, was seen by some Latter-day Saints as jeopardizing the authority of the Bible and challenging the existence of God.[1] Roberts himself, in his seminal 1928 manuscript, "The Truth, The Way, The Life," theorized that Adam and Eve came from another planet to replace an extinct race whose ancient remains would be found in the ground.[2]

During the same period, scholars were scrutinizing the Egyptian papyri that Joseph Smith had purchased in 1836 and claimed to translate into the Book of Abraham. In 1912 Utah Episcopal bishop Franklin S. Spalding submitted facsimiles of the "Abraham" papyri to Egyptologists in Oxford, London, Chicago, and New York. By this time, the Rosetta Stone had been deciphered and linguists had worked out a lexicon of Egyptian hieroglyphics. Spalding's experts determined that the Mormon glyphs were not the writings of Abraham but ordinary funeral scrolls from a later era. They called Smith's translation a "pure fabrication," an "impudent fraud."[3] Roberts endured this assault on Smith's "other translation" and continued to support the Book of Abraham as an authentic chronicle written by the Hebrew patriarch Abraham.[4]

But throughout his career as an LDS general authority, Roberts devoted his primary attention to the book which Joseph Smith said he had translated from gold plates buried in the ground for over a thousand years. In his three-volume *New Witnesses for God* (1909), Roberts looked for convincing arguments to support the book against archeological challenge. In later research, beginning in 1921 at age sixty-four, Roberts took another look from a different point of view. He began to question Smith's claim to have translated an ancient record. From the perspective of orthodoxy, Roberts examined questions that challenged his own core beliefs: He found no answers, yet continued to fulfill his role as church leader and to declare publicly his faith in LDS doctrine. This essay explores the polarities manifest in Roberts's statements during his last years.

To the end of his life, Roberts maintained that he was willing to explore fearlessly all aspects of his religion: "I am taking the position that our faith is not only unshaken but unshakable in the Book of Mormon, and therefore we can look without fear upon all that can be said against it."[5] He made this assertion in response to troubling questions which his colleagues deferred to him in 1921. Consistent with his character, he met the challenge head-on, elaborating the issues in a substantial report which he presented to LDS church president Heber J. Grant and other general authorities beginning in an eight-hour meeting and continuing over a period of three days in January 1922.[6]

"BOOK OF MORMON DIFFICULTIES": ARCHEOLOGY, LANGUAGE, GEOGRAPHY

The questions came from James Fitton Couch, a thirty-three-year-old, non-Mormon chemist from the U.S. Department of Agriculture in Washington, D.C. In August 1921 Couch had read the Book of Mormon during the time he was conducting plant research at the USDA station in Salina, Utah. His summer assistant, William Emerson Riter, a twenty-year-old botany student at Utah State Agricultural College in Logan, discussed religion with his superior prior to serving an LDS mission the next year.[7] Couch responded to Riter with questions about Book of Mormon language and archeology.

Observing that languages change slowly, Couch asked Riter to explain how the language spoken by Book of Mormon people in the fifth century could have multiplied in so short a time into the several hundred distinct Indian languages spoken by Native Americans in the fifteenth century. He questioned how horses, steel, "cimeters,"[8] and silk could be legitimately included in a book set in pre-Columbian America since they are absent from the archeological findings of that period.

On 22 August 1921, Riter sent Couch's inquiries to author and scientist James E. Talmage of the Council of Twelve Apostles, who passed them on to Roberts.[9] Roberts returned to his earlier defense, *New Witnesses for God* (1909), but also began a major reexamination of the issue. Over the next six months, he prepared two lengthy studies: the 141-page "Book of Mormon Difficulties" (1921) and the 291-page "A Book of Mormon Study" (1922). The first treatise dealt primarily with conflicts between Book of Mormon teachings about Indian origins and later archeological discoveries; the second and longer work looked at the possibility that in writing the Book of Mormon, Joseph Smith may have drawn upon an earlier book widely known around Palmyra, New York: *A View of the Hebrews* by Ethan Smith.[10] Five years later in 1927, a third document by Roberts, "A Parallel," more concisely listed the similarities between the Book of Mormon and *A View of the Hebrews.* The three documents, together with related correspondence and journal records, suggest that their author was beginning to see things differently since 1902-03 when he began work on *New Witnesses.*

The voice that emerges in these three important works is amplified in several letters. The first is a cover letter to his "Book of Mormon Difficulties," dated 29 December 1921 and addressed to President Heber J. Grant, the Quorum of Twelve Apostles, and the First Council of Seventy. In it, Roberts compares "Book of Mormon Difficulties" with his earlier published responses to criticism about the Book of Mormon:

> [H]aving devoted some attention to [these questions] while writing my Book of Mormon treatise under the title New Witnesses for God, and knowing that some parts of my treatment of Book of Mormon problems in that work had not been altogether as convincing as I would have liked to have seen them, I still believed that reasonable explanations could be made ... As I proceeded with my recent investigations, however, and more especially in the, to me, new field of language problems, I found the difficulties more serious than I had thought ... I therefore concluded not to undertake an answer to his [Couch's] questions on my own account, but decided to make a study of all the problems he submitted–somewhat enlarging upon them as I proceeded–and then submit the result of my investigations to all of you who are addressed at the head of this communication.

Anticipating the Riters and Couches of the future, Roberts appealed to his colleagues: "I am most thoroughly convinced of the necessity of all the brethren herein addressed becoming familiar with these Book of Mormon problems, and finding the answer for them, as it is a matter that will concern the faith of the Youth of the Church now as also in the future, as well as casual inquirers as may come to us from the outside world."[11]

In the attached manuscript, Roberts examined problems beginning with the identity of the American Indians. In the Book of Mormon, immigrants called Jaredites arrive in the New World around 2200 B.C., followed in 600 B.C. by Lehites who divide into two branches: by 421 A.D. the Nephite branch is succeeded by its more primitive rivals, the Lamanites, ancestors of the Indians. Couch had noted in his questions that no other language groups are mentioned in the narrative and that the closing date of the Book of Mormon does not provide adequate time for the Hebrew language to develop into the diverse idioms spoken by American Indians when Columbus arrived. Roberts acknowledged to his colleagues that

> the time limits named in the Book of Mormon—which represents the people of America as speaking and writing one language down to as late a period as A.D. 400—is not sufficient to allow of these divergencies into the American language stocks and their dialects ... If such other races or tribes existed then the Book of Mormon is silent about them. Neither the people of Mulek nor the people of Lehi or after they were combined, nor any of their descendants ever came in contact with any such people, so far as any Book of Mormon account of it is concerned.[12]

Beyond the issue of language, Roberts asked: Why is there no archeological evidence of the plants, animals, and objects described in the Book of Mormon? In his analysis, Roberts restated the observations heretofore raised by critical outsiders: Plants such as wheat, animals such as horses, technology such as the smelting of iron and steel and the use of wheeled vehicles are all matter-of-factly included in the Book of Mormon. Such things are also described in the Bible but are found widely in Old World archeology. No trace of them has been found in the pre-Columbian New World. At the end of Section II of "Book of Mormon Difficulties," Roberts spelled out the conflict between archeology and faith in the Book of Mormon:

> There can be no question but what the Book of Mormon commits us to the possession and use of domestic animals by both Jaredite and Nephite peoples, and to the age and civilization of iron and steel and of the wheel, and of a written language, by both these peoples. And they, with their descendants, constitute all the inhabitants of the New World, so far as the Book of Mormon informs us, except as to the Gentile races which by the spirit of prophecy it was foreseen would come in later times.
>
> What shall our answer be then? Shall we boldly acknowledge the difficulties in the case, confess that the evidences and conclusions of the authorities are against us, but notwithstanding all that, we take our position

> on the Book of Mormon and place its revealed truth against the declarations of men, however learned, and await the vindication of the revealed truth? Is there any other course than this? And yet the difficulties to this position are very grave. Truly we may ask "Who will believe our report?" in that case. What will the effect be upon our youth of such a confession of inability to give a more reasonable answer to the questions submitted, and the awaiting of proof for final vindication? Will not the hoped-for proof deferred indeed make the heart sick? Is there any way to escape these difficulties?[13]

By the turn of the twentieth century, archeology had identified the ancestors of native Indians as nomadic hunters who crossed the Bering Strait during an ice age approximately 15,000 years ago, long before the Jaredite and Lehite migrations from Israel described in the Book of Mormon. Roberts outlined what would be needed to resolve these findings (subsequently confirmed by radiocarbon dating methods) with the Book of Mormon:

> But what is required is that evidence shall be produced that will give us an empty America 3,000 years B.C., into which a colony from the Euphrates Valley (supposedly) may come and there establish a race and an empire with an iron and steel culture; with a highly developed language of that period; then, after an existence of about sixteen or eighteen hundred years shall pass away, become extinct in fact, as a race and as a nation; this about 600 B.C., leaving the American continents again without human inhabitants.
>
> Then into these second time empty American continents—empty of human population—we want the evidence of the coming of two small colonies about 600 B.C., which shall be the ancestors of all native American races as we know them; possessing as did the former race, domestic animals, the horse, ass and cow; with an iron and steel culture, and a highly developed written literature, the national Hebrew literature in fact.
>
> Can we successfully overturn the evidences presented by archeologists for the great antiquity of man in America, and his continuous occupancy of it, and the fact of his stone age culture, not an iron and steel culture? Can we successfully maintain the Book of Mormon's comparatively recent advent of man in America and the existence of his iron and steel and domestic animal, and written language stage of culture against the deductions of our late American writers upon these themes?[14]

Roberts wanted answers to these questions. According to Wesley

P. Lloyd, who had served briefly in the Eastern States Mission after Roberts and later became Dean of the Graduate School at Brigham Young University, Roberts "went to work and investigated it from every angle but could not answer it satisfactorily to himself. At his request Pres. Grant called a meeting of the Twelve Apostles and Bro. Roberts presented the matter, told them frankly that he was stumped and asked their aid in the explanation."[15]

The meetings on 4, 5, and 26 January 1922 did not produce results that satisfied Roberts. In his own words, these difficulties were answered with "faithful testimonies," a response which disappointed Roberts. Lloyd recorded Roberts's recollection of the leadership's reaction: "[The Twelve] merely one by one stood up and bore testimony to the truthfulness of the Book of Mormon. George Albert Smith in tears testified that his faith in the Book [of Mormon] had not been shaken by the question [but] no answer was available."[16]

At the end of that first day, 4 January, in contrast to the urgency of Roberts's concerns, Apostle Talmage, a geologist by training, recorded this response:

> Brother Roberts has assembled a long list of points called "difficulties," meaning thereby what non-believers in the Book of Mormon call discrepancies between that record and the results of archaeological and other scientific investigations. As examples of these "difficulties" may be mentioned the views put forth by some living writers to the effect that no vestige of either Hebrew or Egyptian appears in the language of the American Indians, or Amerinds. Another is the positive declaration by certain writers that the horse did not exist upon the Western Continent during historic times prior to the coming of Columbus.
>
> I know the Book of Mormon to be a true record; and many of the "difficulties" or objections as opposing critics would urge, are after all but negative in their nature. The Book of Mormon states [that Lehi] and his colony found horses upon this continent when they arrived; and therefore horses were here at that time.[17]

Although Smith and Talmage reaffirmed their faith, they showed that Roberts was asking questions for which neither had an answer. Roberts's dismay at their unresponsiveness indicates that he was not merely playing devil's advocate but had asked questions he personally considered important. The following week, on 9 January, he wrote a follow up letter to President Grant saying: "I was very greatly disappointed over the net results of the discussion. There was so much said that was utterly irrelevant, and so little said if anything at all that was helpful in the matters at issue that I came away from the conference quite disappointed." The brethren had used arguments that Roberts himself had used more than a decade earlier but that he now considered unsatisfactory. He pleaded with Grant:

> I shall be most earnestly alert upon the subject of Book of Mormon difficulties, hoping for the development of new knowledge, and for new light to fall upon what has already been learned, to the vindication of what God has revealed in the Book of Mormon; but I cannot be other than painfully conscious of the fact that our means of defense should we be vigorously attacked along the lines of Mr. Couch's questions, are very inadequate.[18]

Further archeological research has confirmed Roberts's fears. Three decades later, to prove the Book of Mormon, California attorney Thomas Stuart Ferguson convinced church leaders to establish a department of archeology at Brigham Young University and fund the New World Archeological Foundation. After twenty-five years of expeditions to Central America, Ferguson presented his findings to the 1975 Symposium of Book of Mormon Geography at BYU: "It cannot be established factually that anyone, from Joseph Smith to the present day, has put his finger on a single point of terrain that was a Book of Mormon geographical place ... to date there is no Book of Mormon geography."[19] Privately, he recognized the same difficulties that Roberts had confronted. He wrote: "You can't set Book of Mormon geography down anywhere–because it is fictional and will never meet the requirements of the dirt-archeology. I should say–what is in the ground will never conform to what is in the book."[20]

In recent years defenders of Book of Mormon historicity have proposed a revisionist account of Nephite migrations to the New World. They suggest that a small number of Native Americans in a limited region descended from the Lamanites.[21] If the book's description of transoceanic migrations from Jerusalem could be re-oriented to destinations within a limited geographical region (for example, Teotihuacán in southern Mexico), the archeological contradictions might diminish and the problem of numerous Indian languages from a New World populated by one people would be solved. But such a "limited geography" hypothesis strains credibility and contradicts Joseph Smith's revelation that "the Indians [are] the literal descendants of Abraham,"[22] the same message he presented in the Book of Mormon.

In the 1830s the land the American Indians had come from was a mystery. For Christians, Columbus's discovery of the Indians posed a problem because they lay outside the biblical account of human origins; the Bible was therefore dismissed by some as a collection of local stories from the Middle East. Into this breach, Joseph Smith placed the Lamanites as Hebrew tribes that crossed the oceans and resettled the New World as Indians. Now Genesis could account for all humankind. Several Protestant ministers had asserted the same for Indians, that they were of Hebraic descent, but Smith went one step farther–he provided proof in the form of a tangible ancient record inscribed on metallic plates. Smith stated as "revealed" truth that all New World Indians descended from Book of Mormon peoples. He said the angel Moroni, the Hebrew-Indian in the Book of Mormon who had buried the gold plates, told him that the book was "an account of the former inhabitants of this continent, and the sources from whence they sprang."[23]

On 4 January 1833 as he addressed a Rochester, New York, newspaper editor "by commandment of God," Smith defined Book of Mormon people as "the forefathers of our western tribes of Indians ... By it we learn that our western tribes of Indians are descendants from that Joseph which was sold into Egypt, and that the land of America is a promised land unto them."[24] To explain Book of Mormon descriptions of Jaredites that settled "all the face of the land" (Eth. 1:33-34, 42; 2:17, 7:11), an unsigned *Times and Seasons* editorial, under Smith's editorship, stated that the Jaredites "covered the whole continent from sea to sea with towns and cities."[25] In an 1842 letter to John Wentworth, editor of the *Chicago Democrat,* Smith further reaffirmed that "the remnant [of Book of Mormon peoples] are the Indians that now inhabit this country."[26] There is no ambiguity about the claim that the Book of Mormon was the record of the entire American Indian population.

Roberts recognized this central Mormon tenet and followed the tradition recited by leaders before him who understood it in the terms that Joseph Smith had defined for them. For example, at a conference in New York attended by the Quorum of the Twelve Apostles on

27 August 1843, Elder Orson Pratt described the Book of Mormon as "a History of nearly one half of the globe & the people that inhabited it, that it gave a history of all those cities that have been of late discovered by Catherwood and Stephens [explorers of Central American civilizations]."[27] At a 10 September 1843 conference in Boston, at which seven of the Twelve were present, Elder Wilford Woodruff affirmed that the Book of Mormon record "contains an account of the ancient inhabitants of this continent who over spread this land with cities from sea to sea," a restatement that the people of Nephi "did cover the whole face of the land, both on the northward and on the southward, from the sea west to the sea east" (Hel. 11:20).[28] After his death, Smith's teachings about the American Indians continued to be perpetuated by his apostles, bringing the ancient New World populations under the rubric of Christ's church as the Bible does for the Old World peoples. The Book of Mormon, joined to the Bible, united Ezekiel's "two sticks," the divided nations of Israel: Judah, represented by the Bible, and Joseph, represented by the Book of Mormon.[29] Hence, Joseph Smith presented evidence of a world unified by ancient biblical roots. This is the grand Mormon doctrine that Roberts defended against both attack and innovation.

Looking at archeological problems which challenged this doctrine, Roberts asked if there was "any way to escape from these difficulties." He rejected an earlier proposal regarding a limited-geography theory: "Can we answer that the Nephites ... occupied a very much more restricted area of the American continents than has heretofore been supposed" and thus "leave the rest of the continents–by far the greater part of them say–to be inhabited by other races, speaking other tongues, developing other cultures, and making, though absolutely unknown to Book of Mormon people, other histories?" While this would solve some problems such as "the diversity of tongues in the New World," Roberts asked if this was reasonable to think that Book of Mormon people, "part of the time numbering millions and occupying the land at least from Yucatan to Cumorah, and this during a period of at least a thousand years ... [could] live and move and have their being in the land of America and not come in contact with other races and tribes of men." He thought that "to make this possible, the area occupied by the Nephites and Lamanites would have to be extremely limited, much more limited, I fear, than the Book of Mormon would admit of our assuming."[30]

Whatever his personal reservations about the questions Riter raised, Roberts did not share them with this young man. Assisted by second counselor in the First Presidency Anthony Ivins and Elders Talmage and John A. Widtsoe, Roberts wrote a reassuring response that tried to minimize the issues Couch had raised.[31] He declared that the problem of many languages deriving from one was "not that unsolvable." He said that oral language might change quickly and that people speaking in different tongues may have come to North America during the thousand years from the end of Nephite history (A.D. 421) to the coming of Columbus (1492). He also suggested the "possibility that other groups of people may have inhabited parts of the Americas, contemporaneously with the people chronicled in the Book of Mormon, though candor compels me to say that nothing to that effect appears in the Book of Mormon."[32] He said nothing of Couch's question regarding the lack of fossil evidence for such Book of Mormon animals as the horse, although in his "Book of Mormon Difficulties" he told his peers that "nowhere has the evidence for the existence of the horse in America within historic times been found," which he identified as one of "our embarrassing problems."[33]

Roberts presented this reply to the committee appointed to study the problems. He told them he thought "it was an answer that would satisfy people that didn't think, but a very inadequate answer to a thinking man." Nevertheless, "they adopted it by vote and said that was about the best they could do."[34] Here we see two sides of Roberts: While he raised what he felt were significant problems with the Book of Mormon to his colleagues, to an inquiring church member, he gave reassuring answers that would satisfy someone who did not think too far beyond superficial defenses.

"A BOOK OF MORMON STUDY": JOSEPH SMITH AS AUTHOR

Although Roberts fulfilled his formal duty to answer Couch's questions, his own concerns were far from resolved. As he had requested, President Grant approved a committee composed of the most articulate Mormon leaders—Ivins, Talmage, Widtsoe, and Roberts—to further study these questions.[35] In his journal, Talmage noted attendance at meetings through the spring of 1922 in James H. Moyle's home but provided no details.[36] Roberts reported to Lloyd that "they met and looked vacantly at one and other, but none seemed to know what to do about it."[37]

Undeterred by these inconclusive meetings, Roberts worked through the early part of 1922 on a more substantial study of his own. On 29 May he was assigned for five years to be president of the LDS mission in the eastern United States, headquartered in New York City. Before his departure, he wrote a third letter to President Grant, the council, and the Twelve to introduce his 291-page manuscript entitled "A Book of Mormon Study" dealing with "problems ... in addition" to those he had presented to them the previous January.

Roberts urged his associates to continue the discussion in his absence. He recalled for them what he had "stated in my [January 1922] remarks that there were other problems [that] ... would very greatly increase our difficulties."[38]

One of these "other problems" was a book published in 1823, seven years before the Book of Mormon, by a man named Ethan Smith. A Congregational minister in Poultney, Vermont, Ethan Smith summarized various published opinions which supported his viewpoint that Native Americans had descended from the lost tribes of Israel. Roberts wrote to the First Presidency of the "embarrassing" coincidence of themes in the Book of Mormon and Ethan Smith's *View of the Hebrews* which was no doubt available to Joseph Smith "as the book in two editions flooded the New England States and New York."[39] Furthermore, Oliver Cowdery, Joseph Smith's distant cousin and Book of Mormon scribe, lived in Poultney for twenty-two years up to 1825, five years before the Book of Mormon was published; and Cowdery's family attended the congregation which Ethan Smith led from 1821 to 1826.[40] In 1903 I. Woodbridge Riley noted that Ethan Smith's book was "published in Poultney, Vermont, next to Windsor County, where Joseph [Smith's] parents once lived, and by 1825 had circulated to westernmost New York."[41] Roberts referred to Riley in *New Witnesses* but later acknowledged that he was then unfamiliar with Ethan Smith's book "except by report of it, and as being in my hands but a few minutes."[42]

To summarize the first part of his study, Roberts argued that the following similarities between the Book of Mormon and *A View of the*

Hebrews suggested that the latter served as a structural outline for the former:

> 1. Both books maintain that American Indians descended from ancient Hebrew tribes; Ethan Smith wrote that they descended from the Lost Ten Tribes, whereas Joseph Smith limited American Indian ancestry to two Hebrew families, headed by Lehi and Ishmael.
>
> 2. Both open with references to the destruction of Jerusalem.
>
> 3. Both tell of inspired prophets among ancient Americans.
>
> 4. Both quote extensively and nearly exclusively from Isaiah.
>
> 5. Both describe ancient Americans as a highly civilized people.
>
> 6. Both announce the mission of the American nation in the last days to gather these remnants of the House of Israel and bring them to Christianity, thereby hastening the advent of the Millennium predicted in the Bible.
>
> 7. Both mention the "stick of Joseph" and the "stick of Ephraim," which Ethan Smith used to symbolize the Jews and the lost tribes; Joseph Smith advertised the Book of Mormon as "the stick of Joseph taken from the hand of Ephraim."
>
> 8. Both refer to the ancient Urim and Thummim, which Joseph Smith used to translate the Book of Mormon.
>
> 9. Both Smiths referred to Quetzalcoatl, the legendary, white bearded Aztec god. Ethan Smith described him as "a type of Christ," but Joseph Smith saw in the legend evidence that Christ himself had come to the New World.[43]

Beyond any use Joseph Smith might have made of *View of the Hebrews,* Roberts, in the second part of his study, considered the suggestion that Smith himself may have written the Book of Mormon. He discussed technical aspects of the narrative which reflect a youthful naivete consistent with a twenty-three-year-old narrator: the "want of perspective and consistency in the alleged historical incidents," "things miraculous that test credulity," and repetitious plots in various stories. He mentioned long journeys covered in unreasonably short times such as Nephi's 170-mile travel with all the belongings of several families from Jerusalem to the Red Sea in just three days; large cities built too quickly; the construction of a temple like Solomon's "in fine workmanship" with less than 100 people, compared to 30,000 men laboring seven years in the Old Testament to finish Solomon's temple. He noted that the Jaredite and Nephite migrations themselves have parallel story lines: each was a small colony warned to leave—the Tower of Babel in 2200 B.C., Jerusalem in 600 B.C.—because of impending destruction, and each traveled through a wilderness and by a miraculous oceanic voyage to a "land of promise." He compared five nearly identical anti-Christs who experience similar episodes. Speaking of thirteen years of war when none of 2,060 "stripling" warriors are killed, Roberts observed that "the whole matter of war seems to be treated from the amateurish notion that the wicked are invariably punished, the righteous always victorious ... evidence of having originated in one mind and that mind pious but immature."[44] Roberts speculated that the Book of Mormon must have been the product of a relatively unsophisticated imagination and that Joseph Smith, in his early twenties, could have written it: "[T]he evidence, I sorrowfully submit, points to Joseph Smith as their creator." Putting himself in the place of a reader, he asked: "Is all this sober history inspired written and true, representing things that actually happened? Or is it a wonder-tale of an immature mind, unconscious of what a test he is laying on human credulity when asking men to accept his narrative as solemn history?"[45]

Roberts told colleagues he had written "A Book of Mormon Study" "from the viewpoint of an open mind, investigating the facts of the Book of Mormon origin and authorship." In his cover letter he said "that what is herein set forth does not represent any conclusions of mine"—emphasizing the preliminary nature of his research and tending to diminish his role as messenger, thus focusing on the issues which he thought should be considered on their own merits.[46] Some LDS writers have asserted that Roberts played devil's advocate to stimulate discussion only, and they therefore dismiss as academic exercises the archeological difficulties Roberts found in the Book of Mormon. His work was private and never meant to be published, they suggest. In short, Roberts did not believe anything he wrote. Roberts once declared, "If I have caused you to doubt my faith ... let me reaffirm it."[47] Someone reportedly heard Roberts say in 1933 that "Ethan Smith played no part in the formation of the Book of Mormon."[48]

In fact, from 1921 to 1933, Roberts continued to defend the church in public meetings and newspapers. After he completed his "Book of Mormon Study," he asserted in the tract, *Why Mormonism* (May 1922): "The existence of this American Volume of Scripture was revealed to Joseph Smith ... You Reader may know by the power of the Holy Ghost that this Witness to the Deity of the Christ is true, if you will seek that testimony in the way prescribed."[49] A year later, just after he had hand-dated his cover letter to "A Book of Mormon Study," he asserted in an LDS general conference talk: "The Book of Mormon [is] the word of God to the ancient inhabitants of this land of America."[50] Later that year, in an address to the October 1923 conference, he said: "The great outstanding thing in the Book of Mormon is the fact of the visit of the Redeemer to the inhabitants of this western world ... These things being true, makes the advent of the Book of Mormon into the world the greatest literary event of the world."[51]

Yet Roberts's provocative questions speak for themselves. Consider the following selections from his own comments on Ethan Smith's *View of the Hebrews* (emphasis Roberts's; page numbers refer to Brigham D. Madsen's compilation, *B. H. Roberts: Studies of the Book of Mormon*):

1. *View of the Hebrews* was composed of "'common knowledge' throughout the whole region where the Smiths lived from the birth of Joseph Smith in 1805, to the publication of the Book of Mormon in 1829-30" (155).

2. Ethan Smith "quotes chiefly from Isaiah in support of his views concerning Israel, their dispersion, their restoration, and their glorification–and the author of the Book of Mormon, following him, *does the same thing*. ... And many passages quoted by Ethan Smith are identical with passages from Isaiah quoted in the Book of Mormon" (173).

3. "I come now to more specific structural material for the Book of Mormon to be found in the book of Mr. Ethan Smith ... *He assumes a division of the people*, ... [one division] to found cities, build temples, mounds, fortifications, and other traits of civilization, the ruined monuments of which were found by the Europeans upon their arrival in the New World. The other division degenerated to savagery, with the result that a series of 'tremendous wars'

ensued between the savage and the civilized divisions resulting in the *annihilation of the latter* by the savage division, the destruction of civilization ... One acquainted with Book of Mormon historical events will recognize in all this an outline of Book of Mormon 'history'" (188).

4. "Could an investigator of the Book of Mormon be much blamed if he were to decide that Ethan Smith's book with its suggestion as to the division of his Israelites into two peoples; with its suggestion of 'tremendous wars between them'; and of the savages overcoming the civilized division led to the fashioning of chiefly these same things in the book of Mormon?" (192).

5. Roberts inquires "if Ethan Smith's book affords any material that would suggest the Urim and Thummim to the author of the Book of Mormon, and the strange part it took in the alleged translation. There certainly is such material in Mr. Smith's book ... [quoting James Adair] 'The Indian tradition says, that their fathers were possessed of an extraordinary divine spirit, by which they foretold things future; ... *In resemblance of the Urim and Thummim, the American Archimagus wears a breast plate made of a white conch-shell, with two holes bored in the middle of it through which he puts the end of an otter skin strap, and fastens a buck horn white button to the outside of each, as if in imitation of the precious stones of the Urim*' (*View of the Hebrews*, p. 150)" (207-208).

6. "Can it be that it is mere coincidence that these special virtues of Jacob's Lamanites, and Ethan Smith's Indians should run so closely parallel in such a relationship?" (214).

7. "Ethan Smith's book ran through two editions in New England before the Book of Mormon was published. ... [T]he likelihood of Joseph Smith coming in contact with Ethan Smith's book is not only very great, but amounts to a very close certainty. For being published in an adjoining county to the one in which their home had been for so long, and the interest in the subject being very general, not only in New England but in New York also, it would be little short of miraculous if they did not know of Ethan Smith's book" (235).

8. "There is in Ethan Smith's book ... the question that was put to the Delaware Indian Chief–'What did he know of the Christ.' ...

[T]he question suggested the *possibility* of the Indians knowing something of the Christ ... Then there follows the statement quoted from [Alexander von] Humboldt by Smith that the Catholic fathers in Mexico found such traces of resemblances ... [of Christianity and] they persuaded the natives 'that the gospel had in very remote times been already been preached in America'; which would necessarily involve some knowledge of the Christ. This, with the story of Quetzalcoatl ... his being a bearded white man, the mystery of his coming ... [A]ll this, I submit, supplies subject matter overwhelmingly sufficient to suggest the visit of the Christ to the Book of Mormon people and his career among them" (235-36).

9. "[D]id Ethan Smith's *View of the Hebrews* furnish the structural material for Joseph Smith's Book of Mormon? It has been pointed out in these pages that there are many things in the former book that might well have suggested many major things in the other. Not a few things merely, one or two, or a half dozen, but many; and it is this fact of many things of similarity and the cumulative force of them that makes them so serious a menace to Joseph Smith's story of the Book of Mormon's origin" (240).

10. "The material in Ethan Smith's book is of a character and quantity to make a ground plan for the Book of Mormon. ... It not only suggests, but pleads on every page for Israelitish origin of the American Indians. It deals with the destruction of Jerusalem and the scattering of Israel, as the Book of Mormon does. It deals with the future gathering of Israel, and the restoration of the Ten Tribes, as the Book of Mormon does. It emphasizes and uses much of the material from the prophecies of Isaiah, including whole chapters, as the Book of Mormon does ... It holds that the peopling of the New World was by migrations from the Old, the same as does the Book of Mormon. It takes its migrating people into a country where 'never man dwelt,' just as the Book of Mormon takes its Jaredite colony into 'that quarter where there never had man been' ... The savage division utterly exterminates the civilized in Ethan Smith's book; ... [and] quotes Indian traditions of a 'Lost book of god' and the promise of its restoration to the Indians, with a return of their lost favor with the Great Spirit. This is in keeping with the lost sacred records to the savage Lamanites of

the Book of Mormon. ... Ethan Smith's book speaks of the gospel having been preached in the ancient America; the Book of Mormon clearly portrays a knowledge of the gospel had among the Nephites. ... Can such numerous and startling points of resemblance and suggestive contact be merely coincidence?" (240-42).

11. "In the light of this evidence, there can be no doubt as to the possession of a vividly strong, creative imagination by Joseph Smith, the Prophet, an imagination, it could with reason be urged, which, given the suggestions that are to be found in the 'common knowledge' of accepted American antiquities of the times, supplemented by such a work as Ethan Smith's *View of the Hebrews,* would make it possible for him to create a book such as the Book of Mormon is" (250).

12. "And under all the circumstances is it much to [be] wondered at if intelligent people to whom the book of Mormon is presented for consideration, should ask: 'Do we have here a great historical document, or only a wonder tale ... where the miraculous in 'history' is accepted without limitations and is supposed to account for all inconsistencies and lapses that challenge human credulity in the thought and in the easy philosophy *that all things are possible with God*?" (258).

13. "[T]he striking parallelism in these incidents of Anti-Christs of the Book of Mormon, with the strong implication that they have their origin in one mind ... [T]hey are all of one breed and brand; so nearly alike that one mind is the author of them" (271).

14. The story of 2,060 "stripling" warriors "who fought in many battles, *yet none of them were killed,*" is a "[b]eautiful story of faith," but "[i]s it history? Or is it a wonder-tale of a pious but immature mind?" (272-73).

15. Question: are the Nephite and Jaredite wars of extinction all "sober history inspired written and true, representing things that actually happened? Or is it a wonder-tale of an immature mind?" (283).

16. "I think it cannot be questioned but where there is sufficient resemblance between the Book of Mormon instances of religious emotionalism and those cited in the foregoing quotations from

> the works of [Jonathan] Edwards *et al.* to justify the thought that the latter might well have suggested and indeed become the source of the former" (308).

We find two images of Roberts in such passages: faithful in public; questioning, even skeptical, in private. Roberts's critiques of the Book of Mormon were not published during his lifetime; one critique may not even have been delivered to its intended recipients. They were kept private, perhaps because they may have been regarded as damaging to the faith. Whatever ambivalence or difficulty he may have had about putting his questions before the public, Roberts nevertheless persisted in researching and discussing them with his peers in church leadership.[52] He said he had written "A Book of Mormon Study" "for presentation to the Twelve and the Presidency, not for publication, but I suspended submission of it until I returned home" in 1927 from his mission presidency; "I have not yet succeeded in making the presentation of it, although the letter of submission to President Grant was made previous to leaving the E[astern] S[tates] M[ission]. I have made one feeble effort to get it to them since returning home, but they are not in a studious mood."[53]

When he returned in 1927, he wrote a fourth letter, this time to Apostle Richard R. Lyman on 24 October. The letter was accompanied by "A Parallel," an eighteen-page condensation of the similarities between the Book of Mormon and *A View of the Hebrews.* Roberts wanted Lyman to present the summary to the Council of Twelve, perhaps to see how the longer work he had written five years earlier might be received.[54] There is no evidence that Roberts's questions were discussed in further council meetings, although Roberts may have delivered a copy of the longer "Study," along with the "Parallel," to Lyman. The cover letter refers to both the eighteen-page "Parallel" and a lengthy work: "Necessarily the matter presented is rather large in volume, but I hope its interest will excuse its length." If Lyman received the "Study," it is unclear if he passed it on to any of the church councils. Five years later Roberts indicated that he "had not yet succeeded in making the presentation of it."[55]

The letter Roberts wrote to accompany "A Parallel" was informal. Lyman was apparently a close friend. Recalling Lyman's "considerable interest" during his presentation to the council in 1922, Roberts now sent him "a possible theory of the Origin of the Book of Mormon

... which in the hands of [a] skillful opponent could be made, in my judgment, very embarrassing." Roberts noted that in Rochester in 1824, "six years before the publication of the Book of Mormon and within 20 miles of Palmyra," Josiah Priest published *The Wonders of Nature and Providence,* which quoted extensively from *View of the Hebrews.* Roberts warned Lyman that questions may arise some day about the "origin of the Book of Mormon"–if Ethan Smith's book supplied the "structural outline and some of the subject matter of the alleged Nephite record."[56]

ROBERTS'S SILENCE

Little more was heard of Roberts's first two critical works for the next half century. However, ten years after he presented Apostle Lyman with a summary of "parallels" between the Book of Mormon and *View of the Hebrews,* copies were privately circulated in the Mormon community. Elsie Talmage Brandley, daughter of James E. Talmage, gave a copy to Newel K. Young, a member of the church's General Board of Religion Classes and a grandson of Lorenzo Dow Young, younger brother of Brigham Young. Newel, in turn, shared copies with other interested parties, including Sterling M. McMurrin.[57] Since that time, historians and apologists have debated the import of Roberts's comparison. In a 22 July 1939 letter to Ariel L. Crowley, B. H. Roberts's son, Benjamin E., wrote that his father "found nothing in his study which reflected upon the integrity of Joseph Smith's account of the Book of Mormon." Six years later in 1945, Fawn Brodie described Roberts's list of parallels in her biography of Joseph Smith, *No Man Knows My History.*[58] The next year Benjamin Roberts publicly discussed his father's research and distributed copies of his father's "A Parallel."[59] Neither of these discussions mentioned Roberts's 1921 and 1922 studies.[60]

Likewise, in two 1959 *Improvement Era* articles, Hugh Nibley referred to the parallels with *View of the Hebrews* but did not mention the two major studies Roberts had prepared earlier.[61] Several LDS church histories have been written without citing either *View of the Hebrews* or Roberts's studies. His own *Comprehensive History of the Church,* the six-volume revision of his "History of the Mormon Church" that was serialized in the *Americana* magazine (1909-15), screened by a committee of general authorities before publication in 1930, omitted mention of his two studies. Elder Joseph Fielding Smith's *Essentials of Church History* (1922), James B. Allen and Glen M. Leonard's *The Story of the Latter-Day Saints* (1976), and Leonard J. Arrington's and Davis Bitton's *The Mormon Experience* (1979) failed to mention the Roberts studies. Truman G. Madsen's 1980 biography of Roberts followed this cautious precedent, although Madsen was known to be aware of the studies.[62]

Only recently have the two major studies become widely available for examination.[63] In 1979 and 1981 members of the Roberts family gave copies of the manuscripts to the University of Utah and Brigham Young University. These, with descriptive correspondence, were published in 1985 by the University of Illinois Press.[64] Since their reappearance, people have argued about what Roberts really meant. After his death, LDS scholars named him "the most distinguished intellectual in the church's history."[65] Roberts produced numerous articles and over forty books. As a member of the First Council of Seventy (admitted in 1888, president in 1924) and Assistant Church Historian (1902), he compiled the authoritative seven-volume *History of the Church* (1902-11); he wrote his two-volume *Defense of the Faith and the Saints* (1907-12) and the aforementioned *New Witnesses for God* (1909), long the principal scholarly reference work on the Book of Mormon. McMurrin called him "the best historian and theologian that Mormonism produced in its first century."[66] Roberts served in the innermost circles of the church. His later critiques of the Book of Mormon are impressive in part *because* he wrote for insiders and not for publication. They clearly represent his private thoughts and conscience. Some insist that Roberts was primarily a defender of the faith. Others say that after 1921, he questioned Mormon beliefs and lost his faith. Whether this defender of the Book of Mormon came to doubt the book's authenticity is an important question in assessing Mormonism's historical claims.

Attempting to soften the force of Roberts's questions, apologists Truman G. Madsen and John W. Welch emphasize his continued assertions of faith and his never having stepped down from church leadership.[67] Following Madsen's and Welch's lead, Daniel Peterson argues that, "Clearly, B. H. Roberts should not have fallen into serious doubt over five questions such as these," referring to the questions raised by Couch. Peterson believes that Roberts never "explicitly declared his supposed loss of belief" but "continued to testify to the truth of the Book of Mormon right up to his death."[68] Mormon historian Davis Bitton recently reiterated that Roberts's attempts to address these five questions in "three different pieces of manuscript [were] not intended for publication."[69] Wanting to conclude that Roberts "only meant that he was willing to look at every possible challenge while maintaining his longtime convictions," former assistant church historian James Allen looks for inaccuracies in Roberts's "unclear" memory or Lloyd's "misunderstanding of what was said." But Roberts's "disappointment" that his brethren would not take his concerns more seriously does not make sense unless Roberts took them seriously himself.[70] In recollections reported by Madsen about fifty years after the fact, one of Roberts's former Eastern States missionaries remembered that Roberts often said, "I have come to know the book is true."[71] But Roberts's own words leave room for another interpretation. A reading of the critical writings in 1925 led one BYU faculty member to conclude that Roberts had come very close to calling Joseph Smith "a fraud and deceit."[72]

Several missionaries and associates of Roberts recalled a change of heart on the Book of Mormon. Mark K. Allen, secretary to the Eastern States Mission presidency after Roberts, remembered his saying: "We're not through with the Book of Mormon. We've got problems. I could do Volume III of *New Witnesses for God* the other way and be just as convincing."[73] Another missionary in the Eastern States under Roberts remarked that he recommended that missionaries not talk about the Book of Mormon, that Roberts had instructed him "to use the Bible, to approach converts in their own language and avoid the criticism that so often arose from using the Book of Mormon."[74] In Roberts's last years, at least publicly, he continued to voice support for the Book of Mormon, remarking in his last general conference address: "The Book of Mormon [is] one of the most valuable books that has ever been preserved, even as holy scripture."[75]

A month before his death, Roberts spoke perhaps for the last time about the historicity of the Book of Mormon. Wesley Lloyd spent three and one-half hours with Roberts on 7 August 1933 and dictated an account of their conversation to his wife, who wrote it in Wesley's personal journal. Roberts related the contradictions that James Couch had seen in the Book of Mormon and told Lloyd that after he asked

President Grant and the council in January 1922 for help with these problems, the church leadership had been unresponsive. But Roberts continued his interest in these issues: "[Roberts] swings to a psychological explanation of the Book of Mormon and shows that the plates were not objective but subjective with Joseph Smith, that his exceptional imagination qualified him psychologically for the experience which he had in presenting to the world the Book of Mormon and that the plates with the Urim and Thummim were not objective."[76] Roberts also

> explained certain literary difficulties in the Book such as the miraculous incident of the entire nation of the Jaredites, the dramatic story of one man being left on each side, and one of them finally being slain, also the New England flat hill surroundings ... that the entire story [is] laid in a New England flat hill surrounding. These are some of the things which has made Bro. Roberts shift his base on the Book of Mormon.[77]

These are sobering reflections for the great defender of the Mormon faith to come to at the end of his life.

CONCLUSION

During the last twelve years of his life, Roberts spoke with two voices regarding the Book of Mormon. When he could not come up with answers to his questions, he did not find it necessary to abandon his role as a general authority, nor to renounce his faith. But he did share his concerns with colleagues and friends. Fellow defender of the faith Thomas Ferguson followed a similar path after decades of disappointing archeological research. Ferguson would express private views that contrasted with his public pronouncements.[78] Likewise, Roberts said in private that Joseph Smith, a "young" and "imaginative" prophet, produced a work of parable rather than history. Even as Roberts bore his testimony from the pulpit, he drew upon issues of archeology and textual criticism to ask his colleagues to address intractable challenges to the Nephite record.

What significance is there to this dichotomy? That such issues were raised, albeit cautiously, within the highest quorums of the church evokes questions of widespread misgivings about the Book of Mormon within the larger, general membership. Just as we all try to balance our hopes and fears as we confront unfulfilled wishes, more than a few private doubters and public believers must personally share Roberts's questions about the keystone document of their faith. Unfortunately, the taboo against questioning prevents frank discussion of this revered work, although church members, if they were asked, would probably acknowledge that their belief in the Book of Mormon is not measured by the way they view history in general. So, would they benefit from taking Roberts's lead in confronting these questions directly and honestly and attempting to resolve them? Just as the question of historicity held enough merit to be considered by someone known in the church to be the greatest defender of the Book of Mormon, that example may be reason enough to continue such an important inquiry.

NOTES

1. See Gary James Bergera and Ronald Priddis, *Brigham Young University: A House of Faith* (Salt Lake City: Signature Books, 1985), 131-61.

2. Stan Larson, ed., *The Truth, the Way, the Life, An Elementary Treatise on Theology: The Masterwork of B. H. Roberts* (San Francisco: Smith Research Associates, 1994); also an edition edited by John W. Welch (Provo, UT: BYU Studies, 1994). The manuscript was submitted for approval in 1928 to the LDS Council of Twelve Apostles, approval was repeatedly denied, and by 1933 Roberts decided to publish on his own but died before sufficient funds could be raised.

3. Franklin S. Spalding, *Joseph Smith, Jun., as a Translator* (Salt Lake City: Arrow Press, 1912), 24-29, here quoting Dr. Arthur C. Mace, Metropolitan Museum, New York, and Dr. A. H. Sayce, Oxford, England.

4. "A Plea in Bar of Final Conclusions," *Improvement Era* 16 (Feb. 1913): 309-25. Roberts impugned the interpretations of several Egyptologists by pointing out differences in details.

5. Brigham D. Madsen, ed., *B. H. Roberts: Studies of the Book of Mormon* (2nd ed.; Salt Lake City: Signature Books, 1992), 57-58.

6. Apostle George F. Richards recorded in his diary, Wednesday, 4 January 1922: "I made the talk at the temple meeting 9 A.M. and from 10 A.M. to 6 P.M., except while attending to sealing ordinances, was in a meeting of the presidency, the Twelve, and the Council of Seventy hearing Pres. B. H. Roberts present a paper of 141 typewritten pages he had prepared while considering five questions upon the Book of Mormon submitted by a Mr. Couch of Washington, D.C." (in archives, Historical Department, Church of Jesus Christ of Latter-day Saints, Salt Lake City, hereafter LDS archives; see also,

James E. Talmage, Journal, 4, 5, 26 Jan. 1922, Special Collections, Harold B. Lee Library, Brigham Young University, Provo, Utah).

7. Madsen, *B. H. Roberts,* 35-37; Richard F. Keeler, "Mr. Couch and Elder Roberts," *Dialogue: A Journal of Mormon Thought* 29 (Summer 1996): 141-47; Douglas F. Tobler, "Europe, the Church in," in Daniel H. Ludlow, ed., *Encyclopedia of Mormonism,* 5 vols. (New York: McMillan, 1992), 2:471.

8. Scimitar or scimiter is an English term derived from the Persian saber or shamshir. Persian or Turkish sabers date from the 16th-18th centuries A.D. (Leonid Tarassukand and Claude Blair, eds., *The Complete Encyclopedia of Arms and Weapons* [New York: Simon & Schuster, 1982], 416, 419-21).

9. Wesley P. Lloyd, Journal, 7 Aug. 1933, printed in its entirety in Brigham D. Madsen, ed., *The Essential B. H. Roberts* (Salt Lake City: Signature Books, 1999), 358-61. Lloyd, a friend of Roberts, later served as Dean of Men, Dean of Students, and Dean of the Graduate School at Brigham Young University (see George W. Middleton to Richard R. Lyman, 11 Nov. 1921; and Ralph V. Chamberlin to Richard R. Lyman, 3 Dec. 1921, in Madsen, *B. H. Roberts,* 37-45; letters also in B. H. Roberts Collection, Manuscripts Division, Willard J. Marriott Library, University of Utah, and in the Lee Library, Brigham Young University).

10. *A View of the Hebrews; Or the Tribes of Israel in America* (Poultney, VT: Smith & Shute, 1823; 2nd ed., rev. and enl., 1825). In 1964 Modern Microfilm Company (later Utah Lighthouse Ministry), Salt Lake City, photomechanically reproduced Roberts's own copy of the 1825 edition, now at the Marriott Library, University of Utah. Thirteen years later, Arno Press, New York, a subsidiary of the *New York Times,* reprinted the 1823 edition as part of an America-Holy Land Studies sponsored by the American Jewish Historical Society and the Institute of Contemporary Jews at Hebrew University in Jerusalem. In 1996 Charles D. Tate Jr. edited the 1825 edition for the Religious Studies Center, Brigham Young University.

11. Madsen, *B. H. Roberts,* 46-47.

12. Ibid., 92-93.

13. Ibid., 115.

14. Ibid., 142.

15. Lloyd, Journal, 7 Aug. 1933, qtd. in Madsen, *B. H. Roberts,* 22-24.

16. Lloyd, Journal, 7 Aug. 1933.

17. Talmage, Journal, 4, 5, 26 Jan. 1922.

18. Madsen, *B. H. Roberts,* 48, 50.

19. "Written Symposium on Book of Mormon Geography: Response of Thomas S. Ferguson to the Garth Norman and John Sorenson Papers," typescript, 12 Mar. 1975, in Thomas Stuart Ferguson Collection, Marriott Library, and in Stan Larson, *Quest for the Gold Plates: Thomas Stuart Ferguson's Archeological Search for the Book of Mormon* (Salt Lake City: Freethinker Press in association with Smith Research Associates, 1996), 237, 267.

20. Thomas S. Ferguson to Mr. and Mrs. Harold W. Lawrence, 20 Feb. 1976, Ferguson Collection, in Larson, *Quest,* 212, 214.

21. See the work of BYU anthropologist John L. Sorenson, *An Ancient American Setting for the Book of Mormon* (Salt Lake City: Deseret Book; Provo, UT: FARMS, 1985), esp. chapter 1. This study examines textual evidence for a Mesoamerican setting and summarizes information currently available on ancient Mesoamerican cultures that seems to illuminate the Book of Mormon. In 1954 Apostle Joseph Fielding Smith rejected a limited geography thesis: "Within recent years there has arisen among certain students of the Book of Mormon a theory to the effect that within the period covered by the Book of Mormon, the Nephites and Lamanites were confined almost within the borders of the territory comprising Central America and the southern portion of Mexico; the Isthmus of Tehuantepec probably being the 'narrow neck' of land spoken of in the Book of Mormon rather than the Isthmus of Panama. ... This modernistic theory of necessity, in order to be consistent, must place the waters of Ripliancum and the Hill Cumorah someplace within the restricted territory of Central America, notwithstanding the teachings of the Church to the contrary for upwards of 100 years. Because of this theory some members of the Church have been confused and greatly disturbed in their faith in the Book of Mormon" (*Deseret News,* Church Section [27 Feb. 1954]: 2-3). One of the relatively few official statements on Book of Mormon geography is George Q. Cannon, "The Book of Mormon Geography," *Juvenile Instructor* 25 (1 Jan. 1890): 18, discouraging the creation and circulation of "suggestive maps" because of the lack of consensus of their authors and stating that the First Presidency and Twelve have consistently declined invitations to prepare such a map.

22. In his 1835-36 diary, Joseph Smith reflected that at age seventeen when in bed at night, "An angel appeared before me ... He said the Indians were the literal descendants of Abraham" (Scott Faulring, ed., *An American Prophet's Record: The Diaries and Journals of Joseph Smith* [Salt Lake City, UT: Signature Books in association with Smith Research Associates; 1987], 51). On 2 May 1838, the prophet retold this account casting the angel as a "personage" named "Moroni" (called "Nephi" in 1840 in the original publication of the *Times and Seasons* in Nauvoo, Illinois, and in the *Millennial Star* in Liverpool, England; see Dan Vogel, ed., *Early Mormon Documents,* 5 vols. [Salt Lake City: Signature Books, 1986-], 1:64).

23. Joseph Smith Jr., *History of the Church of Jesus Christ of Latter-day Saints,* B. H. Roberts, ed., 7 vols. (Salt Lake City: Deseret Book, 1974), 1:12 (cf. Vogel, *Early Mormon Documents,* 1:64).

24. To N. E. Seaton, in Smith, *History of the Church,* 1:315, 326.

25. *Times and Seasons* 3 (15 Sept. 1842): 922.

26. Qtd. in Roberts, *A Comprehensive History of the Church* (Salt Lake City: Deseret News Press, 1930), 1:167 (cf. Vogel, *Early Mormon Documents,* 1:171).

27. Scott G. Kenney, ed., *Wilford Woodruff Journals* (Midvale, UT: Signature Books, 1983), 2:282.

28. Ibid., 2:300. On 28 July 1847, after the Saints had arrived in Utah, Brigham Young, speaking before the Quorum of the Twelve, stated that "our people would be connected with every tribe of Indians throughout America & that our people would yet take their squaws wash & dress them up teach them our language & learn them the gospel of there forefathers & raise up children by them & teach the children & not many generations Hence they will become A white & delightsome people" (ibid., 3:241). In 1875 Orson Pratt quoted Joseph Smith saying, "The Lord God made a promise to the forefathers of the Indians, about six hundred years before Christ, that all this continent should be given to them and to their children after them for an everlasting inheritance" (*Journal of Discourses,* 26 vols. [Liverpool: F. D. Richards, 1875], 17:299-301). Pratt further asserted that the Indians "have different languages, but the roots of each language indicate that they have all sprung from the same origin" (*Journal of Discourses,* 14:10; 19 Feb. 1871). In 1954 Joseph Fielding Smith, then an apostle, reaffirmed that Nephites "spread over the face of the entire continent" and that "their descendants, the American Indians, were wandering in all their wild savagery when the Pilgrim Fathers made permanent settlement in this land" (*Doctrines of Salvation,* 3 vols. [Salt Lake City: Bookcraft, 1954], 1:151). The church's missionary program to the Indians identifies them as the fallen descendants of the early Book of Mormon peoples (see Orson Pratt, in *Journal of Discourses,* 17:299-301; 14:10; Parley P. Pratt, *A Voice of Warning* [Liverpool: Brigham Young, 1866], 94-109; George Q. Cannon's 6 April 1884 general conference address in *Journal of Discourses,* 25:123-24; and Orson Pratt's 2 December 1877 address in *Journal of Discourses,* 19:170-74). In 1966 Bruce R. McConkie, later an apostle, acknowledged: "It is quite apparent that groups of Orientals found their way over the Bering Strait [and] gradually moved southward to mix with the Indian peoples." However, Indians are still regarded as "chiefly" Lamanites, whom McConkie considered to have come prior to the Bering Strait migrations which archeologists date thousands of years earlier (*Mormon Doctrine* [2nd ed.; Salt Lake City: Bookcraft, 1966], 32-33). Church historians Leonard J. Arrington and Davis Bitton reflect this modified view that the Indian population "apparently mixed with other groups from Europe and Asia [to become] the ancestors of the Indians of the North, Central, and South America" but without discussion of proportions or order of arrival (*The Mormon Experience: A History of the Latter-day Saints* [New York: Alfred A. Knopf, 1979], 14). The traditional view of American Indians as Book of Mormon descendants is continually reaffirmed in church statements and publications, as exemplified by a 1984 article in the *Church News* section of the church-owned *Deseret News* which identified an estimated 177 million Indians of North and South America and Polynesians as Lamanites from the Book of Mormon epic (26 Feb. 1984).

29. John Sorenson argues against Smith and subsequent church leaders,

assuming they were in error, and attempts to proof-text the limited geography hypothesis from the Book of Mormon. He asserts that the text describes foot journeys between Nephi and Zarahemla that took place in some twenty days (approximately 500 miles); a population of about 2,500 assembled in Bountiful in 3 Nephi 10-18 for the visitation of the Savior, and military units at the end of the book numbering in the tens of thousands, not millions. Biblical references, as a possible parallel to "all the land," Sorenson concludes, seem to reflect Hebrew hyperbole rather than exact geographical descriptions (see Josh. 11:23; Isa. 13:5; Jer. 1:18; Matt. 27:45; Luke 23:44).

30. Madsen, *B. H. Roberts,* 92-93; the Hill Cumorah, where Book of Mormon character Moroni is thought to have buried gold records that Joseph Smith found, is about two miles from Smith's home in Palmyra, New York. The archeological problems Roberts confronted remain. For instance, the ancient migration patterns from Africa, north to Europe and east to Asia, then across the Bering Strait into the Americas have been charted by Stanford population geneticist Luigi Cavalli-Sforza who compared archeological, language, and blood/DNA to trace the routes taken by humans in colonizing the earth (Cavalli-Sforza and Francesco Cavalli-Sforza, *The Great Human Diaspora: The History of Diversity and Evolution,* trans. Sarah Thorne [New York: Addison-Wesley, 1995]). In a recent issue of the British journal *Nature*, molecular evolutionary geneticist S. Blair Hedges confirmed this migration pattern beginning in Africa: "The most thorough analysis yet of the divergence of sequences in human mitochondrial DNA has been carried out. The results support the view that modern humans originated in Africa" within the past 100,000 years (Hedges, "Human Evolution: A Start for Population Geonomics," *Nature* 408 [7 Dec. 2000]: 652). Twentieth-century research in archeology, population genetics, anthropology, and linguistics contradicts the theory that Native Americans are of Hebrew origin. It is futile to speculate whether the Nephite horse (missing in pre-Columbian archeology) might really be a tapir (Sorenson, *Ancient American Setting,* 288-99). The Book of Mormon tries to place an Old World Culture into a New World setting that does not fit.

On this point, Yale professor of anthropology Michael D. Coe wrote the following response (28 August 1980) to my questions about the Book of Mormon: "I think that B. H. Roberts's comments about the absence of horses, asses, oxen, cows (same species!), sheep, swine, iron & steel, wheat and barley–and wheeled vehicles–in the pre-Columbian world were and are correct. The horse was present prior to 10,000 years ago as a wild, hunted animal (not ridden)–it was killed off, probably by man, at the end of the Ice Age. Horses are unknown in later times, until the arrival of the Spaniards ... Lastly, it is utterly inconceivable that 10 million people would have lived somewhere in Central America without making contact with other pre-Columbian peoples!" Coe had earlier summarized his widely-quoted professional opinion on Mormon archeology: "Mormon archeologists over the years have almost unanimously accepted the Book of Mormon as an accurate, historical account of the New World peoples between about 2000 B.C. and A.D. 421 ... Let me now state uncategorically that as far as I know there is not one professionally trained archeologist, who is not a Mormon, who sees any scientific justification for believing the foregoing to be true ... The bare facts of the matter are that nothing, absolutely nothing, has ever shown up in any New World excavation which would suggest to a dispassionate observer that the Book of Mormon, as claimed by Joseph Smith, is an historical document relating to the history of early migrants to our hemisphere" ("Mormons and Archeology: An Outside View," *Dialogue: A Journal of Mormon Thought* 8 [Summer 1973]: 41, 42, 46).

31. See Talmage, Journal, 2 Feb. 1922, for the date of the meeting to assist Roberts in preparing the Couch letter.

32. Here Roberts is referring to the position that was beginning to emerge that the Book of Mormon people were one of many groups of ancestors of the present-day Indians.

33. Madsen, *B. H. Roberts,* 107.

34. Lloyd, Journal, 7 Aug. 1933.

35. B. H. Roberts to Heber J. Grant, 1922, hand-dated 15 Mar. 1923, perhaps when he had planned to present the accompanying critique during a spring conference speaking engagement.

36. Talmage, Journal, 29 Mar., 28 Apr., and 25 May 1922. Roberts likely finished the paper in the spring of 1922.

37. Lloyd, Journal, 7 Aug. 1933.

38. Roberts to Grant, 1922.

39. The first edition sold out and the second contained a letter of recommendation, dated 4 Feb. 1825, from Rev. Jaber Hyde of Eden, Erie County, New York, farther west than Joseph Smith's residence in Palmyra and several hundred miles from the publisher in Poultney, Vermont (vi-vii).

40. Madsen, *B. H. Roberts,* 27. Roberts does not seem to connect Cowdery as a possible source of Ethan Smith's ideas for Joseph Smith.

41. *The Founder of Mormonism* (New York: Dodd, Mead, 1903), 124-25.

42. "Objections to the Book of Mormon," in *New Witnesses for God* 3:347-460. "A Book of Mormon Study," in Madsen, *B. H. Roberts,* 152. Roberts noted that Josiah Priest's *The Wonders of Nature and Providence* (Rochester, NY, 1924), which quoted from Ethan Smith's *View of the Hebrews,* was unknown to him as well. George Reynolds of the First Council of Seventy referred to *View of the Hebrews* in the *Juvenile Instructor* (1 Oct. 1902) as providing "strong evidences in favor of the genuineness of the Book of Mormon" (see Madsen, *B. H. Roberts,* 355-57).

43. Summarized from Madsen, *B. H. Roberts,* 240-42.

44. Madsen, *B. H. Roberts,* 251, 260-61, 264-71, 272.

45. Ibid., 283.

46. In a 21 October 1927 letter to Richard R. Lyman, Roberts indicates

that he wrote this second report, "A Book of Mormon Study," before he left for the eastern states but found it impossible to present his report. He apparently never presented it to President Grant (see Lloyd, Journal, 7 Aug. 1933).

47. Truman G. Madsen and John W. Welch, *Did B. H. Roberts Lose Faith in the Book of Mormon?* (Provo, UT: Foundation for Ancient Research & Mormon Studies, Preliminary Report, 1985); John W. Welch, "New B. H. Roberts Book Lacks Insight of His Testimony," *Church News* (15 Dec. 1985).

48. Truman G. Madsen, "B. H. Roberts after Fifty Years," 11-19, Interview with Milo Marsden, 10 July 1983.

49. The Papers of B. H. Roberts, Special Collections, Marriott Library.

50. *Ninety-third Annual Conference of the Church of Jesus Christ of Latter-day Saints* (Salt Lake City: Church of Jesus Christ of Latter-day Saints, Apr. 1923), 64.

51. Ibid., Oct. 1923, 91.

52. During his mission presidency to the eastern states, Roberts visited libraries and museums to study American antiquity and geography (Madsen, *B. H. Roberts,* 25).

53. Roberts to Elizabeth Skolfield, 14 Mar. 1932, qtd. in Madsen, *B. H. Roberts,* 370. See also Roberts to Richard R. Lyman, 14 Oct. 1927, ibid., 58-60.

54. B. H. Roberts to Richard Lyman, 24 Oct. 1927. For "A Parallel," which was attached to Roberts's letter, see the B. H. Roberts Collection, Box 3, Fd 20, Manuscripts Division, Marriott Library.

55. Roberts to Elizabeth Skolfield, 14 Mar. 1932, in Madsen, *B H. Roberts,* 60, 370.

56. Madsen, *B. H. Roberts,* 58-60.

57. Sterling M. McMurrin, interview by author, Salt Lake City, Utah, 19 Jan. 1996. Roberts was the father of McMurrin's aunt, Hazel Roberts Moss, and the McMurrin family called him "Grandpa Roberts."

58. Fawn M. Brodie, *No Man Knows My History: The Life of Joseph Smith* (New York: Alfred A. Knopf, 1945), 45-50. Roberts's two substantial critical studies of the Book of Mormon were still not mentioned in the second edition in 1971.

59. Meeting of the Timpanogos Club, 10 Oct. 1946, in Salt Lake City, Utah. Subsequently, Mervin B. Hogan published the mimeographed list of parallels in *The Rocky Mountain Mason* (Billings, MT, Jan. 1956), 17-31. In 1964 Hal Hougey reproduced Roberts's parallels in a pamphlet entitled *A Parallel: The Basis of the Book of Mormon* (Concord, CA: Pacific Publishing Co., 1963). See Brigham D. Madsen, *B. H. Roberts,* 27, 321.

60. When I consulted the LDS Historical Department archives, it did not, at that time, list either manuscript in its register of Roberts's unpublished works. Family copies were generally unavailable to outsiders until 1979, although Benjamin Roberts showed his copy to Heber Grant Ivins in 1973. Perhaps Benjamin was the source of the "fragments" A. C. Lambert, a member of BYU's faculty, recalls seeing in 1925: "A few of us at BYU got a few fragments

of the manuscript back in 1925, but were ordered to destroy them and to 'keep your mouths shut,' and we did keep our mouths shut. I never got the fragments for my own meager files, which were kept private even then. B. H. Roberts came about as near calling Joseph Smith, Jr. a fraud and deceit as the polite language of a religious man would permit. The grandson who currently owns the manuscript died a few weeks ago as you may already have heard. I have not heard what will happen to the manuscript" (A. C. Lambert to Wesley P. Walters, undated but postmarked 14 Dec. 1978, Special Collections, Marriott Library).

61. Hugh Nibley, "The Comparative Method," *Improvement Era* 62 (Oct. 1959): 10; and ibid. 62 (Nov. 1959): 11.

62. Although Truman Madsen does not mention these works in his biography, *Defender of the Faith, The B. H. Roberts Story* (Salt Lake City: Bookcraft, 1980), he devotes considerable attention to them in "B. H. Roberts and the Book of Mormon" (*BYU Studies* 19 [Summer 1979]: 427-45) and in light of Roberts's commitment to the Book of Mormon in "B. H. Roberts after Fifty Years: Still Witnessing for the Book of Mormon" (*Ensign* 13 [Dec. 1983]: 11-19, quote from p. 17). See also Thomas G. Alexander's review of *Defender of the Faith* in *BYU Studies* 21 (Spring 1981): 248-50, which notes the omission of Roberts's Book of Mormon manuscripts. In his 1983 *Ensign* article, Madsen acknowledges "only two specific similarities," aside from the claim of Hebraic backgrounds, between the Book of Mormon and *View of the Hebrews*: lengthy Isaiah quotes and reference to the urim and thummim. Misdating the second edition of *View of the Hebrews* to 1835, he erroneously asserts that this edition was "published long after the Book of Mormon began circulation [in 1830]," proposing that when *View of the Hebrews* was enlarged, "it surely can also be claimed that Ethan Smith was aware of Joseph Smith's [book]," implying that Ethan Smith may have drawn from Joseph Smith, not vice versa. In his review of Charles Tate's 1996 reprint edition of *View of the Hebrews* (1925 ed.; see n10), Andrew Hedges finds that the "testimonials" of the Indians' Hebrew origins, collected by Ethan Smith, "form a part of the cultural context into which Mormonism was introduced" (*FARMS Review of Books* 9 [1997] 63-68).

63. During the 1979 and 1980 Sunstone Theological Symposiums, Madison U. Sowell and I presented papers discussing Roberts's studies on the Book of Mormon. These papers were later published together, Sowell's "Defending the Keystone: The Comparative Method Re-examined" and my "Defending the Keystone: Book of Mormon Difficulties," *Sunstone* 6 (May-June 1981): 44-54.

64. On 27 December 1979, the University of Utah Special Collections Library received Roberts's 1921 and 1923 papers and correspondence from Adele W. Parkinson, widow of Wood R. Worsley, a grandson of Roberts's first wife, Louisa. On 19 January 1981, Virginia Roberts, widow of Brigham E. Roberts, another grandson of Louisa, gave the library personal copies of the papers. Under an exchange agreement, Brigham Young University Library re-

ceived copies of both sets. The published volume, *B. H. Roberts: Studies of the Book of Mormon,* was introduced and edited by Brigham D. Madsen and prefaced by Everett L. Cooley. It includes a biographical essay on Roberts by Sterling M. McMurrin, a member of the Roberts family.

65. Leonard J. Arrington, "The Intellectual Tradition of the Latter-day Saints," *Dialogue: A Journal of Mormon Thought* 4 (Spring 1969). Twenty-five years later a second poll was conducted by Stan Larson, which continued to rank Roberts as the "foremost intellectual in Mormonism" (see "Intellectuals in Mormon History: An Update," ibid. [Fall 1993]).

66. Madsen, *B. H. Roberts,* xxvi.

67. Madsen and Welch, *Did B. H. Roberts Lose Faith in the Book of Mormon?* 35.

68. See Daniel C. Peterson's review of James R. Spencer, *The Disappointment of B. H. Roberts: Five Questions that Forced a Mormon General Authority to Abandon the Book of Mormon* (Boise, ID, 1991), in *FARMS Review of Books* 9 (1997): 79-81.

69. Davis Bitton, "B. H. Roberts and Book of Mormon Scholarship: Early Twentieth Century: Age of Transition," *Journal of Book of Mormon Studies* 8 (1999): 67. In fact, when I approached Bitton in 1984 about a collection of Roberts's critical studies, he advised against publication because although they may represent important expressions of Roberts's questions, such a volume could "threaten tender testimonies."

70. James B. Allen, "The Story of the Truth, the Way, the Life," in B. H. Roberts, *The Truth, the Way, the Life: An Elementary Treatise on Theology,* ed. John W. Welch (Provo, UT: BYU Studies, 1994), clxvii-clxix.

71. Madsen, "B. H. Roberts after Fifty Years," 11-19, Interview with Jack Christensen, 25 Apr. 25, 1979.

72. See n62.

73. Author's interview, 27 Aug. 1981 and 3 Mar. 1984. Allen was secretary to Eastern States Mission president Rolapp until 1928. Truman Madsen, citing a letter to him from Allen, 20 July 1983, quotes him as saying, "His [Roberts's] faith in the divinity of the book was strong, but he agonized over the intellectual problems in justifying it" and was "uneasy with attempts to build a case out of trivial coincidence and gratuitous parallels" ("B. H. Roberts after Fifty Years," 16). In a letter to Grant Ivins dated 23 Dec. 1973, Heber Holt related comments he remembered Roberts making, which confirms Roberts's desire to rewrite his 1909 *New Witnesses*: "B. H. Roberts was an honest courageous scholar. He said one time he wished to God he had 20 more years to correct some of his mistakes from lack of full information in many subjects."

74. Author's interview, 1 Aug. 1982 and 3 Mar. 1984, with Harold Ellison, former bishop, stake president, and missionary in the Eastern States Mission under Roberts, 1925-26.

75. *One Hundred and Third Annual Conference* (Apr. 1933): 117.

76. Lloyd, Journal, 7 Aug. 1933, in Madsen, *B. H. Roberts,* 22-23.

77. Ibid. Matthew Roper posits that when Roberts was reported by Lloyd to have "shifted his base" on the Book of Mormon, he did not "abandon the battle" as his friend suggested, but "merely [took] up a more defensible position" (review of Jerald and Sandra Tanner, *Answering Mormon Scholars: A Response to Criticism Raised by Mormon Defenders* [Salt Lake City: Utah Lighthouse Ministry, 1996], *FARMS Review of Books* 9 [1997] 1:108). In the same volume, Daniel C. Peterson repeats John W. Welch's assurances that since Roberts wrote his faithfully-drawn intended lesson manual, *The Truth, the Way, the Life,* after his intensive study of the Book of Mormon, "readers can now determine that Roberts did not waiver in his belief because of that study" (review of James R. Spencer, *The Disappointment of B. H. Roberts, FARMS Review of Books,* 83).

78. Although Ferguson concluded that no evidence would be found "in the dirt" to validate the book, he remained within the LDS community, even after he ultimately decided that "all religions [including] Mormonism are, to me, all man-made fabrications." Thomas S. Ferguson to Burt Stride, 15 Sept. 1981, Ferguson Collection, Manuscripts Division, Marriott Library.

6. Isaiah in the Book of Mormon: Or Joseph Smith in Isaiah

David P. Wright

A MAJOR QUESTION IN BOOK OF MORMON (HEREAFTER BOM) scholarship is whether the several chapters or passages of Isaiah cited and paraphrased in the book derive from an ancient text or whether they have been copied with some revision from the King James Version of the Bible (hereafter KJV).[1] (For all other abbreviations used herein, see the end of this essay.) The BoM narrative would have us believe the former, that its citations of Isaiah come directly or ultimately from the brass plates of Laban or from Jesus' recitation where, according to the BoM, he visited the New World peoples shortly after his death. Closer study shows that despite the intent of the story, the Isaiah of the BoM is a revision of the KJV and not a translation of an ancient document. This essay seeks to review and enlarge upon the evidence for this conclusion. It focuses on internal textual evidence where the BoM's Isaiah appears to reflect or respond to the peculiarities and idiom of the KJV text. This analysis demonstrates how intricately and fully the BoM Isaiah is tied to the KJV. The last section reviews and shows the weakness of arguments that the BoM has parallels with ancient manuscripts and translations or that its variants reflect elements of Hebrew style and language.

1. KJV LANGUAGE

One point of evidence, usually set aside in considering the source of the BoM Isaiah, is the general prevalence of KJV language in it. This cannot be ignored. The reality is that, except for a few variants, the BoM text follows the KJV word for word. We do not find significant cases of synonymy, that is, where a BoM passage agrees in idea and content with the corresponding KJV passage but employs different words with variations in syntax, much like what can be found in various modern translations of the Bible.

One might argue that the wording is identical to the KJV because Joseph Smith sought to maintain biblical style. But this could have been done without word-for-word correspondence. For example, Isa. 7:7-9 might be translated independently of the KJV but with a biblical flavor in the following way:

Sample Translation	*KJV*
Thus the Lord God hath said,	Thus saith the Lord God,
It shall not prevail	It shall not stand,
nor shall it be,	neither shall it come to pass.
For the head of Syria is Damascus,	For the head of Syria is Damascus,
and the head of Damascus is Rezin,	and the head of Damascus is Rezin;
But in yet sixty-five years,	and within threescore and five years
Ephraim shall be dismayed	shall Ephraim be broken,
as a people.	that it be not a people.
The head of Ephraim is Samaria,	And the head of Ephraim is Samaria,
and the head of Samaria is the son of Remaliah.	and the head of Samaria is Remaliah's son.
If ye do not trust,	If ye will not believe,
ye shall not be trustworthy.	surely ye shall not be established.

Here the meaning is very close, but the language is significantly different. This is what one would reasonably expect to find between the BoM Isaiah and the KJV if the BoM Isaiah were indeed a translation. The identity between the BoM and KJV is thus no small clue that the former derives from the latter.[2]

2. KJV ITALICS AND BOM ISAIAH

A peculiarity of the KJV is the use of italics to mark words that do not have exact correspondences in the original biblical languages. The KJV was not the first to use italicized words in this way. Sebastian Muenster's Latin translation (1534-35), the French Bible of Olivétan (1535), the Great Bible of Coverdale (1539), and the Geneva Bible (1557-60) also used italics. The original KJV (1611) was printed in black-letter (gothic) with the "added" words printed in small roman type. In 1612 an edition used italics for these words, and this became part of all standard editions of the KJV from that time.[3] Many of the variants in the BoM Isaiah over against the KJV occur precisely at these words. This is a transparent indication that the KJV is the source of the BoM Isaiah text.[4]

Before considering specifically how the BoM varies at italicized words, we should note that circumstantial evidence makes it reasonably clear that Joseph Smith knew, if not with linguistic precision, the basic significance of the italics when working on the BoM. Some Bible reference works of Smith's time explained the reason for italics. A KJV Bible published in New York City in 1818, for example, included the following statement:

> The unlearned reader may find it useful to be informed, that, wherever words occur in the text of the English Bible, printed in Italic character, he is to understand that these words have none corresponding to them in the original Hebrew or Greek text, but that the sense is implied; and that the words are added in the English to complete or make clearer the sense.[5]

Lay readers could have read such statements and circulated the information further by word of mouth. Ministers, too, would have learned the reason for italics either from these sources or through their education and no doubt would have shared it with their congregants.

There is evidence that early Mormons knew the significance and were even, like many at large, suspicious of these italicized words. In July 1833, for example, W. W. Phelps wrote in the Mormon periodical *The Evening and the Morning Star*: "As to the errors in the bible, any man possessed of common understanding, knows, that both the old and new testaments are filled with errors, obscurities, italics and contradictions, which must be the work of men. ... the church of Christ will soon have the scriptures, in their original purity."[6] Note that according to this, the use of italics was something with which people of ordinary knowledge were familiar.

Direct evidence that Smith knew about this issue is found in his work on the revision of the Bible (hereafter JSR), a project which he began in 1830 soon after the completion of the BoM. Robert Matthews, a scholar of the JSR, has noted that throughout the Bible that Smith used, "many italics are crossed out, even when it does violence to the sense. There seems to be little consistency in the cross-outs of italics. Many are not touched; others are crossed out and replaced by words in the manuscripts, and many are not replaced."[7]

The JSR itself manifests the reaction to italicized words. KJV Genesis 20, for example, has twenty-three italicized words. Fourteen of these are associated with variants of some sort in the JSR. One italicized word is simply deleted, six are deleted with accompanying environmental changes, two are retained with environmental changes, and five are replaced with another word. Similar treatment of, and attention to, italics can be found throughout the JSR.

An 1831 article in *The Sun* in Philadelphia indicates that Smith mistrusted the italicized words at the time he worked on the BoM. The article notes that, after an infraction which prevented Smith from being able to translate the BoM for a while,

> Jo [Smith]'s specticles were restored to sight, and he again [was] permitted to open the book.—Jo had, during his spiritual blindness, by the assistance of some one, committed several chapters of the New Testament to memory; and, the better to carry on his deception with the deluded Harris, had inquired, and found out the words inserted by the translators; (which are distinguished by *Italics*, both in the New Testament and the Old.) So, in order to convince Harris that he *could* read from the plates, Jo deposits them in his hat, applies spectacles, and refers Harris to a chapter in the Bible, which he had learned by rote, and which he *read* from the plates, with surprising accuracy; and what astonished Harris most, was, that Jo should omit all the words in the Bible that were printed in *Italic.* And, if Harris attempted to correct Joe, he persisted that the plates were right, and the Bible was wrong.[8]

Although the correctness of certain details throughout the article may be questioned, and although it seeks to ridicule Smith's claims, the account appears to reflect more or less correctly Smith's attitude toward the italicized words and shows that these were of concern early on in the production of the BoM. At least, one cannot argue that ignorance precluded Smith from reacting to italicized words while working on the BoM. Nevertheless, any lingering doubt about the extent of his knowledge is dissipated when looking at the BoM Isaiah evidence itself. Close analysis makes it abundantly clear that the italics were an object of special concern and demonstrates in large measure that the BoM Isaiah derives from the KJV.

The table below shows in a general way how much attention Smith gave the italicized words.[9] It summarizes information from the main chapters or portions of the BoM Isaiah (listed at the top of the table) that are presented as citations and are not clearly paraphrases.[10] The register entitled "Total Variants in the BoM" and the four registers under it ("Variants related/not related to italics") give the number of BoM variants associated and not associated with KJV italicized words. Each word difference in the BoM text counts as one variant.[11] The figures for variants associated with italicized words include instances where these words do not appear in the BoM or where other words stand in their place. They also include cases where italicized words in the KJV still appear in the BoM but with accompanying variants which may have been stimulated by the italicized words (see, below, on these "environmental variants," as I term them). Since these last instances may be open to varying judgments, I have included two figures: a "high count," which is liberal in its inclusion of variants possibly related to KJV italicized words, and a "low count," which is reserved about associating environmental variants with italicized words. These low and high counts show that from 22 percent to 38 percent of all differences between the BoM and KJV Isaiah text are associable with words italicized in the KJV. This correspondence alone suggests that Smith consciously responded to KJV italics.

A count from another and more objective perspective substantiates this impression. The register in the table entitled "Total italicized words in KJV" and the two under it ("Italicized words remaining/lacking ...") show that 40 percent of the words italicized in the KJV are altogether lacking in the BoM Isaiah. The significance of the concentration of variants at italicized words becomes visible when it is realized that only 3.6 percent of the words in the KJV are italicized (see the bottom register of the table). Approximately one-fourth to one-third of

Isaiah chapters	Isa 2	Isa 3	Isa 4	Isa 5	Isa 6	Isa 7	Isa 8	Isa 9	Isa 10	Isa 1
BoM book and chapter	2 Ne 12	2 Ne 13	2 Ne 14	2 Ne 15	2 Ne 16	2 Ne 17	2 Ne 18	2 Ne 19	2 Ne 20	2 Ne 21
Total variants in BoM	97	51	13	34	12	22	13	25	21	2
Variants not related to italics (high count)	71 73%	14 27%	3 23%	8 24%	5 42%	8 36%	11 85%	12 48%	14 67%	2 100
Variants related to italics (high count)	26 27%	37 73%	10 77%	26 76%	7 58%	14 64%	2 15%	13 52%	7 33%	0 0%
Variants not related to italics (low count)	76 78%	17 33%	5 38%	13 38%	6 50%	8 36%	11 85%	15 60%	15 71%	2 100
Variants related to italics (low count)	21 22%	34 67%	8 62%	21 62%	6 50%	14 64%	2 15%	10 40%	6 29%	0 0%
Total italicized words in KJV	23	34	11	31	18	19	17	33	32	2
Italicized words remaining in BoM	12 52%	9 26%	3 27%	13 42%	14 78%	9 47%	15 88%	24 73%	29 91%	2 100
Italicized words lacking in BoM	11 48%	25 74%	8 73%	18 58%	4 22%	10 53%	2 12%	9 27%	3 9%	0 0%
Total words in KJV	568	588	208	866	366	692	558	600	929	51
Percent of italicized words in KJV	4.0%	5.8%	5.3%	3.6%	4.9%	2.7%	3.0%	5.5%	3.4%	0.4

Statistical Data on Italicized Words in the Book of Mormon

a 12	Isa 13	Isa 14	Isa 48	Isa 49	Isa 49: 22–26	Isa 50	Isa 51:1– 52:2	Isa 52: 7–10	Isa 53	Isa 54	
Ne 22	2 Ne 23	2 Ne 24	1 Ne 20	1 Ne 21	2 Ne 6	2 Ne 7	2 Ne 8	Mos 12	Mos 14	3 Ne 22	
0	47	59	129	128	22	104	64	0	5	7	**TOTALS** **885**
0 0%	37 77%	41 69%	77 60%	104 81%	22 100%	64 62%	34 53%	0 0%	5 100%	1 14%	**532** **62%**
0 0%	11 23%	18 31%	52 40%	24 19%	0 0%	40 38%	30 47%	0 0%	0 0%	6 86%	**323** **38%**
0 0%	36 77%	42 71%	97 75%	117 91%	22 100%	68 65%	37 58%	0 0%	5 100%	2 29%	**594** **78%**
0 %	11 23%	17 29%	32 25%	11 9%	0 0%	36 35%	27 42%	0 0%	0 0%	5 71%	**261** **22%**
5	14	29	29	25	5	21	34	0	15	16	**413**
5 0%	7 50%	18 62%	13 45%	17 68%	5 100%	10 48%	16 47%	0 0%	15 100%	13 81%	**249** **60%**
0 %	7 50%	11 38%	16 55%	8 32%	0 0%	11 52%	18 53%	0 0%	0 0%	3 19%	**164** **40%**
47	577	856	621	869	191	365	828	112	387	494	**11,341**
4%	2.4%	3.4%	4.7%	2.9%	2.6%	5.8%	4.1%	0.0%	3.9%	3.2%	**3.6%**

the variants are associated with words that constitute only about one-twenty-fifth of the text.

An examination of variants themselves shows even more clearly that the BoM Isaiah text responds to italicized words in the KJV. Here I limit myself to examining the instances in the BoM chapters listed in the table. One category of variant is where an italicized word does not appear in the BoM. In several of these cases, an absent word has no effect upon the meaning.[12] For example, a relative pronoun or conjunction may be lacking: "for the abundance of milk *that* they shall give ..." > "for the abundance of milk they shall give ..." (Isa. 7:22//2 Ne. 17:22).[13] Once, a pleonastic pronoun is omitted: "Say ye not, A confederacy, to all *them* to whom this people shall say, A confederacy" > "Say ye not a confederacy to all to whom this people shall say a confederacy" (Isa. 8:12//2 Ne. 18:12). An italicized word may be missing, only to be supplied from the same or a synonymous word in a preceding clause: "For the head of Syria *is* Damascus, and the head of Damascus *is* Rezin" > "For the head of Syria is Damascus, and the head of Damascus, Rezin" (Isa. 7:8//2 Ne. 17:8).[14]

The words omitted are those that translators would normally insert during translation for smooth conceptual and idiomatic flow in English. That these italicized words are missing is an indication that Smith was working from the KJV and at times made such modifications rather mechanically.[15] This is more transparent in cases where the want of italicized words yields an ungrammatical and even incomprehensible reading. A recurring phrase in Isa. 5:25; 9:12, 17, 21; 10:4 is that God's "anger is not turned away, but his hand *is* stretched out still." In the BoM parallel passages, the verb "*is*" is absent, producing the syntactically incomplete phrase "his hand stretched out still" (2 Ne. 15:25; 2 Ne. 19:12, 17, 21; 20:4).[16] The difficulty had to be remedied in later editions of the BoM by restoring the verb.[17] The KJV's translation is wholly legitimate here. In Hebrew, nouns, adjectives, and adverbials can stand in predicate relationship to another noun without the verb "to be" being expressly stated. English idiom demands the verb in such cases. The absence of this verb is not only a sign that the italics of the KJV are being deleted but an ignorance of Hebrew (see n49).

Other examples of incomplete and conceptually difficult or impossible readings where italicized words are missing include: "For every battle of the warrior *is* with confused noise and garments rolled in blood, but *this* shall be with burning ..." > "For every battle of the warrior with confused noise and garments rolled in blood, but this shall be with burning ..." (Isa. 9:5//2 Ne. 19:5);[18] "For this *is as* the waters of Noah unto me, for *as* I have sworn that the waters of Noah ..." > "For this, the waters of Noah unto me, for as I have sworn that the waters of Noah ..." (Isa. 54:9//3 Ne. 22:9);[19] "Then said I, Here *am* I" > "Then I said, Here I" (Isa. 6:8//2 Ne. 16:8);[20] "woe *is* me" > "wo me" (Isa. 6:5//2 Ne. 16:5).[21] The change of "their roaring *shall be* like a lion" to "their roaring like a lion" (Isa. 5:29//2 Ne. 15:28) is another case of a syntactically incomplete phrase if it is to come at the beginning of v. 29 as the Hebrew text indicates.[22] These examples remind one of what Matthews observed above in regard to the nonsensical crossing out of italics in Smith's Bible.

Besides cases where the text is incomprehensible, some variants present readings that differ significantly from, and are incompatible with, the Hebrew text. In Isa. 51:17, for example, the KJV reads "thou hast drunken the dregs of the cup of trembling, *and* wrung *them* out"; the BoM has "thou hast drunken the dregs of the cup of trembling rung [sic] out" (2 Ne. 8:17; "rung" here is just a phonetic spelling for "wrung"; there is no difference in meaning). In the BoM the term "rung out" becomes an adjective modifying "dregs" (or perhaps "cup"). The Hebrew, which reads *ʾet qubbaʿ at kôs hattarʿ ēlâ šātît māṣît,* can be construed literally as "the goblet of the cup of reeling you have drunk, you have drained out." It is impossible to get the BoM translation from the Hebrew, and it is unlikely that the BoM is due to a variant in an ancient text. Smith has merely eliminated the italics, producing a reading that is erroneous.

Another erroneous reading that arises from the deletion of an italicized word is at Isa. 54:5//3 Ne. 22:5: "For thy Maker *is* thine husband, the Lord of hosts *is* his name" > "For thy maker, thine husband, the Lord of hosts is his name." The order of the Hebrew words is *kî bōʿ ălayik ʿōśayik,* which, to show the actual order of Hebrew words, could be rendered: "for your husband is your maker" (so REB; see key to abbreviations preceding the endnotes). If the BoM were a translation and if the terms were in apposition as it represents them, one would expect the Hebrew word order *kî ʿōśayik bōʿ alayik*. "For your maker, your husband ..." Here the italicized word was simply deleted and the word order of the KJV retained.

Another category of variant is where other words stand in the place of the italics. These further show that the BoM version is responding to and developing out of the KJV. The BoM sometimes uses a synonym. For example, the relative pronoun "which" appears instead of italicized "*that*": "and in the sparks *that* ye have kindled" > "and in the sparks which ye have kindled" (Isa. 50:11//2 Ne. 7:11).[23] The adverb "yea" appears at times for "*even*": "*even* the son of Tabeal" > "yea, the son of Tabeal" (Isa. 7:6//2 Ne. 17:6).[24] Terms denoting comparison have synonymous variation in Isa. 51:12//2 Ne. 8:12: "the son of man *which* shall be made *as* grass" > "the son of man which shall be made like unto grass." To these examples, compare the variation of the pronominal phrase in Isa. 5:21//2 Ne. 15:21: "Woe unto *them that are* wise in their own eyes" > "wo unto the wise in their own eyes" (cf. a similar variant in v. 22). Some italicized forms of the verb "to be" differ without much or any change in meaning: "*there shall be* no end" > "there is no end" (Isa. 9:7//2 Ne. 19:7).[25]

These variants cannot be explained as the result of translation. Different translations of the same original will produce different but synonymous readings, as noted in Part 1 above. This is not what is happening here. In any of the above noted passages, synonymous variation occurs almost exclusively in regard to the italicized words. The rest of the phrasing closely follows the KJV. Thus the synonymous renderings can only be a reaction to the italics. This conclusion can be brought to bear on cases where the BoM has nonsynonymous words appearing in the place of KJV italicized words. These also result from modification of the italics.[26]

In one case where the BoM has another word for an italicized one, the meaning is significantly changed, but not in accordance with the Hebrew original. The phrase "These two *things* are come unto thee" becomes "These two sons are come unto thee" (Isa. 51:19//2 Ne. 8:19). This is an extremely unlikely reading for any ancient text since the phrase in Hebrew is formulated in the feminine (*šĕtayim hēnnâ qōrʾōtayik*) whereas "sons" (*bānîm*) is masculine. The variant in the BoM is oblivious to the requirements of Hebrew, and it is doubtful that the Hebrew developed from a masculine to feminine formulation. Smith apparently replaced the italicized word, picking up "sons" from the context of vv. 18 and 20.[27]

Besides instances where italicized words are deleted or replaced, there are many examples where words in between and around italics differ from those in the KJV. In some of these environmental variants, words italicized in the KJV also appear in the BOM: "till *there be* no place" > "till there can be no place" (Isa. 5:8//2 Ne. 15:8); "and *there be* a great forsaking in the midst of the land" > "for there shall be a great forsaking in the midst of the land" (Isa. 6:12//2 Ne. 16:12); "for in my house *is* neither bread nor clothing" > "for in my house there is neither bread nor clothing" (Isa. 3:7//2 Ne. 13:7); "I *am* he; I *am* the first, I also *am* the last" > "for I am he, and I am the first, and I am also the last" (Isa. 48:11//1 Ne. 20:12); "they hide *it* not" > "they cannot hide it" (Isa. 3:9//2 Ne. 13:9); "for how should *my name* be polluted?" > "for I will not suffer my name to be polluted" (Isa. 48:11//1 Ne. 20:11).[28]

Sometimes other words appear in the place of some or all of the italics: "that formed me from the womb *to be* his servant" > "that formed me from the womb that I should be his servant" (Isa. 49:5//1 Ne. 21:5); "that I should know how to speak a word in season to *him that is* weary" > "that I should know how to speak a word in season unto thee, O house of Israel, when ye are weary" (Isa. 50:4//2 Ne. 7:4); "*but* not in truth" > "yet they swear not in truth" (Isa. 48:1//1 Ne. 20:1); "For the day of the Lord of hosts *shall be* upon every *one that is* proud and lofty" > "for the day of the Lord of hosts soon cometh upon all nations, yea, upon every one, yea upon the proud and lofty" (Isa. 2:12//2 Ne. 12:12); "upon all the cedars of Lebanon, *that are* high and lifted up" > "upon all the cedars of Lebanon, for they are high and lifted up" (Isa. 2:13//2 Ne. 12:13); "and upon all the hills *that are* lifted up" > "and upon all the hills and upon all the nations which are lifted up" (Isa. 2:14//2 Ne. 12.14), "because *there is* no water" > "because the waters are dried up" (Isa. 50:2//2 Ne. 7:2).[29]

In still other examples, an italicized phrase is wholly or partly missing: "and bind them *on thee* as a bride" > "and bind them on even as a bride" (Isa. 49:18//1 Ne. 21:18); "thy pomp is brought down to the grave *and* the noise of thy viols" > "thy pomp is brought down to the grave, the noise of thy viols is not heard" (Isa. 14:11//2 Ne. 24:11); "utter it *even* unto the end of the earth" > "utter to the end of the earth" (Isa. 48:20//1 Ne. 20:20); "they shall surely gather together, *but* not by me" > "they shall surely gather together against thee, not by me" (Isa. 54:15//3 Ne. 22:15); "or which of my creditors *is it* to whom I have sold you? " > "or to which of my creditors have I sold you, yea, to whom have I sold you? " (Isa. 50:1//2 Ne. 7:1).

It is clear that environmental variants are a consequence of the italics. Actually, there is really not much difference between these and the simpler cases of deletion or replacement noted earlier. It is only that in many environmental variants, deletion and replacement brought in their wake larger contextual revision so that the text would make sense. The attempt to make sense did not always work. For example, the phrase "every place shall be, where there were a thousand vines at a thousand silverlings, it shall *even* be for briers and thorns" becomes in the BoM "every place shall be, where there were a thousand vines at a thousand silverlings, which shall be for briers and thorns" (Isa. 7:23//2 Ne. 17:23).[30] The BoM text is syntactically incomplete and conceptually difficult.[31]

Some of the environmental variants are, like the others, incompatible with the underlying Hebrew. In Isa. 13:3 the KJV reads, "I have also called my mighty ones for mine anger, *even* them that rejoice in my highness." 2 Ne. 23:3 reads, "I have also called my mighty ones, for mine anger is not upon them that rejoice in my highness." The Hebrew phrase that the KJV translates as "for mine anger" is *lĕ-ʾappî,* a preposition plus noun (with possessive suffix). The phrase in the BoM Isaiah involves an entirely different syntax requiring different Hebrew wording, such as *kî-ʾappî,* a conjunction followed by the noun.[32]

A similar problem is found in the case of Isa. 50:2//2 Ne. 7:2. The KJV reads: "Wherefore, when I came, *was there* no man? when I called, *was there* none to answer?" The BoM inverts the italicized words and reads as a statement rather than a question: "Wherefore, when I came there was no man; when I called, yea, there was none to answer." The BoM reading depends on the ambiguity or polysemy of the English "wherefore." In English this word can be an interrogative (why) or a conjunction (therefore). It is an interrogative in the translation of the Hebrew word *maddûaᶜ* "why?" The BoM reading uses "wherefore" as a conjunction, which is not possible for Hebrew *maddûaᶜ,* which reveals the BoM's dependence on the English text.[33]

It is patent from the preceding analysis that many of the variants in the BoM Isaiah came about as a revision of italicized words and of their contexts in the KJV text. While Smith did not revise every italicized word, 40 percent of them were altered. Of the remaining 60 percent, several received environmental changes relating to the italics.[34] Joseph Smith's suspicion of the italics, shared by others of his age, was not well founded, since in most cases the KJV's italicized words simply supply words necessary for the proper rendering of the text's meaning in English. Modern translations of the Bible do not bother with marking literal correspondences since they realize that syntax and structure differ from language to language and that the goal of a translation is to render the text in good idiomatic English that reflects the conception of the original text, rather than giving a word-for-word equivalency. In any case, Smith's suspicion of the italicized words led him to produce a text that sought to obviate the supposed problems they created. But his corrections created their own problems and errors.

3. KJV TRANSLATION ERRORS RETAINED IN THE BOM ISAIAH

Another manifestation that the BoM Isaiah derives from the KJV is its preservation of numerous errors and defects of that translation. The following is a sampling of readings found in the BoM where the KJV is clearly or very likely wrong. It is based on a survey of the Isaiah chapters featured in the statistical table above (though one example is added from Isa. 29). The list is by no means exhaustive; careful readers will find many other cases of clear or suspected errors in the chapters. It selects examples that lend themselves to brief description, those involving, for the most part, single words or short phrases. It does not inventory, for example, cases where larger passages in the KJV are obscure and in need of overall clearer translation (e.g., Isa. 10:16-34; cf. 2 Ne. 20:16-34). The explanations are short. Just enough information is given to point out the difficulties in the KJV. Readers may refer to the modern versions, commentaries, and dictionaries for sample translations, discussion, and documentation.[35]

Isa. 2:6//2 Ne. 12:6: "And they please themselves in the children of strangers." Modern renditions: "They strike hands with foreigners," "make bargain/covenant with foreigners," or "are crowded with foreigners."

Isa. 2:16//2 Ne. 12:16: "Upon all pleasant pictures."[36] Modern renditions: "Upon all grand boats/precious things."

Isa. 3:2//2 Ne. 13:2: "Prudent." Modern renditions: "Diviner."

Isa. 3:3//2 Ne. 13:3: "Eloquent orator." Modern renditions: "Expert enchanter."

Isa. 3:8//2 Ne. 13:8: "To provoke the eyes of his glory." Modern renditions: "Rebel against/defy/insult his glorious presence/glance/gaze."

Isa. 3:18-23//2 Ne. 13:18-22: The meaning of several of the terms in this passage is unclear, and the KJV cannot be considered accurate. Compare the NJPS: "[18] In that day, my Lord will strip off the finery of the anklets, the fillets, and the crescents; [19] of the eardrops, the bracelets, and the veils; [20] the turbans, the armlets, and the sashes; of the talismans and the amulets; [21] the signet rings and the nose rings; [22] of the festive robes, the mantles, and the shawls; the purses, [23] the lace gowns, and the linen vests; and the kerchiefs and the capes."

Isa. 5:2//2 Ne. 15:2: "He fenced it." Modern renditions: "He dug it," "made a trench," "broke the ground."

Isa. 5:17//2 Ne. 15:17: "Then shall the lambs feed after their manner." Modern renditions: "Then lambs shall feed as at their pasture/meadow" or "in their old pastures."

Isa. 5:25//2 Ne. 15:25: "Their carcases were torn in the midst of the streets." Modern renditions: "Their corpses were as refuse in the midst of the streets."

Isa. 5:30//2 Ne. 15:30: "And the light is darkened in the heavens thereof." Modern renditions: "The light is darkened by/in its clouds."

Isa. 6:2//2 Ne. 16:2: "Above it." Most likely to be rendered "above him."

Isa. 7:15//2 Ne. 17:15: "Butter and honey shall he eat, that he may know to refuse the evil and choose the good."[37] The logical relation of the second clause to the first is not clear. It is as if eating butter and honey leads to moral knowledge. Clarification is needed. Compare the NJB: "On curds and honey will he feed until he knows how to refuse the bad and choose the good."

Isa. 8:6//2 Ne. 18:6: "The waters of Shiloah that go softly[38] and rejoice in Rezin and Remaliah's son." The KJV translation of *mĕśôś* (root *śwś)* which KJV translates "rejoice" may be wrong since it does not fit the context. Several read the term as a biform of the root *mss* and translate "but melt [with fear] before Rezin and Remaliah's son."

Isa. 8:12//2 Ne. 18:12: "Say ye not, A confederacy, to all *them* to whom this people shall say, A confederacy."[39] Modern renditions: "... to all that this people calls a confederacy/conspiracy."

Isa. 8:19-20//2 Ne. 18:19-20: "And when they shall say unto you, Seek unto them that have familiar spirits, and unto wizards that peep, and that mutter: should not a people seek unto their God? for the living to the dead? To the law and to the testimony: if they speak not according to this word, *it is* because *there* is no light in them." This is obscure in the Hebrew. The KJV is likewise obscure and the BoM version essentially retains that obscurity.[40] Compare the following modern translation: "And should people say to you, 'Go and consult ghosts and wizards that whisper and mutter'—a people should certainly consult its gods and the dead on behalf of the living! As regards instruction and testimony, without doubt this is how they will talk, and hence there will be no dawn for them" (NJB).

Isa. 8:22//2 Ne. 18:22: "And they shall look unto the earth, and, behold, trouble and darkness, dimness of anguish, and *they shall be* driven to darkness."[41] The Hebrew here is likewise obscure and the KJV offers an unlikely translation, especially of the last phrase. Compare: "Then [he will look] down to the earth, [and] there will be only anguish, gloom, the confusion of night, swirling darkness" (NJB).

Isa. 9:2 (=Heb. 9:1)//2 Ne. 19:2: "Shadow of death." The Hebrew term *ṣalmāwet* which this translates should be simply "darkness." It is not connected with the term *māwet* "death."[42]

Isa. 9:5 (=Heb. 9:4)//2 Ne. 19:5: "For every battle of the warrior *is* with confused noise."[43] Modern renditions: "For every boot that tramps with noise/in battle."

Isa. 10:4//2 Ne. 20:4: "Without me they shall bow down under the prisoners." The KJV takes the Hebrew *biltî* as if it had a suffix pronoun, meaning "without me." This is doubtful. Modern editions take it simply as a negative particle: e.g., "so that they do not cower among the prisoners" (REB); "Nothing remains but to crouch among the prisoners" (RSV).

Isa. 10:15//2 Ne. 20:15: "As if the rod should shake *itself* against them that lift it up, *or* as if the staff should lift up *itself, as if it were* no wood." The KJV is in error. The Hebrew should be translated "as if a rod raised the one[44] who lifted it, as if a staff lifted the one who is not wood."

Isa. 10:27//2 Ne. 20:27: "And the yoke shall be destroyed because of the anointing." The KJV is clearly wrong. It should be translated something like "The yoke shall be destroyed because of fatness." Some emend the text because the Masoretic Text, the main Hebrew Bible text tradition (hereafter MT), does not make clear sense.

Isa. 11:3//2 Ne. 21:3: "And shall make him of quick understanding in the fear of the Lord." The verb *wa-hărîḥô* is unclear but probably does not mean "make him of quick understanding." Compare: "He shall sense the truth by his reverence for the Lord" (NJPS); "And his delight shall be the fear of the Lord" (NAB).

Isa. 13:15//2 Ne. 23:15: "That is joined." Modern renditions: "who are caught/captured."

Isa. 13:22//2 Ne. 23:22: "Wild beasts of the islands." The Hebrew word is not connected with "coast, region"; it should be rendered simply "wild/desert beasts" or specifically "jackals" or "hyenas."

Isa. 14:4//2 Ne. 24:4: "The golden city." The word *mdhbh* is problematic since the root *dhb* is not attested in Hebrew. The KJV is apparently connecting it to Aramaic *dhb* "gold." This translation is therefore doubtful, nor does it fit the context. The text is probably defective, and *mrhbh* "boisterous behavior, frenzy, arrogance" is to be read.

Isa. 29:16//2 Ne. 27:27: "Surely, your turning of things upside down shall be esteemed as the potter's clay." This cannot be correct. A better translation, with the rest of the saying included to show the context, would be: "How perverse of you [or: You turn things upside down]! Can the potter be considered as the clay? Can a work say of its maker, 'He did not make me,' and can what is formed say to the one who formed it, 'He has no [creative] intelligence?'"

Isa. 49:5//1 Ne. 21:5: "Though Israel be not gathered." The negative particle *lōʾ* is no doubt to be read as a preposition plus pronoun *lô* "to him." This forms a nice parallel with the preceding line: "to restore Jacob to him, and that Israel be gathered to him." Modern translations generally follow this or a similar reading.

Isa. 49:8//1 Ne. 21:8: "I have heard thee." The Hebrew is literally "I answer/have answered you."

Isa. 50:4//2 Ne. 7:4: "Know how to speak a word in season."[45] The underlying Hebrew is unintelligible, and the KJV is likely wrong. It is apparently taking the word *laʿūt* to mean "to speak/do in season."

How it is to be understood is not clear. Some modern scholars, with hesitation, take the verb to mean "to aid/help/succor."

Isa. 51:4//2 Ne. 8:4: "And I will make my judgment to rest for a light of the people."[46] The metaphor "make my judgment to rest/repose for a light" is odd.[47] Many modern versions take the verb, which the KJV translates "make rest," with the beginning of the next verse, sometimes with emendation.

Isa. 54:11-12//3 Ne. 22:11-12: Some of the stones and architectural details in this verse have been rendered differently by modern scholarly translations. Compare the REB: "Storm-battered city, distressed and desolate, now I shall set your stones in the finest mortar and lay your foundations with sapphires; I shall make your battlements of red jasper and your gates of garnet; all your boundary stones will be precious jewels."

While other examples could be given,[48] the foregoing short list makes it clear that the KJV has serious deficiencies. Biblical scholarship has grown and advanced considerably since the early seventeenth century through the benefit of new archaeological, textual, and linguistic evidence and through improved methods of study and analysis. The developments are in their own way as revolutionary as those in the sciences, such as in astronomy, physics, chemistry, or medicine. While its language is elegant and the meaning of the original texts is adequately conveyed in many places, the KJV has been superseded, like many of the scientific theories of its age. The BoM conserves unacceptable translations of the KJV now clearly recognized as such from the stance of modern research. If the former were a translation from an ancient text, one would expect it to transcend the limitations of the KJV and even the limitations of modern scholars who still find a number of the noted passages insoluble.

4. DISPARITIES WITH HEBREW LANGUAGE, TEXT, AND STYLE

Some variants reveal a dependence on the English text in ways other than those examined so far. These readings show, on the one hand, an unfamiliarity with Hebrew language, text, style, and context and, on the other, an attachment to the KJV. Three types of variants are of concern here: those reflecting ambiguities of English terminology that do not exist in Hebrew, those showing an ignorance of the meanings of Hebrew words and syntax, and those which upset the smooth poetic style of the Hebrew text.[49]

1. *Variants developing from English polysemy:* There are several cases where the same English word appears in both the KJV and BoM but in the BoM has a meaning different from the underlying Hebrew. In these cases the surface similarity to the English reading but dissimilarity to the Hebrew reveals that the variant comes from revision of the English text. The treatment of italicized words (Part 2, above) presented two examples of this: the word "for" as a preposition in Isaiah 13:3 and a conjunction in 2 Ne. 23:3 and "wherefore" as an interrogative in Isa. 50:2 and a conjunction in 2 Ne. 7:2. These two examples require different underlying Hebrew terms and texts. Other examples can be added:

Isa. 2:10, 19, 21//2 Ne. 12:10, 19, 21: The KJV reads in the three verses: "for fear of the Lord, and for the glory of his majesty." The BoM reads in v. 10: "for the fear of the Lord and the glory of his majesty shall smite thee"; in v. 19: "for the fear of the Lord shall come upon them and the glory of his majesty shall smite them"; and in v. 21: "for the fear of the Lord shall come upon them and the majesty of his glory shall smite them."[50] The word "for" which begins the phrases has different functions in the two versions. In the KJV it is a preposition meaning "because of" and is syntactically part of the previously described action of entering into and hiding in the rocks (see the beginning of vv. 10, 19, 21). In the BoM it is a conjunction, which introduces a syntactically complete phrase with its own verb. Though the English word is the same, two different Hebrew terms are necessary. The Hebrew behind the MT is the preposition *mippĕnê*; the BoM requires a conjunction such as *kî*.[51]

Isa. 5:4//2 Ne. 15:4: This case is like that in Isa. 50:2//2 Ne. 7:2, already noted above but not connected with italicized words. The KJV reads: "Wherefore when I looked that it should bring forth grapes, brought it forth wild grapes?" The BoM's last verb and subject switched places creating a statement: "it brought forth wild grapes." The "wherefore" in the KJV is an interrogative; it translates the Hebrew *maddûa^c* "why." This Hebrew term cannot be taken as the conjunction "wherefore" (="therefore") as in the BoM reading.[52]

Isa. 10:10//2 Ne. 20:10: The KJV reads: "As my hand hath found the kingdoms of the idols." The BoM has a verb which looks similar but has an entirely different meaning: "As my hand hath founded the kingdoms of the idols." The BoM variant is so minor that it may be an English dictation, transcription, or copying error (cf. IVT-1, 49, 114-15). But observe that the idiom of a hand "finding" kingdoms is not a natural English expression. This may have led to an intentional alteration. If so, it is significant since the Hebrew verb underlying "found" in the KJV is *māṣāʾ*, whereas the BoM reading requires *yāsad* ("to found") or a synonym.

Isa. 14:19//2 Ne. 24:19: The KJV reads: "*and as* the raiment of those that are slain." The BoM has: "and the remnant of those that are slain." The underlying words are different: the Hebrew behind the KJV is *lĕbûš,* while the word for the BoM would be *šĕʾār, šĕʾērît* or a synonym. It is possible that this is an English dictation, transcription, or copying error. At the same time, the proximity of italicized words, one of which is deleted, suggests that the change is intentional. The appearance of "remnant" in v. 22 may have suggested the replacement term (cf. IVT-1, 59, 114-15).

Isa. 29:19//2 Ne. 27:30: The KJV reads: "The meek also shall increase *their* joy in the Lord." The BoM reads: "And the meek also shall increase and their joy shall be in the Lord." Though both texts have the word "increase," they require two different Hebrew words. The verb behind the KJV, *wĕyāsĕpû*, is transitive and takes the term *śimḥâ* ("joy") as a direct object. Quite literally it means "they shall add joy." This verb is not used intransitively in the sense of "increase" with reference to the subject, as in the BoM. Another Hebrew verb must be used (e.g., *rbh*). A further sign that this revises the KJV is that the italicized pronoun "their" seems associated with the variant. The BoM reading also upsets the parallelism in the poetry (see below).

Isa. 48:3//1 Ne. 20:3: The KJV reads "and I shewed them; I did *them* suddenly." The BoM reads: "and I shewed them, I did shew them suddenly." The BoM has the word "did" as in the KJV but requires a different underlying Hebrew term. The KJV translates the verb *ʿāśîtî* "I did, performed, acted," as an independent verb. The word "did" in the BoM is not independent but an auxiliary with a following infinitive "shew." The underlying Hebrew would be *hirʾîtîm* ("I showed them"), or better, *hišmaʿtîm* ("I announced them"), the verb which KJV translates "shew" in vv. 3 and 5.[53] A further indication that this variant is English-based is that it occurs next to a word italicized in the KJV.

Isa. 48:16//1 Ne. 20:16: The KJV reads: "from the time that it was, there *am* I"; the BoM: "from the time that it was declared have I spoken." In the BoM the passive participle "declared" is appended after the existing verb "was." This is not possible in Hebrew, which in this case has the infinitive plus pronoun *hĕyôtah* ("it was"). The BoM reading requires replacement of this word with an entirely different Hebrew verb (e.g., *huggad* or *huggĕdâ*). The italicized word "am" is likely part of the motivation for the change. The stimulus for the idea of "declaration" comes from earlier in the chapter in vv. 3, 5, 6, 14.[54]

Isa. 50:2//2 Ne. 7:2: The KJV reads: "I make the rivers a wilderness: their fish stinketh, because *there is* no water"; the BoM: "I make their rivers a wilderness and their fish to stink because the waters are dried up." There are two examples of variants based on English polysemy here. First, the verb "make." In the BoM this serves double-duty, taking both the noun "rivers" and the noun "fish" (with its infinitive "to stink") as objects. This is not possible in Hebrew; the verb *śym,* that lies behind "make" in the KJV, cannot be used as an auxiliary verb with an infinitive ("to stink") to form a causative construction.[55] The BoM needs a separate verb for this such as *ʾabʾîś* ("I cause [something] to stink"). If the BoM text were a translation, one would expect the rendition of separate verbs: "I make their rivers a wilderness, I cause their fish to stink." Similarly, the usage of "because" shows that the English text is being revised. The underlying Hebrew is *mēʾên mayim* ("because there is no water"). The preposition *mē-* (*min*), literally "from," which underlies "because" in the KJV, cannot underlie the BoM since the syntax of the larger clause does not allow for use of the preposition *mē-*. Another word must be used (e.g., *kî* or the simple conjunction *w-*). For further discussion of this passage, see example 23 in Part 6.

Isa. 51:4//2 Ne. 8:4: The KJV reads: "and I will make my judgment to rest for a light of the people." The BoM in the P manuscript and 1830 edition reads: "and I will make my judgment to rest for a light thing of the people."[56] The KJV properly translates the Hebrew word *ʾôr* "light." This does not include the semantic range of lightness in terms of weight. One can compare KJV Isa. 49:6, "Is it a light thing ...?" where the Hebrew term is *nāqēl* (a verb).

2. *Lack of understanding Hebrew syntax and semantics:* This category, similar in some respects to the foregoing, involves cases where vari-

ants create a text markedly at odds with the word order or agreement in the Hebrew text or where the meaning of Hebrew words does not appear to be known. Two cases have already been discussed in detail (see Part 2) in which deletion of italics led to word order and grammatical construction that are notably different from the existing Hebrew text (Isa. 51:17//2 Ne. 8:17: "the dregs of the cup of trembling, *and* wrung *them* out" > "the dregs of the cup of trembling rung [sic] out"; and Isa. 54:5//3 Ne. 22:5: "For thy Maker *is* thine husband" > "For thy Maker, thine husband"). In another case a noun disagrees in gender with the context of the Hebrew (Isa. 51:19//2 Ne. 8:19: "These [feminine] two *things* [feminine] are come [feminine] unto thee" > "These two sons [masculine] are come unto thee").

An additional example, similar to the last mentioned, is in Isa. 5:9//2 Ne. 15:9. The KJV reads: "many houses shall be desolate, *even* great and fair, without inhabitant." The BoM reads: "many houses shall be desolate, and great and fair cities, without inhabitant." The adjectives "fair and great" in the Hebrew (*gĕdōlîm wĕṭôbîm*) agree with the masculine plural noun "houses" (*bāttîm*) in the first clause. The noun "cities" (*ᶜārîm*) is feminine and requires adjectives with different endings.[57]

The BoM manifests an unfamiliarity with Hebrew terminology in 2 Ne. 12:9. The KJV reads: "And the mean man boweth down, and the great man humbleth himself" (Isa. 2:9). The previous verse speaks of the people's idolatry, so their humility in v. 9 seems to pose a contradiction. The BoM reading suits the context better. The P and 1830 texts read: "and the mean man boweth down, and the great man humbleth himself not." The Pc adds "not" after "boweth," apparently for consistency.[58] The problem is that, in the Hebrew, negatives are not needed. The "bowing" and "humbling" are themselves negative in character. Wildberger's commentary, which renders the verbs in the past tense, translates: "Then the human being was bowed down and the man was brought low."[59] The NJPS similarly, though in the future tense, translates: "But man shall be humbled, and mortal brought low." The same verbs are found in Isa. 5:15 where the KJV renders the negative connotation more suitably: "And the mean man shall be brought down, and the mighty man shall be humbled." Compare the verbs in 2:11, 17. Although the BoM seems to react to the inadequate translation of the KJV, it does not realize that the problem is in the rendition of the Hebrew verbs. The ironic thing is that the existence of negative particles in the original text would have created the very contextual problem that the BoM seeks to solve.

3. *Interruption of poetic style:* A characteristic feature of ancient Hebrew poetry, which is found in works such as the Psalms, Proverbs, Job, as well as in many of the prophetic works including Isaiah, is parallelism. This is where a line immediately following another echoes or reflects in some way the thought of the previous line. Parallelistic lines most often occur in pairs; a couplet of this sort is called a bicolon. Sometimes three lines are parallel (a tricolon). Less frequently four or more lines are coordinated in this way. Each grouping of parallel lines is called a strophe. An example of a simple bicolon is found in Isa. 40:31: "They shall run and not be weary, / they shall walk and not faint."[60] "Running" is paralleled by "walking," "being weary" by "fainting," and negative particles appear in both lines.[61]

Several variants in the BoM produce texts that are poetically less elegant than the original Hebrew. This indicates that they are secondary and fits with the thesis that the text is a revision of the KJV. A sampling of cases follows:

Isa. 10:13//2 Ne. 20:13: The KJV reads: "By the strength of my hand I have done *it,* / and by my wisdom: for I am prudent."[62] Here "by my wisdom" parallels "by the strength of my hand," and "for I am prudent" parallels (at least grammatically) "I have done it." In this case the word "my hand" has no parallel but is balanced by inserting the conjunction rendered "for." The BoM has a different word order: "By the strength of my hand and by my wisdom I have done these things, for I am prudent." If we attempt to divide this as a poetic strophe, it appears that the nouns have to be assigned to the first line and the verbs to the second. The BoM reading thus lacks a parallelistic structure. It seems that a motivation for the variant in the BoM is the italicized word "*it.*" This connects the variant specifically with the English text.

Isa. 13:17//2 Ne. 23:17: The KJV reads: "which shall not regard silver, / and *as for* gold, they shall not delight in it."[63] Here "gold" is parallel to "silver," "regard" to "delight in it," and negative particles appear in both lines (the relative pronoun "which" at the beginning is negligible in this analysis). The BoM reads: "which shall not regard silver and gold, nor they shall not delight in it."[64] This puts the word "gold" in the first poetic line and parallelism between the metals does not therefore exist. The bicolon is consequently less artistic than in the Hebrew version. The problem was clearly created by the removal of italicized words.

Isa. 14:11//2 Ne. 24:11: One matter of Hebrew verse that is debated is whether it has meter. Its rhythm is not the same as in western poetry, but patterns appear. The foregoing examples (in the MT) are cases where each poetic line can be analyzed as having three word-stress units, yielding a 3 + 3 pattern. Sometimes, especially in literature connected with lament, a pattern of 3 + 2 appears. This pattern is found for the most part in Isa. 14:4b-21, a lament for the king of Babylon. One bicolon of interest is v. 11a: "Thy pomp is brought down to the grave, / *and* the noise of thy viols." The 3 + 2 pattern can be seen by looking at the distribution of Hebrew words: *hûrad šĕʾôl gĕʾônekā / hemyat nĕbālêkā.* The BoM reading does not follow this pattern: "Thy pomp is brought down to the grave, the noise of thy viols is not heard." Converted to Hebrew, this would read *hûrad šĕʾôl gĕʾônekā / hemyat nĕbālêkā lōʾ nišmĕʿâ.* The pattern here is 3 + 3 (counting *lōʾ,* the negative particle, as a single unit with the verb). Even though some verses in this lament do not have a 3 + 2 pattern, the tendency is toward it; this suggests that the MT is correct. Further inspection makes it clear that the BoM text is secondary and a revision of the English: it has deleted the italicized word "*and.*" This left the second clause, "the noise of thy viols," hanging. Joseph Smith added the verbal phrase "is not heard" to complete the sense.

Isa. 2:12-16//2 Ne. 12:12-16: These verses display a neat poetic pattern in the Hebrew. Here is the Hebrew text with the KJV translation:

A. *kî yôm lyhwh ṣĕbāʾôt*	For the day of the LORD of hosts *shall be*
B. *ʿal kol gēʾeh wārām*	upon every *one that* is proud and lofty,
wĕʿal kol-niśśāʾ wĕšāpēl	and upon every *one that is* lifted up; and he shall be brought low:
C. *wĕʿal kol-ʾarzê hallĕbānôn*	and upon all the cedars of Lebanon,
<*hārāmîm wĕhanniśśāʾîm*>	<*that are* high and lifted up,>

wĕᶜal kol-ʾallônê habbāšān	and upon all the oaks of Bashan,
D. *wĕᶜal kol-hehārîm hārāmîm*	and upon all the high moutains,
wĕᶜal kol-haggĕbāᶜôt hanniśśāʾôt	and upon all the hills *that are* lifted up,
E. *wĕᶜal kol-migdāl gābōah*	and upon every high tower,
wĕᶜal kol-ḥômâ bĕṣûrâ	and upon every fenced wall,
F. *wĕᶜal kol-ʾoniyyôt taršîš*	and upon all the ships of Tarshish,
wĕᶜal kol-sĕkiyyôt haḥemdâ	and upon all pleasant pictures.

Each alphabetic letter designates a strophe. (A) is a monocolon which introduces the series. All of the other strophes are bicola except for (C). The middle line of (C) is probably secondary because bicola appear elsewhere in the series and because this line does not contain the pattern *w-* ("and") + *ᶜal* ("upon") followed by *kol-* ("all/every") and then two words.[65]

It has been argued that the corresponding BoM verses, which have significant variants, are ancient because they manifest poetic parallelism (see IVT-2, 169; IVT-1, 25-26). This argument does not hold. The truth is, the BoM variants break up the neat parallelistic structure of the Hebrew. The BoM text may be laid out as follows (the strophes unique to the BoM are marked with the letters X, Y, and Z, and variants are in bold):

A. For the day of the Lord of hosts **soon cometh**
X. upon **all nations**
yea, upon every one,
B. **yea, upon the** proud and lofty,
and upon every one **which** is lifted up, and he shall be brought low,
Y. **yea,** and **the day of the Lord shall come**
C. upon all the cedars of Lebanon,
for they are high and lifted up,
and upon all the oaks of Bashan,
D. and upon all the high mountains
and upon all the hills,
Z. **and upon all the nations which** are lifted up,
and upon every people,

E. and upon every high tower,
   and upon every fenced wall,
F. **and upon all the ships of the sea**
   and upon all the ships of Tarshish,
   and upon all **the** pleasant pictures.

The additional bicola, (X) and (Z), appear to fit the requirements of Hebrew parallelism in that each second line echoes the first. In fact, they are at odds with the larger pattern seen in the MT. Bicolon (X) does not have the pattern of *w-* + *ᶜal* + *kol* + two terms. Its first line, to convert it schematically to Hebrew, would have only *ᶜal* (no *w-*), *kol*, and one term. The second line is even less apt, having *w-* (for "yea"?), *ᶜal*, and only *kol* (for "every one"), with no word following.[66] Bicolon (Z) similarly, while having the MT pattern in the first line, has only a single term rather than two at the end of the second. Other variants in the passage do not match the neat MT pattern, the first line of (B) lacking the term *kol* "all" and a second term missing at the end of the second line of (D). In addition, (F) has an extra line which makes the strophe a tricolon, inconsistent with the other strophes. It should also be noted that the BoM's unique monocolon (Y) breaks up the flow of the passage. All in all, the BoM text is less consistent and less structured than in the MT, nor can it be claimed that its text "enhances the parallels found in the poetry" (IVT-2, 169). Since the MT text reads so smoothly against the BoM's, the latter must be secondary. It is highly unlikely that scribal omission has occurred to produce the MT (cf. IVT-1, 25).

The BoM variants here can be explained as modifications of the KJV text, especially where there are italics. In (A) "*shall be*" is changed and expanded to "soon cometh upon all nations." The first line of (B), "upon every *one that is* proud and lofty," is expanded to "upon all nations, yea, upon every one, yea upon the proud and lofty."[67] This produces the very problematic strophe (X) and the deficient first line of BoM (B). A minor change of the italicized "*that*" to "which" is made in (B) line 2. The line "*that are* high and lifted up" in (C) becomes the rationale clause "for they are high and lifted up." And in (D) the line "and upon all the hills *that are* lifted up" is expanded to read "upon all the hills, and upon all the nations which are lifted up, and upon every people," which creates (Z). The variant (Y), not connected with italics, is explicable as a revision of the KJV which devotes six words to translating the last single word of (B): *wēšāpēl* "and he shall be brought low." This English translation interrupts the flow of the passage. The added phrase at (Y) acts as a resumptive repetition of line (A) to put the reader back on course. Such a repetition is not necessary in the Hebrew.[68] Finally, the extra line in (F), on the basis of evidence to be considered in Part 6, is clearly an addition.

One might still ask why parallelistic bicola at (X) and (Z), as ungainly as they are, appear at all if this is a revision made by Smith. While he was not a scholar of Semitic languages and the Bible, he seemed to have absorbed a sense for parallelism from the Bible. For instance, parallelistic structures are scattered throughout the Doctrine and Covenants.[69]

In summary, the three classes of variants discussed in this section show various ways in which the BoM Isaiah is not consistent with the Hebrew text in semantics, syntax, or style.[70] This complements the evidence in the first three sections of this essay in two ways, showing how the BoM Isaiah is connected to the KJV English and how distant it is from Hebrew.

5. THE SECONDARY NATURE OF VARIANTS IN THE BOM ISAIAH

Textual criticism uses the terms "plus" and "minus" to refer to elements that a text has or lacks vis-à-vis another text. One of the striking features of the BoM text as compared to the KJV/MT is that it has many more pluses than minuses.[71] Thus, a distinctive feature of the BoM text is that it is a fuller text. Several of the pluses appear to be secondary additions because they explain, clarify, or add definition to the text around them. In one case, there is objective proof that a plus is secondary, as we will see. That these are secondary will circumstantially support the thesis that the BoM text is a revision of the KJV.

The supplemental character is evident in the language used in some pluses and in how they relate to their contexts. Some begin with the focusing or resumptive term "yea" and define or carry further a previous thought, once it anticipates something to come;[72] (a) Isa. 2:5 reads: "O house of Jacob, come ye and let us walk in the light of the Lord." 2 Ne. 12:5 uniquely has after this: "yea, come, for ye have all gone astray every one to his wicked ways." The reason this seems secondary is that it repeats the verb "come" and explains the reason for the call to walk in the Lord's light. (b) The first part of 2 Ne. 24:2, which is the same as KJV Isa. 14:2, says that "the people shall take them (i.e., Israel) and bring them to their place." An ensuing plus notes where this will be and what the people will do: "yea, from far unto the ends of the earth, and they shall return to their lands of promise." (On this further, see Part 6, example 17.) (c) We have already examined the list of persons, places, and objects to suffer on the "day of the Lord" in Isa. 2:12-16 (above, Part 4). This is introduced with the phrase, "For the day of the Lord of Hosts shall be/soon cometh" (Isa. 2:12//2 Ne. 12:12). The BoM has a plus in v. 13 that repeats this language, "Yea, and the day of the Lord shall come." Poetic considerations already noted, along with use of the term "yea" and the repetitiveness, show this to be an addition. (d) 1 Ne. 20:14 (//Isa. 48:14) varies slightly from the KJV by saying that certain persons have had "things" declared "unto them." This is soon followed by the plus, "yea, and he will fulfil his word which he hath declared by them." This expands on and somewhat explains the declarative matter in the previous phrase. (e) In one case, a clause with "yea" precedes a passage to which it relates. Before the beginning of KJV/MT Isa. 50:1, 2 Ne. 7:1 has the following: "Yea, for thus saith the Lord, Have I put thee away or have I cast thee off forever, for [thus saith the Lord ...]." This can be seen as an anticipatory explanation for the questions about divorce that follow. Another sign of secondariness is the repetition of the phrase "thus saith the Lord" of the KJV/MT v. 1. (f) In Isa. 29//2 Ne. 27, a few phrases insert the word "yea," sometimes with accompanying words: e.g., KJV: "shall be as a dream of a night vision. It shall even be as when" (Isa. 29:7-8) > "shall be as a dream of a night vision, yea, it shall be unto them even as unto" (2 Ne. 27:3).[73]

Pluses that begin with the conjunction "for" also display a secondary quality: (a) The plus in 2 Ne. 12:5, noted in the preceding paragraph, uses this conjunction in addition to the adverb "yea." It provides the reason for following God. (b) 2 Ne. 7:1, noted above, uses "for" twice to introduce the clause "thus saith the Lord." (c) Isa. 13:22 ends by saying that Babylon's destruction will be swift. The plus in 2 Ne. 23:22 explains and qualifies what will happen to God's chosen people: "for I will destroy her speedily, yea, for I will be merciful unto my people, but the wicked shall perish." Note here the appearance of "yea" and the twice-occurring "for." These terms provide a two-pronged explanation. (d) In Isa. 29//2 Ne. 27, "for" and some accompanying words embellish the text: e.g., the phrase in v. 9, "cry ye out, and cry," is turned into an explanatory clause in the BoM: "for ye shall cry out and cry" (2 Ne. 27:4). The next verse alters the statement that God "hath closed your eyes" (Isa. 29:10) to an explanatory "for, behold, ye have closed your eyes" (2 Ne. 27:5). The theologically more pleasing reading further indicates its secondariness.[74]

The plus "and it shall come to pass" looks secondary: (a) 2 Ne. 12:10 (see Part 4) uses the word "for" as a conjunction instead of a preposition. The last part of the verse reads: "for the fear of the Lord and the glory of his majesty shall smite thee." The next verse (v. 11) in the KJV reads, "The lofty looks of man shall be humbled. ..." The two verses are somewhat disjointed syntactically. The plus "And it shall come to pass that" in the BoM provides a connection between the verses. (b) Isa. 14:3-4 in the KJV are a syntactically interdependent whole. A variant in the parallel 2 Ne. 24:3 makes this verse independent. Verse 4 is consequently left syntactically incomplete. Hence, "And it shall come to pass in that day," resuming the first part of v. 3, has been added to v. 4 to make it complete. (See Part 6, example 18, for a full discussion of this variant.)[75]

In addition to certain words or phrases as markers of additions, several pluses in the BoM Isaiah define referents–e.g., subjects of verbs or objects of address–and thus appear to be secondary clarifying glosses: (a) The phrase "Therefore, thou hast forsaken thy people" in Isa. 2:6 has sometimes been judged problematic because its subject is not specified. The BoM text provides this: "Therefore, O Lord, thou hast forsaken thy people" (2 Ne. 12:6). (See further, Part 6, example 3.) (b) Isa. 2:10 reads, "Enter into the rock and hide." Who is being addressed? The BoM solves this with: "O ye wicked ones, enter into the rock and hide" (2 Ne. 12:10). (c) Isa. 48:15 reads "I, *even*, I, have spoken." Apparently in part as a reaction to the italics, but also for clarification, the BoM has: "Also saith the Lord, I the Lord, yea I have spoken" (1 Ne. 20:15). (d) The long plus at the start of 1 Ne. 21:1, which begins "And again hearken, O ye house of Israel ..." appears to define the audience intended in the phrase "Listen, O Isles ... ye people" with which the KJV and MT begin (Isa. 49:1; see Part 6, example 22). (e) The question "Is my hand shortened at all ..." in Isa. 50:2 is prefaced by the vocative "O house of Israel" in 2 Ne. 7:2.[76]

One might object to this evidence by saying that terms like "yea," "for," and "it came to pass," as well as terms defining a referent are found throughout the KJV, as are their equivalents in the MT. But consistency in style does not prove originality. The secondariness of such phrases in the BoM seems confirmed by 2 Ne. 27, which paraphrases parts of Isa. 29. Many of these pluses and variants noted in the text and the notes above are interpretive rephrasings to make Isa. 29 apply to the BoM situation, and they use the above-mentioned terms and phenomena in the reformulation.

The circumstantial evidence so far examined can be augmented with objective proof that at least one substantial plus in the BoM is an addition. Isa. 49:25 is cited in two places, 1 Ne. 21:25 and 2 Ne. 6:17, and the versions are different from each other:

Isa. 49:25 (KJV)	*1 Ne. 21:25*	*2 Ne. 6:17*
But thus saith the Lord, Even the captives of the mighty shall be taken away, and the prey of the terrible shall be delivered: for	But thus saith the Lord, Even the **captive** of the mighty shall be taken away, and the prey of the terrible shall be delivered, for	But thus saith the Lord, Even the captives of the mighty shall be taken away, and the pray of the terrible shall be delivered, for **the mighty God shall deliver his covenant people, for thus saith the Lord,**
I will contend with him that contendeth with thee, and I will save thy children	I will contend with him that contendeth with thee, and I will save thy children.	I will contend with them that contendeth with thee.

The plus in 2 Ne. 6:17 is secondary since the version in 1 Ne. 21:25 correlates exactly with the KJV text except for a minor difference at the word "captive." 1 Nephi 21:25 also has the last clause which 2 Ne. 6:17 lacks. It is doubtful that the plus would be dropped from both the other texts or that the last part of the verse would be added to them in exactly the same way.[77]

The accretion in 2 Ne. 6:17 confirms some of the observations made above and implicates other pluses. For instance, the addition contains an explanatory phrase with the conjunction "for": "for thus saith the Lord." It also uses the preexisting "for" to introduce the first part of the gloss. This correlates with the argument earlier that pluses with this conjunction are secondary.

The addition also has the phrase "thus saith the Lord," suggesting that the nearby plus in 2 Ne. 7:1 is secondary since it uses similar language: "Yea, for thus saith the Lord, Have I put thee away or have I cast thee off forever, for. ..." It was already suggested that this plus is secondary because of the appearance of "yea" and the twice-appearing "for." In the next verse, the vocative "O house of Israel" clarifies the audience of the following question. Thus, several indications of secondariness converge in these verses.[78]

An interesting problem arises around the plus in 2 Ne. 6:17. Though the verse has an addition, the text gives no explicit indication that it is to be seen as a secondary. Rather, it appears to be intended as a direct citation from Isaiah. It is true that the citation of Isa. 49 is broken up with interpretation in this chapter. 2 Ne. 6:6-7 cite Isa. 49:22-23, after which comes Jacob's interpretation (2 Ne. 6:8-15), which is then followed by further citation of Isaiah at v. 16. Moreover, the interpretive section paraphrases or makes reference to key ideas and terms in the passage cited (cf. vv. 12-13 against vv. 6-7). But this is not necessarily evidence that the material in the citation itself is to be considered paraphrased. Note how the text speaks of the Isaiah material. Jacob says in 6:4-6a that he "will read you the words of Isaiah ... the words which I shall read are they which Isaiah spake concerning all the house of Israel...now these are the words." The citation follows in vv. 6-7. After the interpretive section, without a new introduction, the quotation continues from 2 Ne. 6:16 to 8:25. This has no break and no clear interpretive comments. After he finishes, Jacob says, "I have read these things," i.e., the passages from Isaiah (2 Ne. 9:1). Too, the text of Isaiah in 2 Ne. 6:16-8:25 in style and in type and distribution of variants is the same in this section as in other passages where Isaiah is cited (cf. 2 Ne. 12-24 and the other chapters listed in the statistical table above). Hence, there is every reason to believe that the citation in 2

Ne. 6-8 is intended as exactly that: a quote without elaboration or secondary expansion.[79]

This means that there is a clear contradiction in the citation at 1 Ne. 21:25 and 2 Ne. 6:17. Note further that just like the citation in 2 Ne. 6-8, the Isaiah text in 1 Ne. 21 claims to be a direct citation of Isaiah like that in 2 Ne. 6. In the introduction in 1 Ne. 19:23-24, Nephi says that he "did read unto them that which was written by the prophet Isaiah." He says to the people, "Hear ye the words of the prophet ... for after this manner hath the prophet written." Like Jacob at the end of his citation, Nephi said that he "had read these things which were engraven upon the plates of brass" (1 Ne. 22:1).

How is this textual clash to be explained? In view of the larger evidence in this essay, it appears that Smith was simply inconsistent in his citation and revision of Isaiah. At one point he cites the verse without elaboration, in the other he cites it with modification. He did not apparently check the later citation against the earlier one because of lack of time, difficulty in sorting back through the manuscript, forgetfulness, or because he felt it unnecessary. The divergent citations suggest that Smith dictated the Isaiah passage directly from the KJV making modifications as he went rather than from some prewritten, revised form of Isaiah (see also n50).[80]

As I explained at the beginning of this section, the BoM, when compared to the KJV and MT, is a fuller text. It has few minuses but many pluses. Its pluses (vis-à-vis the MT/KJV) are not found in other existing ancient versions (see Part 6). This fact alone could lead to the hypothesis that the pluses are secondary. The foregoing evidence gives more detailed reasons why several of these are secondary. In many cases, this judgment is confirmed by a convergence of other sorts of evidence. All of this is consistent with the view that the BoM Isaiah is a revision of the KJV.

6. SUPPOSED PROOFS FOR THE ANTIQUITY OF THE BOM ISAIAH

A few researchers have sought to verify the antiquity of the BoM Isaiah by showing that some variants correlate with ancient versions and manuscripts and that others reflect features of Hebrew language and style.[81] The most extensive recent work of this sort has been done by John Tvedtnes in a FARMS Preliminary Report (TVT-1). He examined the variant readings of the BoM against Hebrew manuscripts, including the large Isaiah scroll from Qumran (1QIsa[a]), and against ancient translations including the Greek Septuagint (LXX), the Aramaic Targum, the Syriac Peshitta, the Old Latin, and Latin Vulgate.[82] His work is valuable for making researchers aware of possible correlations. However, the proposed similarities do not uphold the conclusion that the BOM Isaiah comes from an ancient source.

Because of space limits, I will review here the thirty-six cases that Tvedtnes selected from his Preliminary Report for publication in the proceedings of a conference on "Isaiah and the Prophets" at Brigham Young University held in 1982 (IVT-2). These provide a sufficient sample because he chose them not only "on the basis of the ease with which [he] can explain them to non-Semiticists" but also because of "the favorable light which they shed on the Book of Mormon translation." They include the most probative examples for his case. (For a brief discussion of his other examples, see n150.) The discussion here will deal mainly with Tvedtnes's arguments but will also bring in observations of other researchers on the same passages when pertinent. I begin with the example that has been thought to show most clearly the antiquity of the Book of Mormon text (1), then the other cases in biblical order (2-26), ending with ten instances where a plus of the conjunction "and" is thought to be supported by ancient texts (27).

(1) *Isa. 2:16//2 Ne. 12:16.* The KJV reads: "And upon all the ships of Tarshish, and upon all pleasant pictures." The BoM has an extra phrase or line: "And upon all the ships of the sea, and upon all the ships of Tarshish, and upon all the pleasant pictures." Remarkably, the Septuagint and Targum provide a parallel to the extra line at the beginning of the BoM verse. The Greek reads: *kai epi pan ploion thalassēs kai epi pasan thean ploiōn kallous* "And upon every ship of the sea, and upon every view of ships of beauty." The Targum reads: *wĕᶜal kol nāḥătê sĕpînê yammăʾ wĕᶜal kol dĕšāran bĕbîrānyāt šiprāʾ* "And upon all those who go down in ships of the sea, and upon all those that dwell in palaces of beauty."[83]

While many have cited this passage as an instance where ancient biblical versions appear to support the BoM,[84] the parallel is specious. The MT two-line verse is the original, and the Targum and LXX are interpretive variants of that formulation. Several times in the Targum the term Tarshish is rendered "sea." Instead of the proper noun, one finds simply *yammă*ʾ "sea" (Ezek. 27:12; Jonah 1:3; 4:2). Sometimes it is rendered *mĕdînaṯ yammă*ʾ "city/country of the sea" (Isa. 23:6, 10 for the phrase *bat taršîš;* Isa. 66:19). The phrase *soḥărê taršîš* "merchants of Tarshish" is rendered *taggārê yammă*ʾ "merchants of the sea" (Ezek. 38:13). The specific phrase *ʾoniyyôt taršîš* "ships of Tarshish" is rendered *sĕpînê yammă*ʾ ("ships of the sea") (Isa. 23:1, 14; 60:9; Ezek. 27:25; the Isaiah passages all preface the term with *nāḥătê,* "those who go down," as does 2:16). It should not be missed that in Isaiah the rendering of "Tarshish" as "sea" occurs everywhere the former term occurs. In other words, the Targum is interpreting "Tarshish" as "sea." It is not evidence of an original Hebrew text (i.e., *Vorlage*) with the word "sea" in it.

The LXX reflects this same general interpretive tendency. While it does not display a regular rendering of "Tarshish" as "sea," we do find it in one other passage. In Dan. 10:6, the LXX reads: *kai to stoma autou hōsei thalassēs,* "his mouth (this is a mistake for *soma* "body") was like the sea"[85] for the Hebrew *ûgĕwiyyātô kĕtaršîš,* "his body was like chrysolite/beryl" (here *taršîš* refers to a precious stone, as in Ex. 28:20; 39:13; Ezek. 1:16; etc.).[86]

In view of this evidence, there is no real textual support for the BoM Isaiah variant; the LXX and Targum develop from a text like the MT. So how does the BoM Isaiah come to have a phrase that is so similar to an interpretive reading in the LXX and Targum? It turns out that the understanding of the phrase "ships of Tarshish" as "ships of the sea" was well-known in British and American Bible commentaries in the decades prior to publication of the BoM. The rendering appears in Miles Coverdale's 1535 translation: "upon all shippes of the see [=sea], and upon everythinge y[t] [=that] is glorious and pleasaunt to loke upon."[87]

John Wesley comments on Isa. 2:16 in his *Explanatory Notes upon the Old Testament* published in 1765 (Bristol, Eng.): "*Tarshish*–The ships of the sea, as that word is used, *Psal.* xlviii. 7. whereby you fetched riches from the remote parts of the world."[88] This interpretation is reproduced in Matthew Poole's *Annotations upon the Holy Bible* published in 1801 (Edinburgh).[89]

William Lowth's *Commentary upon the Old and New Testaments: The Prophets,* published in 1727 (London), provided English speakers with the reading of the Septuagint: "... 'ships of Tarshish' signify in Scripture any trading or merchant ships. Accordingly, here the Septuagint render[s] the words, 'ships of the sea,' as our old English translation does, Psal. xlviii 6."[90] John Fawcett cites Lowth's interpretation in his *Devotional Family Bible* published in 1811 (London).[91] The many pre-1829 editions of Thomas Scott's *The Holy Bible Containing the Old and New Testaments* also cite Lowth's comment.[92]

Joseph Smith could have picked up the phrase from any one of these commentaries or, as is far more likely, from sermons he heard or conversations he had on biblical subjects with those who might have known this particular Bible "fact." Smith may have come by this bit of information specifically via Methodist influence since John Wesley's teachings provided the matrix for Methodism and Smith had an attraction to it and attended its meetings.[93]

Corroboration of the unoriginality of the BoM's unique phrase is found in the discussion on Hebrew poetry and the BoM, above (Part 4). The BoM's plus forms a tricolon with the other two lines in v. 16. This is out of place among the bicola in the rest of Isa. 2:12-16, granted the likely emendation in v. 13. Variants in 2 Ne. 12:12-14, part of the same passage, are also tied to the italics, as observed above. The BoM's unique line thus seems secondary and a modification of the English.

(2) *Isa. 2:5//2 Ne. 12:5.* The KJV has: "O house of Jacob, come ye, and let us walk in the light of the Lord." The BoM has a plus following this: "Yea, come, for ye have all gone astray every one to his wicked ways." Tvedtnes (IVT-2, 169; IVT-1, 22) says a two-part textual error must have led to the loss of the BoM's long plus here: (1) the omission of *bʾw* (which he thinks must lie behind "Yea, come") because of its similarity to the *bʾwr* in v. 4 (a type of haplography)[94] and (2) the omission of "for ye have all gone astray every one to his wicked ways" because it would begin with the same conjunction as the beginning of v. 6 (parablepsis).[95] An argument based on such invented textual error in order to provide a parallel for the BoM is highly speculative. That a plausible development can be imagined does not prove that the supposed original text ever existed. It is all the more suspect when it involves multiple stages of supposed development, such as in this particular example. In any case, it is unlikely that the error noted by Tvedtnes occurred. The BoM's plus "Yea, come ..." is resumptive; it picks up and reiterates the "come ye" earlier in the verse. Therefore, one would expect an underlying Hebrew verb to be the same as the

earlier verb, i.e., *lkw,* not *bʿw.* Tvedtnes's further argument that the plus is original because its language is similar to Isa. 53:6 is unconvincing. Smith could have added this phrase which occurs in the most famous chapter of Isaiah for Christian readers. In Part 5 above, reason is given to suspect this plus as being secondary.

(3) *Isa. 2:6//2 Ne. 12:6.* The KJV has: "Therefore, thou hast forsaken thy people the house of Jacob"; the BoM, "Therefore, O Lord, thou hast forsaken thy people the house of Jacob." Tvedtnes argues that the word *ky* ("therefore") may be an abbreviation *k"y* standing for *kî Yhwh* ("Therefore, O Lord") or that a text reading *ky y"* standing for *kî Yhwh* by haplography became simply *ky* (IVT-2, 168; IVT-1, 22-23). It is true that there is contextual evidence for abbreviations in ancient biblical texts.[96] But the argument in this case is only a surmise. Moreover, the versional evidence Tvedtnes refers to for supporting an abbreviation here is in error.[97] Contrary to Tvedtnes, the phrase "O Lord" can be explained as a gloss from Joseph Smith to clarify the subject of the verb "thou has forsaken," as noted in Part 5 above.

(4) *Isa. 2:11//2 Ne. 12:11.* The BoM has at the beginning of the verse the phrase "And it shall come to pass that," after which follows the equivalent of the KJV verse. Tvedtnes notes that 1QIsa[a] and the LXX are in "partial agreement" with the BoM since they have a conjunction at the beginning of the verse (lacking in the MT and KJV).[98] Partial agreement is not strong evidence, especially when it involves only a conjunction (see example 27 below). On the secondariness of the BoM plus, see Part 5 above.

(5) *Isa. 2:12-14//2 Ne. 12:12-14.* Tvedtnes argues that the variants in these BoM lines manifest Hebraic parallelistic structures and hence point to the antiquity of the BoM text (IVT-2, 169; IVT-1, 25-26). This has already been answered in Part 4 above.

(6) *Isa. 2:20//2 Ne. 12:20.* The KJV reads: "In that day a man shall cast his idols of silver and his idols of gold which they made *each one* for himself to worship to the moles. ..." The BoM has the relative clause with a singular verb: "which he hath made for himself to worship." The Codex Alexandrinus of the LXX has a singular verb, *ha epoiesēn proskunein* ("which he made to worship"); so also the Vulgate: *quae fecerat sibi ut adoraret* ("which he had made for himself so that he may worship").[99] Nevertheless, the BoM's variant derives from modification of the KJV. The text is numerically inconsistent: "a man ... they ...

each one for himself." Smith could have simply smoothed out the English. There are several other cases where an attempt to establish consistency can be discerned in the BoM Isaiah: "Say ye to the righteous, that *it shall be* well *with him*: for they shall eat the fruit of their doings" > "Say unto the righteous that it is well with them ..." (Isa. 3:10//2 Ne. 13:10); "Woe unto the wicked! *it shall be* ill *with him*" > "Wo unto the wicked for they shall perish" (Isa. 3:11//2 Ne. 13:11; cf. the previous verse and, in v. 11, "reward of his hands" > "their hands"); "... for them that are escaped of Israel. And it shall come to pass, *that he that is* left in Zion, and *he that* remaineth in Jerusalem" > "... And it shall come to pass [that] them [later editions: they] that are left in Zion and remaineth in Jerusalem" (Isa. 4:2-3//2 Ne. 14:3); "And in that day they shall roar ... and if *one* look unto the land" > "... and if they look unto the land" (Isa. 5:30//2 Ne. 15:30); "and *it* shall return" > "and they shall return" (Isa. 6:13//2 Ne. 16:13). All these cases of numerical smoothing are associable with KJV italicized words. The variant at 2 Ne. 12:20 is likewise associable with italics.

(7) *Isa. 3:1//2 Ne. 13:1.* The KJV reads: "For behold, the Lord, the LORD of Hosts doth take away from Jerusalem and from Judah the stay [*maš*^{c}*ēn*] and the staff [*maš*^{c}*ēnâ*], the whole stay [*miš*^{c}*an*] of bread and the whole stay [*miš*^{c}*an*] of water." For the last phrase, the BoM reads: "the whole staff of bread and the whole stay of water." It is argued that the BoM is more "poetic" here, and hence, so the implication is, more original and ancient. It is also argued that the MT originally had *maš*^{c}*ēnâ* "staff" (in construct state) in the phrase "stay of bread," which by scribal error became *miš*^{c}*an* "stay."[100] The first argument does not hold. The "stay of bread" and "stay of water" line may be secondary in the Hebrew because it does not fit the context.[101] Verses 2-4 speak of leaders; "stay" and "staff" may metaphorically refer to leaders. The "stay of bread and ... stay of water" gives the previous line a new interpretation, perhaps based on v. 7. As a gloss, its goal may not be poetic beauty but prosaic explanation.[102] The second argument does not furnish a mechanism or rationale for haplography and is conjectural. The BoM's variant could have as easily resulted from Smith's attempt to provide the text with balance and sense.

(8) *Isa. 3:10//2 Ne. 13:10.* The KJV has: "Say ye to the righteous, that *it shall be* well *with him*"; the BoM: "Say unto the righteous, that it is well with them." Tvedtnes (IVT-2, 171; IVT-1, 30-31) argues that the

appearance of the preposition "unto" in the BoM is a way of "stressing the preposition" which may have been in the text underlying the BoM reading and which the MT lacks (*ʾimrû ṣaddîq*). Support for the BoM is thought to lie in 1QIsa^{a}, the Peshitta, and the Targum,[103] which have a preposition, all *l-*, and in the next parallel MT line where "wicked" has a preposition before it. This argument appears to presume that the BoM Isaiah is offering a comparative translation that stresses differences with the KJV/MT. This does not make sense as a model of translation. The variant is altogether insignificant and is found in the BoM where prepositions do appear in the MT: 2 Ne. 8:1 (//Isa. 51:1, preposition *ʾel*) and the Decalogue of Mos. 13:13 (//Ex. 20:5, preposition *l-*).

Tvedtnes claims that the Targum's[104] reading of *ṣaddîqayyāʾ* ("righteous ones"), plural, supports the BoM plural pronoun "them," in contrast to KJV "him." The Targum may construe the text according to sense and not reflect an underlying plural term in its Hebrew tradition. The BoM's reading likely arises from a desire to establish consistency, generated in part by the five italicized words in the environment.

(9) Isa. 3:26//2 Ne. 13:26. The KJV reads: "and she *being* desolate shall sit upon the ground"; the BoM reads: "and she shall be desolate and shall sit upon the ground." It is true that the MT construed literally is like the BoM in having a finite verb in the first clause: *wĕniqqātâ lāʾāreṣ tēšēb* ("And she shall be emptied, shall sit on the ground" [NJPS]).[105] And it is true that the LXX has a conjunction before the second clause like the BoM: *kai kataleiphthēsē monē kai eis tēn gēn edaphisthēsē* ("and you will be left alone, and you will be made even with the ground").[106] But the MT and Greek do not each exactly agree with the BoM. The Greek seems interpretive in many respects, and its conjunction may be part of this interpretation. The BoM reading can be explained as a modification of the KJV. The word "*being*" in the KJV is italicized. This spawned a change to the future finite verb form "shall be" which occurs in two other cases (2 Ne. 13:6//Isa. 3:6; 2 Ne. 24:16//Isa. 14:16). With the change to a finite verb, the last phrase "shall sit upon the ground" was left awkwardly uncoordinated and without a subject. Hence, the conjunction was added. In any case, variations in the conjunction "and" are not significant (see example 27 below).

(10) *Isa. 5:30//2 Ne. 15:30.* The KJV reads "and if *one* look unto the

land," while the BoM reads "and if they look unto the land." The LXX offers doubtful support of the antiquity of the BoM (IVT-2, 171; IVT-1, 39; cf. BMCT 1:183 n476). Though it has a plural verb ("they shall look [*emblepsontai*] to the land"), it may itself be rendering as plural a singular form found in the Hebrew text (see example 13, below). The Hebrew of vv. 26-30 has reference to a nation or nations and its military forces in the singular. The LXX renders many of these as plurals. Even the KJV generally renders these as plurals. The variant in the BoM can be explained more simply as a modification of the KJV text. The context of plurals set up by the KJV in vv. 26-30 makes the singular "if one look" seem out of place. This and the italicized pronoun "*one*" provided a trigger for the change in the BoM.

(11) *Isa. 6:12//2 Ne. 16:12.* The KJV reads: "and *there be* a great forsaking in the midst of the land." The BoM has: "for there shall be a great forsaking in the midst of the land." Tvedtnes argues (IVT-2, 171; IVT-1, 42; cf. BMCT 1:185n492) that the BoM has a better rendition of the verb *rabbâ* ("be great"). This is not true. First, the KJV is, in certain respects, a legitimate rendition. It uses a finite form, contrary to what Tvedtnes says, though it is a subjunctive. All the verbs from "until" in v. 11 through v. 12 are subjunctive. Second, the KJV preserves the poetic bicolon in v. 12, whereas the BoM breaks this with its rationale clause ("for there shall be ..."). Third, neither the KJV nor the BoM represents *rabbâ* precisely. The KJV construes it as if an attributive adjective with *hāʿăzûbâ* ("great forsaking"). *Rabbâ* is a verb that, if rendered literally, should be read something like "the forsaking in the midst of the land be/shall be great" (cf. NJPS, NRSV).[107] That the BoM preserves this infelicity is a sign of its dependence on the KJV. Finally, dependence upon the KJV is further marked by the italicized words in proximity to the BoM variant. These likely provided some motivation for the change.

(12) *Isa. 9:3 (Heb. 2)//2 Ne. 19:3.* The KJV reads: "Thou has multiplied the nation *and* not increased the joy"; the BoM lacks the negative: "Thou has multiplied the nation and increased the joy." The traditional reading of the Hebrew is to take the negative particle *lōʾ (lʾ)* as the preposition and pronoun *lô* (usually written *lw*), "to him/it." This yields a positive reading similar to the BoM's: "You have magnified that nation, have given it (literally, 'to it,' as if *lô*) great joy" (so too the NJPS). The Peshitta and Targum have prepositions with pro-

nouns that agree exactly or in essence with this traditional reading (*lh*, "to him/it" and *lhwn*, "to them," respectively). Tvedtnes (IVT-2, 171-172; IVT-1, 46) says that this traditional rereading shows that in antiquity the negative was perceived to be wrong.[108] Instead of providing support for the BoM reading, this simply shows that the negative is problematic and that Smith himself could have deleted it. Observe that the BoM does not manifest the solution of the traditional Hebrew reading: it lacks the preposition and pronoun "for him/it." Part of the impetus for the variant may have been the italicized word "and" that comes just before the negative particle. But there is another difficulty in the text which has not been solved. The word *haggôy* ("the nation") also seems out of place because it does not form a good parallel with *haśśimḥâ* ("the joy") in the next line. It is likely that instead of *haggôy lōʾ* (*hgwy lʾ*), "the nation, not," the text read *haggîlâ* (*hagylh*), "the joy." This yields the nice poetically parallel text: "You have multiplied rejoicing [*haggîlâ*], you have increased joy [*haśśimḥâ*]."[109] Thus the BoM seems to retain a corrupt text.

(13) *Isa. 9:9 (Heb. 8)//2 Ne. 19:9.* The BoM has "inhabitants of Samaria," whereas the KJV has "inhabitant of Samaria." The KJV literally translates the MT's singular, *yōšēb*. Tvedtnes notes that the LXX, like the BoM, has a plural: *hoi enkathēmenoi en Samareia* ("those that dwell in Samaria"). BMCT notes further that the Peshitta and Targum have plurals (1:192n555; cf. IVT-2, 172; IVT-1, 46-47). This is not to say that the underlying Hebrew of these versions had a plural. Elsewhere the LXX has a plural where the MT has singular *yōšēb* (e.g., Isa. 5:3 [though 1QIsa[a] has the plural *yōšĕbê* here]; 8:14 [BHS notes some manuscripts have a plural]; 10:24; 20:6; 22:21; 24:17; 26:21). The Peshitta matches the MT more closely, having plurals at only a few places where the MT has a singular (Isa. 5:3; 8:14; 22:21). But it has plurals where the MT has singulars in other places (such as Judg. 1:17, 21; 3:3; Zech. 12:7, 8, 10). The Targum has a plural noun in the passages just listed for the Peshitta except for Judg. 1:17. While it cannot be denied that the Hebrew texts underlying these versions may have had a plural noun in some cases, this evidence makes it reasonable to suppose that in several places the versions construed a singular as a plural.

The BoM variant could have as easily arisen by revision of the KJV. The context already presupposes a plurality of persons with the initial phrase "all the people shall know." To say "the inhabitants of Samaria" rather than "the inhabitant of Samaria" is more idiomatically suitable in English. Other cases of smoothing the English text are observable (see example 6 above). Furthermore, the BoM often has a plural where the KJV/MT has a singular. This appears to come about in most cases to facilitate English expression: "soul" > "souls" (Isa. 3:9//2 Ne. 13:9); "blossom" > "blossoms" (Isa. 5:24//2 Ne. 15:24); "tempest" > "tempests" (Isa. 54:11//3 Ne. 22:11); cf. "iniquity" > "iniquities" (Ex. 20:5//Mos. 13:13). Note that "face" of Isa. 49:23 is once singular in 1 Ne. 21:23 and plural "faces" in 2 Ne. 6:7.[110] This last case shows objectively that such renderings are not necessarily a sign of translation. One should also not discount the possibility that in some of these cases, BoM variants are English dictation or copying mistakes.[111]

(14) *Isa. 10:29//2 Ne. 20:29:* The KJV has "Ramah," while the BoM has "Ramath." BMCT observes that the Peshitta has *rāmětāʾ* and the Targum *rāmātā,* forms that show a *-t* (=*-th*) ending for the place name.[112] This support fails because these versions generally have a form ending in *-t* where the MT has Ramah (e.g., Josh. 18:25; 1 Sam. 22:6; 25:1; 28:3; 1 Kgs. 15:17, 21, 22; Jer. 40:1; etc.). This, therefore, is a way these versions render the underlying Hebrew *rmh*. Tvedtnes's argument (IVT-2, 172; IVT-1, 50) is of a different sort. He notes that in the development of Hebrew, feminine nouns originally ended in *-at,* which later disappeared in unbound forms yielding an ending *-â* (= *-ah*). The appearance of "Ramath" (a *-t* form) appears thus to display this linguistic fact. Yet, it is not impossible that other occurrences of "Ramath" in the KJV influenced the BoM (Josh. 13:26; 19:8; Judg. 15:17).[113] It is also possible that this is a dictation or copying error.[114] The evidence is not conclusive.

(15) *Isa. 13:3//2 Ne. 23:3:* This is discussed in Part 2 with recapitulation in Part 4, above (IVT-2, 172-73; IVT-1, 52-53).

(16) *Isa. 13:22//2 Ne. 23:22:* The BoM Isaiah reads like the KJV but adds: "for I will destroy her speedily, yea, for I will be merciful unto my people, but the wicked shall perish." There is no "partial confirmation" for this BoM reading as claimed by Tvedtnes (IVT-2, 173; IVT-1, 55). The phrase *tachu erchetai kai ou chroniei* ("it will swiftly come and will not delay") in the LXX is not an added element but an interpretive translation of the last of the MT verse, *wēqārôb lābôʾ ʿittāh wěyāmêhā lōʾ yimmāšěkû,* rendered correctly in the KJV "and her time is near to

come, and her days shall not be prolonged."[115] Some LXX manuscripts appear to have an appended phrase: *kai (hai) hēmerai autēs* (or: *autōn) ou mē ephelkusthōsin*, "and may her [their] days not be drawn out."[116] This recapitulates the last Hebrew line and is not like the BoM plus. The Qumran Isaiah text 1QIsa[a] has only the adverb *ʿôd* ("more") at the end but as part of the last line yielding "her days shall no longer be prolonged." It does not correlate with the BoM plus.[117]

Tvedtnes and BMCT otherwise argue that parablepsis has occurred here, i.e., a scribe's eye skipped from the *kî* ("for") that is found at the beginning of the BoM's extra element to the *kî* ("for") at the beginning of 14:1. This is plausible but still a conjecture. The BoM phrase may be a secondary gloss beginning with the explanatory "for" and tying together the foregoing theme of destruction and desolation and the following theme of mercy (see Part 5 above).

(17) *Isa. 14:2//2 Ne. 24:2:* The first part of the KJV verse reads: "And the people shall take them and bring them to their place, and the house of Israel shall possess them." The BoM has the following plus after "their place": "yea, from far unto the ends of the earth, and they shall return to their lands of promise." 1QIsa[a], which reads "bring them to their land [*ʾel admātām*] and to their place," does not support the BoM as claimed (IVT-2, 173-74; IVT-1, 55; BMCT 1:204n633). The scroll's plus is much too short compared to that of the BoM. Moreover, the scroll places it in a different position than the BoM's unique phrase. The reading of "to their land" rather than "to their place" in two Targum manuscripts and two early printed editions of the Targum also does not support the BoM variant (IVT-1, 55; cf. BMCT 1:204n633). This is simply a variant, perhaps interpretive, of the MT "to their place." Tvedtnes's arguments for how the BoM plus was lost are weak. The phrase "upon their own land" (*ʾel ʾadmātām*) in v. 1 seems much too far away from the BoM plus to have an effect upon it. In any case, Tvedtnes undermines his argument when he says that the phrase "lands of promise" in the BoM phrase was perhaps *ʾărāṣôt habbĕrît* (IVT-1, 55). If the two words for "land" are different (*ʾadāmâ* vs. *ʾarāṣôt*), the mechanism for haplography—such as might be—evaporates. The additional implication that the phrase "land of promise" in the BoM, supposedly containing the Hebrew word *bĕrît* ("covenant," "pact"), was dropped because of similarity to the distant word

byt ("house") in the last line of the MT v. 1 is implausible. The BoM phrase appears to be a secondary gloss.

(18) *Isa. 14:3-4//2 Ne. 24:3-4:* Verses 3-4 in the KJV form a syntactic whole: "[3] And it shall come to pass in the day that the Lord shall give thee rest ... [4] that thou shalt take up this proverb. ..." In the BoM the two verses are independent. Verse 3 has the demonstrative pronoun "that" before "day," making a complete sentence: "And it shall come to pass in that day that the Lord shall give thee rest ..." It also has a plus at the beginning of v. 4, "And it shall come to pass ...," which forms another complete sentence. It is claimed that the BoM variants have parallels in the LXX and to some extent in Hebrew manuscripts (IVT-2, 174; IVT-1, 56-57; BMCT 1: 204nn636-637). In v. 3 the Greek has a demonstrative pronoun with "day": *kai estai en tē hēmera ekeinē anapausei se ho theos* ("And it will be in that day, [that] God will give you rest"). Two Hebrew manuscripts have the pronoun too.[118] Verse 4 in the LXX is independent of v. 3 and (except for the Vaticanus) displays the phrase "in that day": *kai lēmpsē ton thrēnon touton epi ton basilea Babulōnos kai ereis en tē hēmera ekenē* ("and you shall take up this lamentation against the king of Babylon and you shall say in that day").

Despite the similarities, the BoM readings likely arose independently of the ancient texts. It is possible that the ancient texts on the one hand and the BoM on the other separately added the demonstrative "that" under the influence of the forty-two occurrences of "that day" elsewhere in Isaiah.[119] What particularly makes one think the parallel is accidental is that the Greek reading in v. 4 is quite unlike the BoM phrase. It lacks any match to the BoM's "it shall come to pass." The Greek verse is syntactically independent because it is translating the Hebrew which can be construed as "You shall take up. ..." The adverbial "in that day" in the Greek appears in a different place, after the verb "you shall say." It is apparently original in this position since the Greek and Hebrew elsewhere have the verb "to say" followed by "in that day" (12:1, 4; cf. 25:9). What seems to have happened is that after v. 3 was made independent in the BoM, v. 4 was left an incomplete subordinate phrase ("that thou shalt take up ..."). To make it complete, the phrase at the beginning of v. 3 was transferred to the beginning of v. 4. Notably, the beginning of v. 4 is not rendered as "Thou shalt take up this proverb ...," which would be a truer sign of translation. Rather, the BoM preserves the conjunction "that," which is an artifact of the

KJV's translation that syntactically joins vv. 3-4. Thus, not only are the Greek and BoM readings independent, the BoM's has ties to the English. In addition, Tvedtnes's argument for the development of the MT out of a version of Isaiah like that in the BoM requires three stages and is too complex, loose, and improvised to be plausible.

(19) *Isa. 14:32//2 Ne. 24:32:* KJV Isa. 14:32 reads: "What shall *one* then answer the messengers of the nation?" The BoM has the object in the KJV as the subject: "What shall then answer the messengers of the nations?" (2 Ne. 24:32). This is paralleled by the Targum: *ûmāʾ yĕbassĕrûn izgaddê ʿammĕmayyāʾ* ("and what will the messengers of the peoples announce?"). The 1QIsa^a and the LXX follow the same syntax, though they have "kings" instead of "messengers," a matter of a slight variant in the Hebrew *mlky* versus *mlʾky* respectively, *wmh yʿnw mlky gwy* ("what will the kings of a/the nation answer?"); *kai ti apokrithēsontai basileis ethnōn* ("what shall the kings of the nations answer?").[120] Despite these parallels, a more cogent explanation is that the BoM text deleted the italicized word "*one.*" Evidence that this is so is the BoM's retention of the KJV word order which yields a slightly awkward reading. If the BoM reading were a translation, we would expect a more normal, "What then shall the messengers of the nations answer?"[121]

(20) *Isa. 48:11//1 Ne. 20:11:* The KJV reads: "For mine own sake, *even* for mine own sake, will I do it: for how should *my name* be polluted?" The BoM's edited original manuscript has: "For mine own sake, yea, for mine own sake will I do this, for I will not suffer my name to be polluted."[122] Some of the ancient versions have verbs in the first person and some have negative particles like the BoM (IVT-2, 174; IVT-1; 68, BMCT 1:106n781): 1QIsa^a has *lmʿny lmʿny ʾʿsh kyʾ ʾykh ʾyḥl* ("for my sake, for my sake, I will act, for how shall I be polluted").[123] A Targum manuscript reads *bĕdîl šĕmî bĕdîl mêmĕrî ʾuʿăbêd dĕlāʾ ʾittaḥal* ("for the sake of my name, for the sake of my Memra, I will act so that I not be polluted").[124] The Peshitta has *mṭlty ʾʿbd dlʾ ʾtṭwš* ("for my sake I will act so that I will not be polluted"), and the Vulgate, *propter me propter me faciam ut non blasphemer* ("for my sake, for my sake I will act so that I am not blasphemed"). The correspondence of these examples to the BoM reading is inexact. Though there is a first person verb and three versions have a negative particle, the verb is passive in all of them, not active as in the BoM. They also lack the term "my name" in

the clause containing the pollution/blasphemy verb, just as it is missing from the MT and so noted by italics in the KJV. The Greek, the Old Latin (which depends on the Greek), and one Hebrew manuscript have "my name"; these, however, have a third-person verb without a negative: *eneken emou poiēsō soi, hoti to emon onoma bebēloutai* ("for my own sake I will act for you, because my name is polluted"); *propter me faciam, quia nomen meum polluitur* ("I will act for my sake, because my name is polluted"); *ʾykh yḥl šmy* ("how shall my name be polluted"). Hence, no text is, in fact, like the BoM's.

While the term "my name" may have originally been in the text (and it should not be forgotten that the KJV supplies this),[125] other problems remain that make the BoM reading appear secondary. It is not clear that a rhetorical question as in the MT would develop from a simple negative as in the BoM; development in the other direction seems more likely, especially in the versions which are often interpretive in nature. Too, it seems that the third-person verb is original (as in the MT with "my name" as subject) and that the first-person arose when the subject of the third-person verb was no longer present or clear. Hence, the versions with the negative particle and first-person verbs appear to be secondary. Furthermore, the BoM variant can be seen as a response to the italics, as in the line before this where "*even*" becomes "yea" and "*it*" becomes "this." Instead of changing or deleting "my name," the surrounding words were changed. The first person transitive formulation may have been suggested by the first person form in the following line: "I will not give my glory unto another."[126]

(21) *Isa. 48:14//1 Ne. 20:14:* The relevant passage in the KJV has: "... which among them hath declared these *things*?" The BoM has: "... which among them hath declared these things unto them." Nibley's, Tvedtnes's, and BMCT's claim that the Greek has the reading of the BoM is in error.[127] The Hebrew reads: *mî bāhem higgîd ʾet-ʾēlleh* ("who among them declared these things?"). The LXX reads: *tis autois anēngeilen tauta* (literally, "who to them has declared these things?"). The Greek is simply translating the Hebrew *bāhem* ("among them") as *autois* ("to them"), clearly signaled in the one-to-one correspondence of Greek to Hebrew terms and the same word order in both. Tvedtnes argues further that haplography has occurred: *ʾl(y)hm* ("to them") has dropped because of its similarity to *ʾlh* ("these [things]"). This is plausible but a conjecture (see the cautions accompanying example 2). It is

more likely, in view of the evidence above, that the variant in the BoM is an environmental modification reacting to the italicized word "things."

(22) *Isa. 49:1//1 Ne. 21:1:* The BoM Isaiah has a long plus at the beginning of the KJV equivalent of Isa. 49:1. The plus is shown here in bold:

> **And again, hearken O ye house of Israel, all ye that are broken off and are driven out, because of the wickedness of the pastors of my people, yea, all ye that are broken off, that are scattered abroad which are of my people, O House of Israel.** Listen O isles unto me, and hearken ye people from far, ...

Tvedtnes sees a chiastic structure at the beginning of the verse which he believes demonstrates the antiquity of the BoM: (A) Hearken, (B) O ye house of Israel, (C) All ye that are broken off ..., (D) Because of the wickedness ..., (C') Yea, all ye that are broken off ..., (B') ...O house of Israel, (A') Listen, O isles, unto me.[128] He argues that it may be missing from the MT/KJV because of parablepsis between *šimᶜû* ("hearken"), with which the verse supposedly began, and the same verb ("listen") at the beginning of the MT.[129]

This argument is invalid because the chiastic structure he perceives is artificial and the mechanism for parablepsis is doubtful for the following reasons:

1. The last element of the chiasmus (A') is part of a bicolon that includes the line that follows it ("Listen, O Isles ...// and hearken, ye people ..."). One would expect (A') to belong wholly to the chiastic structure or to its bicolon, not both.

2. The chiastic structure here is generally between what might be judged to be poetic lines, but Tvedtnes exceptionally divides the first line into two members to achieve chiastic balance ("hearken" and "O ye house of Israel").

3. There is one too many vocative elements in lines B'-A'. That is, he makes B' parallel to B since both have "O ... house of Israel," but A' with its "O isles" following an imperative verb looks like it should be seen as parallel to A-B taken as a whole. The extra vocative element is what I call "chiastic interference"–a sign that the structure is artificial, an invention of the analyst.

4. In English, the verb at line A in the chiasmus is "hearken" while

at A' it is "listen." If the underlying verb is the same as Tvedtnes claims (i.e., *šimᶜû*), we should expect the English "listen" at the beginning of the BoM verse. The KJV uses "hearken" for another verb, *haqšîbû* (in the line "hearken ye people from far").

5. The argument for parablepsis similarly suffers because of the BoM's initial words "and again." One assumes that this phrase came before the verb "hearken" and its vocative object because it conceptually stands outside the "hearken" phrase. "And again" should have been preserved.

6. In the earlier version of his study (IVT-1, 72-73), Tvedtnes proposed a different chiastic structure which avoided several of the problems noted: (A) Hearken, O ye house of Israel, (B) all ye that are broken off (C) and are driven out, (D) because of the wickedness of the pastors of my people, (B') yea, all ye that are broken off (C') that are scattered abroad, (A') which are of my people O house of Israel. One difficulty with this proposed structure is that the B//B' and C//C' members are not in chiastic order. Another is that A and A' are not exactly parallel. The latter is a relative clause similar to the relatives in lines B, C, B', C'. It also has relationship to the B' and C' lines before it, as D does to B and C, making it somewhat parallel to D. And note the term "my people" that appears in D and A'. These problems, and the fact that two different chiastic structures can be found, suggest that they may be only in the mind of the analyst.

7. Even if one maintains that there is chiasmus here, it cannot be used as a sign of antiquity as Brent Metcalfe has convincingly shown.[130] Chiasmus is found in Smith's scriptural writings that come from his own hand and time (e.g., D&C).

8. Lastly, the plus seems secondary since it explains who is meant by the "isles" and "people from far" (see Part 5).[131]

(23) *Isa. 50:2//2 Ne. 7:2:* The KJV reads: "I make the rivers a wilderness: their fish stinketh, because *there is* no water, and dieth for thirst." The BoM has: "I make their rivers a wilderness, and their fish to stink, because the waters are dried up, and they dieth because of thirst." 1QIsa[a] and the LXX are said to provide support for the originality and antiquity of the BoM reading.[132] This, however, is another instance where the versions are only superficially parallel. The Qumran biblical text and translation read, respectively: *ᵓsym nhrwt mdbr tybš dgtm mᵓyn mym wtmwt bṣmᵓ* ("I make the rivers a wilderness; their

fish dry up, because there is no water, and die from thirst"); *kai thēsō potamous erēmous kai ksēranthēsontai hoi ichthues autōn apo tou mē enai hudōr kai apothanountai en dipsei* ("and I will make rivers a wilderness; and their fish will dry up because there is no water, and they will die from thirst"). These texts read essentially the same as the MT except they have or presuppose *tybš* ("dry up") for *tbʾš* ("to stink").[133] They do not represent a textual tradition significantly distinct from the MT in this particular verse. The verb "dry up" in these versions is not in the same clause as the BoM's verb "dry up."[134] Indeed, an argument that the BoM text is original and that it led to the two different readings in the MT on the one hand and the 1QIsa[a] and LXX on the other (IVT-2, 175-76; IVT-1, 81), or that the BoM brings together the two alternative readings secondarily (IVT-1, 81), requires a highly complex, and hence highly speculative, process of textual alteration with movements of elements between clauses (see the cautions in example 2).

The BoM reading clearly evolves from the KJV. Part 4 above determined that the use of the verb "make" and the preposition "because" (first occurrence) reflect a development on the basis of English polysemy. Furthermore, the BoM variant arises in large part by a reaction to the italicized words "*there is.*" The term "dry up" comes from the influence of the phrase three lines before it which says: "I dry up the sea." There are several cases where changes at the italics reiterate an idea present in the lines or verses just before.[135] The only variant that is susceptible to interpretation as a manifestation of antiquity is "their rivers" instead of "the rivers." The pronoun "their" in Hebrew is written with a suffixed *-m*; since the next word begins with *m-* (*mdbr,* "wilderness"), it could have dropped out because of the similarity. This is not enough, however, to prove antiquity. The pronoun "their" could have as easily arisen in English from assimilation to or influence from the following phrase, "their fish."

(24) *Isa. 51:9//2 Ne. 8:9:* The first part of the verse in the KJV reads: "Awake, awake, put on strength, O arm of the Lord; awake, as in the ancient days, in the generations of old." The BoM lacks the phrase "in the generations of old." Tvedtnes claims, though I cannot confirm, that some Hebrew manuscripts lack the term *dōrôt* ("generations"), thus giving some support for the BoM reading.[136] If this is true, it is still a case of an imperfect match between the manuscripts and the

BoM since the Hebrew manuscripts would presumably still have *ᶜôlāmîm* ("of old").[137]

(25) *Isa. 51:15//2 Ne. 8:15:* The KJV and MT read "his name," while the BoM reads "my name." Tvedtnes (IVT-1, 176; IVT-1, 86) finds support for the BoM's antiquity in the LXX which reads "my name" (cf. BMCT 1:154n248). But contextual smoothing of the KJV may account for the variant (see example 6 above). Verses 15-16 have God speaking in the first person. The third person formulation of the phrase "the Lord of hosts is his name" appears awkward. Hence, a revision to "my name" seems in order. The neighboring italicized word "*is*" may have offered some impetus for this change. The Greek translation may have construed an original third-person pronoun as first person for similar contextual reasons.

(26) *Isa. 54:15//3 Ne. 22:15:* The KJV reads: "Behold, they shall surely gather together, *but* not be me"; the BoM has the variant: "Behold, they shall surely gather together against thee not by me." Tvedtnes (IVT-2, 176; IVT-1, 95) and BMCT (3:1031n859) say that the LXX supports the BoM reading. The LXX reads: *idou prosēlutoi proseleusontai soi di' emou (kai paroikēsousin soi)*[138] *kai epi se katapeuksontai* ("Behold, strangers [or proselytes] shall come to you by my agency, [and they shall live with you], and they shall find refuge with you"). The dative pronoun "to you" in the first line correlates in position with the BoM's variant "against thee."

While this evidence makes one think that the Hebrew texts underlying these translations had a preposition and pronoun in the first clause, it is far from definitive. The Hebrew verse is very difficult and the translations paraphrase rather than offer an exact translation. As for the LXX, Ziegler observes that "the MT of [Isa.] 54:15 was for the LXX quite opaque"[139] and was translated freely in connection with Isa. 55:5 where foreigners run with positive motive to Israel.[140] More specifically, it seems that the LXX assimilated its translation to the wording of the Pentateuchal laws about resident aliens. The MT of Lev. 19:33 reads: *wekî-yāgûr ʾittekā gēr* ("when an alien dwells with you"). The LXX translates this: *ean de tis proselthē prosēlutos humin* ("if a proselyte comes to you"). Here the verb *prosershomai* ("come") is used to translate the verb *gwr* and a dative pronoun *humin* is used to translate the Hebrew preposition and pronoun.[141] However, Isa. 54:15 has nothing to do with resident aliens or dwelling; the verb *gwr* that appears there thrice comes from a homonymous root meaning something like "attack."[142] The LXX, however, took the verb as the *gwr* root dealing with residing and rendered this as *prosershomai* ("come") as in the Pentateuch; it then inserted the subject *proselutos* ("proselyte"). The LXX also could have inserted the dative pronoun *soi* by influence from Pentateuchal formulation.

Even many modern translations provide an object for the verb *gwr*, apparently not on the basis of the ancient texts but simply out of need to make sense. The verses that precede vv. 15 and 17, as well as the ending of these verses, speak of Jerusalem in the second person. In this context it is easy for a translator to add a pronoun referring to Jerusalem. Thus, the NIV translates: "If anyone does attack you"; the JB and NJB have: "should anyone attack you"; and the NEB and REB read: "should any[one] attack you." McKenzie translates: "If anyone assails you."[143]

In view of this, it may be that Smith inserted the prepositional phrase "against thee" for contextual reasons. It clarifies the relationship of "they" and "gathering" to "thou" in the larger context. The wording "against thee" duplicates the same prepositional phrase in "gather together against thee" later in the verse. The stimulus for the change can be seen in the italicized word "*but.*" The awkwardness of the BoM reading is further testimony that we are dealing with a modification of the KJV. The phrase "against thee" replaces the conjunction "*but,*" leaving the KJV's "not by me" poorly coordinated with the foregoing. The Hebrew behind this last phrase is not really clear.[144] If this is a translation, we would expect more clarity overall and not just the insertion of the preposition and pronoun.

(27) *The conjunction "and":* Tvedtnes (IVT-2, 169) lists ten cases where the BoM has the conjunction "and" where ancient translations and manuscripts have it but the KJV does not.[145] These do not provide proof. This minor word can arise independently and coincidentally in texts or translations, especially in a biblical document whose style and/or language allow for conjunctions at the beginning of phrases or as elements in a list.[146] Additional conjunctions could arise in a revision of Isaiah that follows KJV style, as is the case with the Book of Mormon. In view of this, one would expect to see a number of fortuitous coincidences. Not much can be made of this in terms of support for the antiquity of the BoM.

Of Tvedtnes's ten examples, all but one are linked to other environmental changes in the text. Seven are related to the italics (1 Ne. 20:5, 13; 2 Ne. 7:9; 8:18; 13:9, 14, 26) and two are associated with pluses (1 Ne. 20:14, 22).[147] In two instances, the addition of "and" along with pluses disrupts the poetic structure of the text (1 Ne. 20:14; 2 Ne. 7:9). Three of Tvedtnes's examples demonstrate the translator's ignorance of the original text, creating situations that are either syntactically incorrect or incomplete (1 Ne. 20:5, 8; 2 Ne. 8:18). A closer look at these syntactic problems is instructive.

In 1 Ne. 20:5 (//Isa. 48:5), the addition of "and" displays an ignorance of the original. The KJV reads: "I have even from the beginning declared *it* to thee"; the BoM has: "And I have even from the beginning declared to thee." The BoM has the conjunction, according to Tvedtnes, "in a place where MT has the conjunction [*w*-] but [the] KJV did not translate it!" (IVT-2, 169; cf. IVT-1, 66). Actually, the KJV did translate it, as BMCT notes (1:104n766), in the word "even." Thus technically, the conjunction "and" in the BoM is redundant. The KJV did not translate it as "and" because it took v. 4 as a causal clause giving the reason for v. 5: "because I knew that thou art obstinate ... I have even from the beginning declared it to thee."[148] The BoM has a different reading for v. 4, turning it into an independent sentence. This leaves v. 5 unconnected to v. 4 and makes insertion of the conjunction possible. Thus, English-based modifications are responsible for this change. The variant "I did shew them suddenly" in v. 3 is based on English polysemy and an italicized word. This inspired the insertion of "And I did it" at the beginning of v. 4. "And I did it" made v. 4 independent and v. 5, in turn, ready to receive the conjunction. The English basis of the revision is implied further in the deletion or replacement of three italicized words in vv. 4-5.

1 Ne. 20:8 (//Isa. 48:8) reads: "Yea, and thou heardest not." Neither the KJV nor the MT has the added conjunction. But 1QIsa[a] has *wgm* ("and also") at the beginning of the verse and is seen as parallel to the BoM reading (IVT-1, 67; BMCT 1:105n773). The problem is that the BoM has the conjunction after the adverb "yea" and applies it to the first verb in the verse. It is not conjoined to the entire phrase as in 1QIsa[a].[149]

In Isa. 51:18 (//2 Ne. 8:18), the KJV has: "*There is* none to guide her among all the sons *whom* she hath brought forth," whereas the

BoM has a conjunction at the beginning: "And none to guide her among all the sons she hath brought forth." Support for the BoM's antiquity is thought to lie in versions that likewise have a conjunction at the beginning (IVT-1, 87; BMCT 1:155n254): the LXX *kai ouk ēn ho parakalōn se apo pantōn tōn teknōn sou hōn etekes* ("and there was none to console you from all your children whom you bore") and the Syriac *wlyt dmbyᵓ lh mn klhwn bnyᵓ dyldt* ("and there is none to console her from all the children whom she bore"). The parallel is not convincing. The LXX and Syriac are imperfect matches: while having a conjunction, they also have the equivalent of the KJV's "*there is*" which is missing in the BoM. These versions are simply translating the Hebrew. The MT has the equivalent of "*there is*" in its negative existential particle *ᵓên* ("there is not/none"). This means that technically the KJV need not—indeed should not—have italicized "*there is.*" Rather than depending on an ancient text, the BoM's reading arises from the deletion of the KJV's unnecessary italics. Striking "*there is*" yielded an awkward uncoordinated phrase, so "and" was added. I have previously remarked on the tendency for the conjunction to appear at the beginning of phrases or clauses in place of italicized words. The definitive evidence that the BoM's text comes about by the deletion of the italics is that even with the added "and," the larger phrase (even the larger verse) is still syntactically incomplete and does not make sense; it has no main governing verb. Another clue that the conjunction arises from modifying italics is the fact that the BoM deletes or modifies all of the ten italicized words in vv. 17-19 (which further yields several readings completely at odds with the original Hebrew). Thus, a strong case can be made for regarding the ten insertions of "and" listed by Tvedtnes as the result of tampering with the English text rather than reliance on an ancient text.

To conclude here, the proofs ventured by Tvedtnes and others display numerous weaknesses or are in error. The type of evidence that one wants to find in support of the BoM Isaiah is the kind that many have thought 2 Ne. 12:16 (example 1 above) offered: a parallel of a relatively long phrase with context-specific words. The data examined show that this particular case cannot provide that support, and there are no other instances of similar substance or complexity in all the parallels that have been suggested to demonstrate the BoM's antiquity.

The other main cases discussed (2-26) are also problematic as proof. Several proposed parallels are partial or inexact and hence do not provide true textual support (examples 4, 9, 12, 16, 17, 18, 20, 21, 23, 24). In some cases the evidence and/or analysis is highly ambiguous, substantially incomplete, strained, or simply in error (examples 5, 7, 8, 11, 12, 13, 14, 15, 16, 18, 21, 22, 23, 25, 26). The mechanics suggested for error and development in some instances are inexact or highly speculative (examples 2, 3, 5, 7, 13, 15, 16, 17, 18, 20, 21, 22, 23). Some presume that the BoM is an exact translation of Isaiah (examples 8, 9, 10, 13, 14), which is incompatible with other cases where a loose translation is necessary to make the evidence work (2, 11, 15, 22). The general problems associated with the conjunction "and" (example 27) have already been rehearsed in some depth. In contrast to all this, almost every variant can be explained as a modification of the KJV or a secondary development (responses to italics: 5, 6, 8, 9, 10, 11, 12, 15, 19, 20, 21, 23, 26; contextual smoothing or providing consistency as a result of other modifications: 3, 6, 7, 8, 10, 12, 13, 18, 25; developments from English polysemy: 23; secondary glosses or additions: 2, 4, 16, 17, 18, 22).[150]

CONCLUSIONS

Many who maintain the antiquity of the BoM have tried to make sense of KJV language in the BoM by suggesting that Joseph Smith used it when the content of the plates agreed with it. Hugh Nibley, for example, says that "the Book of Mormon follows the language of the King James Bible only as far as the latter conveys the correct meaning of the original."[151] The language comes specifically, according to different versions of this theory, either from Joseph Smith's using an English Bible in the translation process or from revelation without use of the Bible.[152] This theory and its versions are completely untenable in view of the nature of the evidence presented above. They cannot explain the preoccupation with the italics, variants based on English polysemy, and disturbances of Hebrew style. They are chiefly rebutted by the maintenance of KJV translation errors in the BoM as well as by the incomplete and incomprehensible texts in some variants.

A more critical and humanistic version of this argument sees Smith as translating an ancient text while at the same time using the KJV and responding to some of its peculiarities. This accounts for the focus on italicized words, the problems in the BoM Isaiah, and the revisions of the BoM Isaiah that were required.[153] Nevertheless, it is a fragile and illogical theory. It presumes a duplex and contradictory mode of textual production, i.e., derivation of parts of the text by translation from an ancient document on the one hand and, on the other, use of the KJV not only to adopt its idiom but to respond to its unique features and language, often in ways that are inconsistent with the Hebrew text, language, and style of Isaiah.[154]

This sort of theory is advanced in part because its adherents believe there are two types of empirical data, one that shows a connection to the KJV and another which ties the BoM Isaiah passages to ancient texts and Hebrew linguistic features. The present study shows that the ties to the English Bible are far greater than what earlier scholars have recognized or formally laid out and that the evidence connecting the BoM Isaiah text to ancient texts or language matters is insubstantial. Thus, not only in logic but also in factual basis, the foregoing theory is found wanting. The simplest and most logical explanation is that the BoM Isaiah derives directly from the KJV text with some secondary modifications by Smith and that it does not derive from an ancient text through translation.

The larger net of evidence supports this conclusion. Other studies have demonstrated the use of the KJV in the composition of the BoM. Stan Larson has shown that the Sermon on the Mount materials in 3 Ne. 12:1-14:27 are a revision of the KJV Matthew 5:3-7:27.[155] One can add to his insights the observation that several of the variants there are connected with words italicized in the KJV.[156] In another study, I have shown that Smith used the New Testament epistle to the Hebrews in composing Alma 12-13.[157] This is an anachronism in the BoM text, and the language of the parallels reflects the KJV formulation.

Smith's revision of the Bible (JSR) also lends credence to the conclusion here. This work was not a "translation" even though so termed by Smith, but a reworking of the KJV. Though in places it has more substantial pluses than the BoM Isaiah, its basic character is the same. Many variants are associated with italics, develop from English polysemy, contradict Hebrew and Greek language and style, smooth out contextual and theological difficulties, and explain unclear words and ideas. It is also noteworthy that work on the JSR began almost immediately after work on the BoM. When the BoM Isaiah is seen to be a revision of the KJV, the chronological proximity of the two works makes perfect sense. One could even conclude that work on the BoM Isaiah was the training ground for the JSR.

More broadly, the conclusion of this essay is supported by—and in turn supports—arguments that show that the whole of the BoM is not an ancient work but a composition by Smith himself.[158] The book displays cultural, ideational, and textual anachronisms. Much of the work arguing for its antiquity is evidentially or logically incomplete or flawed, highly speculative, and not sufficiently critical. The cases where correlations with the ancient world seem cogent are extremely few and must therefore be the result of coincidence. Certainly the hypothesis of antiquity cannot explain the BoM as satisfactorily as the hypothesis that it was written in the nineteenth century CE. In addition to this, the method of producing the BoM claimed by tradition is most extraordinary and is not verifiable or reproducible scientifically.

Two anachronisms in the book relate to the issue of Isaiah. First, critical scholars have concluded with good reason that much of the biblical Isaiah, especially chapters 40-66, does not come from the eighth century BCE prophet but rather from a later time.[159] The temporal perspective in chapters 40-55 (from which several of the BoM Isaiah chapters come) is that of about 540 BCE. The context is one in which the Jews have recently suffered destruction at the hands of the Babylonians (in 586 BCE).[160] The temple, Jerusalem, and other cities have been destroyed and need rebuilding.[161] Many of the people are now in captivity in Mesopotamia, but Babylonian might is waning[162] and release from captivity is imminent.[163] Cyrus, the Persian king, is the political leader who will effect the release, which occurred ca. 538 BCE.[164] It is not just the mention of specific sixth-century BCE historical figures and events that pin these chapters to that time. Equally telling is that the precision in such descriptions ceases at this point. The era after the release is described in general terms, and this description is in error since bounteous blessing did not ensue.[165] The lack of fulfillment gave Jewish, Christian, and Mormon interpreters cause to reapply the chapters to later events. That Isa. 40-55 were written after the middle of the sixth century BCE is also indicated by their perfect conceptual fit between other prophetic works written in the first half of that century (Jeremiah and Ezekiel) and those written at the end of the century (Haggai and Zechariah 1-8). The mid-sixth-century dating for

Isa. 40-55 means that these chapters could not have been available to Lehi's family when they, according to the story, left for the New World around 600 BCE–and Nephi, Jacob, Abinadi, and Noah's false priests could not have cited from them.[166]

The second anachronism is the BoM's interpretation of Isaiah following many of the cited portions (cf. 1 Ne. 22; 2 Ne. 9-10, 25-33; Mos. 12:25-31; 3 Ne. 23:1-5) and sometimes interspersed within the citations (cf. 2 Ne. 6:6-18; 26:15-27:35). For the most part, it reinterprets the passages to apply to the time of Joseph Smith and the course of Jewish and Christian history up to his time. This reflects the compositional horizon of the book, just as various passages in Second Isaiah (noted above) reflect that work's compositional horizon. Indeed, the course of history that the BoM lays out in its interpretation is clear and defined up to the time of the appearance of the BoM but quite indefinite thereafter, just as Second Isaiah is indefinite about events after about 540 BCE. Furthermore, the BoM shares perceptions about the meaning of Isaiah and methods of prophetic interpretation that were extant among students and readers in the decades just before the BoM came forth. This chronological horizon and these interpretive views are evidence that the interpretation in the BoM is the work of Smith himself.[167]

That the BoM is not an ancient work further coincides with critical study which shows that other supposedly ancient works produced by Smith, such as the revision of the Bible, the Book of Abraham, and temple endowment, do not come from ancient sources but grow out of nineteenth-century influences and sources.[168]

Determining the date, sources, and nature of the text is only the beginning of BoM study. Many significant questions need to be formulated and solved. Theologians, primarily including church leaders, will have the responsibility of re-visioning the spiritual meaning of the book.[169] Historians will need to assess carefully how Smith's context is reflected in the book in order to use it as a guide to his religious thought in his early life. Scholars of the text will need to examine the nature of Joseph Smith's interpretation of Isaiah and his use and interpretation of other biblical material in the BoM.[170]

NOTES

Abbreviations

1830:	First printed edition of the BoM.
1QIsa[a]:	Large Isaiah scroll from Qumran.
BHK:	Rudolf Kittel, ed., *Biblia Hebraica* (Stuttgart: Württembergische Bibelanstalt, 1937).
BHS:	Karl Elliger and Wilhelm Rudolph, eds., *Biblia Hebraica Stuttgartensia* (Stuttgart: Deutsche Bibelgesellschaft, 1984).
BMCT:	*The Book of Mormon Critical Text: A Tool for Scholarly Reference,* 3 vols. (Provo, UT: FARMS, 1984-87).
IVT-1:	John Tvedtnes, *The Isaiah Variants in the Book of Mormon,* FARMS Preliminary Report (Provo: FARMS, 1981).
IVT-2:	"Isaiah Variants in the Book of Mormon," in *Isaiah and the Prophets,* ed. Monte S. Nyman (Provo, UT: Religious Studies Center, Brigham Young University, 1984).
JB:	Jerusalem Bible.
JSR:	Joseph Smith Revision of the Bible (=Joseph Smith "Translation" or the "Inspired Version").
KJV:	King James Version of the Bible.
LXX:	Greek Septuagint translation of the Bible.
MT:	Masoretic Text, the main Hebrew Bible text tradition.
NAB:	New American Bible.
NEB:	New English Bible.
NIV:	New International Version.
NJB:	New Jerusalem Bible.
NJPS:	*Tanakh: A New Translation of the Holy Scriptures* (Philadelphia: Jewish Publication Society, 1985).
NRSV:	New Revised Standard Version.
O:	Original Manuscript of the BoM.
P:	Printer's Manuscript of the BoM, copied from O.
Pc:	Corrections made to P.
REB:	Revised English Bible.
RSV:	Revised Standard Version of the Bible.

1. For a complete list of Isaiah passages cited or paraphrased in the Book of Mormon, broken down according to verse, see Monte S. Nyman, *Great Are the Words of Isaiah* (Salt Lake City: Bookcraft, 1980), 259-81; another list (though with some typographical errors) appears in IVT-1, 6-19. See also recently the list in Royal Skousen, "Textual Variants in the Isaiah Quotations in the Book of Mormon," in *Isaiah in the Book of Mormon,* ed. Donald W. Parry and John W. Welch (Provo, UT: FARMS, 1998), 369-71.

2. See the conclusion of this essay for the implausibility of Joseph Smith's

using the KJV translation and language when it agreed with the BoM Isaiah text.

3. Walter F. Specht, "Italics," *The Oxford Companion to the Bible,* ed. Bruce M. Metzger and Michael D. Coogan (New York: Oxford University Press, 1993), 336-37; Sebastian Bullough, *English Versions of the Bible* (St. Louis: B. Herder Book Co., 1952; reprint: Westport, CT: Greenwood Press, 1972), 324-25.

4. Even tradition-oriented LDS scholar John Tvedtnes recognizes that changes were made at the italicized words (see IVT-1, 106-111). Skousen ("Textual Variants," 381-82) has downplayed the connection. In view of the evidence presented below, it cannot be claimed that "it is doubtful whether Joseph Smith would have even known what the italics meant, especially since no explanation for their use is ever given in the King James Bible." The papers by Calhoun and Robbins to which Skousen refers (written for a 1991 English course at Brigham Young University) lack rigor and detail and are otherwise unconvincing (I thank Brent Metcalfe, who received copies from Skousen, for sharing these papers with me). Finally, Skousen notes that only 29 percent (the errata list to the article notes that the "2 percent" should read "29 percent") of the differences in the BoM Isaiah are linked to italicized words. This amount, which is similar to my totals (see below), is significant. But in the end, it is not merely a quantitative analysis but a qualitative investigation, as presented below, that shows how substantially the BoM reacts to the KJV italics.

5. George D'Oyly and Richard Mant, *The Holy Bible According to the Authorized Version with Notes, Explanatory and Practical,* 2 vols. (New York: T. and J. Swords, 1818-20), vol. 1, the page before the "Introduction to the Old Testament."

6. *The Evening and the Morning Star* (July 1833): [106]. In a previous editorial, Phelps said the BoM was superior to the Bible because "it has not been tinctured by the wisdom of man, with here and there an Italic word to supply deficiencies.–It was translated by the gift and power of God" (ibid., [Jan. 1833]: 2).

7. Robert J. Matthews, *"A Plainer Translation": Joseph Smith's Translation of the Bible: A History and Commentary* (Provo, UT: Brigham Young University Press, 1975), 59. While Matthews suggests that someone other than Smith may have excised these italicized words, it was most likely done under his direction as part of the revision process.

8. "Mormonites," *The Sun* (Philadelphia), 18 Aug. 1831. This was in part cited and discussed by D. Michael Quinn, *Early Mormonism and the Magic World View* (Salt Lake City: Signature Books, 1998), 170-71, 480n308.

9. Since italicized words could vary in different early editions, and since the Bible(s) that Smith had on hand when producing the BoM is (are) not known, I have examined two early nineteenth-century editions to determine a basis for my analysis of Isa. 2-14, 48-54: Thomas Scott, *The Holy Bible Containing the Old and New Testaments with Original Notes, Practical Observations and*

Copious References, vol. 4 (New York: Whiting and Watson, 1812); and Thomas Williams, ed., *The Cottage Bible and Family Expositor Containing the Old and New Testaments,* vol. 2 (Hartford: D. F. Robinson and H. F. Sumner, 1834). As it turns out, the *Cottage Bible* agrees with *The Holy Bible Containing the Old and New Testaments* (Salt Lake City: Church of Jesus Christ of Latter-day Saints, 1979). Scott's edition varies only slightly: it does not italicize "one" in 2:12 (second occurrence), "it" in 3:9, "is" in 3:14, and "by" in 9:1; it does italicize "every" in 2:12 (first occurrence), and "that is" in 4:3 (last occurrence) and 7:22, 14:26 (both occurrences). The concurrence of Scott and the *Cottage Bible* shows a relatively established tradition around the time the BoM was produced. I have used the distribution in the *Cottage Bible* (=1979 LDS ed.) as the basis of this study.

10. On Isaiah in 2 Ne. 6-8 not being a paraphrase, see Part 5 below.

11. More specifically, a plus or minus of one word in the BoM text equals one variant. The appearance of one word in the place of another is one variant; the appearance of two words in the place of one word counts as two variants, and so forth. Transpositions count as one variant. Variants in plural and singular nouns are counted. Insignificant variants (difference in preposition [e.g., "toward" vs. "towards"], spelling variants, hyphenation, word compounding or splitting, etc.) are not counted.

12. There are several cases where the meaning is affected, though minimally, by the lack of an italicized word. See, for absent adverbs and prepositions: "*even*" in Isa. 4:3//2 Ne. 14:3; Isa. 7:17//2 Ne. 17:17; Isa. 51:22//2 Ne. 8:22; "*so*" in Isa. 5:24//2 Ne. 15:24; "*yet*" in Isa. 49:4//1 Ne. 21:4; "*when*" in Isa. 48:21//1 Ne. 20:21; "*namely*" in Isa. 7:20//2 Ne. 17:20; "*on*" in Isa. 7:25//2 Ne. 17:25; conjunctions: "*and*" in Isa. 3:24//2 Ne. 13:24; Isa. 5:19//2 Ne. 15:19; Isa. 9:21//2 Ne. 19:21; Isa. 14:5//2 Ne. 24:5; Isa. 49:7//1 Ne. 21:7; Isa. 51:11//2 Ne. 8:11; Isa. 52:2//2 Ne. 8:25; "*or*" in Isa. 10:15//2 Ne. 20:15; pronouns: "*it*" in Isa. 5:29//2 Ne. 15:29 (his); Isa. 14:27//2 Ne. 24:27; Isa. 48:5//1 Ne. 20:5; "*her*" in Isa. 9:1//2 Ne. 19:1; "*his*" in Isa. 9:7//2 Ne. 19:7; "*their*" in Isa. 3:18//2 Ne. 13:18 (three occurrences; "*about their feet*" is lacking also); Isa. 13:11//2 Ne. 23:11; and the verb "*doeth*" in Isa. 49:18//1 Ne. 21:18. These cases support the conclusion that the text derives from the KJV since the lack of these words creates a choppier English, something not expected from and in a translation. Cases where the meaning changes significantly include: "What mean ye *that* ye beat my people" > "What mean ye? Ye beat my people" (Isa. 3:15//2 Ne. 13:15); "What shall *one* then answer the messengers of the nation?" > "What shall then answer the messengers of the nations?" (Isa. 14:32//2 Ne. 24:32; see the discussion in Part 6, example 19).

13. Additional examples of this type of change are: "yea, thou knewest not; yea, from that time *that* thine ear was not opened, for I knew ..." > "yea, thou knewest not, yea, from that time thine ear was not opened, for I knew ..." (Isa. 48:8//1 Ne. 20:8); "all the sons *that* she hath brought up" > "all the sons she hath brought up" (Isa. 51:18//2 Ne. 8:18); "by the way *that* thou shouldst go" >

"by the way thou shouldst go" (Isa. 48:17//1 Ne. 20:17); "And it shall come to pass, *that* instead of sweet smell" > "And it shall come to pass, instead of sweet smell" (Isa. 3:24//2 Ne. 13:24); "And it shall come to pass, *that he that* is left" > "And it shall come to pass them that are left" (Isa. 4:3//2 Ne. 14:3; "them" appeared in P, 1830, and later editions up to that of 1920 when more suitable English was inserted [BMCT 1:179n443]); "And it shall come to pass in that day, *that* every place shall be" > "And it shall come to pass in that day, every place shall be" (Isa. 7:23//2 Ne. 17:23).

14. Other instances of this kind are: "And they shall look unto the earth ... and *they shall be* driven to darkness" > "And they shall look to the earth ... and shall be driven to darkness" (Isa. 8:22//2 Ne. 18:22); "*he that is* left in Zion, and he *that* remaineth in Jerusalem" > "them that are left in Zion and remaineth in Jerusalem" (Isa. 4:3//2 Ne. 14:3); "How art thou fallen from heaven, O Lucifer, son of the morning, *how* art thou cut down to the ground" > "How art thou fallen from heaven, O Lucifer, son of the morning, art thou cut down to the ground" (14:12//2 Ne. 24:12); "like an abominable branch *and as* the raiment of those that are slain" > "like an abominable branch and the remnant of those that are slain" (Isa. 14:19//2 Ne. 24:19). If the awkward word "and" (before "excellent") in P is incorrect, then another case exists at 2 Ne. 14:2//Isa. 4:2.

15. In some cases, a group of italicized words in series is lacking in the BoM. This makes it appear that occasionally there was a wholesale reaction to the italics. For example, the ten italicized words in Isa. 3:14-24 are lacking in 2 Ne. 13:14-24 (note the six deleted in v. 18), and the ten in Isa. 49:17-19 are either lacking or have other words in their place in 2 Ne. 8:17-19. Cf. Isa. 7:20-23//2 Ne. 17:20-23 where five consecutive italicized words are missing or have alternative readings.

16. Cf. Isa. 14:27//2 Ne. 24:27: "and his hand *is* stretched out, and who shall turn it back" > "and his hand stretched out, and who shall turn it back."

17. See the BMCT on the passages for the textual attestations. The earliest texts, including P and 1830, lack the verb.

18. The verb "is" is missing in P and 1830; later editions restored it (see BMCT 1:192n548).

19. This reading is maintained in the 1981 LDS edition

20. This reading is in P and 1830. Pc and later editions of the BoM have "am" added (see BMCT 1:184n485).

21. So P and 1830; Pc reads "wo is unto me" (BMCT 1:184n481). The next lines of the same verse provide another example: the KJV has "for I am undone; because I *am* a man of unclean lips." P has "for I a man of unclean lips." This is apparently a case of parablepsis where the scribal eye has skipped from the first "I" to the second. The 1830 and Pc editions have: "for I am undone; because I a man of unclean lips." Despite the problems in P, this is a case where the italicized "*am*" was deleted to yield an awkward text. This verb was

inserted back into a further correction of the Pc and appears in printed editions of 1837 and later (BMCT 1:184n482).

22. The printed editions have remedied the problem by placing the phrase at the end of the preceding verse (LDS 2 Ne. 15:28; RLDS 2 Ne. 8:97; and 1830 edition punctuate similarly). This destroys the parallelism of the Hebrew text but saves the syntax by supplying the verb "shall be counted" from two lines before: "their horses' hoofs shall be counted like flint, and their wheels like a whirlwind, their roaring like a lion." Another case where deleting an italicized word creates an awkward text is Exod. 20:10//Mos. 13:18. Note also: "*There is* none to guide her among all the sons *whom* she hath brought forth; neither *is there any* that taketh her by the hand of all the sons *that* she hath brought up" > "And none to guide her among all the sons she hath brought forth, neither that taketh her by the hand of all the sons she hath brought up" (Isa. 51:18//2 Ne. 8:18).

23. Other instances of this type of change are: "and upon every *one that is* lifted up" > "and upon every one which is lifted up" (Isa. 2:12//2 Ne. 12:12); "afraid of man *that* shall die" > "afraid of a man which shall die" (Isa. 51:12//2 Ne. 8:12; cf. Isa. 50:9//2 Ne. 7:9).

24. Other examples are: "*even* the Lord" > "yea, the Lord" (Isa. 13:5//2 Ne. 23:5); "*even* all of them" > "yea, all of them" (Isa. 14:18//2 Ne. 24:18); "*even* for mine own sake" > "yea, for mine own sake" (Isa. 48:11//1 Ne. 20:11); "*even* I have spoken" > "yea, I have spoken" (Isa. 48:15//1 Ne. 20:15).

25. Cf. "*shall be*" > "is" (Isa. 3:10//2 Ne. 13:10); "*is*" > "was" (Isa. 48:4//1 Ne. 20:4); "*had ... been*" > "have ... been" (Isa. 49:21//1 Ne. 21:21). Sometimes the variant verb is more significant: "*are*" > "have been" (Isa. 3:8//2 Ne. 13:8); "*are*" > "shall be" (Isa. 5:28//2 Ne. 15:28). Some italicized pronouns vary without much change in significance (but it should be kept in mind that none of these variants reflect an actual word in the Hebrew): "*with him*" > "with them" (Isa. 3:10//2 Ne. 13:10); "I shewed *it*" > "I shewed them" (Isa. 48:5//1 Ne. 20:5); "I will do *it*" > "I will do this" (Isa. 48:11//1 Ne. 20:11).

26. Cf. "and *are* soothsayers like the Philistines" > "and hearken unto soothsayers like the Philistines" (Isa. 2:6//2 Ne. 12:6); "and if *one* look unto the land" > "and if they look unto the land" (Isa. 5:30//2 Ne. 15:30); "and *it* shall return" > "and they shall return" (Isa. 6:13//2 Ne. 16:13) "and everyone that is joined *unto them*" > "yea, and every one that is joined to the wicked" (Isa. 13:15//2 Ne. 23:15); "to them that *are* in darkness" > "to them that sit in darkness" (Isa. 49:9//1 Ne. 21:9); "the people in whose heart *is* my law" > "the people in whose heart I have written my law" (Isa. 51:7//2 Ne. 8:7).

27. Tvedtnes (IVT-1, 87) recognizes that this variant does not fit the Hebrew and says it could be a change of the italicized word. His alternative suggestion that it is a scribal mistake does not have real foundation. For a similar variant in 2 Ne. 15:19, see Part 4 below.

28. Other examples include: "And I will give children *to be* their princes" > "I will give children unto them to be their princes" (Isa. 3:4//2 Ne. 13:4); "*let*

this ruin *be* under thy hand" > "let not this ruin come under thy hand" (Isa. 3:6//2 Ne. 13:6); "upon all the glory *shall be*" > "upon all the glory of Zion shall be" (Isa. 4:5//2 Ne. 14:5); "but yet in it *shall be* a tenth" > "but yet in it there shall be a tenth" (Isa. 6:13//2 Ne. 16:13); "*and* not increased the joy" > "and increased the joy" (Isa. 9:3//2 Ne. 19:3); "every one *is* an hypocrite" > "every one of them is a hypocrite" (Isa. 9:17//2 Ne. 19:17); "*even* the remnant of Jacob" > "yea, even the remnant of Jacob" (Isa. 10:21//2 Ne. 20:21); "*and* the cedars" > "and also the cedars" (Isa. 14:8//2 Ne. 24:8); "they that see thee shall narrowly look upon thee *and* consider thee" > "they that see thee shall narrowly look upon thee and shall consider thee" (Isa. 14:16//2 Ne. 24:16); "all these gather themselves together *and* come to thee" > "all these gather themselves together and they shall come to thee" (Isa. 49:18//1 Ne. 21:18); "*as* I live" > "and as I live" (Isa. 49:18//1 Ne. 21:18); "everlasting joy *shall be*" > "everlasting joy and holiness shall be" (Isa. 51:11//2 Ne. 8:11); "the Lord of hosts *is* his name" > "the Lord of hosts is my name" (Isa. 51:15//2 Ne. 8:15). Italicized words are also sometimes transposed: "but *it is* in his heart to destroy" > "but in his heart it is to destroy" (Isa. 10:7//2 Ne. 20:7); "And it shall come to pass in that day, *that* a man shall nourish" > "And it shall come to pass that in that day a man shall nourish" (Isa. 7:21//2 Ne. 17:21); cf. Isa. 48:11//1 Ne. 20:12).

29. Other examples include: "Which they made *each one*" > "which he hath made" (Isa. 2:20//2 Ne. 12:20); "the wicked, it *shall be* ill *with him*" > "the wicked for they shall perish" (Isa. 3:11//2 Ne. 13:11); "and will not ye declare *it*? I have shewed thee" > "and will ye not declare them and that I have shewed thee" (Isa. 48:6//1 Ne. 20:6); "I, *even* I, have" > "I, the Lord, yea, I have" (Isa. 48:15//1 Ne. 20:15); "I *am* the Lord thy God which teacheth thee to profit, which leadeth thee by the way *that* thou shouldest go" > "I have sent him; the Lord thy God which teacheth thee to profit, which leadeth thee by the way thou shouldst go hath done it" (Isa. 48:17//1 Ne. 20:17); "*He is* near that justifieth" > "And the Lord is near and he justifieth" (Isa. 50:8//2 Ne. 7:8); "who *is* he *that* shall condemn me? lo, they all" > "and all they which shall condemn me, behold, all they" (Isa. 50:9//2 Ne. 7:9); "I, *even* I, *am* he that" > "I am he, yea, I am he that" (Isa. 51:12//2 Ne. 8:12).

30. The 1981 LDS edition retains the problematic reading.

31. Cf. Isa. 4:2//2 Ne. 14:2: "In that day shall the branch of the Lord be beautiful and glorious, and the fruit of the earth *shall be* excellent and comely for them that are escaped of Israel" > "In that day shall the branch of the Lord be beautiful and glorious, the fruit of the earth and excellent and comely to them that are escaped of Israel." This is found only in P. The 1830 and later editions do not have the "and" after "earth."

32. Tvedtnes's argument that the MT results from textual error is speculative because it requires two separate cases of haplography (see IVT-2, 173; cf. IVT-1, 52-53). A serious problem with his argument is that he discounts the different syntactic use of the word "for," saying that it was added for English

style (IVT-1, 53). One can further note that the BoM reading goes against the parallelism and sense of the verse.

33. Tvedtnes (IVT-1, 35, 80, 116-17) thinks that this variant is due to a misunderstanding by Smith or his scribe. That the variant is, in fact, intentional and from Smith is indicated by the italicized words and the adverb "yea," which suits a change from interrogation to declaration. The variant also appears twice in the passage. (See n52.) A case similar to 2 Ne. 7:2 is found at Isa. 5:4//2 Ne. 15:4; see below. For yet other examples of inconsistency with the Hebrew, see the discussion of Isa. 48:3//1 Ne. 20:3 and Isa. 48:16//1 Ne. 20:16 in Part 4 below. In that section, see also the discussion of how variants around italics in 2 Ne. 20:13 (//Isa. 10:13) and 2 Ne. 23:17 (//Isa. 13:17) produce texts which upset the poetic form of the Hebrew and thus indicate that the readings are not based on an ancient text.

34. Not removing or revising all italics is more or less consistent with Smith's treatment of italicized words in the JSR. Matthews, as cited above, noted that not all of the italics in Smith's Bible, used in producing the JSR, were crossed out. In the example from Genesis 20, noted above, eleven of twenty-three italicized words were retained. This does not undermine the conclusion that they were nevertheless an object of concern. It is simply witness to the fact that either his work was, of necessity, not thorough-going or that he considered many of them to be correct.

35. The versions include the NJPS, JB, NJB, RSV, NRSV, NEB, REB, NAB, and NIV. For the main critical commentaries, see: Bernhard Duhm, *Das Buch Jesaia* (5th ed.; Göttingen: Vandenhoeck & Ruprecht, 1968); Karl Elliger, *Deuterojesaja* 1. Teilband, Jesaja 40, 1-45, 7, Biblischer Kommentar Altes Testament 11/1, fascicles 1-6 (Neukirchen: Neukirchener Verlag, 1978); George B. Gray, *A Critical and Exegetical Commentary on the Book of Isaiah I-XXVII,* International Critical Commentary Series (Edinburgh: T. & T. Clark, 1912); Hans-Jürgen Hermisson, *Deuterojesaja* Jesaja 45, 8-48, 11 (to date), Biblischer Kommentar Altes Testament 11, fascicles 7-9 (Neukirchen: Neukirchener Verlag, 1987-92); Otto Kaiser, *Isaiah 1-12,* Old Testament Library Series (Philadelphia: Westminster Press, 1972); idem., *Isaiah 13-39,* Old Testament Library Series (Philadelphia: Westminster Press, 1974); Edward J. Kissane, *The Book of Isaiah,* 2 vols. (first vol. revised edition; Dublin: Browne and Nolan, Richview Press, 1960, 1943); John L. McKenzie, *Second Isaiah,* Anchor Bible, vol. 20 (Garden City, NY: Doubleday, 1968); Claus Westermann, *Isaiah 40-66,* Old Testament Library Series (Philadelphia: Westminster Press, 1969); Hans Wildberger, *Isaiah 1-12,* Continental Commentaries Series (Minneapolis: Fortress Press, 1991); idem., *Jesaja* 2. Teilband, Jesaja 13-27, Biblischer Kommentar Altes Testament 10/2 (Neukirchen: Neukirchener Verlag, 1978); idem., *Jesaja* 3. Teilband, Jesaja 28-39, Biblischer Kommentar Altes Testament 10/3 (Neukirchen: Neukirchener Verlag, 1982). The dictionaries include L. Koehler and W. Baumgartner, *Hebräisches und aramäisches Lexikon zum Alten Testament,* 4 vols. (3rd ed.; Leiden: E. J. Brill, 1983-90); F. Brown, S. R. Driver,

C. A. Briggs, *A Hebrew and English Lexicon of the Old Testament* (Oxford: Clarendon Press, 1953); David J. A. Clines, ed., *The Dictionary of Classical Hebrew,* 2 vols. to date (Sheffield, England: Sheffield Academic Press, 1993-95); Udo Rüterswörden, D. Rudolf Meyer, Herbert Donner, *Wilhelm Gesenius hebräisches und aramäisches Handwörterbuch über das Alte Testament,* 2 vols. to date (18th ed.; Berlin: Springer Verlag, 1987-95).

36. The BoM has "the" before "pleasant pictures."

37. The BoM has "to" before "choose," which does not affect the meaning.

38. BoM has here "along," which does not affect the meaning significantly.

39. BoM lacks "*them*" but means the same thing as the KJV.

40. The BoM lacks "that" before "mutter" and has "hear from" before "the dead" and "and" before "if they speak," but it essentially follows the meaning and structure of the KJV.

41. The BoM lacks the second pronoun "*they*" (a case of deletion of an italicized word). The meaning of the BoM is nonetheless the same as the KJV.

42. Koehler and Baumgartner, *Lexikon,* 964; Wildberger, *Isaiah,* 386. See in particular C. Cohen, "The Meaning of *ṣlmwt* 'Darkness': A Study in Philological Method," in *Texts, Temples, and Traditions,* ed. M. V. Fox et al. (Winona Lake, IN: Eisenbrauns, 1996), 287-309.

43. BoM lacks the italicized "*is.*"

44. Delete the *w-* on *wʾt* (cf. Wildberger, *Isaiah*, 413). Note that the KJV does not translate this conjunction.

45. The BoM has this phrase, though it has a variant for the following phrase.

46. P and 1830 read: "and I will make my judgment to rest for a light thing of the people" (BMCT 1:153n231). Aside from "light thing" (clearly a modification of the English text), the BoM follows the KJV reading.

47. So Brown, Driver, Briggs, *Lexicon,* 921a.

48. Other examples of the KJV versus modern renditions include: Isa. 6:13//2 Ne. 16:13 ("Whose substance is in them, when they cast *their leaves, so* the holy seed *shall be* the substance thereof"; "Whose stock/stump remains when they are felled [or: their leaves fall]: its stock/stump is the holy seed"); Isa. 8:1//2 Ne. 18:1 ("A man's pen"; "common/ordinary letters" or "common/ordinary stylus"); Isa. 9:1 (=Heb. 8:23)//2 Ne. 19:1 ("Nevertheless the dimness shall not be such as was in her vexation"; "But there will be no gloom for her that was in anguish" [RSV]); Isa. 10:18//2 Ne. 20:18 ("And they shall be as when a standardbearer fainteth"; "And it will be as when a sick man wastes away," "And it will be as when a weak person despairs," or "And it will be as when someone falls in a fit"); Isa. 49:4//1 Ne. 21:4 ("My work [is] with my God" [KJV]; "My recompense/reward is with God"); Isa. 49:24//1 Ne. 21:24//2 Ne. 6:16 ("Or the lawful captive delivered"; "Can ... captives [be] retrieved from a victor?" [NJPS]); Isa. 53:8//Mos. 14:8 ("He was taken from prison and from judgment: and who shall declare his generation?"; "By op-

pression and judgment he was taken away" [NIV], followed by "who could plead his cause" and variations).

49. The BoM is not clear as to whether the Isaiah of the brass plates or the BoM's gold plates were engraved in Hebrew or Egyptian (or an Egyptian script that was purely ideographic and somehow detached from the Egyptian language per se). For problems in the different theories, see Edward H. Ashment, "'A Record in the Language of My Father': Evidence of Ancient Egyptian and Hebrew in the Book of Mormon," in Brent Lee Metcalfe, ed., *New Approaches to the Book of Mormon: Explorations in Critical Methodology* (Salt Lake City: Signature Books, 1993), 329-93. It is likely that the evidence is not clear because of Joseph Smith's own confusion about linguistic matters (cf. Edwin Firmage Jr., "Historical Criticism and the Book of Mormon: A Personal Encounter," in this anthology). At any rate, the BoM, according to its internal assumptions, ultimately depends on a Hebrew text for Isaiah.

50. The inconsistency in the BoM is hard to explain. Perhaps it is evidence of the unsystematic and ad hoc nature of the revision, without reference back to how similar phrases were revised. This lends support to the argument that the quotations derive from working directly with the KJV. The BoM Isaiah shows other inconsistencies: e.g., Isa. 49:25 is rendered differently in 1 Ne. 21:25 and 2 Ne. 6:17 (see the discussion of this, Part 5 below).

51. One could make the argument that the preposition *mippĕnê* is being used as an asyndetic conjunction for *mippĕnê ʾăšer* (for this full conjunctive phrase, see Ex. 19:18; Jer. 44:23). But there are no cases in the Hebrew Bible where *mippĕnê* alone appears as a conjunction. On the other hand, the term as a preposition is found in other cases of hiding (Gen. 3:8; 4:14), which shows that a preposition makes perfect sense here. Tvedtnes (IVT-1, 25) recognizes the problem but has no satisfactory answer in support for the antiquity of the text.

52. It is doubtful that this variant is an accident (so IVT-1, 35, 116-17) since the same sort occurs at 2 Ne. 7:2, which is clearly intentional (see n33). BMCT 1:180n452 (on 2 Ne. 15:4) notes the use of *maddûaʿ* in an indirect question in Ex. 3:3 and the conjunctive translation of the LXX in Isa. 5:4 (*dioti* "for what reason"). This does not change the fact that the Hebrew does have an interrogative in Isa. 5:4 (note the parallelism with the first bicolon in the verse) which should appear as such in a translation that holds to the original. Smith had a predisposition for using "wherefore" as a conjunction (so Tvedtnes observes; cf. also Brent Metcalfe, "The Priority of Mosiah: A Prelude to Book of Mormon Exegesis," in Metcalfe, *New Approaches,* 408-14). This may explain why these changes occurred; the conjunctive use was more idiomatically natural to him, and consequently he reread these KJV Isaiah passages in that way.

53. This is one of the cases where the BoM maintains imprecise KJV language. It could be added to the list of questionable translations in Part 3.

54. Tvedtnes's argument (IVT-1, 71, 114-15) that "declared" is a scribal (dictation) mistake for "there" because they supposedly sound alike does not

hold because there is another variant in the line ("have I spoken") with which "declared" is conceptually consistent and coordinated. Too, a reading like "from the time that it was there have I spoken" does not make much sense, especially against the Hebrew.

55. This type of construction is not attested among the 586 examples of the verb *sym* (cf. the discussion in Brown, Driver, and Briggs, *Lexicon,* 962-64).

56. According to BMCT (1:153n231), Pc and later editions have "for a light for the people." I examined a photocopy of P and it had "for a light thing the people" with "of" written with a caret above and between "thing" and "the." The word "for" is written at a different angle over "thing," and it was not clear to me if "thing" underneath was crossed out. Tvedtnes (IVT-1, 84, 118) says the BoM reading is a scribal error, specifically an "overcorrection." He does not specify who made the mistake and how a word like "thing" could have inadvertently slipped into the text.

57. Tvedtnes (IVT-1, 36-37) recognizes the problem. His suggestion that "MT means to understand 'cities' as conglomerates of 'houses' without writing it" is forced.

58. Cf. BMCT 1:173n373. Tvedtnes (IVT-1, 23, 115) suggests the "not" of the P^c is perhaps a scribal error. This leaves an inconsistency. The addition is conceptually consistent with the negation at the end of the entire phrase.

59. Wildberger, *Isaiah,* 98. He notes (p. 110) that the punitive submission (from God) spoken of in this verse plays against the idolatrous prostration in v. 8.

60. The slash (/) marks the division between parallel lines.

61. A good introductory article is still Norman K. Gottwald, "Poetry, Hebrew," *Interpreter's Dictionary of the Bible,* ed. G. Buttrick, 4 vols. & supplement (Nashville: Abingdon Press, 1962, 1976), 3:829-38. For more detail, see Adele Berlin, *The Dynamics of Biblical Parallelism* (Bloomington: Indiana University Press, 1985); Wilfred G. E. Watson, *Classical Hebrew Poetry,* in the Journal for the Study of the Old Testament Supplement Series 26 (Sheffield, England: JSOT Press, 1986).

62. The Hebrew bicolon is: *bĕkōaḥ yādî ʿāśîtî / ûbĕḥokmātî kî nĕbunôtî.*

63. The Hebrew bicolon is: *ʾăšer kesep lōʾ yaḥšōbû / wĕzāhāb lōʾ yaḥpĕṣû bô.*

64. The double negative "nor ... not" is found in P, 1830, and later editions and was only "corrected" in 1920 (BMCT 1:202n625).

65. So BHS; Wildberger, *Isaiah,* 101; Kaiser, *Isaiah 1-12,* 31; Gray, *Isaiah,* 59.Kissane, *Isaiah,* 1:24, 30, retains the line.

66. Note that in the KJV the word "one" appears twice (strophe B). This word is italicized, which means that the Hebrew has no corresponding individual words. The BoM also has the word "one" twice, correlating more or less with where they appear in the KJV. Because of the correlation with the KJV's term, it is difficult to argue that the BoM text should have a separate Hebrew equivalent of "one" (e.g., *wĕʿal kol-ʾeḥād).*

67. Tvedtnes's textual arguments about this line are confusing (IVT-1, 25).

He is mistaken about 1QIsa^{a}, which in fact lacks *ʿal kol* ("upon every") before *niśśāʾ* ("[a person who is] lifted up"), not before *gēʾeh* ("proud") as he appears to imply. The parablepsis he proposes is problematic. His conversion of the BoM to Hebrew is wrong, as it should read in full: *ʿl kl gwywm wʿl kl wʿl gʾh.* Without *ʿal kol* before *gēʾeh,* the mechanism for textual error is reduced.

68. The verb *wĕšāpēl* itself is a problem and does not fit the context. Scholars have suggested that originally another term meaning "high," similar to other terms in the colon and passage, was here originally (cf. Wildberger, *Isaiah,* 101).

69. Cf. D&C 1:1-6; 3:1-3; 5:19-20; 45:1-9; 76:1-10. The existence and nature of parallelism in biblical poetry was already recognized in popular writings before Smith produced the BoM. For example, the Reverend Dr. John Smith published in 1804 a tract entitled "A Summary View and Explanation of the Writings of the Prophets" of which Adam Clarke cites a substantial portion in the preface to his commentary on Isaiah (*The Holy Bible Containing the Old and New Testaments ... with a Commentary and Critical Notes: Volume IV: Isaiah to Malachi* [Nashville: Abingdon, n.d. (preface date 1823)], 7-13 in the section on Isaiah). The Reverend Smith notes that "the greatest part of the prophetic writings was first composed in verse, and still retains, notwithstanding all the disadvantages of a literal prose translation, much of the air and cast of the original, particularly in the division of the lines, and in that peculiarity of Hebrew poetry by which the sense of one line or couplet so frequently corresponds with that of the other. [He cites Isa. 61:10, in verse form, as an example.] Attention to this peculiarity in sacred poetry will frequently lead to the meaning of many passages ... as the one line of a couplet, or member of a sentence, is generally a commentary on the other." After citing another example, he notes that "it must be observed that the parallelism is frequently more extended." After citing Isaiah 44:3, he says that "the two last lines explain the metaphor in the two preceding" (Clarke, p. 13). One may ask just how familiar Joseph Smith was with this issue as part of his religious education in the various churches he attended.

70. There is one case in which a variant shows a lack of knowledge of cultural-geographical context. In Isa. 9:1//2 Ne. 19:1, the KJV has "by the way of the sea, beyond Jordan, in Galilee of the nations"; the BoM has "by the way of the Red Sea, beyond Jordan in Galilee of the nations." Tvedtnes agrees that the reference to the "Red Sea" does not fit the context (IVT-1, 45, 115), but speculates without warrant that it is the result of "scribal overcorrection, due to prior mention of the Red Sea in the Book of Mormon text."

71. The major minuses are at 1 Ne. 20 (Isa. 48):3, 10, 16; 1 Ne. 21 (Isa. 49):7; 2 Ne. 6:17 (Isa. 49:25); 2 Ne. 7 (Isa. 50):10; 2 Ne. 8 (Isa. 51):1, 9, 15; 2 Ne. 15 (Isa. 5):8; 2 Ne. 19 (Isa. 9):4; 2 Ne. 23 (Isa. 13):8.

72. The term "yea" as a clue to secondariness is seen in other situations. The discussion on italics noted that "yea" often took the place of the italicized adverb "even." This shows that Smith had a preference for this term. The

word also exists as a single plus or in connection with more limited variants in the following cases: 1 Ne. 20:2//Isa. 48:2; 2 Ne. 7:1//Isa. 50:1; 2 Ne. 12:12// Isa. 2:12; 2 Ne. 20:21//Isa. 10:21; 2 Ne. 23:15//Isa. 13:15.

73. Cf. Isa. 29:8//2 Ne. 27:3; Isa. 29:9//2 Ne. 27:4.

74. Cases where "for" appears as a plus in a smaller variant include: 2 Ne. 12:13//Isa. 2:13; 2 Ne. 16:12//Isa. 6:12; 2 Ne. 7:9//Isa. 50:9; 2 Ne. 27:4// Isa. 29:9 (the phrase "For behold ...").

75. See also 2 Ne. 27:6//Isa. 29:11; 2 Ne. 27:15//Isa. 29:11; 2 Ne. 27:34// Isa. 29:13.

76. See also 2 Ne. 27:4//Isa. 29:9.

77. Skousen ("Textual Variants," 386-87) suggests that the missing phrase in 2 Ne. 6:17 may have been accidentally dropped in P when copying from O, which is not extant for this text. But he concludes that "there is probably not enough evidence to actually emend the text of 2 Nephi 6."

78. In view of this, the plus "Also, saith the Lord" in 1 Ne. 20:15 (//Isa. 48:15) appears to be secondary.

79. Tvedtnes believes that the citation of Isa. 49:22-52:2 contains paraphrase. He says: "The best evidence that he [Jacob] is paraphrasing is that, where these same Isaiah passages are cited elsewhere in the Book of Mormon, they are not worded the same as in Jacob's speech" (IVT-1, 80, on Isa. 50:1). 1 Ne. 21:25 and 2 Ne. 6:17 are the only places where there is significant variation. There are only slight variations between 1 Ne. 21:22-24, 26 and 2 Ne. 6:6-7, 16, 18 and between 3 Ne. 20:36-37 (cf. the paraphrase in Moro. 10:31) and 2 Ne. 8:24-25, and none indicates that the verses in 2 Ne. 6-8 are secondary. The rest of the Isaiah citation in 2 Ne. 7:1-8:23 (//Isa. 50-51) has no parallels elsewhere in the BoM (according to Nyman's list, *Words of Isaiah,* 275-76). Tvedtnes's argument that there is a paraphrase in 2 Ne. 6-8 seems geared toward skirting the contradiction between 1 Ne. 21:25 and 2 Ne. 6:17.

80. Another solution is to argue that all of the Isaiah passages in the BoM are paraphrased. That is, when the BoM says it is going to cite Isaiah, it does not mean that it will cite it literally. This would mean that many or all of the pluses and other variants are modifications of a more original Isaiah text. This conclusion brings us by a different route to the conclusion already made in this section of the essay. I doubt, however, that this solution is the right one. It seems that when the characters of the book say they will read from the text, and when the text cites Isaiah for long stretches without any clear interpolation, the text intends this as unalloyed citation.

81. BMCT (see notes passim on Isaiah parallels); Hugh Nibley, *Since Cumorah: The Book of Mormon in the Modern World* (Salt Lake City: Deseret Book, 1967), 129-43; Sidney B. Sperry, *The Voice of Israel's Prophets* (Salt Lake City: Deseret Book, 1952), 90-94; Sidney B. Sperry, *Book of Mormon Compendium* (Salt Lake City: Bookcraft, 1968), 507-12; John Welch, ed., *Reexploring the Book of Mormon: The F.A.R.M.S. Updates* (Salt Lake City: Deseret Book; Provo: FARMS, 1992), 77-79. Cf. Sperry's unpublished study, "The Text of Isa-

iah in the Book of Mormon" (M.A. thesis, University of Chicago, Divinity School, 1926); W. Ham, "A Textual Comparison of the Isaiah Passages in the Book of Mormon with the Same Passages in the St. Mark's Isaiah Scroll of the Dead Sea Community" (M.A. thesis, Brigham Young University, 1961).

82. For these sources, see J. Neville Birdsall, Leonard J. Greenspoon, S. P. Brock, Pierre-Maurice Bogaert, "Versions, Ancient," *Anchor Bible Dictionary*, ed. D. N. Freedman, 6 vols. (New York: Doubleday, 1992), 6:787-803; Melvin K. H. Peters, "Septuagint," *Anchor Bible Dictionary*, 5:1093-1104; Philip S. Alexander, "Targum, Targumim," *Anchor Bible Dictionary*, 6:320-31; D. C. Parker, "Vulgate," *Anchor Bible Dictionary*, 6:860-62. See also the articles in Martin Jan Mulder and Harry Sysling, eds., *Mikra: Text, Translation, Reading, and Interpretation of the Hebrew Bible in Ancient Judaism and Early Christianity*, Compendia Rerum Iudaicarum ad Novum Testamentum 2/1 (Assen/Maastricht: Van Gorcum; Philadelphia: Fortress Press, 1988).

83. Several Targum texts have an alternative reading: *wĕʿal kol dĕyātbîn bĕnêsê yammāʾ* "and against all those who dwell in the islands of the sea" (followed by Bruce D. Chilton in his translation, *The Isaiah Targum*, The Aramaic Bible 11 [Wilmington, DE: Michael Glazier, 1987], 7). One of the points the Targum is trying to make in Isa. 2:16 is that the day of the Lord will be upon the *people* connected with the places or objects mentioned in the Hebrew of that verse.

84. Philip Barlow, *Mormons and the Bible: The Place of the Latter-day Saints in American Religion* (New York: Oxford University Press, 1991), 30-31; Victor Ludlow, *Isaiah: Prophet, Seer, and Poet* (Salt Lake City: Deseret Book, 1982), 90-91; Nyman, *Words of Isaiah*, 33; Sperry, *Voice*, 90-91; Sperry, *Compendium*, 508; Tvedtnes, in IVT-1, 26-27, and IVT-2, 170; Welch, *Reexploring the Book of Mormon*, 78; Church Educational System, *Old Testament: 1 Kings-Malachi (Religion 302) Student Manual* (Salt Lake City: Church of Jesus Christ of Latter-day Saints, 1981). However, none of these have critically examined the issue.

85. So James A. Montgomery, *A Critical and Exegetical Commentary on the Book of Daniel, International Critical Commentary Series* (Edinburgh: T. & T. Clark, [1926]), 409.

86. It is not clear, in view of the Targumic evidence, that Greek *thalassa* ("sea") is a "phonetic development from a transliteration" (Montgomery, *Daniel*, 409). On the LXX being an interpretive translation and the care that must be shown using it in textual criticism, see James Barr, "The Typology of Literalism in Ancient Biblical Translations," *Mitteillungen des Septuaginta-Unternehmens* (MSU) 15, Nachrichten der Akademie der Wissenschaften in Göttingen, Philologisch-historische Klasse (Göttingen: Vandenhoeck & Ruprecht, 1979), 279-325; Ernst Würthwein, *The Text of the Old Testament*, 2nd ed. (Grand Rapids, MI: Eerdmans, 1995), 68-71; Emanuel Tov, *The Text-Critical Use of the Septuagint in Biblical Research* (Jerusalem: Simor Ltd., 1981), 29-72.

87. Myles Coverdale, *The Holy Scriptures of the Olde and Newe Testamente ...*

M.D.XXXV [1535] (London: Samuel Bagster & Sons, 1838 ["reprinted from the copy in the library of His Royal Highness the Duke of Sussex"]).

88. John Wesley, *Explanatory Notes upon the Old Testament,* vol. 3 (Bristol: William Pine, 1765; reprint: Salem, OH: Schmul Publishers, 1975), 1953.

89. Matthew Poole, *Annotations upon the Holy Bible,* vol. 2 (Edinburgh: Thomas and John Turnbull, 1801), 773 (reprint: *A Commentary on the Holy Bible,* vol. 2 [Peabody, MA: Hendrickson, [n.d.]), 331. Its explanation has only a slight variant: "The ships of the sea, as that word is used, Psal. xlviii 7, whereby you fetched riches and precious things from the remote parts of the world."

90. William Lowth, *Commentary upon the Old and New Testaments: The Prophets,* vol. 4 (London: Samuel Bagster, 1809 [original 1727]), 12.

91. John Fawcett, *The Devotional Family Bible Containing the Old and New Testaments,* vol. 2 (London: Suttaby, Evance, & Co. and R. Baldwin, 1811) at 2:16. His explanation has a slight variation: "Ships of Tarshish signify, in scripture, any trading or merchant ships. The Septuagint translation is 'ships of the sea.'"

92. Thomas Scott, *The Holy Bible Containing the Old and New Testaments, with Original Notes, Practical Observations, and Copious References* (Philadelphia: William W. Woodward, 1810-12), s.v., Isa. 2:16. Other editions include: New York: Whiting and Watson, 1812-15; Boston, 1823-24 and 1827. The explanation in Scott reads exactly the same as in Lowth with a reference to Lowth.

93. See Donna Hill, *Joseph Smith: The First Mormon* (Garden City, NY: Doubleday, 1977), 49-50.

94. BMCT (1:172n368) notes that the BoM phrase may have been deleted by haplography. Haplography is a scribal mistake where a letter or group of letters is written once when it is to be written twice.

95. Parablepsis is where a word or phrase is left out because its beginning is the same as the text that follows or its end is the same as the text that precedes (cf. Emanuel Tov, *Textual Criticism of the Hebrew Bible* [Minneapolis: Fortress Press; Assen/Maastricht: Van Gorcum, 1992], 237-40.

96. See Emanuel Tov, *Textual Criticism,* 256-58.

97. He says that the LXX has the reading "Therefore, O Jacob" or in some manuscripts "Therefore, O Israel" (BMCT 1:172n369 also refers to this). This is not attested in the text or apparatus of Joseph Ziegler, ed., *Isaias,* 3rd ed., Septuaginta, Vetus Testamentum Graecum Auctoritate Soceitatis Litterarum Gottingensis Editum, vol. 14 (Göttingen: Vandenhoeck & Ruprecht, 1983) or Alfred Rahlfs, ed., *Septuaginta* (Stuttgart: Württembergische Bibelanstalt, 1935). Nor is it found in the detailed textual notes of Duhm, *Isaiah,* 39-40; Gray, *Isaiah,* 57; Wildberger, *Isaiah,* 99 (or in the Targum, Peshitta, or Vulgate).

98. *w-* in 1QIsa[a] and *gar* in the LXX (IVT-2, 168-169; IVT-1, 24; BMCT 1:173n377). The conjunction, as Tvedtnes notes, may have been lost due to similarity with the *-w* ending the preceding verse.

99. See IVT-2, 170; IVT-1, 27-28; cf. BMCT 1:174n389; Sperry, *Voice,* 91; Sperry, *Compendium,* 508-509.

100. BMCT 1:175n393; IVT-2, 170; IVT-1, 28 (Tvedtnes labels this a scribal error).

101. See Wildberger, *Isaiah,* 124; Kaiser, *Isaiah 1-12,* 39; Gray, *Isaiah,* 63; BHK; BHS.

102. The Aramaic has a variation akin to that in the BoM but with the terms in the order of *smāk, sʿêd, smāk, sʿêd* as opposed the BoM's chiastic ordering.

103. Tvedtnes's data are inexact, perhaps by inadvertence. He notes that the Peshitta has the preposition but then gives the transliteration of the Targum. Both have the preposition: the Peshitta reads *lzdyqʾ* ("to the righteous one" [singular, as indicated by the vocalized editions and the lack of seyame dots in the Brill edition]) and the Targum reads *lṣdyqyʾ* ("to the righteous ones" [plural]). The prepositions in Peshitta and Targum do not mean that their underlying Hebrew texts had prepositions; the translations may be construing according to sense. Though the MT does not have a preposition, it must be construed with one.

104. The description here is based on the correction of data made in the previous note; it is the Targum, not the Peshitta, that has the plural.

105. IVT-2, 171; IVT-1, 34; cf. BMCT 1:178n436.

106. BMCT 1:178n437 correctly notes the parallel in the LXX but wrongly references two other texts. 1QIsa^{a} does not read like the BoM, but like the MT. The Targum does have a conjunction, but it is in the wrong place: *wttrwqn ʾrʿʾ wtḥrwb,* "her land will be emptied out and be desolate" (a reading that is highly interpretive).

107. Cf. Wildberger, *Isaiah,* 248; NJPS; NRSV. Tvedtnes (IVT-1, 42) actually gives the translation "and the forsaking shall be great" but does not draw attention to the discrepancy with the BoM or KJV.

108. See also BMCT 1:191n545; Sperry, *Voice,* 93-94; Sperry, *Compendium,* 511-12. Cf. a similar solution to a problematic negative in Isa. 49:5, noted in Part 3 above.

109. See, for example, Wildberger, *Isaiah,* 386; Anthony Hutchinson, "The Word of God is Enough: The Book of Mormon as Nineteenth-Century Scripture," in Metcalfe, *New Approaches,* 13.

110. Other examples include "depth/height" > "depths/heights" (Isa. 7:11 //2 Ne. 17:11); "forest" > "forests" (Isa. 9:18//2 Ne. 19:18 and Isa. 10:34//2 Ne. 20:34); "nation" > "nations" (Isa. 14:32//2 Ne. 24:32); "iniquity" > "iniquities" (Isa. 53:6//Mos. 14:6); "transgression" > "transgressions" (Isa. 53:8// Mos. 14:8); and "sin" > "sins" (Isa. 53:12//Mos. 14:12).

111. Tvedtnes also argues that the original Hebrew text had an abbreviation *wywš,* as found in 1QIsa^{a}, which he says could have been read as a singular or plural. It is unlikely that the Qumran scroll has an abbreviation. It has no other cases of the participle or substantive *yôšēb* in any of its forms appearing as an abbreviation. Too, the odd *wywš* comes at the end of a line where the acciden-

tal omission of a final letter (i.e., *-b*) seems possible. We may have a scribal mistake rather than an abbreviation. Moshe H. Goshen-Gottstein, ed., *The Book of Isaiah,* The Hebrew University Bible, 3 vols. (Jerusalem: Magnes Press, 1975-93), 1.35, says that the scroll has a lacuna (not an abbreviation): *wyw*[ ].

112. BMCT 1:197n585; cf. Welch, *Reexploring the Book of Mormon,* 77-78.

113. "Ramath" occurs in Judg. 15:17 in the compound place name Ramath-lehi. The term "Lehi" occurs independently in this chapter as a place name in vv. 9, 14, 19. This is the only place in the Bible where this latter term occurs. Of course, Lehi is also the name of the leading patriarch in the BoM story (1 Ne., etc.). One wonders, quite speculatively, if the compound place name Ramath-lehi made an impression upon Smith such that he converted "Ramah" into "Ramath." Note, however, the place name Ramah in Eth. 15:11.

114. The insertion of a *-t* at the end of *ᶜyh* (Aiah) in v. 28 of 1QIsa[a] may not be to show an older form or to conform to an earlier text but simply to correct a mistake, contra Tvedtnes. In any case, it does not provide proof that the BoM reading "Ramath" comes from an ancient source.

115. Note that Edwin Hatch and Henry A. Redpath (*A Concordance to the Septuagint,* 2 vols. [Oxford: Clarendon Press, 1897]) take *tachu* as a translation of Hebrew *qārôb* (2:1339a) and *chroniei* as a translation of *yimmāšēkû* (2:1476b). Joseph Ziegler (*Untersuchungen zur Septuaginta des Buches Isaias,* Alttestamentliche Abhandlungen 12/3 [Münster: Verlag der Aschendorffschen Verlagsbuchhandlung, 1934], 112) also takes the Greek phrase as a translation of the last phrase in the MT.

116. See the critical apparatus in Rahlfs, *Septuaginta,* and Ziegler, *Isaias,* ad loc.

117. BMCT 1:203n632 says that the LXX has eight poetic lines in this verse just as the BoM has eight poetic lines. This is wrong. The BoM has only seven poetic lines (four where it correlates with the Bible and three in its plus). The LXX (including the two pluses noted in the apparatus of Ziegler, *Isaias*) has at most five, maybe six lines. One of the pluses, as just seen in the main text above, is a recapitulation of, or an alternative to, the last line of the MT. The other plus translates part of the second poetic line in the MT (*kai en tois naois tēs spatalēs autēs,* "and in her sanctuaries of luxury") and comes after a line which is also a translation of this same MT line (*kai nossopoiēsousin echinoi en tois oikois autōn,* "and hedgehogs shall make their nests in their dwellings"; note that Hatch and Redpath, *Concordance to the Septuagint,* take *echinoi* as a translation of Hebrew *tannîn* in this line [1:592a], and they note several cases where the Hebrew *hêkāl,* which appears in this line, is translated *oikos* [2:973-982; for the line under discussion here, see 2:980b]). Again, the LXX provides no support for the BoM reading.

118. Cf. Benjamin Kennicott, ed., *Vetus Testamentum Hebraicum cum Variis Lectionibus,* vol. 2 (Oxford: Clarendon, 1780); cf. Goshen-Gottstein, *Isaiah,* ad loc.

119. Isa 2:17, 20; 3:7, 18; 4:1, 2; 5:30; 7:18, 21, 23; 10:20, 27; 11:10, 11; 12:1, 4; 17:4, 7, 9; 19:16, 18, 21, 23, 24; 20:6; 22:8, 12, 20, 25; 23:15; 24:21; 25:9; 26:1; 27:1, 2, 12, 13; 28:5; 29:18; 30:23; 31:7; 52:6 (cf. 2:12; 7:20; 10:3; 13:6, 9).

120. IVT-2, 174; IVT-1, 60. Tvedtnes notes in both of these studies that the Targum has "kings" instead of messengers. This is an error.

121. BMCT 1:207n664 notes that some ancient versions have "nations," as does the BoM, against the KJV/MT "nation." See the discussion of singular/plural variants in example 13 above.

122. The unedited original manuscript reads: "for how should I suffer my name to be polluted" (cf. Skousen, "Textual Variants," 381). If this is the correct reading (simplified by Skousen), then comparison with the following versions that have negative particles is irrelevant. There is no ancient text or version that reads like the unedited O with a causative verb and the noun "my name."

123. A better translation is "be profaned," but I use "be polluted" to show the correspondence between this and the KJV translation.

124. Most manuscripts and early editions have the third person *delā' yittaḥal* ("so that it not be polluted").

125. See Ziegler, *Untersuchungen*, 75; Duhm, *Jesaia*, 364; Hermisson, *Deuterojesaja*, 207. They are not agreed on where the word may have appeared in the verse. For the originality of the term "my name," compare the similarity of Isa. 42:8-9 with 48:11-12.

126. Thus the formulation is not necessarily a manifestation of original poetic parallelism. The idiom in Ezek. 39:7, "I will not let them pollute my holy name any more," may have, but not necessarily, also influenced the formulation of the BoM variant (cf. Ezek. 20:9).

127. Nibley, *Since Cumorah*, 132-134; IVT-2, 174-75; IVT-1, 70; BMCT 1:106 n790.

128. IVT-2, 175; cf. IVT-1, 72-73; BMCT 1:108n811.

129. Nibley's argument (*Since Cumorah*, 134) that the plus is missing because the "doctors of the schools who made both the Septuagint and the Masora" found it offensive is without merit since leaders are elsewhere denounced in prophetic literature. Why delete this instance and not the many other cases?

130. Metcalfe, "Apologetic and Critical Assumptions," 162-69.

131. Cf. 1 Ne. 19:10, 12, 16; 22:3-4; 2 Ne. 10:8, especially vv. 20-21.

132. IVT-2, 175; IVT-1, 80-81; BMCT 1:150nn200-202; Sperry, *Voice*, 93; Sperry, *Compendium*, 509-11.

133. The reading *tbʾš* rather than *tybš* appears to be correct since elsewhere in the Bible there are cases of fish stinking (Ex. 7:18, 21), but not of fish drying up.

134. The comment in BMCT 1:150n202 that the LXX has "dried up" is misleading since it makes it appear as if LXX has the BoM phrase "waters are dried up," which is not the case.

135. Cf. "whose arrows *are* sharp" > "whose arrows shall be sharp" (Isa. 5:28

//2 Ne. 15:28) and the context of the preceding future tenses; "and every one that is joined unto *them*" > "yea, and every one that is joined to the wicked" (Isa. 13:15//2 Ne. 23:15) with "the wicked" in v. 11 and the general context of evil doing; "*but* not in truth" > "yet they swear not in truth" (Isa. 48:1//1 Ne. 20:1) and the preceding "which swear"; "I did *them*" > "I did shew them" (Isa. 48:3//1 Ne. 20:3) and "shew" in the previous line; "I shewed *it*" > "I shewed them" (Isa. 48:5//1 Ne. 20:5) and "I shewed them" in v. 3; "will not ye declare *it*? I have shewed" > "will ye not declare them and that I have shewed" (Isa. 48:6//1 Ne. 20:6) and context of "them" in vv. 3, 5; "from the time that it was, there *am* I" > "from the time that it was declared have I spoken" (Isa. 48:16//1 Ne. 20:16) with "to declare" of v. 15 of BoM; and "I *am* the Lord thy God" > "I have sent him, the Lord they God" (Isa. 48:17//1 Ne. 20:17) with "sent" of v. 16.

136. Kennicott (*Vetus Testamentum Hebraicum*) notes many manuscripts with different spellings of the word but not any that lack the term. BHS and BHK do not note variants. Goshen-Gottstein, *Isaiah,* 3.234, does not list the variant.

137. IVT-2, 176; IVT-1, 84. Tvedtnes is not altogether convinced of the textual parallel. In *The Isaiah Variants* (IVT-1), he says that the BoM reading may simply be an omission due to paraphrasing. On this issue, see Part 5 above.

138. Present only in some manuscripts.

139. "Der MT 54, 15 war für die LXX zu undurchsichtig" (Ziegler, *Untersuchungen,* 164).

140. Ziegler, *Untersuchungen,* 164: "Durch *gwr* des MT dachte sie an die Proselyten und hat sich den Satz frei zurechgelegt im Anschluß an 55, 5." There are several differences between the LXX and the MT which, in view of the difficulty of the MT, seem to be signs that the Greek is not literally translating: (1) the noun (*prosēlutoi*) in the first line of the Greek, where the MT only has a verb; (2) the pronoun *soi* in the Greek, lacking in the MT; (3) the absence of a correspondent in the Greek for *ʾepes*; (4) no correspondent for MT's *mî* ("who") but the appearance of a conjunction (*kai,* "and"); and (5) another conjunction (*kai,* "and") before MT's *ʿālayik yippôl.*

141. The LXX translations of Ex. 12:48 and Num. 9:14 are similar but have *pros humas* instead of the dative pronoun.

142. Koehler and Baumgartner, *Lexikon,* 177b.

143. McKenzie, *Second Isaiah,* 183.

144. Ibid., 139.

145. Most of these are also listed in IVT-1, 98. Tvedtnes's ten examples are: (1) 2 Ne. 13:9//Isa. 3:9; (2) 2 Ne. 13:14//Isa. 3:14; (3) 2 Ne. 13:26//Isa. 3:26; (4) 1 Ne. 20:5//Isa. 48:5; (5) 1 Ne. 20:8//Isa. 48:8; (6) 1 Ne. 20:13//Isa. 48:13; (7) 1 Ne. 20:14//Isa. 48:14; (8) 1 Ne. 20:22//Isa. 48:22; (9) 2 Ne. 7:9//Isa. 50:9; and (10) 2 Ne. 8:18//Isa. 51:18.

146. An example of this is found in sampling the conjunctions in the LXX,

Targum, and Peshitta for Isa. 2-3. These vary in 38 places against the MT, most often with an added conjunction where the MT does not have one. In these 38 instances, the versions all agree in only two places (2:4; 3:9). Two of them agree in 12 places (2:3, 10; 3:2, 3, 7, 8, 14, 19, 20, 21, 22, 25). The other 24 occurrences (almost two-thirds) are in only one version (2:2, 4, 5 bis, 11, 13, 19, 20, 22; 3:2, 5 ter, 7, 8, 9, 13, 14, 16, 18, 19 bis, 26 bis). It is doubtful that, even when two or three versions agree, the variants reflect conjunctions or their absence in the underlying Hebrew text. Many of the discrepancies can be ascribed to the freedom of translators.

147. 1 Ne. 20:22 is actually not an example since Tvedtnes has had to manipulate the Book of Mormon text to produce the parallel. The KJV reads: "There is no peace ..." (MT: *ʾyn šlwm*), while the BoM reads: "And notwithstanding he hath done all this and greater also there is no peace." Tvedtnes says the "also" at the end of the BoM plus should be read with the phrase "there is no peace," which then finds a parallel in 1QIsa[a] (which has a conjunction: *wʾyn šlwm*, "and there is no peace"). This division of the sentence leaves the initial subordinate circumstantial clause hanging: "And notwithstanding he has done all this and greater, also there is no peace." Thus BoM's "also" must go with the preceding clause, and the parallel between the Qumran manuscript and BoM does not exist.

148. Cf. the NJPS, which construes the syntax similarly: "Because I know how stubborn you are (your neck is like an iron sinew, and your forehead bronze), therefore I told you long beforehand."

149. Note that the other instances of *gm* in the verse are rendered "yea" in the KJV (and BoM).

150. This conclusion pertains also to the other examples in Tvedtnes's lengthier work, categories A-D, which he says are "favorable to the authenticity" of the BoM (IVT-1, 96-102). They include: 2 Ne. 12:2 (//Isa. 2:2), a variant at an italicized word; 2 Ne. 13:11 (//Isa. 3:11), which smooths out plural/singular inconsistencies and has no ancient textual support; 2 Ne. 13:12 (//Isa. 3:12), italicized words; 2 Ne. 15:1 (//Isa. 5:1), which Tvedtnes does not show to be a superior translation of the MT; 2 Ne. 15:15 (//Isa. 5:15), where an awkward KJV reading is smoothed out; 2 Ne. 16:9 (//Isa. 6:9), which the textual evidence does not support, especially since the BoM has verbs with different persons (imperative second person versus third person); 2 Ne. 23:4 (//Isa. 13:14), a minor point not necessarily the result of translation; 2 Ne. 24:8 (//Isa. 14:8), connected to the italics (the LXX manuscripts do not support a reading of "and also," and the 3 + 2 pattern may speak against adding *gam*); 1 Ne. 20:6 (//Isa. 48:6), connected to an italicized word (where the Greek reading is contextually different from the BoM and may be the result of interpretation); 1 Ne. 21:8 (//Isa. 49:8), wherein the plus breaks up the neat parallelism of the MT and is therefore secondary; 1 Ne. 21:9 (//Isa. 49:9), for which the proposed textual development is the most elaborately speculative of all that Tvedtnes offers; 1 Ne. 21:18 (//Isa. 49:18), connected to the italics and con-

textual revision of the KJV; 3 Ne. 20:39 (//Isa. 52:6), a paraphrase (and so the textual comparison is unlikely); Mos 12:22; 15:29; 3 Ne. 16:18; 20:32-33 (// Isa. 52:8), regarding which the pronoun "your" in 1QIsa[a] and the Targum appears with the second occurrence of *qôl* ("voice") and thus does not support the appearance of "thy" with the first occurrence of "voice" in Mos 15:29 and 3 Ne. 20:32; too, the variation in the BoM readings indicates that the pronoun may be the result of a BoM paraphrase (cf. esp. 3 Ne. 20:32-33); moreover, the KJV which the BoM otherwise follows is probably erroneous here (cf. the NJPS).

151. Nibley, *Since Cumorah,* 129. Cf. B. H. Roberts, "Bible Quotations in the Book of Mormon," *Improvement Era* 7 (Jan. 1904): 178-92, who says: "When Joseph Smith saw that the Nephite record was quoting the prophecies of Isaiah, of Malachi, or the words of the Savior, he too[k the] English Bible and compared those passages as far as they paralleled each other, and finding that in substance, in thought, they were alike, he adopted our English translation" (183-84). Cf. the similar views of Kent Jackson, "Nephi and Isaiah (2 Nephi 11-25)," in Kent Jackson, ed., *Studies in Scripture, Volume 7: 1 Nephi to Alma 29* (Salt Lake City: Deseret Book, 1987), 139, and Daniel Ludlow, *Companion to Your Study of the Book of Mormon* (Salt Lake City: Deseret Book, 1982), 229-30.

152. See John W. Welch and Tim Rathbone, "The Translation of the Book of Mormon: Preliminary Report on the Basic Historical Information," *FARMS Paper & Reprint WRR-86* (Provo, UT: FARMS, 1986), 14. Although Emma Smith said her husband did not use a book in the translation, she was not a witness to the entire process. Too, she was mainly interested in denying that the Spaulding manuscript was a source of the Book of Mormon.

153. This is implied in IVT-1, passim, especially 96-128, and in BMCT 1:vii. Tvedtnes says: "Joseph Smith made use of the KJV text of Isaiah" (96) and acknowledges the deletion and replacement of italicized words (106-11) but tends to credit errors to scribes (114-18). BMCT says that "B. H. Roberts, H. Grant Vest, and Stanley R. Larson have each convincingly argued that Joseph Smith certainly utilized a copy of the King James Version ... whenever he came to lengthy portions of the text of the Book of Mormon obviously paralleling biblical passages. It is only in such a context that both the real variants upon the plates, as well as Joseph's personal taste are made evident. We have sought to provide access to both phenomena through careful notes and through the insertion of KJV italics into the text of biblical quotations." By "Joseph's personal taste," I understand the BMCT to refer to modifications that are based on italics and perhaps some errors.

154. This approach to the Isaiah problem has resonances with Blake T. Ostler's approach to the BoM at large ("The Book of Mormon as a Modern Expansion of an Ancient Source," *Dialogue: A Journal of Mormon Thought* 20 [Spring 1987]: 66-123). He argues that the BoM has an ancient core which has been significantly expanded by Smith with non-ancient materials. The theory about BoM Isaiah recognizes an ancient core from translation and an elabora-

tion by Smith in response to the KJV. For a critique of Ostler's theory, see Brent Metcalfe, "Apologetic and Critical Assumptions about Book of Mormon Historicity," *Dialogue: A Journal of Mormon Thought* 26 (Fall 1993): 171-74.

155. Stan Larson, "The Historicity of the Matthean Sermon on the Mount in 3 Nephi," in Metcalfe, *New Approaches,* 115-63. Critiques of Larson's argument are found in Daniel C. Peterson, ed., *Review of Books on the Book of Mormon,* vol. 6, number 1 (Provo, UT: FARMS, 1994). Larson's arguments still prevail. In connection with his study, one should read Krister Stendahl, "The Sermon on the Mount and Third Nephi," in Truman Madsen, ed., *Reflections on Mormonism: Judaeo-Christian Parallels* (Provo, UT: Religious Studies Center, Brigham Young University, 1978), 139-54. This shows directly or indirectly the derivative character of the 3 Nephi sermon. See also Ronald V. Huggins, "Did the Author of 3 Nephi Know the Gospel of Matthew?" *Dialogue: A Journal of Mormon Thought* 30 (Fall 1997): 137-48. One should also see Stephen Thompson's review of Metcalfe's *New Approaches* and its critics (*Review of Books on the Book of Mormon* 6:1) in *Dialogue* 27:4 (Winter 1994): 197-206; and Todd Compton's review in *Sunstone* 19/3 (Sept. 1996): 74-81.

156. Examples: "*do*" and "*can*" are deleted (3 Ne. 13:7; 14:18//Matt. 6:7; 7:18); "*are*" becomes "are all" (3 Ne. 12:4, 6, 8, 9, 10//Matt. 5:4, 6, 8, 9, 10); "*is*" becomes "shall be" (3 Ne. 12:12//Matt. 5:12); "*thine*" becomes "your" (3 Ne. 13:2//Matt. 6:2); "*shall he* not much more *clothe* you, O ye of little faith" becomes "even so will he clothe you, if ye are not of little faith" (3 Ne. 13:30//Matt. 5:30); and "thou shalt not be as the hypocrites *are*" becomes "thou shalt not do as the hypocrites" (3 Ne. 13:5//Matt. 6:5).

157. David P. Wright, "'In Plain Terms that We May Understand': Joseph Smith's Transformation of Hebrews in Alma 12-13," in Metcalfe, *New Approaches,* 165-229. The critiques by John Welch and John Tvedtnes in *Review of Books on the Book of Mormon* 6:1 do not invalidate my arguments. Welch (168-81) argues that Genesis 14, not Hebrews, is the source of Alma 12-13. But the Alma chapters have more parallels with Hebrews. He tries to diminish the strength of the Hebrews parallels by noting similar motifs and other elements in other texts. This has no force since he does not present another single text with as many specific terms and motifs as Hebrews. Tvedtnes (19-23) argues that one should look at ancient texts such as 11QMelch and 2 Enoch. These, which I did deal with in my study (cf. nn15, 78, 79 therein), do not provide the parallels of the sort we find between Hebrews and Alma. His comparative analysis lacks rigor and detail, and his logic is not lucid in several places.

158. See the articles in Metcalfe, *New Approaches,* and also the works mentioned in my article there, "In Plain Terms," 165n2. See also Metcalfe, "Apologetic and Critical Assumptions" (William Hamblin responds to this in the *Review of Books on the Book of Mormon* 6:1); Edwin Firmage Jr., "Historical Criticism and the Book of Mormon"; Mark D. Thomas, *Digging in Cumorah: Reclaiming Book of Mormon Narratives* (Salt Lake City: Signature Books, 1999).

159. See Christopher R. Seitz, "Isaiah, Book of (First Isaiah)" and "Isaiah,

Book of (Third Isaiah)," in *Anchor Bible Dictionary* 3:472-88, 501-507; and Richard J. Clifford, "Isaiah, Book of (Second Isaiah)," *Anchor Bible Dictionary* 3:488-501.

160. Isa. 40:1-2; 42:22-25; 43:26-28; 47:6-15; 48:3-4; 49:14-21; 51:19; 54:7-8.

161. Isa. 40:1-2, 9-11; 41:27(?); 44:26-28; 45:13; 49:8, 14-21; 51:3, 17-23; 52:1-10; 54:passim.

162. Isa. 43:14; 47:1-15; 48:14, 20.

163. Isa. 43:5-8; 45:13; 48:20; 49:9-12, 22-26.

164. Isa. 44:28; 45:1-13; cf. 41:2, 25; 46:11; 48:14.

165. Isa. 44:1-5; 48:17-19; 49:20-23; 54:1-5, 9-10, 14.

166. Studies that have argued the unity of Isaiah have not succeeded. Some of these have originated in Mormon circles, including L. Lamar Adams's dissertation ("A Statistical Analysis of the Book of Isaiah in Relation to the Isaiah Problem" [Brigham Young University, 1972]; see also Adams and Alvin C. Rencher, "A Computer Analysis of the Isaiah Authorship Problem," *BYU Studies* 15 [1974]: 95-102), and its critique by A. Dean Forbes, "Statistical Research on the Bible," *Anchor Bible Dictionary* 6:196-97. Forbes concludes that the homogeneity that Adams and Rencher find in Isaiah is "an artifact resulting from inadequate sampling." Avraham Gileadi (e.g., *The Apocalyptic Book of Isaiah* [Provo, UT: Hebraeus Press, 1982]) suggests that Isaiah is a unity on the basis of a complex literary pattern running throughout the book. This conclusion cannot be accepted because the literary pattern lacks specificity; it seems artificial and is likely the result of the interpreter, not the author or editor. If there were such a pattern, it could come from a much later editor. Recent studies of Isaiah are turning toward the book as a whole, in terms of the larger and later editorial concerns that have formed it (e.g., H. G. M. Williamson, *The Book Called Isaiah: Deutero-Isaiah's Role in Composition and Redaction* [Oxford: Clarendon, 1994], who points out [pp. 1-3] that faulting the critical view for its humanistic presuppositions wholly misses the point; to attribute chapters 40-55 to the eighth century BCE creates grave contextual problems).

Another approach to the anachronistic portions of Isaiah is to note that the BoM cites only a limited portion of Isaiah (mainly chapters 2-14, 29, 48-54; a few verses from other chapters are cited or paraphrased; see Nyman, *Words of Isaiah,* 259-81) and argue that only these sections existed in Lehi's time (cf. Nibley, *Since Cumorah,* 143). The problem is that chaps. 48-54 are thematically very much part of 40-47, 55, and reflect the late perspective found in this part of Isaiah. Too, parts of 40-47 are paraphrased or reflected in the BoM: Isa. 40:3//1 Ne. 10:8; 45:18//1 Ne. 17:36. A snippet from Isa. 56-66 is found in the BoM at Jacob 6:4. This loosely quotes Isa. 65:2. A problem for the traditional understanding of the BoM is that this quote is closer to the citation in Romans 10:21 than to Isa. 65:2 itself. Thus, there is a double anachronism here: the BoM not only cites this late portion of Isaiah, it also depends upon the version of KJV Romans.

Another attempt at solving the anachronism of Second Isaiah argues that

Lehi's family obtained the plates of brass as late as 594 BCE, that the writer of Second Isaiah was one of thc prophets of Lehi's day mentioned in 1 Ne. 1:4, and that this writer began his compositions shortly before 594 (William Hamblin, "'Isaiah Update' Challenge," *Dialogue: A Journal of Mormon Thought* 17 [Spring 1984]: 4-7). While this places Second Isaiah closer to Lehi's time, it does not in fact solve the chronological problem. The perspective of Second Isaiah requires a date of 540 BCE or later; Second Isaiah, or its parts, cannot be suitably explained as a work from the first decade of the sixth century BCE.

167. For a detailed analysis, see my article, "Joseph Smith's Interpretation of Isaiah in the Book of Mormon," *Dialogue: A Journal of Mormon Thought* (Winter 1998): 181-206. See also George D. Smith, "Isaiah Updated," *Dialogue: A Journal of Mormon Thought* 16 (Summer 1983): 37-51.

168. On the JSR, see Ronald V. Huggins, "Joseph Smith's 'Inspired Translation' of Romans 7," *Dialogue: A Journal of Mormon Thought* 26 (Winter 1993): 159-82; Anthony Hutchinson, "A Mormon Midrash? LDS Creation Narratives Reconsidered," *Dialogue: A Journal of Mormon Thought* 21 (Winter 1988): 11-74. On the Book of Abraham, see Stephen E. Thompson, "Egyptology and the Book of Abraham," *Dialogue: A Journal of Mormon Thought* 28 (Spring 1995): 143-60; see also the Hutchinson article, just noted. On the temple endowment, see Michael W. Homer, "'Similarity of Priesthood in Masonry': The Relationship between Freemasonry and Mormonism," *Dialogue: A Journal of Mormon Thought* 27 (Fall 1994): 1-113; Edward H. Ashment, "The Temple: Historical Origins and Religious Value," *Dialogue: A Journal of Mormon Thought* 27 (Fall 1994): 289-98; David John Buerger, *The Mysteries of Godliness: A History of Mormon Temple Worship* (San Francisco: Smith Research Associates, 1994).

169. See the suggestions in my article, "In Plain Terms," 211-13; also my article, "Historical Criticism: A Necessary Element in the Search for Religious Truth," *Sunstone* 16:3 (Sept. 1992): 28-38; and especially the valuable approach of Mark Thomas in his *Digging in Cumorah.* The approaches found in Jeffrey R. Holland's "True or False" (*New Era* [June 1995]: 63, which argues that the church falls if the BoM is not an ancient work) and Russell M. Ballard's "Beware of False Prophets and False Teachers" (*Ensign* [Nov. 1999]: 62-64, which essentially dismisses historical critical study of the BoM) are counterproductive in the long run. The call to return to mainstream Christianity by conservative Christians is unrealistic since the same sorts of critical observations made about the BoM are applicable to the Old and New Testaments.

170. See my article, "Joseph Smith's Interpretation of Isaiah in the Book of Mormon"; George D. Smith, "Isaiah Updated"; and Mark Thomas, "A Mosaic for a Religious Counterculture: The Bible in the Book of Mormon," all in *Dialogue: A Journal of Mormon Thought* 29 (Winter 1996): 47-68.

7.

Secret Things, Hidden Things: The Seer Story in the Imaginative Economy of Joseph Smith

Susan Staker

THOSE WHO ASSOCIATED WITH JOSEPH SMITH DURING THE SPRING and summer of 1829 remembered that he used a "seer stone" to dictate both the Book of Mormon and his early revelations.[1] This fact orients Joseph Smith's biography in crucial and important ways, pointing not only backward to his youthful career as glass-looker and treasure seer[2] but forward as well to his emerging work as translator, prophet, seer, and Moses-like leader of a community of believers. This continuity was important for early believers, coming as they did from a world similar to Smith's where the line between magic and religion was fluid and inspiring, not dangerous or degrading.

When Joseph Smith resumed dictating the Book of Mormon in April 1829, evidence suggests that he began where he had left off a year before when Martin Harris disclosed that the 116 pages Smith had dictated were lost.[3] Rather than starting over, Smith continued dictating the story of King Mosiah who, like Smith, was a renowned seer, one who possessed and used special "seer stones" to translate engravings on ancient records, including a set of recently discovered golden plates (Mos. 8). Thus the threshold story of Mormonism, the entrance to surviving portions of the Book of Mormon, is about a man whose plot line mirrors in crucial ways that of the nineteenth-century man with the seer stone who dictated the story. Even more striking, Smith's implied status will become explicit when, near the end of his work on the book some three months later, he dictates a prediction about a "choice seer" of the latter days named Joseph, the son of Joseph (2 Ne. 3:7, 15).

There is no continuous line of priestly office in the Book of Mormon, no continuous line of church leadership or civil leadership or inheritance. The discontinuity narrated in this book can be breathtaking—a world where families divide into warring tribes, where parents kill children and children parents. But threaded through the extremities of this world is one unbroken line, one that is meticulously traced through seer characters who pass records from one generation to the next and are consistently portrayed as conduits for God's power and secrets.

The recurring stories of these powerful seers not only constitute the strand of continuity and authority in the Book of Mormon world but also became the narrative foundation upon which Smith's own authority was established within the community gathering around the Book of Mormon by the time Smith had finished its dictation at the end of June 1829. By then, he had also dictated some dozen revelations that mirrored the Book of Mormon in establishing the importance of a seer and portrayed Smith as the preeminent seer of the latter days. This remarkable flurry of textual activity in the months between the beginning of March and the end of June 1829 initiates the importance of this seer character in Smith's work.

Ultimately, the elaborate and hierarchical structure of priesthood in Kirtland was constructed on this same narrative and so was the story enacted by Nauvoo's secret temple ceremonies of men and women anointed priests and priestesses, kings and queens, gods and goddesses. Again and again, it is the complications within the evolving stories of seer characters that Smith first worked through the problems, challenges, and lures pressing against him and his followers in their nineteenth-century world. His explorations and innovations tend to begin with these narrative revisions. The more overtly discursive or theological passages inevitably extrapolate from distinctive narrative transformations. Again and again, Smith's authority is reconfirmed and enhanced as he asks his followers to live through religious plots first outlined in the texts he had dictated.

This unfolding narrative of the ancient seer comes most clearly into view when traced along the chronology of Smith's dictations, beginning with the Book of Mormon and its environing revelations and continuing with the texts begun a year later in the spring and summer of 1830—further revelations and the first sections from his ambitious "translation" of the King James Bible. Moses emerges within the Book of Mormon narrative as the paradigmatic example of the seer of old times. The Book of Mormon story, for the most part, takes place within the interstices of the King James Bible. Telling and retelling the old-time story of the seer within the confines of the Book of Mormon takes Smith ever closer to the project that will engage him to the end of his life: telling again in ever more striking ways the stories of the King James Bible and, eventually, the history of the gods. When he begins his Bible revision in June 1830, a year after he completes work on the Book of Mormon, he starts with Moses' own prelude to the Bible and then continues with a reworking of the Bible itself. In doing so, he is taking up a task laid out for him in the final weeks of his dictation of the Book of Mormon. He is also already returning to, transforming, and extending the stories of key biblical seers who are prominent players in what were some of the final pages dictated in the summer of 1829: Moses and Smith's namesake, Joseph of Egypt.

If Harris had not lost the 116-page manuscript, the Book of Mormon's internal chronological sequence and Smith's dictation sequence would have roughly paralleled each other. During the two months prior to Harris's blunder, Smith had dictated the story of Lehi and family who left Jerusalem before its destruction and migrated to America about 600 B.C., had worked his way chronologically through Nephite history, and was just beginning what has survived as the book of Mosiah. These pages, telling the chronological beginning of the Lehite story, were the pages that were lost. When he returned to the project a year later with his scribe Oliver Cowdery, who came to Harmony, Pennsylvania, to replace Harris, Smith began somewhere in the first chapters of the book of Mosiah. During the months of April and May 1829, he dictated the remainder of Mosiah and then continued on through the end of Nephite history, including Moroni's abridgement of Jaredite history. Finally, after relocating to Fayette, New York, in early June, he began dictating what is now the opening portion of the Book of Mormon, known as the small plates of Nephi (1 Nephi-Words of Mormon). These plates recorded first-person accounts of Nephi, Jacob, Enos, and others and replaced the lost third-person summary known as the "Book of Lehi" (see Preface, Book of Mormon, 1830 edition). Mosiah's story, halfway through the chronological plot, thus survives as the beginning of the dictation sequence or plot. It therefore becomes important to follow the stories of the seers along the contours of this dictation history.

KING MOSIAH'S STORY

Mosiah's story is thus the earliest surviving narrative dictated by Joseph Smith, partly as a matter of chance. However, even viewed from the end of Smith's career in Nauvoo, it seems rather fitting to begin with the story of a seer, the guardian and conduit for God's sacred secrets. Mosiah's seership is defined explicitly as a topic of discussion between King Limhi, the sovereign of a group long separated from the main body of Nephites, and Ammon, a subject of King Mosiah who has gone into the wilderness looking for this group. King Limhi is looking for someone who can translate an ancient record engraved on golden plates which has come into his hands. Limhi believes that these records may unlock the secret to the destruction of this lost civilization.

Responding to Limhi's query, Ammon makes clear that Mosiah's prestige is as much tied to his seership as to his kingship. In describing the king's reputation, Ammon introduces a profile of the seer which gathers together themes that will be repeated throughout the Book of Mormon. This profile also provides a framing introduction to Smith's own work as he negotiates the borderland between his early involvement in occult treasure seeking and the world opening up to him as "choice seer" and guardian of God's secrets in the last days.

An item associated with treasure seeking is singled out by Ammon as the defining sign of anyone with such a calling. A "seer," Ammon says, is one commanded by God to gaze at stones. Mosiah is "a man that can translate the records; for he has wherewith that he can look, and translate all records that are of ancient date: and it is a gift from God. And the things are called interpreters. ... And whosoever is commanded to look in them, the same is called seer. And behold, the king of the people who are in the land of Zarahemla is the man that is commanded to do these things, and who has this high gift from God" (Mos. 8:13, 14). Later these "interpreters" are described as "two stones which were fastened into the two rims of a bow" (Mos. 28:13). Further, it is confirmed that "whosoever has these things is called seer, after the manner of old times" (v. 16).

As the conversation continues, Ammon evokes several God-sanctioned uses of the stones. Responding no doubt to Ammon's emphasis on Mosiah's prestige as seer and king, Limhi proposes that "a seer is greater than a prophet" (Mos. 8:15). Ammon goes him one better, continuing that "a seer is a revelator, and a prophet also; and a gift which is greater, can no man have, except he should possess the power of God, which no man can; yet a man may have great power given him from God" (v. 16). Ammon's most immediate claim is striking. Within a hierarchy of power, only God has more power than the seer. As recipient of God's "high gift," the seer's power encompasses that of a revelator and prophet and goes beyond, obtaining to the "greater" gift and the "great" power of God.

It is at the site of these proliferating superlatives that the substance of this singular calling is elaborated by Ammon. He begins by making explicit the gifts implied by the terms "revelator" and "prophet": "But a seer can know of things which are past, and also of things which are to come; and by them shall all things be revealed" (Mos. 8:17)—in other words, revelation. Ammon then pauses, more carefully singling out the revelatory function: "Or rather, shall secret things be made manifest, and hidden things shall come to light, and things which are not known shall be made known by them, and also things shall be made known by them which otherwise could not be known" (v. 17). In other words, the seer comes closest to God's power because he controls earthly access to God's secrets. He is the one to whom God reveals and prophesies. He is the one called to write and to translate sacred secrets. Evidence of the power of these secrets will always follow in the wake. Ammon concludes: "Thus God hath provided a means that man, through faith, might work mighty miracles; therefore he becometh a great benefit to his fellow beings" (v. 18).

Following through on the logic of Ammon's insistence that this high gift is associated with God's secrets, King Limhi anticipates Mosiah's translation of the golden plates: "Doubtless a great mystery is contained within these plates, and these interpreters were doubtless prepared for the purpose of unfolding all such mysteries to the children of men" (Mos. 8:19). In other words, because these records have been hidden, because they have found their way to a seer, guardian of God's secrets, they must contain God's mysteries or secrets.

King Mosiah presides and rules in a world that inextricably links magic and religion. He has been singled out by God to use magic artifacts, seer stones, to discover God's secrets and become a conduit for God's power. Specifically translations, revelations, and miracles are evoked as God-sanctioned activities, the signs which mark a seer's access to God's secrets and power.

The details of Mosiah's story, in the book bearing his name, point to the importance of a seer's work with written texts, guarding, translating, and revealing records. His story begins and ends with a scene of succession in which the sacred cache of records is passed from one generation to the next and the departing leader delivers a written revelation. King Mosiah is introduced when he receives the records and artifacts from his father, King Benjamin, and gathers the people together so they can hear his father's revelation.

Each scene in which Mosiah appears concerns this cache of ever expanding records. His second scene as a character in this drama comes when Limhi and his offshoot group and their records are finally united with the main body of Nephites. In the scene of unification, the focus is kept squarely on the additional records: "And it came to pass that Mosiah received them with joy; and he also received their records, and also the records which had been found by the people of Limhi" (Mos. 22:14). The next scene in which Mosiah appears is another unification event, this time when a group led by Alma Sr. becomes subject to King Mosiah. To celebrate their unification, Mosiah calls the entire population together and reads to them the records of the various groups: "And it came to pass that Mosiah did read, and caused to be read, the records of Zeniff to his people. ... And he also read the account of Alma and his brethren" (25:5, 6).

Mosiah's final scenes portray another ritual of succession. The narration confirms that Mosiah has translated the golden plates using the seer stones, has caused his translation to be written down, and has shared the contents with his subjects (see especially Mos. 28:18). He then turns the cache of records over to his designated successor, Alma Jr. (Alma, son of Alma). The records now include not only the brass plates and the Nephite records but also those of the Jaredites and of Zeniff and Alma. Like his father before him, Mosiah too has written down a final revelation, delivered as part of this ritual of succession (Mos. 28-29).

This ritual repeats itself in each succeeding generation, often a scene rather elaborately dramatized within the text. Alma Jr. passes the records to Helaman, and they are passed in an unbroken line which is carefully traced within the text until they come to Mormon, who gives them to his son Moroni, the final guardian seer in the book's chronological timcline.

That the seer is the one continuous thread in the flux and change of such a world already comes clearly into view by considering what endures and what changes between the rituals of succession at the beginning and end of the Book of Mosiah. As we have seen, Mosiah receives the Nephite tokens of power and authority at the beginning of the book and Alma Jr. at its end. However, the structure of Nephite community and governance, both civil and religious, has been entirely reconfigured between these two scenes. The importance of what remains unchanged is italicized by the radical developments that intervene in the middle. At the beginning, Mosiah inherits both kingship and seership from his father. By the end, he abdicates his throne and convinces his nation to hold elections. Alma Jr. is elected. Not only is Alma Jr. no relation to Mosiah, he is from a group that was not even subject to the monarchy when Mosiah became king. In other words, the transition from monarchy to democracy punctuates the social changes as various groups join the main body of Nephites. A church was founded by Alma Sr. in the wilderness, and Mosiah allows him to continue as autonomous leader of the church after the separate populations are unified. Mosiah blesses the expansion of this church into the larger population. Alma Sr. passes the leadership of the church to his son Alma at about the time he is also elected to head the new government. Thus at the end of his story, Mosiah passes only the seer stones and sacred cache of records to Alma Jr. Mosiah is no longer king, no longer sovereign, no longer religious leader.

AT THE BOUNDARY BETWEEN HEAVEN AND EARTH

Mosiah is the only character within the world of the Book of Mormon who is specifically called a "seer." The word will not appear again in the dictation timeline until near its end, this time applied to Joseph Smith himself, written into the Book of Mormon plot as a Joseph Jr., son of Joseph, the "choice seer" of the latter-days (2 Ne. 3).[4] However, Mosiah stands at the beginning of the following line of men, all who warrant this title on the basis of the definition introduced by Mosiah's story: King Benjamin, Mosiah, Alma Jr., Helaman, Shiblon, Helaman II, Nephi, Nephi Jr., Amos, Amos Jr., Ammaron, Mormon, and Moroni. In addition, from the final stories dictated by Joseph Smith in the spring of 1829, we can add Nephi, Jacob, Enos, Jarom, Omni, Amaron, Chemish, Abinadom, Amalek, and finally back again to King Benjamin.

These characters tend to share a recognizable profile organized around the ensemble of characteristics introduced by King Mosiah. Not only do they guard the same sacred cache of records, they stand nearest in proximity to God and become the conduit for his secrets and power. In addition to possessing the high gift of translating and revealing God's "hidden things, secret things" with stones, seers come to be associated with other miracles as well, in particular with the ministering of angels, visits by God himself, and with the possibility of being "translated" or "transfigured" and becoming in effect angels themselves. The seer is portrayed as a liminal character situated at the border between earth and heaven. In fact, the curve of the Book of Mormon dictation timeline is to bring the seer ever nearer to heaven and to God.

The portrait of Mosiah's father, which dominates the opening pages of the book of Mosiah is already structured by this seer profile. King Benjamin consistently associates himself with God's mysteries and secrets. Twice in his first remarks to his sons, he reiterates that the purpose of the records is that "we might read and understand of his [God's] mysteries" (Mos. 1:3, 5). He emphasizes the difficulties associated with reading these records which have been kept in the "language of the Egyptians" (v. 4), a language which he implies is largely unavailable to the population. He has taught his sons the language so that they will have access to the mysteries of God–the sacred secrets found in the records. In other words, he seems to be passing not only the cache of records and artifacts but also the key to decoding the records, the language of the Egyptians.

The grand public ceremony marking Mosiah's succession as king and guardian is climaxed by the reading of a revelation, the unveiling of a secret, that punctuates Benjamin's dual career. Introducing the theme of ministering angels that will become associated with these inheritors of secrets within the Book of Mormon world, King Benjamin explains that the written revelation he will read has been dictated to him by "an angel from God" (Mos. 3:2).[5]

The joyous secret delivered by the angel at the beginning of the Book of Mormon dictation timeline is that a secret Christian tradition has existed, going back to the beginnings of time, that God will become a man. This mystery has been revealed to God's holy prophets (seers) throughout history. Viewed within this context, the Law of Moses is to be seen, according to Benjamin, as an encoded or encrypted (Benjamin uses the terms "types" and "shadows") set of rituals and laws pointing forward to the Christian story (Mos. 3:13-15). Thus the Book of Mormon's enduring focus on Christ is introduced within a context already structured around the sacredness and secrecy associated with God's line of seers. Moses is introduced within this context as the prototypical Old Testament seer. Certainly he fits the seer profile: not only did he too teach the great Christian mystery, as King Benjamin suggests, he too kept sacred records. He too was associated with miraculous events.[6]

As if to confirm the importance of the Book of Mormon's secret, another version of this great Christian mystery is soon embedded within the frame of Mosiah's story. It turns out that the offshoot group of Nephites led by King Limhi have been keeping their own records. Immediately following the exchange between Ammon and King Limhi (Mos. 8), these two records appear in the text. Taken together, the stories of Zeniff and Alma Sr. make clear that God has indeed been revealing this secret tradition of Christ to his prophets and seers.

Within the story told by the records of Zeniff and Alma, a figure named Abinadi receives an independent revelation which recapitulates the angel's revelation to King Benjamin. Abinadi's words are warranted by God and come by supernatural means. God makes it impossible for Abinadi's enemies to kill him until he has delivered his revelation. Abinadi is drawn as a kind of Moses, the same Old Testament seer evoked in Benjamin's story: "Now it came to pass ... that the people of king Noah durst not lay their hands on him, for the Spirit of the Lord was upon him; and his face shone with exceeding luster, even as Moses' did while in the mount of Sinai, while speaking with the Lord. And he spake with power and authority from God ..." (Mos. 13:5-6). Abinadi explicitly confirms what King Benjamin had suggested, that Moses had revealed this secret to his people: "For behold, did not Moses prophesy unto them concerning the coming of the Messiah, and that God should redeem his people?" (v. 33).

Alma Jr., who in the final pages of the book of Mosiah receives the sacred records and artifacts, in effect becomes the heir of both the revelation of King Benjamin and the independent revelation of Abinadi. Alma Jr.'s father, Alma, had heard and believed Abinadi's Christian message. Although Abinadi was put to death by King Limhi's wicked father, Alma Sr. had escaped into the wilderness and there founded a Christian church. At the unification of these peoples, Alma Sr. unites the two separate Christian traditions under the umbrella of one expanding church. This is the church he turns over to his son.

Alma Jr.'s life is a litany of miraculous occurrences. He is struck down and converted to Christianity by the visit of an angel. He heals people and is delivered from prison through supernatural intervention. He is again visited by angels.[7] As with Abinadi, the Book of Mormon sets up an explicit comparison between Alma Jr. and Moses. This comparison introduces a recurring miracle plot associated with the seer characters: the possibility that a seer may escape conventional mortal death. The Book of Mormon compares Alma Jr.'s end to the end of Moses, which the King James Bible leaves similarly open-ended: "And it came to pass that [Alma Jr.] was never heard of more; as to his death or burial we know not of. Behold, this we know, that he was a righteous man; and the saying went abroad in the church that he was taken up by the Spirit, or buried by the hand of the Lord, even as Moses. But behold, the scriptures saith the Lord took Moses unto himself; and we suppose that he has also received Alma in the spirit, unto himself; therefore, for this cause we know nothing concerning his death and burial" (Alma 45:18-19).

The life of Alma Jr.'s grandson Nephi also includes an impressive range of miracle stories. He is able to prophesy the future by announcing the murder of the chief judge and identifying his murderer. He calls down first famine and then rain. Angels are associated with his work. For example, he and his brother are encircled with fire and visited by an "angel of God" when they are cast into prison.[8] That such miracles take this seer to the very boundaries of heaven is emphasized explicitly by the text itself which reports that the people say of him, "Behold, he is a god, for except he was a god he could not know of all things" (Hel. 9:41). It is fitting then that the text opens up for this seer the same possibility of escaping death accorded to his grandfather and the Old Testament seer Moses: "Then [Nephi] departed out of the land, and whither he went, no man knoweth" (3 Ne. 1:3). As if to underscore this odd detail, it is repeated again several pages later: "And Nephi, who was the father of Nephi, who had the charge of the records, did not return to the land of Zarahemla, and could nowhere be found in all the land" (2:9).

Nephi's son Nephi is the seer living when the resurrected Christ visits America after his New Testament death. Before this event occurs, Nephi Jr. already demonstrates the miracle profile of his father, even shadowing Jesus himself who will make his appearance in the Book of Mormon world on the next page. Like Jesus, Nephi Jr. casts out devils and unclean spirits, heals those with sicknesses and infirmities, and raises a man, his brother, from the dead. The details of the characteristic ministering of angels emphasize how special Nephi was: "[So] great was his faith on the Lord Jesus Christ that angels did minister unto him daily" (3 Ne. 7:17-26). At the moment when Jesus, the Son of God, will physically come into this world, the seer's attributes are dramatized as being very nearly those of the God who will disclose himself. That Nephi Jr. inhabits the border between worlds is emphasized by the fact that this seer, "after the manner of old times," is the first of twelve disciples chosen by Jesus among the Nephites. Nephi is the first one among the twelve who is baptized with the new baptism Christ institutes.

The last Nephite seer, Moroni, provides a final paradigmatic example of the seer character. His ending, if for no other reason than that he cannot narrate his own death, is left in suspense like that of Alma and Nephi (and Moses) before him.[9] Certainly Smith's own story of his miraculous encounter with the ancient guardian of the records cache in New York dramatizes that Moroni has in fact become a ministering angel. Continuing the arc which finds the seer increasingly traversing the borderland between natural and supernatural, Moroni is the first Nephite to privately see not just the emissary of God, a ministering angel, but God himself: "And then shall ye know that I have seen Jesus, and that he hath talked with me face to face, and that he told me in plain humility, even as a man telleth another in mine own language, concerning these things" (Eth. 12:28-41).

Moroni brings the cycle of stories about seers back to where the record began, with King Mosiah, the seer who used stones to translate the ancient gold records of the Jaredites (Mos. 28:11-19). It is never made clear what happened to Mosiah's translation, but it seems that Moroni, the final Nephite seer, must repeat this work, presumably using the seer stones to again translate these same records. Moroni includes a summary of his translation within the text Smith dictates. The summary emphasizes the experiences of men within the Jaredite tradition who receive the revelation of the Christian mystery, employ sacred stones, and guard a cache of records and artifacts. In fact, Moroni begins with the story of a seer, the "brother of Jared," who creates gold plates and produces a set of interpreters or stones, presumably the ones employed by King Mosiah.[10]

In telling the brother of Jared's story, Moroni returns to the same themes associated with Nephite seers. But the brother of Jared's encounters with the divine consistently intensify the, by now, familiar ensemble of themes and evokes this profile of the seer in an ever more miraculous context. The setting of this story gives it precedence even over the story of Moses. The Jaredites begin at the Tower of Babel, long before the beginning of Moses' story. God allows them to escape the confusion of languages which occurs at Babel. This means that the language of the Jaredite record is more unique and preciously guarded than the Egyptian tradition kept by the line of Nephites. The Jaredite record is presumably written in the pure Adamic language.

The portrait of the brother of Jared can be seen to organize itself into a plot which recapitulates even as it tropes the story of Moses in the Old Testament. His life not only repeats but elaborates and makes more miraculous, italicizes the priority of coming first in God's scheme of things. It dramatizes itself not only as a story of the ultimate origins of the Book of Mormon seers but even more generally of a line of seers going back into the Old Testament beyond the time of the Jewish wanderings. Like Moses, the brother of Jared and his brother, Jared, lead their people into the wilderness. As with the children of Israel, God leads them from within a cloud. Like Moses, the brother of Jared performs miracles of nature. Whereas Moses parted the Red

Sea, the brother of Jared rather stunningly moves a mountain (Eth. 12:30). As is the case with Moses, God shows the brother of Jared the history of the earth beginning with its creation. Ths seer writes a record which sounds very like the account traditionally attributed to Moses: "[T]he first part of this record, which speaks concerning the creation of the world, and also of Adam, an account from that time even to the great tower, and whatsoever things transpired among the children of men until that time" (1:3).

Like Moses, the Jaredite goes into the mountain where he sees the Lord face to face. His revelation of the Christian mystery is made even more spectacular than that of Benjamin or Abinadi because he sees God as the Son long before God assumes a body on earth. Whereas Moses is only able to lead the Israelites to the border of the promised land, the brother of Jared leads his people across the ocean to a new promised land in the new world. He does so by spectacular means acquired during his encounter with God.[11] Before ascending the mountain, the brother of Jared prepares sixteen stones which "were white and clear, even as transparent glass" (Eth. 3:1). The Lord touches these stones to provide light for the long voyage. It is implied that the seer stones Mosiah acquires have their origin in this miraculous encounter (3:22-28).

It is on the mountain that the brother of Jared is shown the earth's history from beginning to end. He writes what he has seen and thus begins the cache of records which eventually passes to Moroni, the final Nephite seer. Moroni emphasizes the secrecy associated with these records that God specifically commands him to "write these things and seal them up; and I will show them in mine own due time unto the children of men" (Eth. 3:27).

Moroni's summary of this epic ends with the profile of another seer whose story mimes Moroni's own. Like Moroni, Ether witnesses and writes of the final destruction of his people. Like Moroni, he gathers together the records and miraculous artifacts associated with the work of the seer. He hides up the Jaredite artifacts "in a manner that the people of Limhi did find them" (Eth. 15:33). These artifacts are among those which Moroni similarly hides up in the manner that, according to Smith, they were ultimately found. Ether's last words confirm the recurring theme often associated with the seer in Nephite history–words that might serve for Moroni's own: "Whether the Lord will that I be translated, or that I suffer the will of the Lord in the flesh, it mattereth not, if it so be that I am saved in the kingdom of God" (v. 34). In Ether's case, the ambiguous end of the seer, the implicit possibility of translation, seems to have become something of an expectation.

THE MARCH AND APRIL 1829 REVELATIONS: JOSEPH SMITH THE SEER

The distance Smith travels along a transformative path between the time he dictates Mosiah's seer story in early April 1829 and the time he completes Ether's account in late May or early June is rather remarkable. His role will soon correspondingly expand from translator-seer to seer-revelator.

Smith's first revelation, dictated in July 1828, came in response to his translation crisis (Doctrine and Covenants 3; hereafter D&C). Prior to Oliver Cowdery's arrival, he had dictated two other revelations. The first came in February 1829 when he was visited by his father and the second in March when visited by Martin Harris, who was still seeking forgiveness for the previous year's disaster. By the end of April, when Smith would have finished dictating the frame of Mosiah's story, he had received four more revelations, these addressed to his new scribe, Cowdery. Already, the March and April revelations demonstrate the complicated ways the Book of Mormon narrative and Smith's own world would mirror and interact over the course of the spring and summer. Ultimately, the complicated logic of the seer stories can be traced only when the dictation plot for the spring and summer of 1829 is expanded to include the chronology of Smith's work on both the Book of Mormon and its environing revelations. Indeed, the energy that drives and structures the complex seer narratives in both the ancient and modern texts seems derived as much from the problems facing Smith in 1829 as by problems within the Book of Mormon world.

The March revelation to Harris (Book of Commandments IV, hereafter BC; D&C 5), probably dictated about the same time Smith was returning to Mosiah's story, begins precisely where Mosiah's story begins and ends, with the ancient cache of records and artifacts. Underscoring the place of the seer and the artifacts, the first-person voice of God introduces these as objects of sacredness and secrecy as well as the focus of belief and the reward for faithfulness. The first sentence echoes the explanation within Mosiah's story that "whosoever has these things is called seer, after the manner of old times." The earliest extant manuscript of the revelation begins: "Behold I say unto you that my servant [Martin Harris] hath desired a witness that my servant Joseph hath got the things which he has testified that he hath got" (cf. BC IV:1).[12] "The things" of which God speaks are the very things which Mosiah receives and passes on to Alma Jr. At various times, Smith spoke of receiving not only the ancient records but also the Book of Mormon seer stones ("interpreters") and the sword of Laban, also associated with Mosiah.

Certainly then, Mosiah's story brings an authoritative frame for interpretation to the story Smith has been telling since 1823 about the cache of records and artifacts he has received from Moroni, their ancient guardian. Smith is placed quite literally into an unbroken line of seers called to guard the records and tend God's secrets. Further, this threshold revelation focuses rather narrowly on the same activities which are most closely associated with Mosiah by the end of his story. Just as the Book of Mormon dictation timeline will expand and elaborate on the possibilities of this role, so too will the revelations increasingly expand and elaborate on the possibilities for Smith's work as seer.

Following through on the theme of secrets and mysteries which Mosiah's story introduces as a seer's special domain, the March revelation dictated by Smith takes up the theme of secrecy. God specifically assumes responsibility for the secrecy surrounding the cache of records: "I have caused him that he should enter into a covenant with me that he should not show them except I command him" (cf. BC IV:2). God then holds out the possibility that a few faithful witnesses might penetrate this veil of secrecy and be rewarded with a view of the sacred artifacts: "[Y]ea & the testimony of three of my servants shall go forth with my word unto this Generation yea three shall know of surety that those things are true for I will give them power that they may Behold & view these things as they are" (cf. v. 4). The final passage sets up the conditions under which a believer might become one of the three witnesses to the reality of God's secret.

Not only does the opening passage point to the ancient artifacts as the focus of belief for those attracted to Smith's story, it also makes explicit that Smith's work is parallel to Mosiah's once the leadership of the nation and of the church have been ceded elsewhere: the seer's work with stones and records. This same responsibility is underscored as the only work assigned by God to Smith: "[H]e has a gift to translate the Book & I have commanded that he shall pretend to no other gift for I will grant unto him no other gift" (cf. BC IV:2).

The question of what, precisely, is involved in the seer's ability to translate ancient records becomes a recurring and explicit theme within the curve of the April 1829 revelations Smith received during the first month of his association with Cowdery. These revelations plot a mini-drama wherein God first holds out to Cowdery the possibility that he too will be given the high gift to translate but then ultimately tables the offer because of what is described as a failure on Cowdery's part. Like the March revelation, the communications of April focus on the issue of seership. Any distance between the exclusive focus on Smith's ability to translate "the book" (singular) and that evoked in the series of revelations after Cowdery's arrival is not to be found in the nature of the work licensed for Smith. A key theme in April is the multiplicity of records which Smith will be called to translate. This is arguably a swerve from the rather narrow but emphatic emphasis of the March revelation which allowed him to "translate the book" and pretend to no other gift.[13] Prior to Cowdery's arrival, it was not clear that Smith would be able to finish the translation, at least not in a timely fashion. Now, with the Book of Mormon dictation progressing rapidly, the revelations for the first time hint at a continuation of Smith's role as seer-translator beyond the Book of Mormon. For the first time, his revelations broach the subject of other hidden records awaiting translation.

Arguably, this glimpse into Smith's future mimes Mosiah's story, which includes the discovery of several new records, including the gold plates of the Jaredites and the records of Zeniff and Alma. The latter two records are immediately embedded within the book of Mosiah. Strikingly, Smith enacts this same sub-plot within the frame of his own story during the time he is dictating Mosiah. He too embeds an ancient record within his record. One April revelation is a restoration of the actual words of John, one of the disciples of Jesus.[14] This short fragment, in fact, forecasts the project that Smith will take up the following summer of 1830, a work more and more explicitly prepared for in the final portions of the Book of Mormon: a revision or "translation" of the narratives told within the King James version of the Bible itself.

Like Mosiah's story and the March revelation, the April revelations privilege secret and hidden things as the special concern of one possessing the gift of translation. Evidence suggests that Cowdery had shared with Smith his own experience of growing up in a world that accepted magic or occult links to the supernatural. The first of these April revelations, addressed to Cowdery, begins at the fluid borderland where Smith in 1829 is making his journey from treasure seer to prophet, seer, and revelator. Cowdery is enjoined to "seek not for riches but for wisdom, and behold the mysteries of God shall be unfolded unto you, and then shall you be made rich. Behold he that hath eternal life is rich" (BC V:3).[15] The connection between mysteries and hidden records, such as in the discussion between Ammon and King Limhi, can be seen when God explicitly holds out to Cowdery the possibility that he, like Smith (and like Mosiah), will be allowed to translate: "[I]f you have good desires, a desire to lay up treasures for yourself in heaven [again, the contrast between buried treasure and sacred secrets], then shall you assist in bringing to light, with your gift, those parts of my scriptures which have been hidden because of iniquity" (BC V:12).

Within the April revelations, the task of translation recalls Mosiah's work in other crucial ways. As in Mosiah's story, access to secrets and power is linked to magic or occult expertise. But instead of seer stones, the April revelations focus on another kind of magic tool: divining rods.[16] Smith was known to use a rod in his earliest days as a treasure seer. As the April revelations make clear, Cowdery was also familiar with divining rods. Within the world of the Book of Mormon, Mosiah's abilities may be linked rather closely to the seer stone, but in the environing revelations which tell of Smith's story and that of his associates, seer stones must not necessarily be employed. Instead, Cowdery's gift to translate is juxtaposed to his expertise with the rod: "Now this is not all, for you have another gift, which is the gift of working with the rod: behold it has told you things: behold there is no other power save God, that can cause this rod of nature, to work in your hands, for it is the work of God; and therefore whatsoever you shall ask me to tell you by that means, that will I grant unto you, that you shall know" (BC VII:3).

Just as both the book of Mosiah and the April revelations license expertise with magic objects such as seer stones or diving rods, they both assume that access to God's secrets depends on and is intertwined with miracles, demonstrated along a similar spectrum in both Mosiah's story and Smith's own. In the wake of secrets, God's power may be manifest in translations, revelations, and miracles. The most encompassing term used for the gift is the "Spirit of revelation." Cowdery is told in a third revelation (BC VII) that his desire to translate depends on the gift of this spirit: "[Y]ou [shall] receive a knowledge of whatsoever things you shall ask in faith, with an honest heart, believing that you shall receive a knowledge concerning the engravings of old records, which are ancient" (v. 1). This gift of translating or revealing ancient secrets is tied to nature miracles such as those associated with Moses in the Old Testament: "Now, behold this is the Spirit of revelation:—behold this is the spirit by which Moses brought the children of Israel through the Red sea on dry ground: therefore, this is thy gift" (BC VII:2).

That Moses is evoked within the April revelations, as he was within the frame of Mosiah's story, as the prototype of older times is significant. He is also mentioned within an overtly magic context when God approves the use of the divining rod to receive revelation. Although no explicit connection is explored, the juxtaposition of Mosiah's nature miracles with the discussion of divining rods hardly seems accidental. One follows immediately on the other within the revelation (BC V). This juxtaposition is best explained within nineteenth-century occult tradition where one would call his divining rod a "Mosaical rod," recalling the miracles performed by Moses with his rod in dueling competition with the Egyptian pharaoh and his magicians.[17]

MORMON'S STORY

By the end of May, at the point Smith was finishing Ether's story, one particular worry was pressing against him. He would now have to replace the 116 pages of manuscript lost by Martin Harris a year earlier. In the next of the revelations, received in May, God himself takes up the dangers of this task and the threat it poses to the authority of Smith's high gift: "And behold, satan has put it into their hearts to alter the words which you have caused to be written, or which you have translated. ... because they have altered the words, they read contrary from that which you translated and caused to be written; and on this wise the devil has sought to lay a cunning plan, that he may destroy this work; for he has put it into their hearts to do this, that by lying they may say they have caught you in the words which you have pretended to translate" (BC IX:2).[18]

God then discloses his solution:

> And now, verily I say unto you, that an account of those things that you have written, which have gone out of your hands, are engraven upon the plates of Nephi; yea, and you remember, it was said in those writings, that a more particular account was given of these things upon the plates of Nephi. And now, because the account which is engraven upon the plates of Nephi, is more particular concerning the things, which in my wisdom I would bring to the knowledge of the people in this account: therefore, you shall translate the engravings which are on the plates of Nephi, down even till you come to the reign of king Benjamin, or until you come to that which you have translated, which you have retained; and behold, you shall publish it as the record of Nephi, and thus I will confound those who have altered my words. ... Behold they have only got a part, or an abridgement of the account of Nephi. Behold there are many things engraven on the plates of Nephi, which do throw greater views upon my gospel: therefore, it is wisdom in me, that you should translate this first part of the engravings of Nephi, and send [it] forth in this work. (IX:9-11)

This May revelation explains the striking narrative transformation that has occurred within the pages Smith has been dictating over the previous few weeks. As his dictation of the Book of Mormon progressed into the early summer days of 1829, a first-person narrator, Mormon, the penultimate Nephite seer, had unexpectedly disclosed himself within the pages of the dictation plot. Mormon does so in order to clarify his place in creating the version of the story that Smith is dictating. As it turns out, this version is a summary or abridgement, Mormon's own reading of one set of records long included among those in the seer's cache. Even as this ancient editor continues to narrate his story of past seers, he gradually discloses a mini-plot of his own. Digging deeper into the cache of records, he discovers a set of ancient plates that will solve Smith's problem—a way for Smith to return to the story told in the 116 pages and tell it in a new way. In service of this end, the third-person narrative characteristic of the first two hundred-plus pages of the Book of Mormon dictation timeline gradually morphs into a mosaic of first-person accounts by the seers themselves.

The Book of Mormon dictation begins at the story of King Mosiah in a kind of third-person discourse that would have been familiar to nineteenth-century readers of the King James Bible. The source of narration in the Bible is mysterious, impersonal, unsituated. Its authority comes from its magisterial aura, able to narrate even God creating the world. Through more than sixty percent of the total Book of Mormon pages Smith finally dictated, the Book of Mormon is characterized by this same authoritative third-person discourse.

And then, quite unexpectedly, the voice of a first-person "I"-narrator appears, jumping forward to talk about the end of the narrative not yet lived through: "And behold, in the end of this book ye shall see that this Gadianton did prove the overthrow, yea, almost the entire destruction of the people of Nephi. Behold I do not mean the end of the book of Helaman, but I mean the end of the book of Nephi, from which I have taken all the account which I have written" (Hel. 2:13-14).

These personal words are jarring, disorienting for the reader whose attention has been strung along the dictation timeline. Who is this "I" speaking for the first time in the narrative? Quite unexpectedly, the reader must confront herself as exactly that, a reader, situated in front of a printed page, following along word for word, wondering about the shape of an ending. Not only is the reader abruptly wrenched from the comfortable fiction created for her in a magisterial third-person narrative—a privileged and omniscient viewing perch for the unfolding events of history—but this same reader, only just finding herself a reader, is confronted with the possibility of not just one textual ending coming into view but rather at least two—not just the end of the book of Helaman, the title of the section the reader is contemplating, but also "the end of the book of Nephi, from which I have taken all the account which I have written."

Once this initial, unexpected, authorial intrusion is passed, this first-person "I"-narrator begins more and more to break into the authoritative, third-person scriptural narrative. As announced by the first break in third-person, the preoccupations of this at first unnamed speaker announces himself as yet another of the seers lined in by the dictation timeline of the Book of Mormon story. The "I"-narrator is preoccupied with the concerns of guarding and generating the records of God's story in the Book of Mormon world.[19]

In particular, the "I"-narrator, who finally identifies himself as Mormon (3 Ne. 5), returns again and again to the subject announced in his first authorial intrusion–the multiplicity of records available to tell the Nephite story. The Nephites have produced many records, and Mormon has created his abridgement from the more detailed version of the story engraved on the plates of Nephi. In this environment, Mormon will finally discover God's solution to Smith's problem of the lost pages of manuscript.

The dictation timeline, which has wound its way through the books of various seer characters–Mosiah, Alma, Helaman, Nephi–comes to the section called the "Book of Mormon" which finally tells Mormon's story within the chronological sequencing of the book. Ammaron, the previous seer who had buried the records, singles out the ten-year-old Mormon and tells the boy where to find the buried plates of Nephi: "And behold, ye shall take the plates of Nephi unto yourself, and the remainder shall ye leave in the place where they are; and ye shall engrave on the plates of Nephi all the things that ye have observed concerning this people" (Morm. 1:3-5). Eventually, Mormon does as Ammaron tells him, but in addition, he makes an abridged record on another set of plates. It is his words on this second set of plates that the reader of the composite Book of Mormon encounters: "And behold I had gone according to the word of Ammaron, and taken the plates of Nephi, and did make a record according to the words of Ammaron. And upon the plates of Nephi I did make a full account of all the wickedness and abominations; but upon these plates I did forbear to make a full account of their wickedness and abominations" (Morm. 2:17-20). Eventually, Mormon passes the sacred records and the role of seer to his son, Moroni: "[H]aving been commanded of the Lord that I should not suffer the records which had been handed down by our fathers, which were sacred, to fall into the hands of the Lamanites, (for the Lamanites would destroy them) therefore I made this record out of the plates of Nephi, and hid up in the hill Cumorah all the records which had been entrusted to me by the hand of the Lord, save it were these few plates which I gave unto my son Moroni" (Morm. 6:6).

A rather more elaborate account of this handoff from Mormon to

Moroni is provided in a second book bearing Mormon's name, the "Words of Mormon." Evidence suggests that this book was probably dictated after the first-person accounts of Nephi and his immediate descendants and was thus the final section of the book to emerge. This would have been in late June 1829. It stands as a coda to the dictation timeline which began with the narrative of Mosiah, eventually disclosed to be an abridgement created by the same Mormon. Arguably, even more records and a more precise version of their significance came into view during the dictation of the final set of first-person narratives which would, in the end, begin the Book of Mormon narrative.[20]

According to Mormon, once he had abridged Nephi's plates through to the reign of King Benjamin, he discovered an additional set of small plates that contained much the same story, including the words of Nephi and of the other seers from Jacob to King Benjamin. Impressed with these records, he decided to include them with the others: "Wherefore, I chose these things, to finish my record upon them, which remainder of my record I shall take from the plates of Nephi; and I cannot write the hundredth part of the things of my people. ... And I do this for a wise purpose; for thus it whispereth me, according to the workings of the Spirit of the Lord which is in me" (Words of Mormon 1:5-6). Of course, the wise purpose was to provide an alternate version of the 116 missing pages.

The first-person mode of narration loosed into the story by Mormon's asides about the records comprising his work comes to more and more characterize the final part of the Book of Mormon. Such interpolations are characteristic of the summary of Jaredite history made by Mormon's son, Moroni. This gives way to first-person narrative in the letters and sermons of Mormon and Moroni and finally in the autobiographies of Nephi and his immediate ancestors.

NEPHI'S STORY

The autobiographies comprise the final movement of the epic story within the dictation plot, replacing the first version of the story lost with the 116 pages. Nephi's profile of his father, Lehi, immediately situates him within the tradition introduced within Mormon's abridgement and reconfirmed within Moroni's. Nephi's father is introduced with language alluding to Moses, the prototypical Old Testament seer who has returned again and again within the Book of Mormon: "And it came to pass as [Lehi] prayed unto the Lord, there came a pillar of fire and dwelt on a rock before him; and he saw and heard much; and because of the things which he saw and heard he did quake and tremble exceedingly" (1 Ne. 1:6). After this miraculous experience, Lehi receives yet another version of the revelation of the ancient Christian mystery, that God will come to the earth as Jesus. Like the revelations of Benjamin and Abinadi and the brother of Jared before him, within the dictation timeline, this revelation of the secret that God will be born within the mortal world as Jesus is greeted with great joy.[21] Like the previous Christian revelations, this one is warranted by miraculous occurrences: "[Lehi] was carried away in a vision, even that he saw the heavens open, and he thought he saw God sitting upon his throne, surrounded with numberless concourses of angels in the attitude of singing and praising their God" (1 Ne. 1:8). Again, following the plot of Moses' story and the brother of Jared's, Lehi is told to lead his family into the desert and eventually to a promised land. As with other seers whose stories Smith and Cowdery have dictated in the preceding weeks, Lehi makes sure that these revelations are written down. According to the explanation provided by Nephi, who in these first paragraphs is quickly situating himself into the line of seers, he has abridged his father's records, to include with his own, in the tradition of Mormon and Moroni.[22]

Similarly, Nephi situates himself within this long line of seers. He too has visions and is visited repeatedly by angels. An angel appears to Laman and Lemuel in order to save Nephi from their hostilities and to authorize Nephi's leadership over them (1 Ne 3:30). An angel brings Nephi the extended vision of the future of the world, which includes a view of the twelve disciples and angels ministering to them (esp. 1 Ne. 11:30). Angels visit him after his father's death.[23]

Nephi also continues the project begun by Mormon and continued by Moroni of mapping the line of Book of Mormon seers, the crucial thread of continuity stretching across the entanglements and disjunctions of the book's history, out into the encompassing events of biblical tradition. In Mormon's narrative, the visit of Christ to America forges one crucial link of adjacency between the worlds of the Bible and the Book of Mormon. Moroni's narrative traces the Jaredite line of seers back beyond the Mosaic period to the Tower of Babel and, in the process, provides a story of origins for some of the sacred records and artifacts. Nephi's narrative similarly traces the Nephite line back beyond Hebraic history. In doing so, Nephi lines in more of the story of the record's origins. He pushes this privileged tradition of continuity forward beyond the boundaries of the Bible and draws Smith's nineteenth-century story into the narrative cycle of seers.

Like the story of the brother of Jared and the stones, Nephi's story of origins reaches back beyond the story of Moses. Nephi presents yet another story of succession, the sacred records passed from one guardian to another. The violence of this succession story underscores the lengths to which God may press his chosen ones in the service of God's secrets and power. Nephi recounts that Lehi receives yet another vision, or dream, this one that his sons should return to Jerusalem and retrieve the records engraved on brass plates. A man named Laban guards these records, and according to Nephi, the plates have been kept within the extended family since the time of Joseph of Egypt. Lehi and his family are descendants of Joseph. So too is Laban, who has inherited this work of keeping records from his fathers. But Laban is not a seer chosen by God.[24]

The lengths to which God will go with Lehi's sons underscores the importance of the cache of records guarded by Book of Mormon seers and now kept by the nineteenth-century seer dictating the bloody story. When Laban refuses to relinquish the cache of records, the "Spirit of the Lord" commands Nephi to kill him with his own sword (a sword added to the cache of artifacts and eventually inherited by Smith). "It is better that one man should perish," writes Nephi, "than that a nation should dwindle and perish in unbelief" (1 Ne. 4:13). It is this cache of records dating back to Joseph of Egypt, obtained at great cost, which Lehi and his family take with them to America and which become the first records in the priceless cache. The seers are thus situated by Nephi's story in a genealogy extending back to Joseph of Egypt and to the stories of the patriarchs recounted in Genesis, the first book of the Old Testament.

These links going back to Joseph of Egypt become the explicit focus during the following, rather more peaceful and ritualized scene of succession. Near the end of his life and near the end of the Book of Mormon dictation timeline, Lehi passes his advice and the tokens of his power to his sons just as King Benjamin did at the beginning of the timeline. Nephi narrates in expansive detail the suite of scenes associated with this ritual of succession and continuity which make him heir to the records. Like Benjamin, Lehi has a document read as part of the succession narrative. And like Benjamin, Lehi reveals a secret to his sons—or more precisely, Joseph of Egypt reveals this secret. For the revelation which Lehi reads to his sons, in particular to his son named Joseph, is dramatized as quoting Joseph of Egypt's own words engraved on the ancient record purchased, at God's insistence, with a human life.

Just as the April revelation to Smith and Cowdery had presented previously unknown words spoken by the biblical character John, Lehi now presents previously unknown words written by another biblical character, Joseph of Egypt. The fact of these written words places Joseph of Egypt in the line of old-time seers. No longer a narrative lined in the interstices of the King James Bible, this scene from Lehi's succession ritual directly engages and extends the Bible and can be seen to initiate the project that Smith will take up in earnest a year later, his own "translation" of the Bible. This is underscored by the fact that Smith will embed a version of these words of Joseph, quoted by Lehi, within the fiftieth chapter of Genesis in his version of the Bible.

The words of Joseph, so singular within the frame of the Book of Mormon story, foretell the birth of two holy men, both descendants of Joseph, both like him standing in the line of seers. The births he prophesies are of two descendants. The first descendant will be Moses, the character who has been repeatedly evoked within the Book of Mormon dictation timeline as a prototypical "seer after the manner of old times." The second descendant will be a latter-day seer named Joseph Jr. This is the first time that the specific term "seer" has appeared within the text since it was used to set up the work of King Mosiah in the beginning pages of the dictation timeline: "A seer shall the Lord my God raise up, who shall be a choice seer unto the fruit of my loins. ... And his name shall be called after me; and it shall be after the name of his father. And he shall be like unto me; for the thing, which the Lord shall bring forth by his hand, by the power of the Lord shall bring my people unto salvation" (2 Ne. 3:6, 15). In a rather breathtaking conclusion to the story, Smith himself is written into the Book of Mormon story in the company of Joseph of Egypt and Moses.[25]

If Joseph of Egypt explicitly compares the "choice seer" of the latter-days to himself, God is quoted as comparing Joseph Smith Jr. to Moses: "And he shall be great like unto Moses, whom I have said I would raise up unto you, to deliver my people, O house of Israel. ... I will raise up a Moses; and I will give power unto him in a rod; and I will give judgment unto him in writing" (2 Ne. 3:9, 17). God himself, in the extended passage encompassed within the above ellipses, emphasizes several of the key themes which have been associated with the work of the seer and which were evoked several months earlier when Smith dictated the March and April revelations. This passage from near the end of the Book of Mormon dictation timeline was probably produced some time in June.[26] God again confirms the continuum for the seer's gifts which already appeared in the spring: not only to reveal or translate God's secrets but also to perform miracles and to demonstrate other expertise with the supernatural.

In the passage dramatized as excerpted from the writings of Joseph of antiquity, God comes very close to quoting the March revelation which told Harris that Smith "has a gift to translate the book, and I have commanded him that he shall pretend to no other gift, for I will grant him no other gift" (BC IV:2). God says to Joseph of Egypt, "And I will give unto him a commandment, that he shall do no other work, save the work which I shall command him" (2 Ne. 3:8). Here, God has already dropped that narrow reference to Smith's "gift to translate the book" and has modulated it into the rather more broadly conceived discussion of a gift to translate in general, as in the April revelations. But the emphasis otherwise remains firmly focused on Smith's calling to translate and reveal God's secrets. His work of writing down God's words is compared to that of Moses who, according to tradition, not only received the revelation of the law but was also the author of the first five books of the Old Testament, the so-called books of Moses: "I will give judgment unto him in writing. ... I will write unto him my law" (2 Ne. 3:17).[27]

God is also returning to the April 1829 revelation which juxtaposed Moses' miraculous powers with the gift of working with the rod. The comparison which was implicit there is made explicit here. Both Moses and his latter-day double have "power unto him in a rod" (2 Ne. 3:17). It is this power of the seer, to not only translate or reveal God's secrets but to perform miracles as well, which Lehi emphasizes when he finishes quoting from the ancient record by Joseph of Egypt: "And there shall rise up one mighty among them, who shall do much good, both in word and in deed, being an instrument in the hands of God, with exceeding faith, to work mighty wonders, and do that which is great in the sight of God, unto the bringing to pass much restoration unto the house of Israel, and unto the seed of thy brethren" (2 Ne. 3:24).

TRANSLATING THE OLD STORY

From this singular platform of authority created by the book he finishes at the end of June 1829, Joseph Jr. launches a fifteen-year odyssey that will ultimately lead to the sacred secrets of Nauvoo and to his murder there in the summer of 1844. He is Joseph, son of Joseph, descendant of Joseph, choice seer of the latter days, like unto those of old: Joseph and Moses. The community that is gathering around belief in his book is thus given a framework that can sustain a commitment to him through the dangerous and exhilarating twists and turns of his odyssey. These same claims will provide the framework to sustain the intense opposition of enemies, for Smith ventures into highly charged territory as he begins, in the texts he dictates, to rewrite the Bible and canons of traditional Christian theology.

Certainly this intense period of transformation in Smith's career—from treasure seer and glass looker to prophet, seer, and revelator in the illustrious biblical tradition of Joseph of Egypt and Moses—is a lucky opportunity for the student of Mormon origins, coinciding as it does with such a profusion of texts. Focused and concentrated in the remarkable output of three months during the summer of 1829, in literally hundreds and hundreds of pages, can be found both the narrative themes that will spin out over the next fifteen years and culminate in a new religious tradition and the structures of life and thought that will characterize Smith throughout his career.

By the end of the Book of Mormon dictation plot, the seer narratives have become not only the major thread of continuity within the Book of Mormon but also the thread along which a broader history of the world is being plotted. The Book of Mormon reaches back towards biblical beginnings and then moves forward to Smith's own work as the latter-day Joseph of Egypt, a latter-day Moses, and God's "choice seer."

These seer narratives in the Book of Mormon are already laying the groundwork for what will become the most radical and enabling impulse within Smith's religious economy. By the time of his death, he will not only have written into one encompassing plot the old and new worlds, the Old and New Testaments, and biblical and contemporary histories, he will also have written God and man into one interlinking cosmic narrative. As the final revision of his writing and rewriting of biblical narratives, Nauvoo's secret temple rituals will plot the life story of earthly man (and by Nauvoo an earthly woman) becoming king (and queen), priest (and priestess), god (and goddess). Looking backward to Smith's threshold narratives about God's seers in the Book of Mormon and its environing 1829 revelations, it is possible to see man becoming god as the final emplotment of the life story of the seer which preoccupied and fascinated Smith from the beginning: the story of an earthly being who comes near to God, learns his secrets, and wins the possibility of being transformed, pushing beyond the limits circumscribed by the natural world and human mortality.

As Harold Bloom has suggested in his appreciative reading of Smith in the 1992 volume, *The American Religion*, Smith was consistently fascinated with those in whom "the distinction between God and man wavers." Bloom focuses on characters whom he describes as "man-become-angel." He correctly observes that Smith's radical theology of God and man required two interrelated moves: bringing God closer to earth and man closer to heaven. Bloom celebrates this double move as "Smith's radical sense of the theomorphic patriarchs and anthropomorphic gods." He writes that "what theologians deprecate as an anthropomorphic Yahweh is the necessary correlative of the Hebrew Bible's vision of theomorphic men and women: Abraham, Jacob, Joseph, Tamar, David. The religion-making genius of Joseph Smith, profoundly American, uniquely restored the Bible's sense of the theomorphic."[28]

The man-become-angel who most fascinates Bloom in Smith's work is Enoch, a character who will appear at the threshold of the dictation plot for Smith's rewriting of the King James Bible begun in 1830. During that first year, Smith's work would employ the term "seer" twice, once applied to himself in the revelation dictated at the organization of the Church of Christ on 6 April 1830 (D&C 21:1) and once to apply to Enoch, the seer who in Smith's translation of the

Bible performs miracles such as moving mountains and manages to have not only himself but also his whole city translated (Moses 6:36, 38). Although Bloom does not acknowledge Enoch's textual genealogy, even these abbreviated details suggest the way in which Enoch will continue to push at the curve of the seer story we have already explored–continuing the impulse to return to origins and to bring the seer ever nearer to the border between God and man.

If read against the backdrop of the Book of Mormon seer, Bloom's description of Enoch can be a useful frame for considering what is at stake in the insistent preoccupation with the seer character in Smith's textual economy:

> Smith was haunted by the figure of Enoch, who in ancient Jewish texts was transmogrified into the angel Metatron, sometimes called the lesser Yahweh. A giant in size, radiant with light, this patriarch-angel was renowned for his total knowledge of the secrets of God. If the distinction between God and man wavers anywhere in Kaballah, that wavering is most incessant in the fused figure of Enoch-Metatron. Enoch, who walked with God, is taken up by God, and so does not die. The Kabbalists interpreted Enoch's ascent as the restoration of the state of Adam, not Adam in the Garden but a preexistent cosmic anthropos, at once God, angel, and man. ... [E]soteric traditions always had exalted Enoch as the archetype of man-become-angel, and even become God. The revelation of Enoch was made to the Prophet Joseph precisely as it was made to the Kabbalists, to grant unto us a more human God and a more divine man.[29]

This Enoch character, however striking his portrait within Smith's revision of the King James Bible, is only one version of the man-become-angel story within Smith's dictation timeline. What Bloom misses in his discussion is the richly detailed backdrop provided for Enoch by the Book of Mormon cycle of transcendent seers. Bloom fails to appreciate how much more enduring and central to Smith's imagination will be the dramatic and ongoing transformations in the story of Moses, Smith's prototypical version of the seer in old times, the man become angel. While many characters come and go within Smith's texts, Moses remains an enduring presence into Nauvoo and a key character for tracing the narrative transformations and, through them, Smith's religious innovations.

Bloom's reading provides not only a useful frame for considering the narrative importance of the seer character, located as it is at the boundary between earth and heaven, but also for considering the structure and method of the Book of Mormon and the concurrent revelations in the spring and summer of 1829. The work of the seer within the Book of Mormon is focused in the high gift of "translation"—with all the suggestive possibilities of this richly nuanced word. As Mormon and Moroni make clear, this work is often as much reading and interpreting, abridging and summarizing an ancient text as it is transmuting a text from one language into another. That Smith will apply the term to his revision of the King James Bible, where the focus is on inspired rereading of the text, not on "translation" in any traditional sense, emphasizes that for Smith, the process is characterized by reading, rereading, and transforming.

Rather than apologizing for this revisionary impulse, Bloom celebrates it as constitutive of Smith's creativity and an organizing source of energy and innovation. He locates Smith's Bible revision as the ultimate wellspring of this animating energy: "He was anything but a great writer, but he was a great reader, or creative misreader, of the Bible. Mormonism is a wonderfully strong misprision, or creative misreading, of the early history of the Jews." On first hearing, Bloom's compliment can easily be taken as a putdown. It is important to understand that in describing Mormonism as "a wonderfully strong misprision, or creative misreading" and Smith as a "great reader, or creative misreader," Bloom is paying a compliment to Smith's imaginative and religious power.[30] According to Bloom, poetry itself is a matter of creative misreading: "Strong poets make history by misreading one another, so as to clear imaginative space for themselves. ... Weaker talents idealize; figures of capable imagination appropriate for themselves."[31]

His notion of strong reading provides a crucial tool for understanding the power of an imagination as dependent as Smith's on an earlier text. For however long and with whatever heat the various camps in Mormon letters argue over Smith's sources, all would agree that the Bible constituted a major source of borrowings for his work. Bloom makes clear that a dependent imagination, one which comes late in a tradition, is not lesser or doomed to derivative repetition. Rather, the power of such an imagination comes in bold and self-enhancing swerves in relation to earlier texts, its negotiations of strategic space in a world overcrowded with already-written books and already-imagined stories. Reading is a tool, in this view, for creative energy, for revelation. A way of making something new, something authoritative in an old world.[32]

The complicated path of reading and rereading in 1829 can be glimpsed by returning to Smith's text of Joseph of Egypt embedded in the scene in which Lehi passes the tokens of seership to his son Nephi, the last great scene of succession dictated by Smith. As already suggested, Joseph of Egypt comes very close to quoting the words of God to Martin Harris in the March revelation. But already, the distance opened between the March and April revelations is arguably captured in Joseph of Egypt's Book of Mormon words. In the March revelation, Smith is told quite plainly that he "has a gift to translate the book, and I have commanded him that he shall pretend to no other gift, for I will grant him no other gift" (BC IV:2). The April revelations hinted at possible translations of other books (BC VIII:1). This broader version is echoed in the passage from Joseph of Egypt in the Book of Mormon, dictated some two months after the April revelation: "And I will give unto him a commandment, that he shall do none other work, save the work which I shall command him" (2 Ne. 3:8). More than a year later in 1830, Smith will return to this passage as part of his translation of the Bible, embedding an expanded version in the fiftieth chapter of Genesis. Here the description of Joseph Jr.'s calling has been modulated again to encompass the ever expanding responsibilities he is carrying within the community of faith: "And he shall do whatsoever work I shall command him" (JST Gen. 50:28). Certainly it is striking that the story of the choice seer, Joseph Jr., has been written into the King James Bible itself.

Smith will return to this theme one final time as he prepares the March 1829 revelation for publication in the 1835 Doctrine and Covenants, prepared in Kirtland about two years after discontinuing work on the Bible. Here, in the final version of the words that have echoed and re-echoed across the borders of the ancient and modern texts dictated and translated by Smith in the six years between 1829 and 1835, there is little room for ambiguity: "And you have a gift to translate the plates; *and this is the first gift that I bestowed upon you*; and I have commanded that you should pretend to no other gift *until my purpose is fulfilled in this*; for I will grant unto you no other gift *until it is finished*"

(D&C 5:4; emphasis added). By 1835, it is clear that the Book of Mormon was indeed only the first task for God's choice seer.

When Smith reworked the passage in 2 Nephi 3 for inclusion in his version of the King James Bible sometime in 1833, he made another significant change to this passage, first embedded within the Book of Mormon as a fragment from Joseph of Egypt looking forward to the birth of Moses and the birth of Joseph Smith. This change effaces the focus in the Book of Mormon's version of Moses' (and by implication Smith's) power in using the rod, the same rod that is the focus of Cowdery's attempts at translation in the April 1829 revelations. The passage in the Book of Mormon closely aligns two themes associated with the seer, the use of magic artifacts such as seer stones and the calling to guard and create records: "I will give power unto him in a rod: and I will give judgment unto him in writing" (2 Ne. 3:17). In the version prepared for the Bible revision, this same passage reads: "I will raise up Moses, and a rod shall be in his hand, and he shall gather together my people, and he shall lead them as a flock, and he shall smite the waters of the Red Sea with his rod. And he shall have judgment, and shall write the word of the Lord" (JST Gen. 50:34-25).

By the time Smith reached this passage, probably sometime in 1833, the stories of the seer and of Moses were still transforming within the confines of the texts Smith was dictating. This revision brought the passage more in line with the evolving narrative. When Smith had taken up the story of Moses again in the summer of 1830, a year after completing the Book of Mormon, he began with a prologue story about Moses (Moses 1). In this prologue, Moses appears again as a seer. But the emphasis is no longer on Moses and the rod as it was the year before, but rather on his power as a more direct revelator of God's words. In a similar move, Smith himself had left behind his seer stones and received his revelations more directly in a manner that again mimed the experience of Moses in the texts of 1830. In the summer and fall of that year, Smith was elevated to a singular position within the new church on the basis of his likeness to Moses. A September 1830 revelation declares that Smith is the only one who may receive commandments and revelations: "[F]or he receiveth them even as Moses. ... for I have given him the keys of the mysteries and the revelations which are sealed" (D&C 28:2; cf. BC XXX:2). Like Moses, Smith is now "head of the church" (D&C 28:6; cf. BC XXX:6).

Ironically enough, this revelation was received in response to a member of the community who was using a seer stone to receive revelations purported to be from God for the group.[33]

When Smith returned to the April revelations as part of his work leading up to the 1835 version of the Doctrine and Covenants, he reworked the passages on the divining rod just as he had done when he returned to the passage on Moses two years before. Rather than "the gift of working with the rod," Cowdery is now told that he has "the gift of Aaron" (D&C 8:6). By then, the story of Moses and his brother Aaron had been contextualized within the expanding seer story which had become, at this point, the story of the Melchizedek and Aaronic priesthoods.[34]

These echoing versions of the passages concerning the work of the old-time seer capture the expansive and fluid nature of the story as it plays itself out through many repeating versions strung along the timeline of the narratives and texts Smith dictates between 1829 and 1844. Following the complications of this story is one crucial way of finding entrance into the story of Mormon origins.

NOTES

1. Michael Quinn describes at least three seer stones which were associated with Joseph Smith but suggests that the sources most consistently describe a brown stone. This would be the same stone he used to translate the Book of Mormon and to receive the revelations which environed his translation of the Book of Mormon, March through June 1829. D. Michael Quinn, *Early Mormonism and the Magic World View* (Salt Lake City: Signature Books, 1987), 38-41.

2. For other discussions of Smith as a treasure seer during the period he was communicating with the guardian of the golden records, see H. Michael Marquardt and Wesley P. Walters, *Inventing Mormonism: Tradition and the Historical Record* (Salt Lake City: Smith Research Associates, 1994), 63-116; Richard Van Wagoner and Steven Walker, "Joseph Smith: 'The Gift of Seeing,'" *Dialogue: A Journal of Mormon Thought* 15 (Summer 1982): 48-68; John Brooke, *The Refiner's Fire: The Making of Mormon Cosmology, 1644-1844* (Cambridge: Cambridge University Press, 1994), 150-57.

3. For a summary of evidence supporting the order of the dictation plot as described in this essay, see Brent Lee Metcalfe, "The Priority of Mosiah: A Prelude to the Book of Mormon Exegesis," in *New Approaches to the Book of*

Mormon: Explorations in Critical Methodology (Salt Lake City: Signature Books, 1993), 395-444; see also Edwin Firmage, Jr., "Historical Criticism and the Book of Mormon: A Personal Encounter," in this collection.

4. The term appears one final time in 2 Ne. 27:5, again in a passage which is prophesying the work of Smith, this time in the passage of the learned man who says that he cannot read a sealed book.

5. Prior to reading the revelation in public, King Benjamin spoke privately with his son about the angel's secret, telling Mosiah that he "shall give this people a name, that thereby they may be distinguished above all the people which the Lord God hath brought out of the land of Jerusalem" (1:11). This implies that the significance of a name is something new, not previously known.

In public, King Benjamin again underscores that he is telling them something previously unknown (Mos. 3:1-4). Like his words to his son, this passage depends for its effect on a mystery, and his introduction heightens the sense of expectation and teases his listeners with a secret of miraculous proportions.

6. For a reader accustomed to reading the Book of Mormon chronologically, it is easy to miss the ways in which the content of King Benjamin's address is dramatized as something new and unfamiliar. The first-person narratives attributed to Nephi and his immediate descendants, which tell the beginnings of Nephite history, speak freely and in great detail about God's coming to the earth as Jesus. Read within the chronological plot as coming after these detailed discussions, Benjamin's enthusiastic emphasis does not make sense and, as a result, is easily missed. Viewed within the dictation timeline, it is possible to see a discussion about Christ develop gradually. This is first introduced in rather broad outlines, and only later is the idea that Jesus will visit the Nephites introduced (Alma 16:20). The detailed prophecies, viewed within the dictation timeline, are in a sense retrospective accounts. For a discussion of the arc of development of Jesus' appearance, see Brent Metcalfe, *New Approaches*, 416-418.

7. An angel appears both to Alma and Amulek prior to their mission (Alma 9, 10). Alma often preaches about angels and revelation, saying that they are sent to prophets to declare the coming of Jesus (Alma 13:22-26). They can appear to women (Alma 32:23). He has personally received revelations from angels (Alma 36:5-8).

Other angelic visits include: when Ammon is spared because of God's promise to his father, Mosiah, and King Lamoni's household is converted (Alma 19) and when Samuel the Lamanite's mission is revealed (Hel. 13:7). Even in these somewhat tangential cases, the event is associated with seers.

8. A mass conversion follows the visitation of angels and encircling fire (Hel. 5:23-52).

9. It is interesting to note that "translation" (later specifically applied to another seer, Ether) will be generalized beyond the seers to three Nephites at once. A recurring impulse for Smith was to generalize by way of community or

friendship—for instance, in extending the opportunity to Oliver Cowdery to translate texts, in the expanding community of "witnesses," lay priesthood, and then godhood as the mechanisms by which the role of seer is generalized to the community of believers.

10. Confusion exists regarding Mosiah's seer stones and those of the Jaredites. Mosiah already has a reputation as a stone gazer before he receives the Jaredite artifacts. That there might be more than one set does not present insuperable problems within this accepting and fluid narrative.

11. Within the dictation timeline, Jesus' appearance to the Brother of Jared occurs after Jesus' visit to America. It is thus, in one sense, a retrospective on 3 Nephi.

12. I quote the earliest extant version from the manuscript in the Newell K. Whitney collection, library, Brigham Young University, Provo, Utah. This version predates the 1833 Book of Commandments (chapter IV), which contains significant changes—although not as many as in the 1835 version in the Doctrine and Covenants. For all three versions, see Karl F. Best, "Changes in the Revelations, 1833 to 1835," *Dialogue* 25 (Spring 1992): 92-97; see also H. Michael Marquardt, *The Joseph Smith Revelations: Text and Commentary* (Salt Lake City: Signature Books, 1999), 26-28.

13. Emphasis on the singular book, swept away within a month, is mine. See Book of Commandments, Chapter IV (now D&C 5). I rely on the Book of Commandments because the passage was substantively revised for the 1835 Doctrine and Covenants, muting the emphasis on the singular. For the various versions, see Robert J. Woodford, "The Historical Development of the Doctrine and Covenants" (Ph.D. diss.; Provo, Utah: Brigham Young University, 1974), I:149-200.

14. This ancient revelation links men—the unbroken line of seers—rather exclusively to the possibility of being translated rather than submitting to a conventional death. When the revelation was published in 1832 (B&C VI), the detail was added that it was a translation of an ancient parchment "written and hid up by" John, the disciple of Jesus. Later accounts mentioned that the revelation was received through the seer stone in response to a question about what became of John. The 1835 D&C revised the text to reflect the increasing importance of Peter, James, and John as a First Presidency and the restorers of the Melchizedek priesthood. Only Peter and John are in the version that appeared in 1832. For a description of this textual history, see Woodford, "Historical Development of the Doctrine and Covenants," 176-184.

15. The command to search not for treasure but for "mysteries" calls up King Benjamin's comment: "My sons, I would that ye should remember that were it not for these plates, which contain these records and these commandments, we must have suffered in ignorance, even at this present time, not knowing the mysteries of God." Underscoring this link between the records and secrets, Benjamin refers to "these things, which have been kept and pre-

served by the hand of God, that we might read and understand of his mysteries" (Mos. 1:3, 5).

16. As the Book of Mormon comes to propose a variety of ways in which a seer might have access to God—through seer stones, angelic visits, dreams, the Liahona, or a direct visit from God himself—the April revelations similarly begin to generalize in providing multiple models. After the flurry of activity translating and receiving revelation in the spring of 1829, Smith will for the most part abandon use of physical devices to assist in his approach to God.

17. For Smith's and Cowdery's connection to divining rods, and also the "Mosaical rod," see Quinn, *Magic World View,* 32-34.

18. In the current Doctrine and Covenants, the date for Section 10 is given as the summer of 1828. However, the date May 1829 appeared in all versions printed during Smith's lifetime. For a discussion of this, see Woodford, "Historical Development of the Doctrine and Covenants," 200-17.

19. Mormon's interpolations focus on sources. He describes the multiplicity of records (Hel. 3:13), mentions that secret oaths were not included in Helaman's account (Hel. 6:25), describes the plates of Nephi and his own abridgment (3 Ne. 5), discusses what the Lord has told him to include or to leave out of the compilation (3 Ne. 26:6), speaks about events that will surround the book's appearance in the latter days (3 Ne. 29), and describes the record keeping of Nephi and subsequent seers (4 Ne. 1:11-23).

20. The story of multiple records unfolds gradually and is not entirely coherent. The first time Mormon mentions an alternative account, it seems to be associated with Nephi Jr., the seer who was alive when Jesus comes to America (3 Ne. 5). Later, these records are associated with Nephi, son of Lehi. In the Words of Mormon, written near the end of the dictation timeline, Mormon describes finding yet another set of Nephi plates. These are eventually used to replace the missing 116 manuscript pages. In late May or early June, while seeking a copyright for the Book of Mormon and presumably before dictating the Words of Mormon, Joseph Smith produced a title page which he said he found at the end of the plates. It describes Mormon's and Moroni's abridgments but omits mention of the alternative small plates. See Metcalfe, "The Priority of Mosiah," 398, 403.

21. As with Benjamin, this family maintains the ability to read Egyptian.

22. For mention of records written by Lehi, see 1 Ne 1:17; 6:1.

23. Nephi's brother Jacob is also visited by an angel, who reveals to him the name of Jesus (2 Ne. 10:3).

24. For discussion of the genealogy of the line of men who have produced and guarded these records, see 1 Ne. 5:16; 6:1-2.

25. The final use of the term "seer" within the dictation timeline will also call up Joseph Smith and go into even more detail about Smith's earthly life including the fact that he will deliver a book to a man who will say he cannot read it because it is sealed (2 Ne. 27).

26. Evidence suggests that the title page was written by 11 June, before

Smith began dictating the first-person narratives (1 Nephi through Words of Mormon) which comprise the beginning of the Book of Mormon text. Considered within this context, the passages in 2 Nephi which I discuss would have been dictated rather more near the end of June (see Metcalfe, "Mosiah Priority," 403). The title page emphasizes the themes of sacred secrets and translation: "Written and sealed up, and hid up unto the Lord ... To come forth by the gift and power of God unto the interpretation thereof ... The interpretation thereof by the gift of God."

27. The April revelation and this passage from the Book of Mormon also parallel each other in structural ways which further emphasize their shared interest in secrecy. As we have seen, an "ancient record," the words of Jesus' disciple John, was embedded within the revelations. In the same way, this "ancient record" of Joseph of Egypt is embedded in the final text. Both hidden records turn on secrets or mysteries. This embedding of secret records within secret records was already set up at the beginning of the dictation timeline in the Book of Mosiah with the records of Zeniff and Alma.

This is actually an oversimplification of the Chinese-box structure at this point in the text with its overdetermination of secrets within secrets. The prophecy of Joseph of Egypt is said to be taken from the brass plates, a record still hidden from Book of Mormon readers. The details of what might be found in this hidden source are mentioned throughout the final portions of the dictation.

In addition, evidence suggests that Smith himself came to a "knowledge" of the two sets of plates of Nephi rather late in the process. This passage from the brass record appears on the "small plates of Nephi." Arguably, the distinction between the "large" plates of Nephi (which presumably contained the Book of Lehi, whose translation was lost by Martin Harris) and the "small" plates of Nephi (which contained the first-person replacement narratives) does not exist until introduced in 1 Nephi chapters 6 and 9. Both the title page and the revelation describing how Smith was to proceed in replacing the missing manuscript (BC IX; D&C 10) describe a single record, the "plates of Nephi." See Metcalfe, "Priority of Mosiah," 403.

28. Harold Bloom, *The American Religion: The Emergence of the Post-Christian Nation* (New York: Simon & Schuster, 1992), 84, 99-100.

29. Ibid.

30. The magnitude of Bloom's compliment is gauged by the fact that he nearly gives Smith priority over his own habitual literary heroes: "I myself can think of no other American, except for Emerson and Whitman, who so moves and alters my own imagination. For someone who is not a Mormon, what matters most about Joseph Smith is how American both the man and his religion have proved to be. So self-created was he that he transcends Emerson and Whitman in my imaginative response, and takes his place with the great figures of our fiction, since at moments he appears far larger than life, in the mode of a Shakespearean character. So rich and varied a personality, so vital a

spark of divinity, is almost beyond the limits of the human, as normally we construe these limits" (ibid., 126-27). His own admiration for, and self-identification with, Smith's audacity leads him to overlook just how male-identified Smith's imaginative world is.

31. Harold Bloom, *The Anxiety of Influence: A Theory of Poetry* (Oxford and London: Oxford University Press, 1973), 5.

32. Mormon scholar David Wright has also linked the Book of Mormon and Smith's bible and Book of Abraham as "readings" of the King James Bible. As Wright points out, Smith applied the term "translation" to all three projects. Certainly there are differences in the three texts, but as Wright argues, there is a consistency in approach and method: "He is not working in any of them with ancient languages ... and in all them there is attention (to a greater or lesser degree) to revising or responding to the King James Version." See David Wright, "In Plain Terms That We May Understand": Joseph Smith's Transformation of Hebrews in Alma 12-13," in Metcalfe, *New Approaches*, 211.

According to Wright, Smith relies on "textual conservation, the retention of elements in the biblical text," on "solving problems in the biblical text," and on "midrashic transformation or expansion of textual implications." Further, "to save text, to solve problems, or to develop implications, the biblical phraseology and ideas were placed in a new context." He describes three recurring strategies for creating new contexts: generalizing or universalizing, primordializing or moving to origins, conflating or collocating previously unrelated material.

Wright fails to emphasize the part that narrative per se plays in this. His focus is on "principles and ideas"–propositions and theology–and on "biblical phraseology." But it is usually because of narrative characters and by living through their stories that Smith first works through problems, challenges, and the lures that press against him. Even more specifically, it is by way of characters conceived in relation to the grand fund of sacred narrative made available by the biblical tradition that Smith's explorations and innovations tend to begin. The more overtly discursive, theoretical, or theological passages in Smith's texts are inevitably propped on and extrapolated from distinctive readings of biblical narratives. The process of interpretation or commentary gives way to discussion and theologizing rather late within the recurring arc of development in Smith's texts.

As Wright emphasizes, Smith conserves more often than contradicts the biblical text. He prefers to expand and add within the interstices what he considers to be the missing plain and precious parts. Within this context, the Book of Mormon can be seen as a narrative interpolation drawn in the margins of the Bible. Certainly Smith will, on occasion, delete portions of the text, and he will also, on occasion, change portions of the text in a way which contradicts entirely or revises directly the previous meaning of the passage. But because these latter changes are relatively rare, they are in effect underscored, advertised as "exceptional"—a transformation of last resort.

I agree with Wright's focus on problem-solving as a force that drives Smith. In one recurring set of revisions in his new translation of the Bible (especially in the Old Testament portion), the blame for behavior perceived to be less than exemplary (anger, revenge, the need to repent) is shifted from God to his prophets and wayward children. Perhaps even more striking is the inclination to solve immediate problems. Narrative interpolations mirror and shadow the nineteenth-century world, especially the community of believers gathering around Smith. These parallels become scripts for life for those in the latter-day church. Thus, for example, when in December 1830 Smith dictates the story of Enoch and his Holy City for his revision of Genesis 5, it is because his own community, suddenly the size of a small city in the wake of the first missionary successes in Kirtland, is in need of a model for their own Zion.

I also agree that Smith's revisions usually construct new frames or contexts for earlier readings. These tend to knot together into an encompassing story various strands of narrative which, until that point, might have been adjacent to each other in time or space. A new frame provides a way of directing the attentions and inattentions of the reader, provides in effect directions for what can be ignored, what should be privileged.

Plotting fragmented narratives into a unified chronology is one characteristic way that the texts reframe characters and plots into master narratives. Evoking the power and authority of origins, chronology is traced backwards in time ever closer to the beginning and forward to the end of time. Smith's most radical theological innovations which will play themselves out in their fullest form in Nauvoo—the notion that God was once a man and that men (and women) can become gods—can also be seen as teasing out a narrative logic. The final encompassing master narratives extend back beyond the world's creation and forward beyond the world's end. God and humans are plotted into one encompassing narrative. Viewed in this context, it is possible to see the beginnings of this narrative logic in Smith's revisions between 1830 and 1835. For example, the vision of multiple heavens dictated in February 1832 begins to make the scene of God's story continuous with the unfolding sketch of man's story: if righteous enough, certain privileged men can come to live in the same place God lives. (Attention to the story of women will largely await further expansion of the marriage narratives.)

What all of this means is that Smith's imaginative economy with its decided inclination towards conservation and collocation, saving and gathering together, generates a body of work characterized by increasingly intricate and overdetermined intertextuality. The further along an intertextual arc of revision and translation traveled, the more complicated and encompassing are the tasks which a text must negotiate in order to clear its own space and assert its own authority.

33. For a description of the events leading up to this revelation, see Wood-

ford, I:404-408. There are no substantive revisions to this revelation for the 1835 D&C.

34. For discussions of the extensive revisions to the March and April 1829 revelations, see Woodford, I:132-99.

8.

Echoes of Anti-Masonry: A Rejoinder to Critics of the Anti-Masonic Thesis

Dan Vogel

In recent years Mormon apologists have begun to challenge what many researchers, myself included, long regarded as obvious: the Book of Mormon's reflection of the cultural milieu of early nineteenth-century America, particularly the anti-Masonic controversy that pervaded western New York during the late 1820s.[1] If the similarities between Masonry and the secret societies described in the book are not apparent to some modern readers, they were to its first readers, Mormon and non-Mormon, who almost immediately associated its warnings of latter-day "secret combinations" with the dreaded Masons.[2] Despite the book's use of the term "secret combinations"—a favorite anti-Masonic epithet—several scholars now, for various reasons, object to the connection and, in some instances, offer alternative interpretations. In particular, I will examine and respond to the arguments put forth by Richard L. Bushman, Blake T. Ostler, D. Michael Quinn, and Daniel C. Peterson.

In his 1984 book, *Joseph Smith and the Beginnings of Mormonism,* Richard Bushman acknowledged "a few obvious similarities" between the Book of Mormon and anti-Masonic rhetoric but contended that such parallels are superficial.[3] While he discounted the possibility of environmental influence on the Book of Mormon, Blake Ostler tried to account for similarities between the book and its environment in his 1987 article, "The Book of Mormon as a Modern Expansion of an Ancient Source," suggesting that what occurs in the book is "Joseph Smith's independent commentary on Masonry, sparked by his reflection on Nephite secret combinations."[4] Disregarding the many early accounts that describe Smith's translation method as a mechanical process of reading the English text as it appeared in the stone,[5] Ostler embraced a liberal view of translation in which Smith played an active role as inspired commentator and expander of the ancient text. Thus, he accounted for the presence of anti-Masonic rhetoric while at the same time defending the book's ancient origin.

Ostler's apologetic has yet to find much favor among fellow defenders of the faith who typically see his position as subversive to the foundational claim regarding "the most correct of any book on earth."[6] In fact, backlash from his concessions resulted in a reiteration of Bushman's position, with subsequent apologists willing to acknowledge only the most superficial similarities between anti-Masonry and the Book of Mormon. In his apparent rejection of Ostler's translation thesis, Michael Quinn not only dismissed anti-Masonic parallels as shallow but argued in his 1987 book, *Early Mormonism and the Magic World View* (and again in the 1998 revision), that the book's "secret combinations" actually refer to witchcraft and occult murders.[7] While Quinn's novel interpretation received scant support, some of his arguments against the anti-Masonic thesis have been employed by later apologists.

In his 1990 "Notes on 'Gadianton Masonry,'" Daniel Peterson attempted to refute many of the claimed similarities between nineteenth-century Masonry and the Book of Mormon's secret societies, particularly those I advanced in a 1989 essay, "Mormonism's 'Anti-Masonick Bible.'" Drawing on the arguments of Bushman, Quinn, and Ostler, he concluded that there is "no reason to insist upon a simple one-to-one equation between the Gadianton robbers and any single modern organization."[8] Hailed by some as near-definitive,[9] Peterson's article represents the current apologetic against the anti-Masonic interpretation.

While each of these authors varies from the others in approach and conclusion, they are united in attempting to rescue the Book of Mormon from anti-Masonry thesis. It is hoped that what follows will clarify the issues and raise the ongoing debate to a more productive level of discussion. I have elected to follow a point-for-point format. In doing so, I respond to all of the major and most, if not all, of the minor arguments against the anti-Masonic thesis.

BUSHMAN'S ARGUMENTS FROM SILENCE

1. According to Bushman, "critics in Joseph Smith's own day made ... little of anti-Masonry in the Book of Mormon" (131; cf. Peterson, 213). Here—the first of several arguments from silence—Bushman is incorrect. For, many in Smith's day, including Alexander Campbell in 1831, Eber D. Howe and Jason Whitman (separately) in 1834, and Edward Strut Abdy in 1835, to name a few, identified the Book of Mormon's ancient secret societies and modern "secret combinations" with Freemasonry.[10] Bushman is also wrong about critics after Campbell ignoring the point in order to credit Solomon Spalding with "authorship" (131). Howe, Whitman, and Abdy came after Campbell, and Mormon convert Oliver B. Huntington's experience in New York in 1843 demonstrates that this interpretation was far from dead:

> In the course of the day we went over to Mr. Lewises, about 40 rods distant and there found one Mr. Millard one of the devils minute men standing like a soldier of no Sense at all to fight against truth and reason. He said he knew all about Mormonism and what it sprang from, it sprang from masonry or the death of [William] Morgan, that Mormon was derived from the word Morgan. ... He said he would prophesy in the name of the Lord Jehovah that Mormonism did spring from the death of Morgan.[11]

Bushman's impression that the Spalding theory overshadowed other explanations is simply untrue. In Howe's 1834 book, for instance, he presented the Spalding theory along with environmental explanations for the book's origin. These are not mutually exclusive. Those who advocated the Spalding theory usually believed that the manuscript had been reworked by Joseph Smith, Sidney Rigdon, or both. Bushman overstates his case when he says Campbell "accepted the Spalding-Rigdon hypothesis despite the contradiction with his own 1831 [environmental] analysis" (231n37). That Campbell advocated the Spalding theory does not mean he "dropped the point about

Masonry," (131). Bushman also reads too much into Campbell's later neglect of the Book of Mormon since Campbell came to ignore the subject of Mormonism altogether.

2. Speaking of first-generation Mormons, Bushman argues that "the people who knew anti-Masonry and the Book of Mormon in the 1830s made less of the connection than critics today" (131; cf. Peterson, 213). Founding Mormons did make the connection–a point that Bushman could have addressed at greater length. On 15 March 1831, Ohio's *Geauga Gazette* quoted early convert Martin Harris that the Book of Mormon was "the Anti-Masonick Bible." The *Ohio Star* for 24 March reported: "The Mormon Bible is anti-masonic, and it is a singular truth that every one of its followers, so far as we are able to ascertain, are anti-masons." Given the fact that the two major anti-Mormon works of the day–Campbell's 1831 critique and Howe's 1834 book–criticized the presence of anti-Masonry in the Book of Mormon, some subsequent reticence is understandable. Either those who believed in the book had no answer or, unlike modern apologists, did not perceive a real conflict.

Bushman asserts that "converts paid no attention to anti-Masonry" (131; cf. Peterson, 204-205). He does not explain how he knows this. One should not make too much of such an argument in any case since it could also be said that early converts paid no attention to teachings on the godhead, baptism, spiritual gifts, or church government. In fact, the earliest Mormons lived in a culture of biblical hegemony and rarely referenced the Book of Mormon on any subject. Rather, many of the retrospective accounts emphasize their quest for religious authority, which the Book of Mormon offered.[12]

Bushman argues that "Lucy Mack Smith [Joseph Smith's mother] said nothing about masonry, [William] Morgan, or anti-Masonry in her autobiography. Joseph was equally neglectful" (131; cf. Peterson, 204-205).[13] Disappointingly, however, the Smith histories are silent on Joseph's use of a stone to hunt for buried treasure in Manchester; his 1826 trial for glass-looking in Bainbridge, New York; his participation in Palmyra's debating club and his involvement with Methodists; the differing religious views of his parents; and Joseph Sr.'s drinking problem. Considering these lapses, the failure to mention the William Morgan excitement of the mid-1820s is hardly significant. Yet, we do know that the Morgan affair was important and had a negative effect on attendance at Palmyra's Mount Moriah Lodge, which counted Joseph's older brother Hyrum as one of its members.[14] That the histories of Joseph (1838)[15] and his mother (1845) were written when the subject had largely disappeared from local and national discourse may indicate that anti-Masonry was no longer as important as it once seemed.[16]

3. The complaint is made by Bushman that Book of Mormon groups known as Gadianton "were not one continuing society, like the Masons, but five distinct combinations that sprang up among the Nephites and Jaredites" (130; cf. Ostler, 74-76).[17] The Book of Mormon actually describes the ebb and flow of Gadianton bands depending on the wickedness or righteousness of the Nephite nation, implying ontinuity. The groups are said to have been used by God to humble the Nephites. Bushman sees the term "Gadianton robbers" as simply a convenient label for distinct groups, but after Mormon describes the founding of the Gadianton band, he observes that "in the end of this book ye shall see that this Gadianton did prove the overthrow, yea, almost the entire destruction of the Nephite people" (Hel. 2:13). Apparently, transmission between the first and second bands was accomplished through records hidden in the earth (Hel. 11:10, 26). Succeeding robber bands claimed Gadianton as their founder and held the belief that their oaths were "of ancient date" and "handed down" (3 Ne. 3:9). The secret societies that appeared among the Nephites after the visit of Jesus and eventually led to their destruction were not independent, for Mormon states that "the wicked part of the people began again to build up the secret oaths and combinations of Gadianton" (4 Ne. 1:42). Thus, the treatment of secret societies is not as fragmentary as Bushman states.

On the other hand, international Freemasonry was not as unitary as Bushman claims. It was generally recognized to be divided among distinctive orders and rites with two competing grand lodges in New York alone.[18] The disunity of Masonry was noted by Henry Dana Ward, who wrote in 1829 that "the present convulsed state of Mexico, is principally owing to the secret operations of two masonic parties, the York masons, and the Scotch masons."[19]

Ultimately, Bushman's complaint is irrelevant since it was not imperative that Smith follow either a unitary or diversified history of Masonry. He was free to adapt such cultural borrowings to the requirements of his own work. The historical and literary critic seeks evidence of environmental influence, not exact replication. An author uses his life's experiences to create something both familiar and unique, and some differences, especially of traits not considered particularly distinctive, should be expected.

4. Bushman expresses surprise that "the murder of the Masonic traitor William Morgan in 1826, had no equivalent in the Book of Mormon" (131). Again, one should not expect an exact, duplicate plot line. By 1830, Morgan's murder had become less relevant to anti-Masons who were expanding their rhetoric to include accusations of other Masonic murders.[20] Moreover, if the Book of Mormon is viewed as anti-Masonic, one should expect to find Morgan portrayed as a hero, not as a "traitor." While anti-Masons were aware of Morgan's former Masonic affiliation, from their point of view, he had been killed for exposing Masonry's true character. The Reverend David Pease's 1830 sermon provides a good example of how the other side—the anti-Masons—regarded Morgan:

> More than one hundred ministers of the gospel have renounced and denounced it. ... But it was reserved by the providence of God, for Capt. Wm. Morgan to openly commence the attack upon this potent foe, which had secretly interwoven itself with all our civil, religious and even domestic concerns. ... [H]e bravely opened the war against that power ... and though he fell as a martyr in the cause, he tore away the strongest pillars. ... The spell with many was now broken. A ray of *light* ... found its way into the chamber of darkness.[21]

The Book of Mormon image of prophets being martyred at the hands of "secret combinations" could be loosely inspired by Morgan's death (Al. 37:30; 3 Ne. 6:19-30). Regardless, the principle upon which anti-Masons believed Morgan's murder had been carried out is expressed: "And whosoever of those who belonged to their band should reveal unto the world of their wickedness and their abominations, should be tried, not according to the laws of their country, but according to the laws of their wickedness, which had been given by Gadianton and Kishkumen" (Hel. 6:24). Later, as he worked on his Inspired Revision of the Bible in October 1830, Joseph Smith would make an addition to Genesis with a more direct comparison to the Morgan affair. His revision disclosed that Lamech murdered Irad, the son of Enoch, "for the oath's sake," because Irad began to reveal secret oaths to the sons of Adam (Moses 5:47-50). This undoubtedly reminded many in western New York of Morgan's violent murder.

5. Bushman insists that "in the supposed anti-Masonic passages in the Book of Mormon, nothing was said about Masonic degrees or elaborate initiation rituals" (131; cf. Ostler, 74; Peterson, 186). This carries little weight because the Book of Mormon repeatedly explains the omission. Moroni, for instance, states that he does not describe the "oaths and combinations" of the Jaredites, "for it hath been made known unto me that they are had among all people, and they are had among the Lamanites" (Eth. 8:20; see also Al. 37:29). He directly associates the Gadianton oaths with those practiced by latter-day "secret combinations" (Eth. 8:20-21). This connection was not unique to New Yorkers who had already heard about Masonry in ancient America. John V. N. Yates and Joseph W. Moulton, in their 1824 *History of the State of New York,* made the following statement:

> Travellers describe certain private societies among the Indians which apparently resemble our lodges of freemasons. Their rules of government and admission of members are said to be the same. ... They have different degrees in the order. The ceremonies of initiation, and the mode of passing from one degree to another, would create astonishment in the mind of an enlightened spectator. ... We receive the information from Governor Clinton, to whom it was communicated by a respectable Indian preacher, who received the signs of the mystery from a Menonie chief. ... They are said to have secret signs, and pretend that the institution has existed from eternity.[22]

It was unnecessary to repeat the secret oaths because readers were familiar with them. In addition, a book purporting to be a history of Jewish migrants with scant details of their elaborate rituals and customs could hardly be expected to record rituals that were considered satanic.

Contrary to Bushman, the Book of Mormon alludes to "secret signs," "secret words," death-oaths, and possibly the initiatory "Cable-Tow" ritual. While Bushman insists that the Book of Mormon should have mentioned "Masonic degrees," many in Smith's day, including Masons, believed that the elaborate system of degrees was a modern invention, whereas the oaths, signs, and key words were ancient.[23] While not giving the details of the oaths, the Book of Mormon does provide general information that the first readers would have easily associated with Freemasonry.

Mormon not only mentions that the Gadiantons, like Masons, had "their signs, yea, their secret signs, and their secret words" (Hel. 6:22), he explains the purpose of such devices in language reminiscent of anti-Masonic rhetoric. The Gadianton bands, he explains, adopted their secret signs and words "that they might distinguish a brother who had entered into the covenant, that whatsoever wickedness his brother should do he should not be injured by his brother" (Hel. 6:22). He charges that initiates promise that "they would protect and preserve one another in whatsoever difficult circumstances they should be placed, that they should not suffer for their murders, and their plunderings, and their stealings" (v. 21).

By the time the Book of Mormon appeared, anti-Masons had widely published the secret Masonic oaths and rituals including its "signs" or "passes" (hand grips) and accompanying secret "words" or "names."[24] Masons who received the secret word for the second degree were told that it was "used by our ancient brethren to distinguish a friend from foe."[25] Anti-Masons charged that the oaths were designed "to protect their brethren from the lash of the civil laws ... whether guilty or not guilty, treason and murder not excepted; and although they may be obliged to swear falsely to clear the guilty brother, they must do it, or incur the penalty of secret death."[26]

In the Book of Mormon, Akish's Jaredite secret combination included a death-oath requiring initiates to "swear unto him, by the God of heaven, and also by the heavens, and also by the earth, and by their heads, that whoso should vary from the assistance which Akish desired should lose his head; and whoso should divulge whatsoever thing Akish made known unto them, the same should lose his life" (Eth. 8:14). It was well known in Smith's day that Masonic degrees included "penal signs" and death-oaths which describe various ways life might be taken.[27] Anti-Masons became especially concerned about such penalties after Morgan was reportedly found in Lake Ontario with his throat cut, the victim of Masonic vengeance. The penalty for the first degree's Entered Apprentice mentions having one's throat cut. Not until the higher degree of Knight Templar do we find mention of having one's "head struck off,"[28] but the wording of Akish's oath is probably an anti-Masonic rhetorical expansion based on Matthew 5:33-37

(//3 Ne. 12:33-37; see also Morm. 3:9-10, 14)–hence the choice of decapitation.

Despite the assertion that the "elaborate initiation rituals" are absent from the Book of Mormon, researchers have long believed that 2 Nephi 26:22 alludes to the Masonic initiatory cable-tow ritual. In describing the corrupt churches and priestcrafts of the last days, Nephi adds: "And there are also secret combinations, even as in times of old, according to the combinations of the devil, ... and he leadeth them by the neck with a flaxen cord, until he bindeth them with his strong cords forever" (2 Ne. 26:22). In the Masonic ritual, the initiate is blindfolded and led into the lodge by a rope around his neck, the cable-tow.[29]

Peterson associates Nephi's "flaxen cord" with the ancient custom of "leading human captives by means of a rope around the neck" and argues that Nephi's imagery is not sufficiently specific to be Masonic (200-201). To the contrary, the specific image of humans being led by the neck with a rope appears only once in the Book of Mormon and never in the Bible. This image appearing in the context of latter-day "secret combinations" argues against the suggestion that Nephi used a "natural" image to describe bondage to Satan.

Peterson asserts that similar imagery appears elsewhere such as in Isaiah 52:2: "[L]oose thyself from the bands of thy neck, O captive daughter of Zion" (//2 Ne. 8:25; 3 Ne. 20:37). However, in this instance as well as in the examples from Egyptian and Near Eastern art to which Peterson refers, the rope leads captive humans to their destinations, whereas in 2 Nephi the people are enticed but not yet captive. The "bands of thy neck" in Isaiah symbolizes Israel's captivity. In 2 Nephi the "flaxen cord" represents an allurement, not imprisonment. Nephi states elsewhere: "[T]he devil ... leadeth them away carefully down to hell" (2 Ne. 28:21). While many Book of Mormon passages link satanic "captivity" to chains (e.g., 2 Ne. 1:13, 23; 9:45; 28:21, 22; Al. 12:11), 2 Nephi has the only verse mentioning satanic binding with cords, imagery also absent from the Bible.

Attempting to discount the uniqueness of 2 Nephi, Peterson connects the "flaxen cord" imagery with passages that describe Satan leading the unwary, unencumbered by ropes, or grasping the wicked with "everlasting" or "awful" chains (2 Ne. 28:19, 22). He then asks, in a bait-and-switch tactic, "Where is the Masonic parallel for the chains?" (201).

His apologetic aside, the word "leadeth" is central to Nephi's "flaxen cord" imagery. In verse 24, Nephi contrasts this with the image of Jesus dying that "he may *draw* all men unto him" (2 Ne. 26:24, emphasis added; cf. Jn. 12:32; 3 Ne. 27:14, 15). Recognition that chapters 25-33 are, in part, a commentary on Isaiah is also important. Isaiah is quoted at great length in chapters 12-24, and the next chapter begins with: "Now I, Nephi, do speak somewhat concerning the words which I have written, which have been spoken by the mouth of Isaiah" (2 Ne. 25:1). The reference to Satan leading his dupes by the neck seems to be an interpretation of Isaiah 5:18: "Wo unto them that *draw* iniquity with cords of vanity, and sin as it were with a cart rope" (emphasis added; //2 Ne. 15:18).

Nor can one ignore this metaphor's rhetorical setting. It matters little that similar imagery appears in Egyptian art or Near Eastern literature when Nephi is directing his comments to a latter-day audience. Can anyone seriously doubt that many, if not most, nineteenth-century readers understood these words to refer to the Masonic cable-tow?[30] This conclusion is supported by an early newspaper account of Mormon missionaries preaching in Ohio: "[The Book of Mormon] predicts, we understand, almost all events which have come to pass, such as the American Revolution, &c. and that there should be *secret societies,* and that men should be led on to destruction as by a *rope of flax,* said to mean *Cable tow.*"[31]

Bushman is incorrect that the Book of Mormon contains no references to Masonic oaths, and he and Peterson are misled in discounting the rhetorical and cultural milieu in which the author and reader communicated.

OSTLER DRAWS DISTINCTIONS THAT ARE TOO NARROW

6. Blake Ostler states: "A frequent charge against Masonry, also absent from the Book of Mormon, was that it displaced Christianity by being a religion itself. ... Book of Mormon bands of robbers were not a quasi-religious fraternity" (74; cf. Peterson, 212). It is true that anti-Masonic rhetoric initially focused on the fraternity's assumed threat to Christianity. But following the apparent murder of Morgan in 1826,

the concern shifted to the implied erosion of civil liberties and free government. By the 1828 election, this had become a highly politicized topic as anti-Masons organized to prevent the election of Andrew Jackson to the presidency.[32] Religious concerns were not entirely displaced, but political and legal arguments dominated.[33] One should not really expect to find the Gadianton robbers described as a religious organization.

Anti-Masons came to see their nemesis as an evil subversion of religion and feared that it could destroy, rather than replace, Christianity. In the introduction to Morgan's 1827 *Illustrations of Masonry,* David C. Miller declared: "Masonry is to the modern world what the whore of Babylon was to the ancient; and is the beast with seven heads and ten horns, ready to tear out our bowels, and *scatter them to the four winds of heaven.*"[34] The *Palmyra Freeman* for 17 November 1829 alleged that Masonry was "a secret COMBINATION to destroy liberty and religion." On 23 November 1828, the *Republican Monitor* of Cazenovia, New York, declared that it was "a dark, iniquitous, and corrupt combination against truth, equity, and the church of Christ" and a "deep and broad conspiracy, against republicanism and christianity." Within months following the Book of Mormon's publication, the Reverend Lebbeus Armstrong called Masonry a "work of darkness," inspired by Satan to "oppose, root out, destroy, and, if possible, exterminate true religion from the world."[35]

Consistent with this view, the Book of Mormon portrays Gadiantons as a threat to the true church. Mormon describes the purpose of the society formed about 29 C.E. to be that of protecting corrupt judges who were secretly executing the prophets (3 Ne. 6:19-30). Alma concurs that "secret combinations" were responsible for murdering the prophets (Al. 37:30; see also Eth. 8:25). Concerning the last days in particular, Nephi and Moroni warn of the corrupting effects of "secret combinations" on the church (2 Ne. 26:20-33; Morm. 8:27-41); Moroni speaks of "the blood of [God's] saints, which shall be shed by them" (Eth. 8:22).

Nevertheless, Ostler's description of Gadiantons as a secular robber band is incomplete since there are also hints that their oaths included religious elements. Initiates "entered into a covenant" by "swearing by their everlasting Maker" (Hel. 1:11; cf. Eth 8:14). Mormon mentions that Gadianton did not obtain his "secret oaths and covenants" from Jaredite records but rather by revelation from Satan (Hel. 6:26). It does not appear that the Gadiantons would have agreed with this assessment, however. Contrary to their negative portrayal, one leader declares that their works are "good" and "of ancient date" and argues that they seek only to "recover their rights and government" (3 Ne. 3:9, 10).[36]

In light of the shifting emphasis after the Morgan affair, one finds the Gadiantons described as might be expected—that is, with Book of Mormon prophets controverting Gadianton claims of religious, just, and "good" ideals with a portrayal of them as a Satan-inspired cult designed to destroy true religion and subvert free government.

7. Ostler argues, "Nowhere in anti-Masonic rhetoric were Masons referred to [as] a distinct band of robbers. ... The Masons were never identified as a group which held out in the mountains and attacked as marauding robbers. ... The Nephites tried the robbers under martial law, and assigned responsibility for dealing with them to the military. Americans looked to their civil sheriffs, and Masons stood trial in the usual criminal courts" (75). In this instance, Ostler places undue emphasis on the guerrilla aspects of the Gadiantons who did not originate in the outback but began as a social subculture intent on infiltrating Nephite government by assassination. They fled to the wilderness only under extreme pressure (Hel. 1-2). Their oaths, signs, and secret words to "distinguish a brother" from the uninitiated (Hel. 6:21-22) indicate their intercultural presence. Despite Ostler's assertion, the wilderness condition was not a foreign idea. According to Masonic lore, "before lodges were erected," ancient Masons met on the "highest hills" and the "lowest vales" because it was "better to guard against cowans [intruders] and enemies, either ascending or descending, that the brethren might have timely notice of their approach to prevent being surprised."[37] Some lodges were themselves referred to as "encampments."[38] Thus, the Reverend Peter Sanborn worried in 1829 that Masonry was "an encampment, intrenched on a high and *inaccessible* mountain; ready to rush down upon our country, like an irresistible tornado."[39] Whether in legend or metaphor, the wilderness imagery was there to expand upon.

Ostler is similarly incorrect about Masons not being classed with robbers. The *Wayne Sentinel* for 26 September 1828 reprinted an article alleging that Masonry's real "object is anarchy and PLUNDER."

Anti-Masons attacked the fraternity's attempt to gain unfair economic advantage over the uninitiated and frequently quoted Volney's statement that "every association which has mystery for its basis, or an oath of secrecy, is a league of robbers against society."[40] Joseph Smith may have transformed Volney's metaphor into a dramatic portrayal or simply assumed that Masons forced into encampments would degenerate into robber bands (see 3 Ne. 4:5).

The argument is otherwise flawed because the Book of Mormon's description of ancient societies should not be read as a literal reflection of what was actually happening in Jacksonian America. This requires from the book something that it never says. Rather, the Nephite writers warned later Americans that what had happened anciently could happen to them. Thus, Moroni warned readers to "awake to a sense of your awful situation" to avoid the fate of the Jaredites and Nephites (Eth. 8:24). The book described, not what Masons were currently doing, but what their political and criminal potential was.

Yet, in view of the 1828 rhetoric about Andrew Jackson's involvement with the Aaron Burr conspiracy in the western territories (in 1805 and 1806), which anti-Masons believed included a Masonic cover-up, the idea that plots to overthrow the government would come from the "wilderness" was not unrealistic. It remains unclear what Burr's full intentions were as he plotted his western coup, but he gained lasting notoriety as a traitor, and Jackson's involvement, though perhaps innocent, hurt him in the 1828 campaign.[41] Concerning the Burr conspiracy, anti-Masonic writer Henry Dana Ward declared:

> The injury done to our national character by Burr's conspiracy was of the highest magnitude; the private correspondence of that conspiracy was carried on in the *Royal Arch cypher,* which is a proof that the agents were exalted Freemasons. This accounts, also, for their escaping the vengeance of the law: the evidence of their guilt was chiefly in the mystic characters of Freemasonry, and the Royal Arch breasts, and thus closed against the search of human tribunals by the profane oath, and impious penalty of a Royal Arch Mason's obligations.[42]

QUINN'S EISEGETICAL ERROR

8. That "the vast majority of anti-Masons ... had always seen Freemasonry as a strictly modern development" (161-63; cf. Peterson,

188-89) is Michael Quinn's assumption, which he contrasts with the Book of Mormon view that "secret combinations" originated with Satan and Cain (Hel. 6:26-27; 3 Ne. 6:28; Eth. 8:15, 25). In fact, anti-Masons tended to favor one of two rhetorical responses to the claim of divine and ancient origin–one line of reasoning even describing Adam and other Old Testament patriarchs as Grand Masters.[43] The majority of antiMasons certainly followed the course Quinn mentions, arguing that Masonry had a strictly modern origin.[44] Others, hoping to avoid the fruitless debate over the antiquity of the organization, claimed that the secret society originated with Cain, the first murderer. Thus, Peter Sanborn, explaining Masonry's "real origin," argued that "the truth may be, that the first grand arch mason, was Satan; the first secret lodge, in Eden, between *him* and Eve. ... Cain, like Nimrod, rebelled against the priesthood and government of Adam; he, with Tubal Cain, no doubt, were masons."[45] The two approaches were logical avenues of the debate and needed little encouragement.

Quinn is right that the second path stemmed more from necessity than from a sincere belief in the antiquity of Masonry. But in making this observation, he is perhaps too dismissive, for such subtlety may have escaped Joseph Smith. If anti-Masonic writers separated fact from rhetoric, it does not necessarily follow that their audiences did. It is also possible that Smith, as author of the Book of Mormon, was creating his own rhetoric for the sake of making a point. Regardless, the possibility that Smith adopted an anachronism should not come as a surprise since one can also find evidence of a similar approach to Christian chronology in the Book of Mormon (see Ostler's discussion, 79-87).

That Smith connected the origins of Masonry with Cain receives support from his subsequent "Inspired Revision" of Genesis. Dictating what might be called an anti-Masonic interpretation of Cain's murder of Abel sometime between June and October 1830, Joseph Smith revealed that Cain had secretly covenanted with Satan to murder Abel for gain (Moses 5:29-32). He then added a most revealing passage to Genesis: "And Cain said: Truly I am Mahan, the master of this great secret, that I may murder and get gain. Wherefore Cain was called Master Mahan, and he gloried in his wickedness" (Moses 5:31). If Smith intended "Master Mahan" as a play on "Master Mason," the name given to third-degree Masons, he reinforced the link already made in the Book of Mormon between Cain and the origin of secret oaths and combinations (Hel. 6:27; Eth. 8:15).[46]

9. "Whereas anti-Masons typically claimed that Masonry was a fraternal organization dedicated to overthrowing Christianity and monarchy," Quinn asserts, "the Book of Mormon ... repeatedly claimed that the main purpose ... [was] to murder and plunder, ... and that the subversion of governments was necessary only for gaining the power to protect these murders and plunders" (164). To establish an occult thesis for Book of Mormon culture, Quinn diverts attention from the political context in which the Book of Mormon describes the Gadianton bands. However, political objectives are a major feature of these subsocieties. One finds little in the Book of Mormon to support Quinn's assertion that the Gadiantons infiltrated government only to protect their crimes. Political power certainly had this added benefit (Hel. 7:4-5), consistent with a major feature of anti-Masonic rhetoric following the Morgan affair. One 1827 anti-Masonic broadside from Monroe County, New York, called on voters to put down Masonry's statewide corruption of government:

> The masonic fraternity have outraged humanity, and violated all law. The nature of their offence is so complicated–the offenders so numerous–and their evasions have been so manifold–that justice has only been enabled to pursue her course with tardy and faltering steps. In a dark day of the [Morgan] investigation, we supplicated the legislature to quicken her pace, and strengthen her arm, but it was a MASONIC LEGISLATURE, and we were coldly repulsed! We now appeal to the SOVEREIGN PEOPLE. Let *their* verdict be awarded upon the merits of this question.[47]

Quinn is nevertheless wrong about the Gadianton bands. If anything, "secret combinations" seek power and wealth (cf. 1 Ne. 22:23; Eth. 8:22, 23; 11:15) and resort to murder and robbery as the quickest means of obtaining them. Political power and the overthrow of government are major goals.

The first secret society among the Nephites was formed about 52 B.C.E. to protect Kishkumen, who had assassinated Pahoran, the chief judge (Hel. 1:9-12). Gadianton becomes the leader of Kishkumen's band and seeks to become chief judge himself. He promises his co-conspirators that "if they would place him in the judgment-seat he would grant ... that they should be placed in power and authority among the people" (2:5). To place Gadianton in power, Kishkumen tries to assassinate Helaman, who had replaced Pahoran as chief judge. Thus Gadianton's band is formed to advance political intrigue. This is the opposite of what Quinn asserts, for rather than seeking civil office for protection, Gadianton and his band derive protection from oaths obligating them to secrecy while they plot political gain (6:21-23).

Before Kishkumen is killed, he reveals to one of Helaman's servants that "it was the object of all those who belonged to his band to murder, and to rob, and to gain power" (Hel. 2:8). Even from its founding, political objectives were integral, not peripheral, to Gadiantonism.

A subsequent Gadianton group, organized about 16 C.E., proclaimed its intention to overthrow the Nephite government by force if necessary. Giddianhi, the "governor" of the Gadiantons, writes an epistle to Lachoneus, leader of the Nephites, asking him to surrender the reigns of government or be destroyed. In his letter, Giddianhi imparts some Gadianton political philosophy: "I hope that ye will deliver up your lands and your possessions, without the shedding of blood, that this my people may recover their rights and government" (3 Ne. 3:10). This hardly sounds as though Gadianton political objectives were of incidental interest.

The secret society organized about 29 C.E. to protect corrupt judges (3 Ne. 6:19-30) similarly challenges Quinn's assertion that Gadiantons infiltrated government for protection. In this instance, the secret society protects public officials, not the reverse. This same society conspires to establish one of its members, Jacob, as king (6:30; 7:1-12)—demonstrating again that political power was a major objective.

The secret society among the Jaredites had similar political origins. In this case, Jared and Akish conspire to assassinate King Omer (Eth. 8:7-15; 9:1-6). Moroni describes the oaths administered by Akish, which had existed since the days of Cain and were designed "to help such as sought power to gain power, and to murder, and to plunder, and to lie, and to commit all manner of wickedness and whoredoms" (8:16). Jared's conspiracy, like that of Gadianton's, sought political rule.

This brief overview shows the Book of Mormon to be in line with what Quinn acknowledges for anti-Masonic rhetoric: that Masonry was dedicated to the overthrow of "Christianity and monarchy," or more accurately in America, the overthrow of republican government. The *Wayne Sentinel* for 18 July 1828 reported that anti-Masons objected to the institution because "[i]t affords opportunities for the corrupt and designing to form plans against the government." The *New England Anti-Masonic Almanac* for 1831 recognized that Masonry "is *peculiarly adapted* to *Political* intrigue."[48]

One should not push too hard for exact parallels, as I have argued, since the Gadiantons are only intended to be analogous to Jacksonian America as a warning of potential dangers. One should not expect to find Masons accused of assassinating public officials or forming military coups in the wilderness. Instead, one should view such elements as a reflection of Joseph Smith's imagination—his attempt to create for readers frightening images of what Masonry could become.

In constructing various scenarios for the Gadianton bands, the author may have been inspired, at least in part, by the anti-Masonic view of the French Revolution. Anti-Masons believed that the revolution was the result of Masonic conspiracy. Henry Dana Ward said in 1829: "The horrors of the Revolution in France are, however, clearly traced to the hand of this midnight Order."[49] Arguing that George Washington had changed his views on Masonry before his death, even renouncing his own membership, the *New England Anti-Masonic Almanac* for 1831 claimed: "He saw Masonry in France and Germany throw aside the veil that concealed its haggard features and boldly avow the detestible principles of Atheism, and the Illuminati. He saw the infamous Duke of Orleans at the head of the masonic combination in France, carrying on the bloody work of the Revolution, whose excesses were but the natural fruit of this poisonous tree."[50]

Particularly suspect were the Jacobins, a small group of radical revolutionaries who met in closed meetings, had great influence over the masses, and unofficially oversaw the revolution. The Jacobins became known for their barbarism during the Reign of Terror (1793-94) which culminated in the "great purification." Anti-Masons believed that the Jacobins had ties to the Illuminati, an exclusive group of Bavarian Masons organized, it was believed, with the sole purpose of overthrowing world governments and destroying Christianity.

Many conservatives in late eighteenth-century New England, such as the Reverend Jedidiah Morse, feared that the Illuminati were at work in America and were being aided by liberal Republicans.[51] In a sermon delivered in 1798, Morse declared: "There is great reason to believe that the French revolution was kindled by the *Illuminati.* ... The successes of the French armies, many of them, can be traced to the influence and the treacheries of different branches of this society. There are too many evidences that this Order has had its branches established, in some form or other, and its emissaries secretly at work in this country, for several years past."[52] Morse continued: "It is not improbable that the affiliated *Jacobin Societies* in this country were instituted to propagate here the principles of the illuminated mother club in France."[53]

In many ways, the political anti-Masonry of the late 1820s and early 1830s was simply a revival of the Illuminati agitation that had already occurred in New England. The *Wayne Sentinel* for 26 September 1828 alleged that "Freemasons have been the cause of all the 'seditions, privy cons[p]iracies, and rebellions,' which, for the last thirty years, have afflicted Europe. ... The Freemasons are, therefore, radically and essentially, demagogues, jacobins, conspirators, assassins, infidels, traitors, and atheists. ... [T]heir secret is the watch-word of sedition and rebellion–their object is anarchy and plunder. ... [U]nless they are suppressed, there will soon be neither religion, morals, literature, nor civilized society left!"

Much like the ebb and flow of the Gadiantons, anti-Masons believed that America had narrowly escaped destruction during Jefferson's administration. The Reverend David Pease sermonized in 1830:

> Freemasonry, like the sweeping plagues of Egypt, had come up and filled the whole land, infesting all our religious and civil institutions, perverting justice, and threatening our liberties. It had seated itself in the temple of the MOST HIGH. It had nearly secured the reins of government ... and had not the slumbers of the people been timely broken by a cry from the *west,* Freemasonry, in all probability would soon have been in America, what it was in France in the reign of anarchy and cruelty.[54]

Resurrecting these images of the revolution and the Illuminati, the Reverend Armstrong declared in 1830:

> And ere the Commonwealth was apprised of the imposture, or discovered omens of danger, the chains of masonic despotism were forging and preparations fast making to bind the nation in its power. ... After all this preparation, suppose a plot had been formed to overthrow our dear-

> bought Republican Government, to erect a throne in this western world, and place on it a Grand, Sublime, Royal, Ten Times Thrice Illustrious, and Absolutely Sovereign Masonic King. ... Under such circumstances, what could have prevented the total overthrow of our national government, and the establishment of an absolute Masonic Monarchy? If the government of France was revolutionized in *three days,* might not the government of these United States have been changed to Monarchy in *one* day by the Mystic Power of Masonic Stratagem? Nothing could have prevented such a revolution, but the interposition of that Divine Providence. ... The God of Israel has interposed. Glory be to his name; the Lord of Hosts has hitherto prevented our national ruin.[55]

Shifting his concern to the contemporary Masonic threat, Armstrong feared that the situation could still, at any moment, erupt into "civil war," include Jacobin-like purges on anti-Masons, and culminate in the establishment of a monarchy. He warned: "Let masonry prevail and prosper, and the deplorable results may be looked for, of a Masonic Monarchy for our form of government; a masonic established religion; a masonic church; a masonic way to a masonic heaven; and blood and massacre, and destruction to all who subscribe not to support the Monarch, who sways the energies, and rewards the services of the works of darkness. Then might be written with tears and blood, America is fallen!"[56]

Of relevance to the Book of Mormon is the fear that Masonry was conspiring to establish a king in America.[57] While the first secret society in the Book of Mormon conspired to infiltrate Nephite government and make Gadianton the chief judge, a subsequent combination infiltrated the judicial system, then sought to "destroy the governor, and to establish a king" (3 Ne. 6:30). About 30 C.E., this combination assassinates the chief judge and divides the Nephites into competing tribes, thus destroying the "regulations of the government" (7:1-6). Gathering strength, they appoint one of their own to be a king, "whom they did call Jacob; ... and he was one of the chiefest who had given his voice against the prophets who testified of Jesus" (vv. 9, 10). Despite their losses, the various tribes unite against this "secret combination," causing Jacob to retreat with his band into "the northernmost part of the land" (vv. 11-12). From his newly established headquarters in the city Jacobugath, the king begins to curry support for his ambition to control all the land (v. 12; see also 9:9).

Given anti-Masonic concerns about a monarchy in America, one might reasonably wonder if the Book of Mormon character, Jacob, is loosely based on Andrew Jackson. Another clear allusion, of course, is to the Jacobins. Similar to the Book of Mormon's portrayal of Jacob, the conservative reaction to Jackson focused on four issues: (1) his Masonic membership, (2) his potential use of military force, (3) his intention to decentralize the federal government, and (4) his promotion of the separation of church and state, which conservatives saw as an attempt to demoralize America and weaken the church. Jackson's association with the Jacobins would have been reinforced in the minds of readers by his decisive, harsh actions as a military general, a fact that his opponents exploited during the 1828 election. What many believed were acts of extreme patriotism, conservatives interpreted as erratic and dangerous behavior. Recalling the days prior to Jackson's election, New York governor Martin Van Buren said that many who otherwise supported Jackson were kept "in constant apprehension that he would, through passion or ill advisement commit some rash act" and then confessed that he too had shared "not a little of the same feeling." Van Buren reported that his friend Thomas Richie of the *Richmond* (VA) *Enquirer* "scarcely ever went to bed in those exciting times without apprehension that he would wake up to hear of some *coup d' etat* by the General ... and his letters to me were filled with remonstrances and cautions upon the subject."[58]

In this context, the Book of Mormon's repeated anti-monarchical stance is more than a mere reflection of early American sentiment but a clear warning against an imminent danger (e.g., Mos. 29:5-39). Speaking of latter-day America, Nephi's brother Jacob proclaims: "And this land shall be a land of liberty unto the Gentiles, and there shall be no kings upon the land, who shall raise up unto the Gentiles. ... For he that raiseth up a king against me shall perish. ... Wherefore, for this cause, ... I must needs destroy the secret works of darkness, and of murders, and of abominations" (2 Ne. 10:11, 14, 15).

While King Jacob gathered strength in his northern headquarters, the prophet Nephi began a three-year ministry among the Nephites, warning them of the impending destruction to occur at Jesus' crucifixion. Much like Smith, Nephi had been "visited by angels and also the voice of the Lord" (3 Ne. 7:15) and had a dead brother whom Nephi brings back to life (v. 19). The Book of Mormon prophet experiences a measure of success, performing miracles and baptizing many. But his mission is brief, for as predicted, many cities, including the headquarters of the secret society headed by Jacob (9:9), are destroyed by the upheavals that accompany Jesus' crucifixion. Only the righteous remained to greet their resurrected savior. Although an obvious expansion of Matthew's account of the crucifixion, the magnitude of the destruction is more analogous to the apocalyptic events associated with Jesus' anticipated Second Advent, allowing first readers to more easily identify with the Book of Mormon's account of "secret combinations" preceding Jesus' arrival.

Perhaps Smith imagined a similar end to his own career. In a letter he wrote to N. C. Saxton, editor of a newspaper published in Rochester, New York, dated 4 January 1833, he wrote: "And now I am prepared to say by the authority of Jesus Christ, that not many years shall pass away before the United States shall present such a scene of *bloodshed* as has not a parallel in the hystory of our nation pestalence hail famine and earthquake will sweep the wicked off this generation from off the face of this Land to open and prepare the way for the return of the lost tribes of Israel from the north country."[59]

Regardless of one's interpretation of "secret combinations," it should be clear that Quinn's deemphasis of the Gadiantons' pursuit of political power is misguided. It should be equally apparent that first-generation readers would have had no difficulty understanding the anti-Masonic implications of the Book of Mormon's treatment of ancient societies.

10. Bushman disagrees with Quinn and suggests that the Gadianton bands "could with equal ease be perceived as modern terrorist guerrillas, dissenters at war with the old order, penetrating villages on the margins of official control, undermining from within, and attacking openly when they had strength. Viewed in context, the Masonic-like oaths and covenants were secondary to direct attacks on government through assassinations and military raids" (131). In other words, Bushman wants to emphasize the political context and downgrade the secret oaths which the Book of Mormon presents as an integral part of its description. The oaths and covenants were central to the Gadianton plan of infiltration as well as to their cohesion and identity (Hel. 6:18-30). Alma considered the oaths and covenants crucial enough to command his son to "retain" them from the people, "lest

peradventure they should fall into darkness also and be destroyed" (Al. 37:27); the oaths were also the "means of bringing down the people unto destruction" (Hel. 6:25). Thus, one cannot with "equal ease" apply the Book of Mormon's description of the Gadianton bands to terrorists.

In the context of the 1828 election, Jackson and his followers *were* the "dissenters at war with the old order." It was a period of extreme tension and represented a major shift in the balance of power in the United States. Not surprisingly, many predicted doom upon the young nation and feared that the situation would degenerate into civil war.[60] Given Masonry's own militaristic imagery–its reference to "encampments" and "knights"–together with its apparent union with the liberal democrats headed by the famous General Jackson, whose brutality was a feature of the opposition's campaign rhetoric, Joseph Smith would not have had to stretch his imagination too far to come up with the militant Gadianton bands.

11. Ostler assumes that the Jaredite and Nephite secret societies were transmitted to the Americas from the Near East (73-76; cf. Quinn, 165), and Peterson repeatedly compares the Gadiantons to Middle Eastern robber bands (201-202, 209-10).[61] Ostler's theory seems to be disallowed by the Book of Mormon. The first secret society does not appear among the Nephites until about 52 B.C.E., nearly five centuries after Lehi's family settled in the New World. Furthermore, Mormon mentions that "those secret oaths and covenants did not come forth unto Gadianton from the records which were delivered unto Helaman; but behold, they were put into the heart of Gadianton by that same being who did ... plot with Cain, that if he would murder his brother Abel it should not be known unto the world" (Hel. 6:26-27). Thus, the Near Eastern comparisons are irrelevant as far as the Book of Mormon is concerned.

Ostler's further statement that "[t]he Book of Mormon secret societies differ from Masons in the precise ways they are similar to ancient Near Eastern bands of robbers" (74; cf. Quinn, 165) is true only in the sense that Masonry in 1829 was not considered a marauding robber band. Again, the Book of Mormon merely describes this potential. However, the Gadiantons were insiders who emerged, following a hotly contested election, to hatch an internal political plot (Hel. 1-2). Only later do they take on the characteristics that Ostler and Peterson emphasize.[62] Regardless, the robber bands Ostler and Peterson described are not unique to any one civilization.

12. Quinn argues that the Book of Mormon's prediction of latter-day "secret combinations" and "secret murders" really refers to witchcraft and occult murders (164) but offers little evidence to support his occult thesis. He places considerable weight on "a well-established tradition that sorcery originated with Cain" and a separate and unrelated charge that "[t]he devil hath taught man *sorcery* or *witchcraft*" (167) without explaining how such claims were brought together or found their way into a supposedly authentic ancient history of America. Significantly, unlike the anti-Masonic interpretation, Quinn cannot quote any of the book's first readers who believed its "secret combinations" referred to the occult. The major flaw in Quinn's thesis, as I see it, is that he fails to place witchcraft and occult murders into the political and national setting required by the Book of Mormon (Eth. 8). Obviously, the "secret combination" seeking to destroy the latter-day American government, that Moroni warned of, was something more pervasive and threatening than witchcraft or the occult, although many religious anti-Masons regarded Masonry as an occult-like institution. But on the political and national level, the "secret combination" which many in the late 1820s and early 1830s feared would destroy America was Freemasonry, especially following its perceived alliance with the Jacksonians.

PETERSON'S UNREASONABLE DEMAND FOR OVERWHELMING EVIDENCE

13. Peterson finds that "one of the major difficulties" with the anti-Masonic interpretation is that "one must see Joseph Smith as a vocal and committed anti-Mason in 1830 who then, only twelve years later, enthusiastically joined the Masons and, as some would have it, borrowed the most sacred rituals of his religion from them. ... Where, then, is the evidence of his alleged conversion from anti-Masonry in the late 1820s (during the translation of the Book of Mormon) to pro-Masonry in the 1840s (when he was revealing the ordinances of the temple)?" (181-82, 200). There were several factors involved in Smith's decision to become a Mason. Given the political climate in Illinois at the time, he undoubtedly believed it was advantageous.[63] But his "conversion" was not complete, for soon after joining the Masons on 15

March 1842, he devalued the system by claiming it was a corrupt version of his temple endowment.[64] No matter what interpretation one holds of the Book of Mormon and Masonry, one must acknowledge that Joseph Smith joined the order before he opposed it.

Peterson knows that in 1839 Smith spoke against "the impropriety of ... bands or companies [being organized] by covenant or oaths[,] by penalties or secrecies. ... Pure friendship always becomes weakened the very moment you undertake to make it stronger by penal oaths and secrecy" (182).[65] Smith's change of attitude did not go unnoticed. Ebenezer Robinson said: "Heretofore the church had strenuously opposed secret societies such as Freemasons, [and] Knights of Pythias ... not considering the 'Order of Enoch' and 'Danites' of that class; but after Dr. [James C.] Bennett came into the Church a great change of sentiment seemed to take place."[66] James C. Brewster, who became the leader of a dissident Mormon group, saw the endowment as a contradiction of earlier teachings. In 1849 Brewster declared that the church had fallen by "imperceptible degrees" until 1842 when "the fatal step was taken by the introduction of a secret order in direct violation of almost every command in the gospel of Christ."[67] "The priesthood does not consist in high sounding titles, in secret combinations, in key words and mysteries," he wrote.[68]

Smith's Masonic membership poses problems for all interpreters, not just those proposing an anti-Masonic approach to the Book of Mormon. Ultimately, Smith himself is responsible for such inconsistencies, and no one should feel compelled to create harmony where real contradiction exists. If he reversed himself on Masonry, it was not the only instance. He subsequently changed his mind on the nature of the godhead and the duration of hell and punishment, for example, which were Book of Mormon doctrines.[69]

Although Peterson seems aware that the resemblance between the LDS and Masonic ceremonies is more than striking, he defends a divine origin for the endowment by arguing that "the short interval between Joseph's Masonic initiations on 15 and 16 March 1842 and the introduction of the full endowment ceremony on 4 May 1842 would have left him little leisure for the massive reorientation of the Masonic rites that would be required on this hypothesis" (183-84). He, of course, exaggerates. There was no "massive reorientation" of Masonic rites but rather a selective borrowing. Additional variances were introduced later. Hence, a period of about seven weeks would be sufficient for the task. The argument is further weakened by the fact that Masonic ritual had been widely published since William Morgan's 1826 exposé.[70] Edward Giddins perhaps gave the clearest indication of how familiar the secrets of Freemasonry had become to western New Yorkers when he remarked in 1830 that "[t]hese mysteries, so sublime, and once so sacred, are now familiar with boys; and they practice them in the streets for their amusement."[71]

Quinn, on the other hand, assumes an even more indefensible position by arguing that "the Mormon temple endowment reflected the ancient and occult mysteries far closer than Freemasonry" (185-89). Comparison of the endowment, particularly the earliest versions, with Masonic ritual reveals that they are nearly identical in key places.[72] Smith took fundamental elements and recast them into another theological setting, one that was more Christ-centered and organized around the doctrine of three heavens. Whatever differences existed, such as the candidate's assent into the third heaven in the endowment, early Mormons attributed to Smith's attempt to "restore" corrupted Masonic ritual.[73]

The position taken by Michael Homer is more intellectually honest and apologetically advantageous. In a 1994 essay comparing Masonic ritual with the Mormon endowment, he concluded: "Dilemmas in church history are more easily understood if one acknowledges that Joseph Smith used his own imperfect thought processes, that the language he used represented the cultural context in which he was situated, and that he adapted recognizable texts and documents through creative inspiration."[74] Given Quinn's and Peterson's resistance to word-for-word similarities, one wonders if they could ever acknowledge more subtle correspondences between Masonry and the Gadianton bands.

14. Peterson believes that in Joseph Smith's day the phrase "secret combinations" referred generically to "guerrilla warriors" (189-97, 209-13). Specifically, he disagrees with David Persuitte, Robert Hullinger, and myself that anti-Masons used the term to identify Freemasonry. Persuitte's and Hullinger's purpose was to show anti-Masonic influence on the Book of Mormon, mine was to explain why many of the book's first readers believed it referred to Freemasonry. Peterson particularly attacked my assertion that "at the time of the Book of

Mormon's publication the term 'secret combinations' was used almost exclusively to refer to Freemasonry" (180, 191).[75]

My intention was to show that in the context of the 1828 U.S. presidential campaign, the phrase had become politically charged, not that anti-Masons had invented the phrase. Andrew Jackson's opponents, especially in western New York, incorporated this phrase into their stock of political buzz-words. In this setting, it was anything but generic and anyone using it in another context ran the risk of being misunderstood. Perhaps the best example comes from the *Morgan Investigator,* a periodical published at Batavia, New York, which declared in its 29 March 1827 issue: "BEWARE OF SECRET COMBINATIONS. These are the dying words of General George Washington. ... Do not these words ... point with an index that cannot be mistaken, to the society of Freemasons?" Of course, Washington himself was a Freemason and had only warned of "combinations," not "*secret* combinations."[76] Anti-Masons had thus expanded on Washington's own words to make it appear that he agreed with them. In such an environment, the Book of Mormon's use of the phrase would have been understood as an unmistakable reference to Freemasonry.

Joseph Smith was aware of the Masonic connotation, and his use of the phrase was clearly intentional. For example, he could have used any number of less problematic words, had he wanted to avoid misunderstanding: secret societies, for instance, secret alliances, secret leagues, confederacies, plots, conspiracies, schemes, or clandestine activities. It was not necessary to use the specific phrase "secret combinations." Obviously, Smith used the term to convey the meaning and comparison he intended.

Ignoring my qualification, "*almost* exclusively," as well as the cultural and time limitations of my statement, Peterson went to extraordinary lengths to find exceptions to the meaning. Based on a preliminary survey of late nineteenth-century legal documents, which yielded ten cases, all of them decades after Joseph Smith's death, he found the term "secret combinations" used in a different context and therefore predicted that a more thorough search would turn up earlier, time-appropriate examples of non-Masonic uses of the phrase (190-95). He may be correct, but one should bear in mind Mark Thomas's observation, after examining court cases involving "combinations" in labor disputes between 1806 and 1829, that the term "*secret* combination" was not used, although "combination" appeared frequently. As a result of his own search, Thomas concluded: "Peterson's hypothesis that 'secret combinations' is a vague, generalized symbol with no specific referent cannot be substantiated by the very legal documents where he suggests the evidence will be found. If the evidence presented here is representative of the pre-1830 vocabularies, Peterson's post-1850 legal examples of 'secret combinations' are not typical of the 1830 language surrounding Joseph Smith."[77] Even if Peterson's hoped for evidence did exist, legalese was not the language of Joseph Smith, nor was it the language of his intended audience. It seems fruitless to search legal archives for exceptions to the interpretative rule that clearly dominated Smith's cultural milieu. It is irrelevant what the phrase "secret combinations" meant in technical language at the time, even if it did have a separate legal definition. It only matters what the phrase meant to Smith and others in his cultural environment. To understand the language of the Book of Mormon, one must search the literature of pre-1830 western New York, something Peterson seems unwilling to do.

In a subsequent essay, Peterson tried again to produce a variant meaning for "secret combination" by quoting from a letter dated 15 December 1826 from Andrew Jackson to Sam Houston in which Jackson protests Henry Clay's accusation that Jackson and his wife were unmarried. There was some question about the legitimacy of the marriage since it was uncertain if Jackson's wife had a legitimate divorce. In the letter, Jackson declares his intention to "unmask such part of the Executive council, as has entered into the combination to slander and revile me" and to expose Clay's "secrete movements" and his efforts "*secretely* to carry his cowardly and base purpose of slander into effect." Finally, Jackson complains that his wife cannot escape Clay's "secrete [sic] combination of base slander."[78] While it is possible that Jackson used "secret combination" descriptively, it is equally possible that the term was a subtle response to the administration's barbs about Jackson being a Mason. Even Quinn criticized Peterson's use of the Jackson letter, noting that Peterson "acknowledged that Jackson was an active Freemason attacking a lapsed Freemason, Henry Clay." Given the possible "sarcastic use of an anti-Masonic phrase by one Freemason against another," Quinn concludes that Jackson's 1826 letter "does not support Peterson's claim that the letter 'definitively' disproves all claims for the exclusively anti-Masonic use of the phrase 'secret combination.'"[79] Regardless, the term "secret combination" did not take on its full anti-Masonic meaning until 1827-28 when it became clear—at least to anti-Masons—that William Morgan's murder would go unpunished due to a Masonic conspiracy.

Also irrelevant is Joseph Smith's later use of the term in non-Masonic contexts. Once the term had taken on a pejorative connotation, thereby increasing its propagandistic value, it was only a matter of time before it was used as a slur against other groups. As they began to develop their political platform and seek to justify their legitimacy as a political party, anti-Masons themselves would use the term to include other organizations. The platform of the anti-Masonic Convention in Baltimore in September 1831 declared that one purpose of the new party was "diffusing information upon the subject of freemasonry, *and other secret combinations* against the equal rights of mankind, and other free institutions," although no other group than the Masons was named.[80] Clearly, the expanded use of the term would not have been possible had it not been first popularized as a weapon against the Masons both in the 1828 presidential election and in the 1830 New York state elections.

15. Rejecting the connection I made between the "secret combinations" of the Doctrine and Covenants (42:64; hereafter D&C) and Jacksonian Masons (27), Peterson suggested that they "were simply persecutors, the mobs with whom Mormons would become so wearily well acquainted" (197-98). In historical context, it is clear that the D&C describes something more vast than Mormon persecutors, something which functions independently of Mormons. What is more, contrary to Peterson's assertion that "there is no reason to suppose that the 'secret combinations' alluded to in the Doctrine and Covenants have any connection at all with Freemasonry" (199), there are in fact several good reasons to suppose so.

On 9 February 1831, shortly after Smith arrived in Ohio, he dictated the revelation announcing that Mormons were to gather to the New Jerusalem. It directs: "[L]et him that goeth to the east teach them that shall be converted to flee to the west, and this in consequence of that which is coming on earth, and of secret combinations" (D&C 42:64). This document returns to the theme of an earlier revelation which explained that a desolating war "is coming on earth":

> Behold, the enemy is combined. And now I show unto you a mystery, a thing which is had in secret chambers, to bring to pass even your destruction in process of time, and ye knew it not. ... And again, I say unto you that the enemy in the secret chamber seeketh your lives. Ye hear of wars in far countries, and you say that there will soon be great wars in far countries, but ye know not the hearts of men in your own land. ... Wherefore, for this cause I gave unto you the commandment that ye should go to the Ohio (D&C 38:12-13, 28-29, 32).

Mormons are warned to flee those who plan their destruction in "secret chambers," a term sometimes applied to Masonic lodges.[81] More important is the prediction that war is about to break out. The close association of "secret combinations" with the coming war makes Peterson's interpretation of Mormon persecutors too narrow.

The connection with war extends back into the Book of Mormon. Speaking to the latter-day workers of "secret abominations," Moroni declares: "Behold, the sword of vengeance hangeth over you; and the time soon cometh that he avengeth the blood of the saints upon you, for he will not suffer their cries any longer" (Morm. 8:41). Moroni later expresses hope that his history will cause the American gentiles to repent "and suffer not that these murderous combinations shall get above you ... to your overthrow and destruction if ye suffer these things to be" (Eth. 8:23). The Book of Mormon was a jeremiad addressed to Jacksonian America, warning them that what happened to the Nephites and Jaredites was about to happen again. With numerous burial mounds dotting the Great Lakes region, this aspect of the Book of Mormon had frightening implications for its first readers.

The subject of "secret combinations" and civil war did not conclude with D&C 42:64. The following month, on 7 March 1831, Smith dictated a revelation on the same subject: "Ye hear of wars in foreign lands: but, behold, I say unto you, they are nigh, even at your doors, and not many years hence ye shall hear of wars in your own lands." (D&C 45:63-64). It should be added that Smith was not alone in making such predictions. Many conservatives worried that Jackson's election would result in war.[82]

In November 1832 fears about the president's election seemed on the verge of fulfillment. South Carolina rejected the Federal Tariff Acts of 1828 and 1832 and Jackson threatened to take military action. The following month, Smith dictated his famed "Prophecy on War" which predicted that civil war would "shortly" consume America, escalate into a world war, and culminate in the "full end of all nations" (D&C 87). What many overlook is that this revelation was a continuation of themes discussed in the Book of Mormon (3 Ne. 21:12; Morm. 5:19-24). The Doctrine and Covenants predicted that the coming war would involve Indians (v. 5) and avenge the murdered true believers (v. 7). The wording echoes Moroni's statement about nations upholding secret combinations and vengeance for the murdered saints (Eth. 8:22; see also 8:24; Al. 37:30-31; Morm. 8:40-41). This was perhaps the cause of some anxieties between Mormons and their neighbors in New York.

A glimpse into this tension is provided by an early source that recently came to light. Following Hyrum Smith's flight from Manchester, New York, in October 1830 to evade creditors, his mother reported her bewilderment over his departure since "the secret combinations of his enemies were not fully developed."[83] A short while later, a group of men claiming to represent Dr. Alexander McIntyre ransacked the Smiths' cabin looking for Hyrum. When Joseph learned of the incident, he warned his brother in a letter dated 2 December 1830 to "beware of the freemasons, [Alexander] McIntyre heard that you were in Manchester and he got a warrant and went to your father's to distress the family but Harrison [Samuel Harrison Smith] overheard their talk and they said that they cared not for the debt, if they could obtain your body. They were there with carriages. Therefore beware of the Freemasons."[84] Masonic records indicate that the Smith family physician, Alexander McIntyre, and Levi Daggett, who sued Hyrum and issued a warrant for his arrest, were both members of Palmyra's Masonic lodge.[85] In his letter to Hyrum, Joseph not only revealed an anti-Masonic bias but also expressed his belief that Masons were among the chief persecutors of the Mormons in New York.[86]

Clearly, the "secret combinations" of the Doctrine and Covenants cannot reasonably be isolated from the larger context of potential war in America. In the context of 1828 campaign rhetoric, Jackson led a "secret combination" to overthrow the government and establish himself as a king–actions which would ultimately embroil the country in war.

16. Peterson notes that "the vast majority of the anti-Masons joined the rising Whig party–but at least in Kirtland, the Mormons

were 'Jacksonians almost to a man'" (203).[87] It is true that Mormons voted for Jackson's party, but in an environment where political deals and compromise were the norm, voting is not the best index of ideological stance. Rather than voting conscience, Mormons voted as a block to maximize political clout. In Ohio, Mormons unhappily found themselves in counties where the anti-Masons were also anti-Mormons. To repeat what I wrote in 1989: "[I]n the political environment of Ohio where the Mormons found themselves in counties dominated by National Republicans (later Whigs) the Mormons quickly learned that the best way to break the economic and political hegemony of the Whigs and establish themselves in the area was to support Jackson and his party."[88] They voted for him—even though his party stood for liberalism, separation of church and state, and the harboring of infidels and Masons—because their political choices were limited, not because their ideologies were in alignment with the Jacksonians.

17. "The translation of the Book of Mormon did not occur in Palmyra, but rather, for the most part, in Harmony, Pennsylvania," Peterson argues. "In other words, for almost every dated Palmyra article commonly adduced, Joseph was two or three or perhaps even four days distant (in an age that lacked telephone, radio, and television). ... But the fact remains that frantically anti-Masonic quotations from *Palmyra* newspapers have no clearly demonstrated direct relevance to the mind of Joseph Smith" (206-7). On the contrary, Masonry was extensively discussed long before Smith's departure from Palmyra in December 1827.[89] He left at a time when the excitement over the subject was high. New York had just completed its state and county elections, which in Smith's region were dominated by Masonic issues. In August 1827 Palmyra Baptists passed a resolution forbidding Baptists from becoming Freemasons.[90] According to historian William H. McIntosh, the Palmyra lodge "prospered till the Morgan excitement, when their charter was surrendered to the Grand Lodge."[91] Significantly, unlike other years, Palmyra's Mount Moriah Lodge was unable to pay its dues that year.[92]

Smith retained contact with Palmyra through the frequent visits of his family and friends and his own return visits. Nevertheless, the Masonic issue was certainly not isolated to Palmyra, let alone to western New York. Even a superficial survey of the subject reveals that Masonry was a persistent national issue dating back to the early days of the republic.[93] When one examines the early nineteenth-century sources in the New York counties of Ontario, Wayne, Seneca, Chenango, and Broome, and Susquehanna County, Pennsylvania, it becomes evident that Masonry was a subject that could not be avoided.

Peterson wonders, without checking, if "anti-Masonry was all the rage in Harmony as well, ... so far as I am aware, nobody has attempted to adduce proof" (207). Because Harmony was essentially a rural community and, unlike Palmyra, had no newspaper, it is difficult to recover the specifics of its political and religious culture. The only newspaper in the county–the *Susquehanna Register* in Montrose–was considered a "Masonic press" for its support of Jackson. Nevertheless, it published an account from the *New York Spectator* (21 Sept. 1827) of Morgan's abduction and murder; a report of the anti-Masonic convention in Le Roy, New York (14, 21 Mar. 1828); extracts from the oaths of the "Royal Arch Degree" and "Order of the Cross" (21 Mar. 1828); mention of an anti-Masonic meeting in nearby Gibson (31 Oct. 1828); the resolutions of another anti-Masonic meeting (5 Dec. 1828); a notice dated 6 April 1829 and published several times announcing that an anti-Masonic meeting was being rescheduled; and a report that an anti-Masonic state convention was held 25 June in Harrisburg (3 July 1829).

A letter published in the *Register*, dated 27 October 1828 from Montrose and signed "A Young Politician," defended Jackson against insinuations that "the whole Masonic Fraternity in the Union are acting in concert to elevate Gen. Jackson to the presidency on his masonic merits." The writer pointed out that some Masons favored Adams's reelection but complained that some Adams supporters "in the eastern part of the county are so much heated with enthusiasm that they insinuate to the people that Jacksonianism and Freemasonry are synonimous" (31 Oct. 1828).

Anti-Masons meeting in Gibson on 18 November 1828 declared, among other things:

> That of all secret societies, the masonic institution, from its numbers, wealth, and the corruption of its members, is the most dangerous to civil liberty now in existence. ... That we consider the institution of Freemasonry as immoral in its tendency, anti-republican in its principles, and dangerous in the extreme. ... That we concur in the sentiments so commonly expressed by our fellow citizens in the state of New York and else-

where, that speculative Freemasonry is dangerous to man, wicked in its ceremonies, detrimental to religion and dangerous to the administration of justice (5 Dec. 1828).

Although Masonry was widely discussed in Susquehanna County, anti-Masons seemed to be in the minority. Henry Dana Ward listed fifteen anti-Masonic counties of Pennsylvania, of which Susquehanna was not one.[94] Yet, there were anti-Masonic meetings in the area. Unlike his experience in Palmyra, Smith may have felt overwhelmed by the pro-Jacksonian and pro-Masonic attitudes, making the message of his book all the more important.

Nevertheless, only the most naive researcher believes that passages from Palmyra newspapers, or even from the *Susquehanna Register* for that matter, represent the mind of Joseph Smith. Even if it could be demonstrated that Smith was in the vicinity of Palmyra or Harmony when a specific anti-Masonic editorial was published, it would not reveal his state of mind since it could not be demonstrated that he read or considered it unless he explicitly quoted from it. Most researchers have cited local newspapers only to demonstrate that the subject was being discussed.

At best, literature–like any artifact–facilitates a fragmentary reconstruction of the past; moreover, newspapers were not the only sources of information. In other words, an author's inspiration is largely untraceable. Historical and literary criticism can only make indirect connections between a written work and its cultural environment. Most researchers appreciate the limitations of their work and proceed cautiously.

APOLOGETIC NEGLECT

Apologists have focused their attention on the Gadianton bands. Of greater significance is the prophecy of a specific latter-day "secret combination." Identification of this secret society is essential to understanding the Book of Mormon's analogous use of Gadianton bands in warning Jacksonian America. The apologists' neglect of this aspect of the text is a serious flaw in their critique of the anti-Masonic interpretation. The following discussion not only illuminates this blind-spot but reinforces and supplements aspects of the above examination.

Moroni declares that the Book of Mormon will "come in a day

when the blood of the saints shall cry unto the Lord, because of secret combinations and works of darkness" (Morm. 8:27); Nephi's prediction about "secret combinations" in the "last days" concerns "the days when the Lord God shall bring these things [the Book of Mormon] forth unto the children of men" (2 Ne. 26:14, 22); and in 1831 Joseph Smith's revelations confirmed the presence of "secret combinations" in the United States (D&C 38:12-13, 28-29, 32; 42:64). Clearly, we are dealing with a subject of immediate concern to the Book of Mormon's first readers. Moreover, Smith's early Zionic (utopian) goals and the urgency with which he carried them out exclude concerns about the twentieth century.[95] A revelation dictated in March 1829 captures the millenarian spirit of his early mission:

> And now if this generation do harden their hearts against my word, behold I will deliver them up unto satan, for he reigneth and hath much power *at this time*, for he hath got great hold upon the hearts of the people of this generation: and not far from the iniquities of Sodom and Gomorrah, do they come *at this time*: and behold the sword of justice hangeth over their heads, and if they persist in the hardness of their hearts, the time cometh that it must fall upon them (BofC 4:6, emphasis added).

Smith believed that America was in the midst of a crisis, that "secret combinations" were threatening the young nation's survival, and that civil war was about to destroy the republic. Thus, his message, especially during the early years when he was trying to establish his New Jerusalem in Missouri, pertained directly to his contemporaries, not to future generations.

Moroni describes both the religious and political threat, imbedded in a larger discussion about latter-day churches being "defiled" and "polluted," which was a major concern for religious anti-Masons (Morm. 8:25-39). For instance, an anti-Masonic committee which met in January 1830 in Waterville, New York, two months before the first copies of the Book of Mormon were issued, declared:

> After a patient and thorough investigation, we are led to the belief, that masonry is one of the greatest sins that now infests the Church—that it is utterly opposed to the pure and simple spirit of the Gospel of Jesus Christ—that it retards the growth of grace in the heart of the Christian, and tends to lull the sinner into a false security—that it is prejudicial to re-

> vivals of religion, and that it must be eradicated before the splendor of the Millenial morn can break upon the world. ... If these things are so, is it not the solemn duty of the Christian public to awake to a sense of them? ... Come then, one and all, and help to purge away the iniquity.[96]

The call is strikingly similar to Moroni's exhortation that America must "awake[n] to a sense of your awful situation, because of this secret combination which shall be among you. ... Wherefore, I, Moroni, am commanded to write these things that evil may be done away. ..." (Eth. 8:24, 26). However, where Waterville anti-Masons called for a cleansing of the church, Moroni demanded the purging of America.

Nevertheless, Moroni's criticisms echoed the concerns of religious anti-Masons. Addressing his latter-day audience, Moroni queried: "Why have ye transfigured the holy word of God, that ye might bring damnation upon your souls?" (Morm. 8:33). The Reverend Armstrong reflected the same attitude when he charged in 1830: "Freemasonry perverts the holy scriptures by introducing masonic traditions, and interpolations, to supply pretended deficiencies of the bible."[97]

Moroni also asked, "Why are ye ashamed to take upon you the name of Christ?" (Morm. 8:38). While this passage reflects a complaint of primitivists, anti-Masons were also concerned with the absence of Christianity from Masonry. Again, Armstrong declared, "The institution of Freemasonry acknowledges no human depravity which needs a Saviour's atonement, and records neither the sufferings nor triumphant glories of the Saviour of men." Quoting Acts 4:12, he reminded Masons that "there is none other name under heaven given among men whereby we must be saved."[98] One anti-Mason complained in 1828 that "Free Masonry makes many prayers, but they are prayers without the acknowledgment of a Savior. Our Savior has not told us that we may worship God without mentioning his name."[99] "You are members of a secret society," another declared in 1829, "in whose ritual of religious worship the name of the holy Redeemer is not found!"[100]

Moroni writes further: "Yea, why do ye build up your secret abominations to get gain, and cause that widows should mourn before the Lord, and also orphans to mourn before the Lord, and also the blood of their fathers and their husbands to cry unto the Lord from the ground? ..." (Morm. 8:40). For those who believed Moroni was addressing Freemasons, his words carried subtle irony, for Masonry had its own imagery of widows and orphans. Masonry's central figure, Hiram Abiff, was "a widow's son," and the Masonic sign of "grief and distress" included the words: "O Lord, my God! is there no help for the widow's son?"[101] Although Masonry claimed "to receive the sufferings of the widow and the orphan," Presbyterian minister Nathan N. Whiting of Waterville, New York, charged that the Masonic murder of Morgan had produced an "agonized widow" and the "lamentations of the fatherless children."[102]

When Moroni revisits the subject of latter-day "secret combinations" (Eth. 8), his approach is more political than religious. In fact, his warning is an excursus following the introduction of a secret political society among the Jaredites. Jared's daughter conspired to help her father become king by plotting the assassination of her grandfather, King Omer. In an effort to recruit an assassin, she dances before Akish, who asks Jared for her hand in marriage. Jared will grant his wish if he will bring to him the head of his father, King Omer. To keep the conspiracy secret, Akish founds a "secret combination, even as they of old" (8:9-18). Omer is warned in a dream to flee; in his absence, Jared is made king anyway.

While many see the obvious comparison to Herod's promise to Salome, who danced for John the Baptist's head (Matt. 14:6-12),[103] there is more to consider here. Anti-Masons often referred to Herod when appealing to Masons to renounce their oaths. The Reverend Whiting argued, "If no distinction is to be made between lawful and unlawful oaths, we have committed a mistake in supposing Herod deserved censure, when the gory head of the Baptist testified to the 'lords and high captains,' that murder should (as in later times) be committed for an 'oath's sake.'"[104] The *Anti-Masonic Review and Magazine* for 1829 warned that "nothing short of renunciation of their oaths, will deliver them from the danger of Herod's transgression."[105] So the association of Herod's oath with the Jaredite "secret combination" was natural.

Significantly, in warning America of political dangers, Moroni employs the term in the singular, as if he has a specific group in mind, saying that it will be "because of *this* secret combination which shall be among you; or wo be unto *it*, because of the blood of them who have been slain; for they cry from the dust for vengeance upon *it*, and also upon those who built *it* up. For it cometh to pass that whoso buildeth *it* up seeketh to overthrow the freedom of all lands" (Eth. 8:24-25, emphasis added). In my 1989 essay, I suggested that the "secret combination" (singular) threatening America, as perceived by anti-Masons, was Jackson and his political followers. Nothing apologists have said in the last decade has come close to refuting this thesis.

Below is a brief review of the characteristic traits of the Book of Mormon's latter-day "secret combinations" in light of the above discussion. Because the Book of Mormon uses Gadianton bands in an analogous fashion, some elements are applicable to this latter-day group.

1. They are present when the Book of Mormon comes forth (2 Ne. 26:14, 22; Morm. 8:27; D&C 42:64).

2. They are not in the wilderness but "among you" (Eth. 8:24).

3. They are identified as "secret combinations" and "works of darkness" (2 Ne. 26:22; Morm. 8:27), and when discussed in a political context, the singular–"secret combination"–is used (Eth. 8:24-25).

4. They are bound by death-oaths and use "secret signs" and "secret words" for protection (Eth. 8:20; Hel. 6:22).

5. They claim an ancient origin (2 Ne. 26:22; 3 Ne. 3:9, 6:28; Eth. 8:15, 18, 10:33).

6. They seek political "power and [economic] gain" (Eth. 8:22; Morm. 8:40).

7. They infect and defile the churches, change or distort the Bible, and are not true Christians (Morm. 8:27-41).

8. They are responsible for secret murders, especially of the prophets and the saints (Morm. 8:27, 40; Eth. 8:22, 23, 25; 3 Ne. 7:6, 10).

9. They seek to infiltrate and overthrow the United States government (Eth. 8:24-25).

10. They seek to "overthrow the freedom of all lands, nations, and countries" (Eth. 8:25).[106]

11. They threaten to cause civil war in America (Morm. 8:41; Eth. 8:23; D&C 38:28-29, 42:64; 87:1-8).

12. They seek to establish a monarchy (3 Ne. 6:30, 7:9-10; cf. 2 Ne. 10:11-15).

Obviously, Freemasonry in general, and the Jackson party in particular, is the group that most logically meets these requirements, at least through anti-Masonic and anti-Jacksonian eyes.[107] Significantly, none of the book's first readers who expressed an opinion on the matter were confused about this. Commenting on the prophesy in Ether 8, for instance, Alexander Campbell stated that Moroni "laments the prevalency of free masonry in the times when his Book should be dug up out of the earth."[108] One should be cautious about embracing an interpretation of "secret combinations" that conflicts with the consensus of the book's first audience.

CONCLUSION

Despite the efforts of Bushman, Ostler, Quinn, and Peterson, anti-Masonry remains the probable source of inspiration for the Book of Mormon's Gadianton bands. The declarations of some apologists—for example, William J. Hamblin's statement that the "supposed Gadianton-Masonry connection has been debunked," or John Gee's assertion that the anti-Masonic thesis has been "conclusively demonstrated to be a mirage"—are premature and naive.[109]

For those interested in the historical and literary anachronisms in the Book of Mormon, a search through Joseph Smith's cultural environment for possible influences is a profitable enterprise. For those of us so engaged, the apologetic demand for an exact correspondence between Masonry and Gadianton bands is unnecessary and irrelevant. The parallels are so striking that any reasonable person should acknowledge them, whatever their subsequent interpretation of their significance may be. The question is no longer whether Joseph Smith used Masonic and anti-Masonic elements from his environment to create something both similar and unique in the Book of Mormon, but rather to what extent. Nothing the apologists have suggested thus far has rendered unlikely the conclusion that Joseph Smith clearly intended the Book of Mormon to adopt an anti-Masonic posture.

NOTES

1. I wish to acknowledge the research and advice of David J. Buerger, Rick Grunder, Kathleen Smith Kutolowski, Brent Lee Metcalfe, Mark Thomas, John E. Thompson, Kent Walgren, and Wesley P. Walters. For those who have previously discussed anti-Masonic influence in the Book of Mormon, see I. Woodbridge Riley, *The Founder of Mormonism: A Psychological Study of Joseph Smith, Jr.* (New York: Dodd, Mead and Co., 1902), 160-63; Walter F. Prince,

"Psychological Tests for the Authorship of the Book of Mormon," *American Journal of Psychology* 28 (July 1917): 376-77; S[amuel] H. Goodwin, "Mormonism and Masonry–Anti-Masonry in the Book of Mormon," *The Builder* 10 (Nov.-Dec. 1924): 323-27, 346-48, 363-67; Fawn M. Brodie, *No Man Knows My History: The Life of Joseph Smith the Mormon Prophet* (2nd ed.; New York: Alfred A. Knopf, 1976), 63-66; Thomas F. O'Dea, *The Mormons* (Chicago: University of Chicago Press, 1957), 35; Sidney E. Ahlstrom, *A Religious History of the American People,* 2 vols. (Garden City, NY: Image Books, 1975), 1:606-8; Robert N. Hullinger, *Joseph Smith's Response to Skepticism* (Salt Lake City: Signature Books, 1992), 99-120; Jerald Tanner and Sandra Tanner, *Mormonism: Shadow or Reality?* (5th ed.; Salt Lake City: Utah Lighthouse Ministry, 1987), 69-72; David Persuitte, *Joseph Smith and the Origins of The Book of Mormon* (Jefferson, NC: McFarland and Co., 1985), 176-79; and Dan Vogel, "Mormonism's 'Anti-Masonick Bible,'" *John Whitmer Historical Association Journal* 9 (1989): 17-30.

2. This evidence is reviewed in Vogel, ibid., 17-19.

3. Richard L. Bushman, *Joseph Smith and the Beginnings of Mormonism* (Urbana: University of Illinois Press, 1984), 128-31.

4. Blake T. Ostler, "The Book of Mormon as a Modern Expansion of an Ancient Source," *Dialogue: A Journal of Mormon Thought* 20 (Spring 1987): 73-76.

5. The evidence for Smith's claim to a mechanical, literal translation is most conveniently found in Richard Van Wagoner and Steven Walker, "Joseph Smith: The Gift of Seeing," *Dialogue: A Journal of Mormon Thought* 15 (Summer 1982): 48-68; and James E. Lancaster, "The Translation of the Book of Mormon," in *The Word of God: Essays on Mormon Scripture,* ed. Dan Vogel (Salt Lake City: Signature Books, 1990), 97-112.

6. This was Smith's own description of the Book of Mormon. See Joseph Smith Jr., *History of the Church of Jesus Christ of Latter-day Saints,* ed. B. H. Roberts, 7 vols. (2nd ed. rev.; Salt Lake City: Deseret Book, 1948 printing), 4:461.

7. D. Michael Quinn, *Mormonism and the Magic World View* (Salt Lake City: Signature Books, 1987), 160-64; and his 1998 revised edition by the same publisher, 202-10. Unless otherwise noted, references in this essay are to the first edition.

8. Daniel C. Peterson, "Notes on 'Gadianton Masonry,'" Stephen D. Ricks and William J. Hamblin, eds., *Warfare in the Book of Mormon* (Salt Lake City: Deseret Book Co.; and Provo, UT: Foundation for Ancient Research and Mormon Studies, 1990), 174-224.

9. E.g., William J. Hamblin, "An Apologist for the Critics: Brent Lee Metcalfe's Assumptions and Methodologies," in *Review of Books on the Book of Mormon* 6, 1 (1994): 499-500.

10. See Vogel, "Mormonism's 'Anti-Masonick Bible,'" 17-19.

11. Oliver B. Huntington, Diary, typescript (2 vols.), 1:12, Special Collections, Harold B. Lee Library, Brigham Young University, Provo, Utah.

12. On this matter, consult Dan Vogel, *Religious Seekers and the Advent of*

Mormonism (Salt Lake City: Signature Books, 1988), chap. 2; and Grant Underwood, *The Millenarian World of Early Mormonism* (Urbana: University of Illinois Press, 1993), chap. 8.

13. See also Grant Underwood, "The Earliest Reference Guides to the Book of Mormon: Windows into the Past," *Journal of Mormon History* 12 (1985): 81-82, who finds an apparent lack of attention by early Mormons to anti-Masonry.

14. W[illiam] H. McIntosh, *History of Wayne County, New York* (Philadelphia: Everts, Ensign and Everts, 1877), 143. See also discussion in Dan Vogel, *Early Mormon Documents*, vol. 3 (Salt Lake City: Signature Books, 2000), 452-56).

15. Smith's 1832 history abruptly ends with the commencement of the Book of Mormon's translation and thus does not describe its contents.

16. For a discussion of the Mormon shift from concern about "secret combinations," see Vogel, "Mormonism's 'Anti-Masonick Bible,'" 28-29.

17. The term Gadianton is not used to describe the secret society that existed among the Jaredites.

18. On the fragmentary condition of Freemasonry, see, e.g., Michael W. Homer, "'Similarity of Priesthood in Masonry': The Relationship between Freemasonry and Mormonism," *Dialogue: A Journal of Mormon Thought* 27 (Fall 1994): 9-10.

19. *The Anti-Masonic Review and Magazine* 1 (1828-29): 296-97.

20. Lebbeus Armstrong declared that "many of the numerous murders which have polluted this, and other lands, with blood, which horrid deeds have been palmed on some innocent, or unknown persons, have been really the bloody fruits of masonic executions" (Lebbeus Armstrong, *Masonry Proved to Be a Work of Darkness, Repugnant to the Christian Religion; and Inimical to a Republican Government* [New York: Printed for the Author, 1830], 11). He also said: "It is awfully to be feared, that when the light of eternity shall shine on the deeds of darkness, and every secret thing shall be brought into judgment, it will then be found, that many of the sudden deaths in the world have been the result of masonic VENGEANCE, in the execution of penalty in a lodge-room, or personal dispatch by poison, or assassination, as the ghosts of the murdered Artemas Kenedy, near Boston, the poisoned Simmons, of Albany, and a host of others, would, doubtless, testify now, were they permitted to speak" (ibid.).

21. David Pease, *The Good Man in Bad Company: Or Speculative Freemasonry a Wicked and Dangerous Combination. A Sermon Delivered in Belchertown (Mass.), July 8, 1830* (Brookfield, MA: Printed by E. and G. Merriam, 1831), 13.

22. John V. N. Yates and Joseph W. Moulton, *History of the State of New York* (New York: A. T. Goodrich, 1824), 55-56.

23. E.g., Armstrong, *Masonry Proved to Be a Work of Darkness,* 15.

24. E.g., William Morgan, *Illustrations of Masonry* (Rochester, NY: David C.

Miller, 1827). Originally published in 1826, this work was advertised for sale in the columns of the *Palmyra Freeman* (2 Dec. 1828): 3.

25. Ibid., 68-69.

26. *Ontario Phoenix* (17 Sept. 1828): 2.

27. E.g., Morgan, *Illustrations of Masonry,* 15, 22, 53, 77; and *Wayne Sentinel,* 14 Mar. 1828.

28. *Wayne Sentinel,* 14 Mar. 1828.

29. Morgan, *Illustrations of Masonry,* 18.

30. Similar metaphorical use of the cable-tow was made in the *Morgan Investigator* for 29 March 1827, which declared: "Those men are fastening a 'Cable Tow' about their necks, which will have a more comfortable set than those they have worn in the lodge, and which they will in all probability wear to their graves." Edward Giddins may have had this in mind when he said: "What a state of things is this! and how degraded to our nation, that with all her boasted freedom, she yet bears upon her bosom a secret society of men, who are applying the halter of despotism to the necks of the people, and that halter has been drawn closer and closer and that without murmur for half a century" (*The Anti-Masonic Almanack, for the Year 1828* [Rochester, NY: Edwin Scrantom, [1827]], 13-14).

31. *Auburn* [NY] *Free Press,* as reprinted in *Philadelphia Album,* 18 Dec. 1830. Thanks to Dale Broadhurst for bringing this to my attention.

32. This was in part the burden of my 1989 essay (see Vogel, "Mormonism's 'Anti-Masonick Bible,'" 22).

33. For the shift from religious to political anti-Masonry following Morgan's disappearance, and especially during the 1828 presidential election, see William Preston Vaughn, *The Antimasonic Party in the United States, 1826-1843* (Lexington: University Press of Kentucky, 1983), 21-34.

34. Morgan, *Illustrations of Masonry,* vii-viii.

35. Armstrong, *Masonry Proved to Be a Work of Darkness,* 17.

36. Peterson recognizes that Ostler's statement needs modification, stating: "[T]he fact that the Book of Mormon authors elected to treat Gadiantonism as a secular robber gang does not necessarily make them such. A close reading of the text even in its present tendentious state demonstrates that Gadiantonism was an ideological movement and an alternative religious vision of considerable seductive power" (212).

37. Morgan, *Illustrations of Masonry,* 44.

38. E.g., *The Anti-Masonic Review and Magazine* (New York) 1 (1828-29): 81, 205, 223, 362; *Wayne Sentinel,* 14 Mar. 1828.

39. P[eter]. Sanborn, *Minutes of an Address Delivered Before the Anti-Masonic Convention of Reading, Mass., January 15, 1829* (Boston: Free Press, 1829), 19.

40. *The New England Anti-Masonic Almanac for the Year of Our Lord 1831* (Boston: John Marsh and Co., [1830]), 24; Pease, *The Good Man in Bad Company,* 11. See also Vogel, "Mormonism's 'Anti-Masonick Bible,'" 23.

41. See the *Wayne Sentinel,* 8 and 15 Aug. 1828; see also James B. Ranck,

"Andrew Jackson and the Burr Conspiracy," *Tennessee Historical Magazine* (1930): 17-28; and Joe Gray Taylor, "Andrew Jackson and the Aaron Burr Conspiracy," *West Tennessee Historical Society Papers* (1947): 89.

42. *Anti-Masonic Review and Magazine* 1 (1828-29): 297.

43. E.g., George Oliver, *The Antiquities of Free-Masonry, Comprising Illustrations of the Five Grand Periods of Masonry, from the Creation of the World to the Dedication of King Solomon's Temple* (London: G. and W. B. Whittaker, 1823), which not only describes Adam as a Mason and Eve as "mother of all Masons" but states that Cain "apostatized from Masonry" (39, 43, 46).

44. E.g., *Anti-Masonic Review and Magazine* 1 (1828-29): 32, 52, 99.

45. Sanborn, *Minutes of an Address,* 16.

46. Quinn suggests that "Mahan" could be linked to Satan, "Mahoun" (pronounced "Mahan"), in use during the early nineteenth century (167). Although this would assign a nineteenth-century source for Smith's revision of Genesis, the full term "*Master* Mahan" is closer to Masonic usage.

47. *Monroe County Antimasonic Broadside,* Oct. 1827, Cornell University Collection of Regional History, qtd. in Lee Benson, *The Concept of Jacksonian Democracy: New York as a Test Case* (Princeton, NJ: Princeton University Press, 1963), 17n31.

48. *New England Anti-Masonic Almanac,* 32.

49. *Anti-Masonic Review and Magazine* 1 (1828-29): 296.

50. *New England Anti-Masonic Almanac,* 30.

51. See Vernon Stauffer, *New England and the Bavarian Illuminati* (New York: Russell and Russell, 1967) esp. 229-360.

52. Jedidiah Morse, *A Sermon, Delivered at the New North Church in Boston* (Boston: Samuel Hall, 1798), 23.

53. Ibid., 24.

54. David Pease, *The Good Man in Bad Company,* 11.

55. Armstrong, *Masonry Proved to Be a Work of Darkness,* 22-23.

56. Ibid., 24. In his 1827 book, *An Inquiry into the Nature and Tendency of Speculative Free-masonry* (3rd ed.; Utica, NY: Northway and Bennett, 1827), John G. Stearns "led the way in expounding the theory that Masonry was a state within a state and that one day Masons would overthrow the democratic government of the United States and would crown one of their 'grand kings' as ruler of this nation" (Vaughn, *Antimasonic Party,* 20).

57. Nor were anti-Masons pleased that some Masonic officials were already designated Kings and Grand Kings. The *New England Anti-Masonic Almanac* for 1831 worried that "there are as many as five hundred Masonic Kings in the United States ... [and] many subordinate Kings in each state" (32).

58. Martin Van Buren, *Inquiry into the Origin and Course of Political Parties in the United States* (New York: Hurd and Houghton, 1867), 322-23. For attempts by Jackson supporters to mitigate such fears, see: *Address of the Republican General Committee of Young Men of the City and County of New-York, Friendly to the Election of Gen. Andrew Jackson to the Presidency, to the Republican Electors of the State*

of New-York (New York: [General Committee of Young Men], 1828), 13; and "The Fear of Military Chieftainism," *Wayne Sentinel*, 26 Sept. 1828.

59. See Dean C. Jessee, ed. and comp., *The Personal Writings of Joseph Smith* (Salt Lake City: Deseret Book, 1984), 273-74.

60. Vogel, "Mormonism's 'Anti-Masonick Bible,'" 19-21, 22, 26-27.

61. See also Peterson, "The Gadianton Robbers as Guerrilla Warriors," in *Warfare in the Book of Mormon*, 146-73.

62. Interestingly, immediately following the founding of Kishkumen's secret society, Smith chose to name a Lamanite king Tubaloth (Hel. 1:16), a name that appears nowhere else in the Book of Mormon. If this is a blending of Tubal Cain, the name of the Master Mason's sign, and Shibboleth, the name of the Fellow Craft's sign, it is an indication of what was on the author's mind when he introduced the concept of political combinations (see Morgan, *Illustrations of Masonry*, 108, 109).

63. See Mervin B. Hogan, *Mormonism and Freemasonry: The Illinois Episode* (Salt Lake City: Campus Graphics, 1980). Michael Homer argues that "Smith was not a lukewarm Mason" and that the "Mormons were not using Masonry only to gain a political foothold in Illinois" (Homer, "'Similarity of Priesthood in Masonry,'" 68). Political incentives nevertheless contributed to Smith's decision to promote a Mormon/Mason alliance.

64. See David John Buerger, "Development of the Mormon Temple Endowment Ceremony," *Dialogue: A Journal of Mormon Thought* 20 (Winter 1987): 45-46; and Homer, "'Similarity of Priesthood in Masonry,'" 68-69.

65. Dean C. Jessee, ed., *The Personal Writings of Joseph Smith*, 405. Peterson, who notes that Hyrum Smith was a co-signer, concludes that Hyrum must not have seen anything in the letter that was contradictory or insulting to his Masonic membership. In fact, Hyrum seems to have been a rather lukewarm Mason. The only record (returns filed with the Grand Lodge in New York City for 1827-28) listing a "Hiram Smith" as a member of the Palmyra lodge was likely another "Hiram Smith" who appears in other Manchester township records. While Nauvoo records state that Hyrum's membership was transferred from Palmyra, the fact that his name is missing from the records suggests that he was not a zealous Mason. See Vogel, *Early Mormon Documents*, 3:452-56.

66. *The Return* 2 (June 1890): 287.

67. *Olive Branch* 2 (Dec. 1849): 90.

68. Ibid. 2 (Dec. 1849): 93; see also 1 (Mar. 1849): 146; 1 (Nov. 1849): 72; 2 (Feb. 1850): 122-27.

69. See Dan Vogel, "The Earliest Mormon Concept of God," in *Line upon Line: Essays on Mormon Doctrine*, ed. Gary James Bergera (Salt Lake City: Signature Books, 1989); and Dan Vogel, "Anti-Universalist Rhetoric in the Book of Mormon," in *New Approaches to the Book of Mormon: Explorations in Critical Methodology*, ed. Brent Lee Metcalfe (Salt Lake City: Signature Books, 1993), 21-52. Perhaps of more direct relevance is Smith's reversal on polygamy (cf. Jac. 2:23-24 with D&C 132:38-39; see also Edward H. Ashment, "The LDS

Temple Ceremony: Historical Origins and Religious Value," *Dialogue: A Journal of Mormon Thought* 27 [Fall 1994]: 289-98).

70. The *Wayne Sentinel* (14 Mar. 1828) published the script for the fourth through the seventh degrees. See also Buerger, "Development of the Mormon Temple Endowment Ceremony," 45-48.

71. Edward Giddins, *Anti-Masonic Almanac, For the Year 1831* (Utica, NY: William Williams, 1830), 3-4.

72. Michael W. Homer's essay comparing Masonic ritual with the Mormon temple ceremony clearly demonstrates that the similarities are more than "superficial" (Homer, "'Similarity of Priesthood in Masonry'"; see also Buerger, "Development of the Mormon Temple Endowment Ceremony," 36-46).

73. See Buerger, ibid., 45-46; and Homer, ibid., 67-75. Passing to higher degrees in Masonry could have suggested an ascent into heaven. Also, the signs and tokens of Masonry were believed to have been used to facilitate movement into various rooms in Solomon's temple.

74. Homer, ibid., 112.

75. Vogel, "Mormonism's 'Anti-Masonick Bible,'" 18. In a recent essay, Peterson stated, "On 26 August 1989, Vogel and his sometime coauthor Brent Metcalfe, in a Salt Lake City conversation with me and my colleague, Prof. Stephen D. Ricks, declared flatly that the phrase 'secret combination' was never used at the time of the translation and publication of the Book of Mormon, except to refer to Freemasonry" (Daniel C. Peterson, "'Secret Combinations' Revisited," *Journal of Book of Mormon Studies* 1 [Fall 1992]: 185n5). What I said was that after extensive reading in the primary pre-1830 sources, I had been unable to find another use for the term and doubted that one would be found. I remain skeptical, but wisdom dictates that the door be left open slightly in case someone on the margins of popular nineteenth-century culture happened to have used the term in a non-Masonic context.

76. See *Ontario Phoenix*, 31 Mar. 1830. This paper was edited by W. W. Phelps, who later joined the Mormon church.

77. Mark Thomas, *Digging in Cumorah: Reclaiming Book of Mormon Narrative* (Salt Lake City: Signature Books, 1999), 212.

78. Peterson, "'Secret Combinations' Revisited," 187. For a transcript of the entire letter, see John Spencer Bassett, ed., *Correspondence of Andrew Jackson*, (Washington, D.C.: Carnegie Institution of Washington, 1928), 3:325. A discussion of the historical context of the letter can be found in Robert V. Remini, *Henry Clay: Statesman for the Union* (New York and London: Norton, 1991), 340.

79. Quinn, *Early Mormonism and the Magic World View* (2nd rev. ed., 1998), 202, 511-12n216.

80. *The Proceedings of the Second United States Anti-Masonic Convention, Held at Baltimore, September, 1831* (Boston, 1832), 5, emphasis added.

81. E.g., *Republican Monitor* (Cazenovia, NY; 23 Nov. 1828): 1, which declares that Masonry's murderous plots are proof of the "iniquity of their secret

chambers"; and *Proceedings of the Sangerfield Meeting, Held at the Presbyterian Meeting House in the Village of Waterville, January 14, 1830* (Utica, NY: William Williams, 1830), 10.

82. This point was emphasized in my 1989 essay.

83. Lucy Mack Smith, *Biographical Sketches of Joseph Smith the Prophet, and His Progenitors for many Generations* (Liverpool: S. W. Richards, 1853), 162; also in Dan Vogel, ed., *Early Mormon Documents,* 5 vols. (Salt Lake City: Signature Books, 1996-), 1:432-33 (hereafter EMD).

84. Joseph Smith to Colesville Saints, 2 Dec. 1830, Newel Knight Journal, 206-207, ca. 1846, in private possession (see EMD 1:22).

85. See "Return of the Mount Moriah Lodge No. 112 held in the Town of Palmyra in the County of Wayne and State of New York from June 4th AL 5827 [1827] to June 4th AL 5828 [1828]," Grand Lodge of Free and Accepted Masons of the State of New York, Chancellor Livingston Library, New York, New York; Levi Daggett vs. Hyrum Smith, Nathan Pierce, Docket Book (1827-30), 76b (entry of 28 June 1830, etc.), and "execution" order of 14 August 1830 (separate sheet kept with book), Manchester Township Office, Clifton Springs, NY.

86. William Van Camp, editor of the *Wayne Democratic Press* at Lyons, New York, saw both anti-Masonry and Mormonism as "off-shoots of the parent stock *Ancient Federalism*" (9 June 1858). Elsewhere, Camp declared that "Joe [Smith] was a firm believer in anti-Masonry" (*Rochester Union Advertiser,* 27 May 1857, 2).

87. Peterson quotes Underwood, "Earliest Reference Guides to the Book of Mormon," 82. Justice of the Peace J. C. Dowen of Painesville, Ohio, remembered that "the Majority of the Mormons were Democrats" (J. C. Dowen, Affidavit, 2 Jan. 1885, Arthur B. Deming Collection, Chicago Historical Society, Chicago, IL). Joseph Smith himself said in 1838 that "the Politics of this Church (with but few exceptions only) is that of Democracy" (Scott H. Faulring, ed., *An American Prophet's Record: The Diaries and Journals of Joseph Smith* [Salt Lake City: Signature Books in association with Smith Research Associates, 1987], 181).

88. Vogel, "Mormonism's 'Anti-Masonick Bible,'" 28-29. See also Marvin S. Hill, *Quest for Refuge: The Mormon Flight from American Pluralism* (Salt Lake City: Signature Books, 1989), 64-66.

89. E.g., *Palmyra Register,* 19 Mar. 1819; *Wayne Sentinel,* 12 July 1825; 18 Aug., 13 Oct., 3, 10, 24 Nov., 8 Dec. 1826; 19 Jan., 2, 16, 23 Feb., 6, 13, 27 Apr., 4 May, 15 June, 26 Oct. 1827.

90. See "Book of Records for the first Baptist Church in Palmyra 1813," 1813-28, entry for Aug. 1827, Baptist Historical Society, Rochester, New York.

91. McIntosh, *History of Wayne County,* 143. If McIntosh's report is true, the charter was surrendered only briefly since there does not appear to be a significant gap in the returns of the Palmyra lodge.

92. "Return of the Mount Moriah Lodge," 4 June 1827-4 June 1828.

93. See Homer's review of the literature in "'Similarity of Priesthood in Masonry,'" 4-25.

94. *Anti-Masonic Review and Magazine* 1 (1828-29): 375-77. Ward states that the difficulty anti-Masons experienced in Pennsylvania resulted from its "laboring against a powerful and secret combination" (374).

95. On the early Mormon concept of the imminent return of Jesus and the approach of the Millennium, see my discussion in *Religious Seekers and the Advent of Mormonism,* 181-213.

96. *Proceedings of the Sangerfield Meeting,* 6.

97. Armstrong, *Masonry Proved to Be a Work of Darkness,* 4.

98. Ibid., 7.

99. *Anti-Masonic Review and Magazine* 1 (1828-29): 99.

100. Ibid., 312.

101. Morgan, *Illustrations of Masonry,* 69, 76.

102. *Proceedings of the Sangerfield Meeting,* 9, 13.

103. E.g., Brodie, *No Man Knows My History,* 62-63; O'Dea, *The Mormons,* 38; Tanner and Tanner, *Mormonism,* 74; and Ostler, 76.

104. *Proceedings of the Sangerfield Meeting,* 14-15; see also Armstrong, *Masonry Proved to Be a Work of Darkness,* 20.

105. *Anti-Masonic Review and Magazine* 1 (1828-29): 142.

106. Anti-Masons claimed that no less than New York governor DeWitt Clinton admitted in 1825 that Masonry was a dangerous institution because "it has conspired against all governments" (*Proceedings of the Second United States Anti-Masonic Convention,* 27). In 1829 the Massachusetts convention declared: "[Masonry] is directly calculated to overturn every religion, and every civil government on earth" (*An Abstract of the Proceedings of the Anti-Masonic State Convention of Massachusetts, Held in Faneuil Hall, Boston, Dec. 30 and 31, 1829, and Jan. 1, 1830* [Boston: John Marsh, 1830], 15).

107. Certainly Masonry is preferable to the groups Peterson flippantly suggests–i.e., United States Bar Associations and the Phi Beta Kappa (195-97).

108. Alexander Campbell, "The Mormonites," *Millennial Harbinger* 2 (1831): 90.

109. See *Review of Books on the Book of Mormon* 6, 1 (1994): 499-500, 76n88. Hamblin and Gee are referring to Peterson's work. In fact, Peterson barely dealt with the issues raised in my 1989 article, his neglect no doubt stemming from his being "a medieval Islamicist, not an American historian." He then asserts: "[S]ince my own desultory readings on American history and politics have supplied this counterexample, one can confidently predict that a true search of period writings could furnish many more" ("'Secret Combinations' Revisited," 186, 187-88).

9.

Joseph Smith: Inspired Author of the Book of Mormon

Robert M. Price

IN 2 KINGS 22, WE WITNESS A PIVOTAL SCENE FOR THE HISTORY OF the ancient Kingdom of Judah, one with far-reaching echoes that continue to sound in the present day. Two particular notes in this echo concern us here. The scene is a familiar one to lovers of scripture. The priest Hilkiah sends word to Josiah the King, words simple but heavy with omen: "I have found a book." At the king's direction, he had been busy locating certain funds to be used to compensate the workmen hired to refurbish the temple when suddenly the shrouding dust and shadows disclosed a surprising secret, a moldering scroll. Perhaps thinking at first it might be an old parish ledger, a record of the money he is seeking, he opens the volume and scans a page or two. A gasp signals the others present that their task has turned out to be anything but mundane; what seemed but an extensive spring cleaning proved to be an excavation. For the old book is nothing less than the Book of the Covenant or what we today refer to as the Book of Deuteronomy (at least the core of it, chapters 4-33). Hilkiah knows at once it is something the king must see.

When the young sovereign hears the contents read, he is stunned.

Perhaps tempted to doze during the long sections of tort law and ritual etiquette, Josiah is rudely jolted awake by the litanies of blessings and curses that give Deuteronomy its unique theology. He hears the words like a death sentence, for up until his reign, Judah has been ruled by a sorry succession of perverts and apostates whose outrages have been catalogued in the preceding chapters of 2 Kings. Josiah recognizes in the lists of banned and interdicted deeds a virtual resume of his predecessors. Eager though he is to make amends before God, he is told by Huldah the Prophetess that it is too little too late, though he himself will be spared seeing the sad ending. Josiah might well have spoken the words later attributed to Louis XIV of France: "*Après moi, la déluge!* [After me, the flood!]"

The passage is important for many reasons, not the least of which is that it provides priceless information about the emergence of the Book of Deuteronomy. We only wish we had such revealing clues at other points in the history of the biblical canon. We may suppose, however, that the story of Josiah, Hilkiah, and the book strikes deeper resonances for Latter-day Saints than for any other Christian group. This is because of the similarity to the conditions in which the Book of Mormon came to light. It, too, is said to be an ancient scripture long buried in a time of religious and national crisis, only to resurface long afterward when its forgotten message should be heard anew.

We may set the tales of the rediscovery of the books of Deuteronomy and Mormon alongside those of the twin discoveries made roughly fifty years ago of the Dead Sea Scrolls at Qumran in Israel and of the Nag Hammadi Gnostic Library near Chenoboskion, Egypt. As if replaying the story of Mormon and Moroni racing to finish the epic of salvation history in America before persecution should overtake them, these latter two discoveries enable us to piece together the events that led to their hiding.

In the one case, the Dead Sea Scrolls had been taken out of Jerusalem and buried at various points around the Judean desert to save them from being torched by Roman troops should their siege of the city finally succeed, as indeed it did.[1] (Even with the traditional view,[2] if the scrolls were the library of an Essene monastery at Qumran itself, their hiding was still an attempt to protect them from the Romans.)

In the case of the Nag Hammadi Library, it now appears that it belonged to the first known Christian monastic community, that of Saint

Pachomius. We may envision the brethren in the Eastertide of the year 367 C.E. perusing the Paschal Encyclical of their bishop Athanasius with increasingly furrowed brows. The epistle listed the twenty-seven New Testament books we now have and declared that no one must consult any other scripture. In view, no doubt, were the very sort of writings the brethren cherished: *The Gospel of Thomas,* the *Gospel of Truth,* the *Gospel of Philip,* the *Gospel of Mary Magdalene,* the *Secret Book of the Great Invisible Spirit,* the *Apocryphon of John,* the *Apocalypse of James,* the *Prayer of Paul the Apostle, Thunder: Perfect Mind,* and others. Wordlessly the monks exchange troubled glances; they know what will come next: a visit from Athanasius's inquisitors, who will ask them to hand over any non-canonical books for burning, just as their pagan Roman predecessors required the canonical books themselves for destruction. The shovels are distributed, the books carefully packed up.[3] Thus, two great sectarian libraries were bequeathed, like a message in a bottle, cast forth on the ocean of the future for someone to find and read for whatever edification he might gain.

And so the trembling hands of young Joseph Smith uncovered the buried golden plates of Mormon and Moroni, lost chapters of an undreamed-of history of Israelite tribes and the Christian Savior in the New World. As the depraved Lamanites had pursued the Nephite Mormon and his son to death, so did young Smith feel besieged by the competing claims of rival evangelists and revivalists in his "Burned-Over District."[4] It was no surprise that the analogous tale told in the plates struck a note deep within him. And as the Nephites had long survived as a parallel branch of biblical Israel in the western hemisphere, so would the Church of the Latter-day Saints make its lonely but triumphant way through the generations as a parallel version of the Christian religion shared, at arm's length, by most other Americans.

One of the chief points of contention and division between the Mormon church and its "separated brethren" ironically harks back to the discovery of the lost Book of Deuteronomy in 2 Kings 22, for today virtually all critical scholars are agreed that the tale of Josiah and Hilkiah tries to hide the very thing it hints at: that the book was not discovered and dusted off but actually created by Hilkiah, Huldah, Jeremiah, and others of the "Deuteronomic School" who thus sought to win the impressionable young king to their religious agenda. What is set forth in 2 Kings as reactionary (restoring the past) was really revolutionary (pressing on into a new future). Though it no doubt contained much traditional material, both from Israel in the north and from Judah in the south, Deuteronomy was essentially a new book, a "modern" revision and updating of previous laws collected in the Yahvist Epic (the "J Source") and Elohist Epic (the "E Source"). On the basis of a platform of a newly streamlined monotheism (or at least monolatry) and a humanitarian regard for slaves, animals, and employees, Hilkiah, Huldah, and the others hoped to avert God's wrath for the abuses they had witnessed with increasing disgust for far too long. Thus they penned the book in secret, much like the framers of the United States Constitution, delegates commissioned for one purpose, strengthening the Articles of Confederation, who in fact accomplished another, creating the Constitution.

Again, virtually all critical scholars agree that Joseph Smith did not discover the Book of Mormon but rather created it. His goal would have been as analogous to that of Hilkiah as his methods had been: in response to his confusion over which nineteenth-century version of Christianity to embrace—none seeming to have any particular advantage over the others, all seeming to be severely in want of something—Smith tried to make a clean break with the recent past and to go on into a new future by invoking a more distant past. And in so doing he had created something new, an imaginary Sacred Past, the way it *should* have been.

NEPHITES AND NEOPHYTES

As Jacques Derrida has indicated,[5] all attempts to critique the present by comparing it to a pristine past are in reality self-deceptive paradoxes of the same kind we have just described, in that every model of a pristine past superior to the present (e.g., Voltaire's "noble savage," Marx's "primitive communism," Margaret Mead's innocently promiscuous Samoans) is inevitably a kind of fiction. Since we cannot actually return to the past, at least until someone invents a time machine, we can only surmise, speculate, and make educated guesses about it, and more often than not, our guesses presuppose that the present stage of things represents a declension from a superior level in the past, a fall from Eden, an Age of Lead following ages of Gold, Silver, and Bronze. We sincerely imagine ourselves to have recovered the true past, but often it is instead a vision, an agenda, of the way we wish the present were and the future to be.

The scholarly quest for the historical Jesus has provided a double example. Historical-critical scholars from Hermann Samuel Reimarus in the eighteenth century to John Dominic Crossan today have maintained that the way Jesus is portrayed is not a simple description of the historical Jesus. Rather, it represents a portrait overlaid by many successive layers of repainting as Jesus was gradually retouched and transformed into the likeness of the churches' evolving dogma. Partisans of various sides of various christological disputes tried to refashion a Jesus who would provide an authoritative pedigree for their own views (e.g., on fasting, the mission to the gentiles, the question of circumcision). In an effort to strip away the falsifying alterations, critical scholars have sought to rediscover the historical Jesus so that his radical teachings might once again challenge and energize modern men and women and shake Christianity out of its dogmatic slumber.

Have they succeeded? The idea of a restored, pristine, authentic Jesus has indeed caught fire; many people are excited by it and motivated to great deeds. But all we can be sure of is that the new portraits of the historical Jesus are powerful. What we can never be sure of is that we got it right. We may have somehow hit the bull's-eye, but we can never know. What we *can* be sure of is that our "historical Jesus" construct is a christological model we have devised, based on our own selective sifting of the scriptural evidence, just as Athanasius, Apollinarius, and Nestorius did. And we have "marketed" it as a new alternative to the old church model of Jesus. Thus any historical Jesus construct is certainly a new christological option even if it also happens to hit upon what Jesus of Nazareth was really like. Albert Schweitzer, in his great book *The Quest of the Historical Jesus,* skewered most of the previous attempts to restore the "historical Jesus," showing how each theoretical Jesus "just happened" to mirror the theological preferences and social agendas of the scholar himself.

In other words, the scholars were doing pretty much the same thing the early Christians were: imagining a Jesus in their own image. Their historical Jesuses are not so much what Jesus *was* as what he *should have been.* The sort of Jesus who could serve as the figurehead for the creation of a desirable kind of Christianity. So what tries to be the rediscovered past is really a novelty, pointing the way not to the past but to the future. We might sum up the tendency of all such "reconstructions" with the popular movie title *Back to the Future.*

Seen this way, similarities between the Latter-day Saint movement and the Campbellite Restoration movement make new sense. When the Campbellite sects blazed a trail "back to the Bible"—that is, to the early church of the New Testament—they unwittingly retrojected onto the past their own ideas of how the church *ought* to be. Obviously, Alexander Campbell and the others derived their ideals from a selective reading of New Testament documents, noticing certain things and ignoring others, so it was not as if they had created their scriptural prototype out of thin air. And by the same token, neither had Joseph Smith. Assuming he was the author of the Book of Mormon, Smith's picture of a pristine American Christianity was in fact his own biblically-informed ideal of what American Christianity in his own day ought to become. And for a great many Americans, it would. His creation and retrojection of a superior biblical past is simply the most dramatic and thorough-going of all "restorationist" creations.[6]

Thus far, I have suggested that if Joseph Smith is to be considered not the excavator and translator but the author of the Book of Mormon, the situation is far removed from that of some crude hoax or practical joke. The creative fabrication of an ancient document is in natural continuity with the process of historical reconstruction. Just as the latter is an attempt to move from ancient evidence to a new product synthesizing some of that evidence, so is the former. The difference between them is important, but only in some senses, not in others. The pseudepigraphist understands that he is fashioning a version of events that almost certainly never actually occurred. It would be the wildest stroke of luck if he had chanced upon an ancient reality, and he would never be able to know that he had. But really, how much different is the position of the historian? He, too, is exercising historical imagination to paint a plausible picture of what *might* have happened in the past. True, he is bound to the extant evidence more closely than the pseudepigraphical writer who feels free to imagine new characters and events. But the historian, too, may posit characters of which he knows nothing but who are likely enough to be equivalent to real characters who must have played analogous roles, even though no specific evidence of them happens to survive. Surely Napoleon had various advisers. If no evidence of their identities and words happens to survive (there is no real reason it should), then may we not sketch out such characters and assign them names? Journalists do this all the time. Granted, the historian may not feel entitled to do it, but historical novelists do. And the farther we go into the past, the smaller the gap between historians and historical novelists. Granted the analogy between Joseph Smith and historical critics eventually runs thin and peters out, but that it extends so far is the surprising thing.

NARRATIVE WORLDS WITHOUT END

Where that analogy ends, another, even closer one begins. I already referred to the analogy between the books of Deuteronomy and Mormon, both being judged by modern critics as unhistorical pseudepigrapha (scriptural texts penned under the name of an ancient author). What Joseph Smith did, as historical critics understand the matter, is exactly what all ancient pseudepigraphists did, and he belongs to an illustrious company including authors of the Book of Daniel, the Book of Deuteronomy, the *Book of Zohar*; the Pastoral Epistles (1 and 2 Timothy, Titus), not to mention a greater or lesser number of other epistles attributed to Paul; 1 and 2 Peter; 1, 2, and 3 Enoch; 1, 2, and 3 Baruch; the *Apocalypse of Moses*, Madame Blavatsky's *Book of Dzyan*, and a number of "rediscovered" Tibetan Buddhist texts.[7] But is this group a company of saints or a rogues' gallery? Traditionally, apologists and polemicists alike have equated "pseudepigraphist" with "fraud" or "liar." There is a trivial sense in which such a characterization is correct.

The pseudepigraphist is a liar in the same sense that a fiction writer is a liar and a deceiver. That is, even though the book jacket be labeled "fiction," the writer strives to woo the reader into a state of "temporary willing suspension of disbelief" that Coleridge called "poetic faith." For the time being, the reader, as also the viewer of a play, allows himself or herself to be drawn into the events, to be moved by the fortunes and misfortunes of the characters. One enters a fictive, narrative world in order to feel and experience things one would never otherwise experience. We now recognize, as Aristotle did, the wholesome and edifying function of temporarily suspending disbelief. But it has not always been so. Shakespeare and others were obliged to reassure their audiences that what they were about to see or read was "The *True History* of Richard III," or whomever.[8] Some were not able to understand the difference between fiction and lying. The problem was that of "bifurcation," the reduction of a complex choice to an over-simple one. One's alternatives are *not* either "fact or deception," "hoax or history." Were the parables of Jesus factual or deceptive? Did he intend anyone to think he was talking about the case of a real prodigal son of whose improbable homecoming he had yesterday read in the *Galilee Gazette?* Of course not; he knew that his audience knew he was making it up as he went. And this is pretty much the same kind of "deception" practiced by the scriptural pseudepigraphist, whether ancient or modern.

It may help at this point to remind ourselves of the distinction between the *author* of a story and the *narrator.* The author is the actual person composing and producing the text. Let Herman Melville serve as an example. The narrator, on the other hand, is one of the characters in the story, from whose viewpoint the story is related. So the textual self-designation "I" refers not to the author but to the narrator. "Call me Ishmael." Does this mean that Melville is trying to deceive us as to what his name is? No, of course not. We once again temporarily suspend disbelief, entering into a narrative world. While inside it, we listen to the narrator, a fictive construct of the author. For the meantime, the author is forgotten. "Ishmael is certainly a tough old salt!" one reader may remark to another. But when they have both laid the finished novel aside, they will begin to speak of Melville's, not Ishmael's, literary strengths and weaknesses. Accordingly, we ought to realize that for Joseph Smith to be the author of the Book of Mormon, with Nephi, Mormon, and Moroni as narrators, makes moot the old debates over whether Smith was a charlatan.

Following Hans Frei, many recent Protestant theologians (George Lindbeck, William C. Placher), recognizing the narrative nature of the Bible including both its largely fictive character and the pseudonymity of most of the writers, bid us enter into that narrative world, that sacred epic, ourselves and so become real-life participants in the drama of salvation history.[9] We transcend the mundane world by bathing it with the illumination of our narrative imagination. We think this or that "is going on" in the real world, that life is "about this or that"; in short, we identify which dramatic scenario we symbolically play out on the stage of life. If we choose a scenario in which things are tending toward a happy ending when nice guys finish first, we no doubt choose to act in that role as best we can. If we imagine no story to be taking place around us, we may stop trying to get somewhere; we may conclude that life is meaningless and we may stop trying to achieve anything. All meaning is the imposition of a narrative world onto the ambiguous text of life. Joseph Smith afforded people the opportunity to write themselves into the plots of both the epic of biblical Israel and that of American pioneer Christianity. Like Civil War reenactment hobbyists who relive a saga of the past or we who do the same every Sunday in a worship service. We have sought out a brief vacation in what Berger and Luckmann (*The Social Construction of Reality*) call a "finite province of meaning"[10] where, for the duration, we believe not in electric lights and the radio, as Bultmann said, but in demons, angels, and spirits.[11] Afterward we return to the larger, public world of experience where none of these stories seems to describe current events.

Devout Mormons, like other Christians, have internalized the narrative world of scripture so that they carry it with them and see all experience through the colored lenses it provides. Just as Don Quixote, living in the benign delusion of a chivalric romance, saw his Lady Dulcinea in the tattered rags of a peasant wench, so does the Christian see his Lord, the Son of Man, in the smudged and blood-shot face of "the least of these my brethren." So does the Mormon Christian, but he also sees the epic of Israel replaying itself in the pioneer struggles of the North American continent. The meaning of our lives resides in the particular story we choose to live out by way of exemplar or of script. In creating the whole saga of the Nephites and Lamanites in America, Joseph Smith created a new world of meaning in which millions of people continue to find rewarding and fulfilling roles to play. In this, his achievement as a foundational figure may be compared with that of Christ: "If anyone is in Christ, there is a new creation. Behold, the old has passed away, the new has come" (2 Cor. 5:17).

"WHY IS IT THAT YOU ASK MY NAME?"

Envision the situation that led to the production of pseudepigrapha in the ancient world and in the modern alike. It all began with the process of closing the canon of scripture. Josephus informed his readers that the authority of the Jewish priests and scribes had come to substitute for that of the ancient prophets since the voice of prophecy had long ago fallen silent. Christians reading Josephus often read him naively at this point. They cite Josephus and then point to John the Baptist as a renewal of prophecy after centuries of silence. They fail to realize that Josephus was giving a *pre*scriptive account, not a *de*scriptive account. The priestly and scribal establishment position had officially closed the canon of prophecy. It wasn't that new prophets were no longer forthcoming. Rather, the point was that they were no longer welcome.[12]

The Bible makes clear that prophets had never been particularly welcome. Like Homer's Cassandra, their voices usually went unheeded and were often silenced by force. If a prophet were sufficiently popular, the authorities had to appear to take him seriously to maintain credibility with their flock (cf. Mk. 11:27-33). The first step was to silence the prophet; the second was to domesticate his inconvenient oracles by a process of official exegesis. Jesus satirized this as an adornment of the tombs of the old prophets while secretly building new ones for their present-day successors (Matt. 23:29-31). "Blessed are you when all men despise you and cast out your name as evil, for so they did to the prophets who were before you. But woe to you when all men speak well of you, for so they extolled the false prophets" (Lk. 6:22, 26) of the past—*and* the *true* prophets after they *killed* them!

In view of this situation, what was a new visionary to do? He had a message to declare, but there was no point in simply announcing it publicly, only to be carried away and executed. Then who would hear the message? So pseudepigraphy was born. Whereas the old prophets had *spoken* their messages, the new ones, the pseudepigraphists, *wrote* their oracles and circulated them in this form as an underground *samizdat.* They knew it was important even when speaking in the name of the Lord, to be speaking also in the name of a famous prophet. One might have established one's own prophetic charisma by personal appearances as Isaiah and Jeremiah had, but personal appearances were dangerous. To gain a hearing, to have their oracles taken seriously, they wrote under the names of Enoch, Moses, Daniel, and Baruch. The words may have rung true enough on their own, but they first had to be read, and that was the trick. So one put Daniel's or Moses' name on it, and the reader soon found himself recognizing the Word of God no matter the name of the human channel through which it may have come. Did it matter much to an ancient Jewish reader that the Word of God had come through Isaiah or through Jeremiah? No more than it does to most modern readers. All that matters is that it is the prophetic Word of God. And then, it ought to hardly matter if the writer is Isaiah of Jerusalem or a later visionary appropriating his name as in the cases of the Second and Third Isaiah and the *Ascension of Isaiah*.[13]

The closing of a canon is momentous in the history of any religion. It signals that the establishment, which caused the canon to be closed and decided what belonged in it and what did not, has decided that the formative period is over and that the religion must be standardized and consolidated.[14] You are setting about building the ark of salvation, and you don't want anyone rocking the boat after you've built it. You don't want to hammer out a doctrine of the Trinity only to find some prophet popping up who announces the revelation of a *fourth* person in the Godhead![15] So the guardians of the newly minted orthodoxy, disdaining the doctrines taught in this or that gospel or prophet, cross these off the canonical list. They claim the prerogative of interpreting the contents of what remains: "First of all, you must know this: no prophecy of scripture is a matter of one's own interpretation" (2 Pet. 1:20). Thus the long unwillingness of Roman Catholicism to open the Bible for everyone's scrutiny. Zechariah knew the situation well: "And if anyone again appears as a prophet, his father and mother who bore him will say to him, 'You shall not live, for you speak lies in the name of Yahve' ... On that day every prophet will be ashamed of his vision when he prophesies; he will not put on a hairy mantle [the distinctive uniform of prophets] in order to deceive, but he will say, 'I am no prophet, but I am a tiller of the soil. ...'" (Zech. 13:3-5).

In fact, these very oracles are in a section of the book that critical scholars dub Deutero-Zechariah. The original Zechariah was some sort of cultic prophet attached to the temple and its hierarchy, the very group who were trying to clamp the lid on populist prophecy. In order to still have a chance to be heard, someone—one of those later prophets "ashamed of his vision" and not daring to publish it under his own name—retreated behind the pen name of an older prophet. Having discovered his imposture, though not his real name, we still call him "Deutero-Zechariah" or "the Second Zechariah." But the name hardly matters; the content does, and this is why "Deutero-Zechariah" set pen to paper. If the sharp edges of the old prophets and seers have been smoothed out by harmonizing exegesis, then it is the pseudepigraphist's aim to sharpen that edge again by introducing new and harsh words under the prophets' names. All right, the new visionary may not dare appear in public, but the authorities will not dare to condemn "newly discovered" writings by the old, canonical prophets. In this way, the newer prophets sought and managed to slip under or over the fence built around the canon.

It may seem a great irony that a religion whose leaders claim the prophetic word as their charter of authority will at the same time be opposed to receiving any new prophecy. But it is no irony at all, for the very notion of a canon of scripture denotes that the living voice of prophecy has been smothered out and replaced by scribal authority exercised by the official exegetes who make the old oracles ring not with God's voice but with their own. As Paul declares: "I have no word from the Lord, but I give my opinion as one who by the grace of the Lord has been found trustworthy" (1 Cor. 7:25; cf. 2 Tim. 1:2-3). Jesus "taught them as one who had authority, and not as the scribes" (Mk. 1:22)–which is why the scribal establishment decided they had to be rid of him. It is well depicted in Dostoyevsky's "Parable of the Grand Inquisitor" in *The Brothers Karamazov.* Jesus reappears on earth–and the first thing the church does is to arrest him and condemn him to the stake. It has taken the church long enough to consolidate its absolute power over the minds and consciences of the faithful, and they are not about to allow Jesus' living voice to return to stir things up. These are the battle lines: canon versus prophecy. The guardians of the canon use the fossil-prophecy of the past in order to turn back the challenge of living prophets by using their own weapon against them. "We know that God has spoken to Moses, but, as for this man, we do not even know where he comes from!" (Jn. 9:29).

In short, both the new prophets and the establishment are trying to hide behind the names of the ancient, canonical prophets in order to claim authority for what each side is saying. The establishment scribes are using the corpus of the scriptural prophets as something of a ventriloquist dummy to spout their own views, but just as surely, the pseudepigraphists are impersonating the old prophets, speaking with their own voices while donning the deceptive Esau-mask of pseudepigraphy. The question is: who wears the mantle of the old prophets?

We see exactly the same situation repeated only a couple of centuries later when both orthodox bishops and heretical dissidents alike claimed apostolic succession. If the Pope of Rome claimed to be the successor of Linus, Peter's appointed successor in Rome, Basilides the Gnostic claimed to have received his *gnosis* at the hands of Glaukias, the secretary of Peter. Both are vying for recognition as the true heirs of the apostle. No wonder so many New Testament pseudepigraphs were penned in the early church, and no wonder so many of them were excluded from the official established list. The same thing would happen yet again some centuries later when Muslim scholars decided they had to establish criteria for sifting out false *hadith* (tradition) from genuine ones, since all tried to claim the authority of a traditional saying of Muhammad in order to promote their own views.

Even so, Joseph Smith, disillusioned by the strife and confusion of rival Christian sects, each of which claimed the authority of the Bible for its distinctive teachings, finally decided to cut the Gordian Knot of Bible exegesis by creating a new scripture that would undercut the debating of the denominations and render them superfluous. He sought to found a new Christianity on a completely new basis: a new scripture, a third testament called the Book of Mormon, from an old source, the Bible. And just as the theologians of the Protestant sects followed the example of the Pharisees of old, resting upon the scribal authority of exegeting *ancient* revelation, Smith was wise enough to adopt the old strategy of putting forth his own revelations in the outward form of an *ancient* manuscript, a pseudepigraph. If only old prophets are to be taken seriously, then by all means let's write one! It's the only way left to gain media access!

Smith hardly intended to reopen the gates of prophecy to all who might feel themselves inspired. His own pseudepigraph served rather as a new and ready-made canon, an authoritative pedigree to root his new community in the holy past, to give it instant venerable equality with even superiority over—the established Protestant sects. Prophecy would continue, but only through his own mouth, as he soon stipulated.

So far, I have tried to indicate that, far from being a mischievous or malicious hoaxer, Joseph Smith was simply doing what the authors of the various biblical and extra-biblical pseudepigrapha were doing. If we still wish to dismiss Smith as a hoaxer and a liar, or, to put it another way, if we feel entitled to decree that God could never sink to inspiring a pseudepigraph[16] (and if we are privy to the literary tastes of the Almighty, we are claiming to be prophets ourselves!), then we have no option but to dismiss the *biblical* pseudepigraphs along with the Book of Mormon. What's good for the goose is good for the gander. What's good for the stick of Ephraim is good for the stick of Judah. This point hardly escaped the literalistic biblicists of the past who tried to defend the historical genuineness of 2 and 3 Isaiah, 2 Zechariah, Deuteronomy, Daniel, and the Pastoral Epistles just as zealously as they sought to debunk the Book of Mormon. A case in point would be Gordon H. Fraser, author of the polemical *What Does the Book of Mormon Teach?* One can scarcely imagine him welcoming Higher Critics of scripture to apply the same critical tools on Fraser's beloved Bible as he himself has used in vivisecting the Mormon scripture.[17]

Such apologists/polemicists professed to see no problem in accepting the claim of the Book of Daniel to have been penned in the Babylonian and Persian periods and then sealed away to be discovered by Jews living at the time of the events predicted in the book (Dan. 12:4, 9), the period immediately preceding the ejection of the Seleucid tyranny from Judea. No matter that the historical descriptions nearer the ostensible time of Daniel are filled with linguistic and historical anachronisms while the sections closer to the end are eagle-eyed in their predictions of Antiochus IV Epiphanies, even of his troop movements in Palestine. When Gabriel directs Daniel to seal up the prophecy and stash it away for the benefit of readers hundreds of years into the future, the same alarm ought to be going off in the fundamentalist apologist's head as when faced with Mormon claims that Joseph Smith found a book on Hill Cumorah. Of course, he does not see them the same way since Daniel is part of his Protestant canon, while Mormon is not. Thus the latter may be safely debunked and discredited and thus kept safely outside the charmed circle of the canon, as if by a fiery sword that turns every way, while the former must be kept safe lest it lose its favored position and be "cast forth as an unclean thing" (Ezek. 28) from the Garden of God's Word.

In the wake of historical criticism, which one cannot keep out as long as one resolves with Martin Luther to admit the Grammatico-Historical Method to the study of scripture, reading scripture as any other human writing, most theologians have come to accept that God might inspire an authoritative pseudepigraph as easily as a parable. There no longer seems anything incompatible between a book being scripturally inspired and authoritative on the one hand and being a historically spurious but fictively edifying pseudepigraph on the other. Deuteronomy and its theology are probably taken with much greater seriousness than ever before in Christian history now that its character, and thus its intention, can be truly understood for the first time. In the same way, a new treasure house of riches may be disclosed in the pages of the Book of Mormon once one comes to recognize the skill and the goal of the theological artistry exercised by Joseph Smith as author, not just translator.

I have already indicated that Smith adopted the form of an ancient manuscript as a metaphor for saying that the coming of this Word was "from of old, from ancient days" (Mic. 5:2). If we dismiss his book as a spurious fake, we show the same theologically tin ear the opponents of Jesus had when they said, "How can this man say, 'I came down from heaven'?" "You are not yet fifty years old and you have seen Abraham?" Presently, I will attempt to demonstrate that Smith also followed pretty much the same method of composition as biblical pseudepigraphists. Thus he will come to look more and more like what we are suggesting he was: a writer of new scripture, not merely a discoverer or translator of ancient scripture. But we must first pause to ask if, however consistent with the goals and methods of biblical pseudepigraphists, such a role for Smith would not be incompatible with his own claims for himself and Latter-day Saint claims about him.

In a word, no. We have already recalled the fact that, after setting forth the Book of Mormon, Smith began to prophesy in his own voice. The Mormon canon contains many such inspired speeches by the Mormon prophet. The work of a prophet is not that of a transcriber or translator. To equate the two is to deny the vast gap between Moses and the latter scribes, the distance between the prophet Jeremiah and his secretary Baruch, or between the Gnostic Revealer and the shepherd Muhammad 'Ali al Samman, who chanced upon the Nag Hammadi texts while hiding from his enemies in an Egyptian cave. According to the traditional story of the origins of the Book of Mormon, when read the traditional way, the role of Smith was like that of John the Baptist, hardly that of a prophetic revealer in his own right but rather the herald for *another* who *would* be a prophetic revealer; in Smith's case, a book. Yet this picture belies the central importance of

Smith as revealer, prophet, and Moses-like founder of the Latter-day Saint community. He was a living prophet whose voice was the mouthpiece for God to issue regulations for the fledgling nest of faith, not a mere forerunner or scribal translator.

The closest history-of-religions parallel would be the prophet Muhammad. Like Joseph Smith, Muhammad claimed to be the one to disclose the revelations of a hitherto unknown book. These revelations include hitherto secret histories of prophetic personalities including Noah, Moses, and Jesus. In the case of Muhammad, this book was the "Mother of the Book," the heavenly prototype of the Qur'an (Koran). Muhammad would simply speak forth the revelations dictated to him by the angel Gabriel who read them off the pages of the heavenly original. But this did not make Muhammad any less of a prophet since the book from which he believed himself to be "quoting" ("Qur'an" means "repetition") was a celestial object (analogous to the "Akashic Records") unavailable to human beings in any other form. To say one is conveying the unseen text of a heavenly volume is to say one is the channel for the revelations as they enter into human eyes and ears for the first time. Thus Muhammad was no mere recording secretary but rather a prophet in the strict sense of the word. Later tradition depicted the caliph Uthman as commissioning Zaid ibn Thabit to bring together all extant Qur'an manuscripts and standardize them into a textus receptus, and thus Zaid would be a closer analogy to Joseph Smith on the traditional understanding of Smith as a transcriber and translator of the golden plates. But clearly, Smith is supposed to be on Muhammad's level, not on Zaid's. If Smith were simply equivalent to Zaid or to Baruch instead of Jeremiah, we would have a problem accounting for the full prophetic dignity subsequently ascribed to him. Would not his new character as a prophetic revealer have to be understood as a self-exaltation against the ostensibly sufficient revelation of Mormon and Moroni? Would not Smith actually be interposing himself between the scripture and the faithful? Would it not make better sense all around to suppose that the Book of Mormon itself was the first revelation to come by Joseph Smith, its author? Seen this way, Smith's authorship of the Book of Mormon would simplify rather than complicate, vindicate rather than discredit, his claim to prophetic inspiration.

REFORMED EGYPTIAN AS GLOSSOLALIA

The clue to this as the true scenario lies in Smith's supposed use of the oracular glasses of the urim and thummim. These are said to have enabled him to find clear meaning in a text that was to him but a "field of signifiers" (Roland Barthes) or perhaps to *create* meaning there. The metaphor of the urim and thummim glasses is exactly parallel to Paul's characterizing glossolalia not as a human language unknown to the speaker, an indefensible and absurd claim, but as the ecstatic "tongues of angels" which sing the glories "which man may not utter." While no mortal may render their meaning exactly, it is nonetheless possible, Paul says, to "interpret" them (1 Cor. 12-14). But this is closer to interpreting omens or nonverbal dreams than it is to translating a text. Apollo's oracle at Delphi, overcome with volcanic sulfur fumes, would mumble on in ecstatic gibberish which an interpreter standing by would render roughly into human conceptuality. To imagine glossolalia as a translatable language, as many Pentecostal defenders of the practice do, is to bring the practice into needless discredit since linguistic analysis has more than once demonstrated that there is no syntactical structure among the glossolalic sounds.[18] Pentecostal literalists fear that if they admitted that glossolalia is simply the inspired product of the Spirit-energized glossolalist, rather than of a stenographer taking dictation, the divine quality they attribute to the sounds would be gone. Likewise, we fail to grasp the metaphor of the urim and thummim if we imagine Joseph Smith was simply using something like a translating program on a computer.

If we have ears to hear, we will recognize the urim and thummim tale as a metaphor for Smith looking at America through the lens of the Bible and at the Bible through the lense of the American experience. The Book of Mormon was the inspired result, not an ancient, translated text but a creative extended metaphor. To defend the notion of a genuine ancient manuscript that was translated from an imaginary "Reformed Egyptian" language out of fear that the Book of Mormon will otherwise forfeit its authority is like the Pentecostals trying to convince themselves and others of the truly miraculous character of speaking a genuine ancient language unknown to themselves.

In both cases, the proof of the pudding would seem to reside in the eating, not in the package design and advertising slogans. Why defend a metaphor as if it were a literal fact when factually it is manifestly false and symbolically may be profoundly true? Tongues-speaking is not speaking a genuine foreign language. The Book of Mormon never existed as a set of golden plates in an untranslatable language, either. Neither is the point. Speaking mysteries in the spirit *is* genuinely revelatory and so is a book which translates the frontier heritage of America into the language of the Bible.

Even the designation of the supposed original language of the Book of Mormon can be taken as a clue to the real state of affairs: the term "Reformed Egyptian" carries resonances, first, of the biblical exodus of Israel from Egypt. Americans from Benjamin Franklin onward have seen it as a paradigm for the journey of American colonists and immigrants to freedom in the American "land of promise." And of course, Smith and his followers repeated the Exodus story in their own experience as they moved from the hostile East to the Promised Land of Utah where they could sit in peace, each beneath his vine, and where, delivered out of the hand of their enemies, they might worship without fear. Like Moses, Smith was not destined to enter the land with them, and at the same time, we cannot help but be reminded of "Joseph in Egypt," the persecuted young visionary despised by his contemporaries but called to great things.

Second, the enigmatic term "Reformed Egyptian" signifies the new start Christianity was making in America under Smith's own leadership. Smith had begun what he regarded as a new Reformation in Protestant Christianity. Hence "Reformed Egyptian": that is the language Smith and his Book of Mormon were speaking. It was no more a genuine ancient language than Pentecostal glossolalia is, but it was every bit as much a super-verbal metaphor for new inspiration.

To say the book was rendered from reformed Egyptian was, then, to carry the foundation myths of biblical Israel and Protestant Christianity into modern America. It was to say that that great epic of salvation history was far from over, that it continued to unfold here and now. A powerful image for this is the discovery in one's own time of an ancient American bible. An even more potent image is of *writing* a new chapter of the biblical epic in modern America. This is just what Smith did. There are not *two* authorities vying for priority in Mormonism, Smith's prophecies versus the letter of the inspired text of the Book of Mormon. No, there is only *one* authority: the divinely inspired prophecy of Joseph Smith. And the Book of Mormon *is* the fundamental prophecy of Joseph Smith.

LATTER PROPHETS AND LATTER-DAY SAINTS

Thus far, I have been applying to the study of the Book of Mormon a technique called "form criticism" by some and "genre criticism" by others. Usually, when we speak of the "forms" of biblical literature, we are referring to self-contained passages within a larger book: a type of psalm (a lament, coronation, song of ascents or pilgrimage, wisdom, acrostic, a hymn of praise), a kind of story (controversy, miracle, discipleship paradigm, pronouncement or apophthegm, parable) or saying (aphorism, proverb, Christological "I-saying," a sentence of holy law, a passion prediction), prophecy (oracle of doom, promise of hope, apocalypse), and so on.[19] By contrast, when we speak of *Gattung* or genre, we have in mind a larger literary unit as a whole. Here we might contrast a prophetic book like Isaiah with an apocalypse like Revelation, Daniel, or 4 Ezra. We might contrast Luke's Gospel, a book much like a Hellenistic hero biography,[20] with his Book of Acts, resembling contemporary historical and picaresque novels.[21] We might compare the Pauline corpus with various kinds of ancient correspondence including the personal letter (Philemon), the treatise put in epistolary form (Romans), the church order (cf. the *Manual of Discipline* or the *Didache of the Twelve Apostles to the Gentiles*), or the pseudepigraphical epistle (those attributed to the Cynics, Plato, or Apollonius of Tyana). What we are looking for in all cases is a set of distinctive formal marks identifying a passage or a whole book with others of the same type and function in order to place it in a larger, common category. This may help place it in the stream of evolution of forms and genres. For instance, narratives like those of the Transfiguration of Jesus or of his walking on water, which look much like scenes involving various Greco-Roman "son of god" or "divine man" figures, seem to presuppose a setting in the wider Hellenistic world and thus an origin after Christian missionaries had penetrated the Mediterranean world.

Further study will reveal specific formal categories for individual Book of Mormon passages, but thus far, it is quite clear that the book as a whole fits very comfortably into that broad class of pseudepigrapha which seek, as late-comers, either official entry into the canon or similarly high credibility by using an ancient authority's name. We might get more specific and suggest that the Book of Mormon conforms to the genre of "the Latter Prophets" rather than that of the "Former Prophets." The difference between these two species of biblical books is that the Former Prophets are collections of prophetic oracles or speeches, gathered and recorded by their hearers and disciples (think here of the Book of Isaiah, the Book of Jeremiah, the Qur'an). The Latter Prophets are a series of edifying and usually semi-legendary histories written from the moralistic standpoint of the prophets: when the people are faithful, God's reward follows them. When the nation is unfaithful, they have only God's wrath to look forward to. Since the Babylonian Exile made it clear that the prophets had been quite right about all this, the exiled scribes and priests of Judah compiled what we call the Deuteronomic History (Joshua, Judges, Samuel, and Kings) according to the prophetic philosophy of history. They assembled historical stories, sagas, and legends, welding them into one overarching unity. All victories were made into deliverances by God, defeats and oppressions into divine scourges. When a king goes against God's Word, he is punished, while the faithful kings are honored by God. Another book of this kind, though written too late for inclusion in the "Prophets" category, is the Chronicler's history (Ezra, Nehemiah, 1 and 2 Chronicles). It is clear that the Book of Mormon belongs with these works. It is a sort of Deuteronomic history of ancient America, illustrating its preachings with object lessons of the fates of wicked Lamanites and virtuous Nephites. It represents an artificial effort to extend the biblical histories up nearer our own day.

It may help to remind ourselves what sort of book the Book of Mormon is *not.* For one thing, it is not a Gospel, does not even contain a Gospel, even though Jesus Christ appears as a character in the Book of Mormon. He appears there almost in passing, just as the Deuteronomic historians found space for several long and short episodes of Elijah and Elisha and their miracles and disciples. There are epistles, at least letters, but these are embedded, "imbricated" (Roland Barthes), in the surrounding narrative, playing a role analogous to that of a Greek chorus in a play, commenting on the action as it moves along so the reader can keep up with the flow. Luke uses such letters throughout the Book of Acts. Luke has much in common with the Old Testament Deuteronomic history, as recent scholars have noted. So does the Book of Mormon.

PROPHECY AND PALIMPSEST

Recently scholars have reopened an old debate over biblical narrative books, a debate that has interesting implications for our estimation of the Book of Mormon. Critical analysis of the Bible began with seventeenth-century French physician Jean Astruc who suggested that the Pentateuch was less likely a single work from the pen of Moses than a compilation of pre-existent source documents. These, he reasoned, might be distinguished from one another and reconstructed by means of distinguishing the names used for the Deity: Yahve ("Jehovah"), Elohim, Adonai, Elyon, etc. Not long thereafter, Baruch Spinoza, a Jewish philosopher and mystic, carried this study further, as did a whole series of eighteenth- and nineteenth-century German savants culminating with Julius Wellhausen (*Prolegomena to the History of Israel*). Wellhausen believed, and most scholarship follows his lead, that virtually every verse of the Pentateuch could be confidently assigned to one or another of these earlier source documents (J, E, D, and P). The stylistic and theological features of each source were so distinctive that there was seldom any danger of confusing them. Wellhausen spoke about each of the early documents as if it were the unified work of a single creative author. Wellhausen crowned the Yahvist writer, J, the great literary genius of the Pentateuch, the Priestly writer, P, the worst of the four because of his endless windy repetition and love for great masses of dry statistics.

Wellhausen's astonishingly comprehensive book was eventually to sweep the field and become critical orthodoxy. But Herman Gunkel arose with form criticism to challenge Wellhausen's conclusions.[22] He pointed out that the narratives of the Pentateuch, and of the Deuteronomic History as well, bore the tell-tale marks of transcribed oral tradition. This meant that Wellhausen's four authors were rather more like collectors or compilers of popular traditional stories, analogous to the Brothers Grimm who fanned out over the German countryside to interview old nurses and grandmothers about the earliest extant versions of the old fairy tales before they became lost to history.

Gunkel's approach was by no means incompatible with Wellhausen's since the latter had never claimed that the Yahvist, the Elohist, and the Priestly writer were composing out of whole cloth from their own imaginations. The only adjustment one need make in Wellhausen's theory was to see the four Pentateuchal writers and the Deuteronomic historians as compilers who naturally put their own stamp on their material as they retold it and worked it up into a consecutive narrative. The result was that scholars would look both for signs of earlier oral transmission of a particular passage ("pericope") and for signs of the individual compiler's rewriting or redaction of the passage. Both techniques together illuminated the texts to an even greater extent than Wellhausen's original source criticism. Now one could try to demonstrate both the nature of the source material and what the author had done with it. The comparison would often yield new data on what goal or effect the writer or redactor was trying to achieve by editing in the precise way he did. This method became known as "redaction criticism." Much was learned by applying these critical tools to the Old Testament and, later, to the New Testament as well.[23]

But in recent years some scholars have questioned both the presuppositions and the methods of form criticism. Beginning with Güttgemanns (*Candid Questions concerning Form Criticism*), many scholars have turned the microscope on the narrative materials of both testaments. Frank Kermode, Robert Fowler, Werner Kelber, and Frans Neirynck[24] have shown how deeply the distinctive vocabulary and structure of the evangelist Mark penetrated his text. There seems to be less and less need to posit a traditional basis for biblical narratives, or rather perhaps, one may minimize the extent to which the biblical narrators were dependent upon any prior sources they may have used. In the latter event, the biblical authors would have simply derived ideas from traditional stories but retold them entirely from their own standpoint, just as one might today compare Hollywood Bible epics with the underlying Bible stories.

The more of the narrative that makes sense as the product of the author's skill, the less sure we can be that there ever *was* a source. He may have been, as we have just observed, less slavishly bound to the source's wording, but then, are we sure we are justified any longer in believing he was dependent upon a prior document at all? The evidence for a source has faded as scholars are now beginning to move toward a very different approach. It may be, say scholars like Randel Helms, Thomas L. Brodie, and John Dominic Crossan, that the Gospel writers did not so much employ oral traditions as the basis for their work as they have perhaps rather taken Old Testament texts, disregarded the plots, and reshuffled various descriptive details and narrative sequences abstracted from the larger story to use as building blocks for their own new stories, which are then provided with a definite biblical ring and yet without recalling a particular story.

Helms, Brodie, and Crossan all break down numerous Gospel stories into various phrases and motifs derived from this and that Old Testament story. Crossan isolates all the Old Testament passages which the Gospel crucifixion narratives cite as prophetic predictions of the death of Jesus and proceeds to demonstrate how the Gospel stories seem to have been composed not from historical memory of the events but by connecting the dots provided by the Old Testament passages. It is not that Mark's account is simple reportage of events that mirrored the "predictions" of Psalm 22. Mark does not even refer to Psalms. It begins to appear as if Mark possessed no traditional story, only the bare preaching that Jesus had died on the cross. The rest he had to fill in. As his material, he used the collection of Passion "testimonia" drawn by early Christian preachers from the scriptures, especially the Psalms.[25]

Brodie, to take but a single example, derives Luke's story of the anointing of Jesus (Lk. 7:36-50) from the tales of Elisha in 2 Kings 4:1-37 involving the widow with the vessels of oil and the Shunammite woman. As Brodie sees it, Luke derived the character of Simon the Pharisee, Jesus' rather chilly host, from the Shunammite who is pictured as initially wary of Elisha and from Elisha's disciple Gehazi who fails in the healing mission. The sinful woman who anoints Jesus is a character combining traits of the Shunammite and the widow of the guild prophet who, at Elisha's direction, pours out the self-replenishing oil to pay her creditors. The creditors in Jesus' parable of the two debtors, contained in the anointing story, were suggested by the creditors of the prophet's widow who threatened to take her two children as collateral for her debts. Simon's invitation to Jesus was derived from the Shunammite's invitation to stay with her. Her miraculous conception of a son led Luke to imply, Brodie thinks, that Simon the Pharisee had a change of heart, a sort of rebirth. The debt of the sinful woman is a moral one, while that of the guild prophet's widow is a financial one. Both debt crises are mediated by the prophet, Jesus in the one case, Elisha in the other. Thus the Jesus story has been derived from the two Elisha tales, while not actually modeled upon them.[26]

Helms concentrates on the Gospels, but here is an example of his work on another narrative, one from the Acts of the Apostles. He traces a series of probable connections between the opening chapters of Ezekiel in the Greek Septuagint translation and the story of Peter's vision in Acts 10:9-16. Ezekiel has a series of visions which teach him what he will have to endure as a prophet of God. In the first one (Ezek. 1:1), Ezekiel sees heaven opened (*enoichthesan hoi ouranoi*), while in Acts 10:11 Peter sees "heaven opened" (*ten ouranon aneogmenon*). In a second vision, Ezekiel is shown a honeyed scroll and told to eat (*phage*) it (Ezek. 2:9), while Peter is shown a great sheet of sailcloth containing all manner of animals, including those deemed unclean by Leviticus. He, too, is commanded, "Arise, Peter, kill and eat (*phage*)!" In a subsequent vision, Ezekiel is told to eat bread baked over a dung fire, something ritually unclean, which he, as a priest, is ill-inclined to do. He retorts to God: "By no means, Lord!" (*Medamos, Kyrie*), just as Peter does at the command to prepare unclean food: "By no means, Lord!" (*Medamos, Kyrie*). It is hard to resist the conclusion Helms reaches: Luke has invented the episode of Peter's vision based on the series of visions in the beginning of Ezekiel. Luke didn't even have to read very far into Ezekiel to find enough details to mix together a new story.[27]

While this sort of cannibalizing of old texts to fashion new ones may seem arbitrary to some readers, we must note that the technique is not merely the product of modern theory, as if modern scholars had simply inferred that the Gospel writers *must* have been doing something of the kind. These practices of recombining bits and pieces from this and that to create, in effect, a new Bible verse have long been familiar as a standard exegetical procedure of the old rabbis. For instance, Mark's citation of Isaiah (in Mk. 1:2-3, "As it is written in Isaiah the prophet, 'Behold. I send my messenger before thy face, who shall prepare thy way; the voice of one crying in the wilderness: Prepare the way of the Lord, make his paths straight.'") turns out, in fact, to be a conflation of three Old Testament passages: Malachi 3:1 ("Behold I send my messenger ["angel"] to prepare the way before me, and the Lord whom you seek will suddenly come to his temple; the messenger [angel] of the covenant in whom you delight, behold, he is coming, says the Lord of hosts"); Exodus 23:20 ("Behold, I send an angel [messenger] before you, to guard you on the way and to bring you to the place I have prepared"); and Isaiah 40:3 ("A voice cries: 'In the wilderness prepare the way of the Lord, make straight in the desert a highway for our God'").

Notice the effect produced by the silent juxtaposition of the three verses. Taking "my messenger" from Malachi with "to prepare thy way" from Exodus and "Behold, I send [my] angel/messenger before ..." from both texts (a similarity that had already led Jewish scribes to conflate the two verses even before Mark's time), Mark creates a new text. Additionally, Mark alters Isaiah 40:3 slightly, making it say "a voice crying in the wilderness, [saying] 'Prepare the way of the Lord'" instead of, as originally, "a voice crying, 'In the wilderness prepare the way of the Lord.'" In the latter instance, "wilderness" denoted the preparation of a clear path for the Jewish exiles from Babylon back through the desert to Canaan, while in the former the voice itself is in the "wilderness" and the way is metaphorical; a similar shift in meaning also occurs in the Dead Sea Scrolls' citation of this Isaiah verse. Obviously, none of the three passages originally meant anything like what Mark makes of them in combined form. We might question whether this sort of treatment of the biblical text even counts as exegesis, but in fact, it was characteristic of Mark's time and of esoteric Jewish exegesis for long afterward.

Here we have the distinctly unProtestant notion that, being a divinely inspired book, the Bible was susceptible to all manner of clever manipulation. It meant whatever one might make it seem to mean since it could be no coincidence that the text should yield up such fortuitous recombinations. God must have intended any message the imaginative exegete could squeeze out of it by hook or by crook.[28] There are well-known Kabbalistic methods including *Temurah* (reading the Hebrew text from left to right like a word search puzzle to find hidden "backward masking" revelations), *Notarikon* (reading each letter of a word as the first letter of the words in an implied sentence of cryptic revelation), and *Gematria* (reading the letters as if the digits stood for numbers so that a word could be interchanged with any word elsewhere in scripture that added up to the same sum). New revelations excavated by such methods were called "combinations," and to devise striking new ones was a mark of spiritual enlightenment. In Isaac Beshevis Singer's novel *Satan in Goray,* one particular Kabbalistic guru, Reb Gedaliya, is acclaimed for this: "[H]e ... adorned his speech with mystical combinations and permutations."[29] An angel proclaims, "All the worlds on high do tremble at the unions he doth form. The power of his combinations reaches even to the heavenly mansions. From these combinations seraphim and angels twist coronets for the Divine Presence."[30]

In all the cases treated by Crossan, Helms, and Brodie,[31] the verbal parallels and motifs are clear enough that we can see the use of Old Testament materials. It would be extremely difficult to try to break down an Old Testament story into such building blocks from earlier sources. But in the heyday of form criticism, scholars identified passages in Mark's Gospel that seemed to derive from orally transmitted traditions, something like the individual *hadith* of the prophet Muhammad. As we have seen, scholars now attribute more and more of the stories to Mark himself. Yet, even here, it is sometimes possible to spot pre-existent oral forms, as Dennis R. MacDonald tries to do in *The Legend and the Apostle: The Battle for Paul in Story and Canon,* dislodging three of the major stories of Paul from the literary tapestry of the *Acts of Paul.* As we read them now, the tales are woven into the seamless fabric of the work as a whole, but there are still some formal factors giving evidence of an earlier, traditional form, despite the thorough retelling in the author's own vocabulary.[32]

It would take a large-scale scrutiny of the Book of Mormon, and in minute detail, to determine if there is evidence of oral, preliterary traditions underlying the stories of the book. If scholars were to conclude that the narrative of the Book of Mormon had been worked up from traditional material, this would go a long way toward vindicating the claim of the book to be based on ancient accounts of ancient events, even though such a conclusion would not fit very well the accounts given in the book of its own composition by eye-witnesses. But on the whole, thus far it appears that the Book of Mormon is the product of the kind of process discussed by Helms, Brodie, and Crossan: the scrambling of motifs and distinctive phrases from previous *literary texts* in order to produce a new text of the same basic type.

By way of contrast, in Smith's Inspired Version of the Bible, we have something very much like the tendentious spot-revisions that traditional redaction critics traced in the use that both Matthew and Luke made of Mark. If it were determined that Joseph Smith's *Grundschrift* ("ground work") for the Book of Mormon was the *View of the Hebrews*[33] rather than the Bible, we could do more traditional redaction criticism as a prior stage of analysis. He might be shown to have utilized many elements from the earlier work and yet fleshed them out in a completely distinctive way, much as the evangelist John has done with the traditions he had in common with the Synoptists Matthew, Mark, and Luke.

If the Book of Mormon is the literary creation of Joseph Smith, who wrote new biblical-sounding stories by combining familiar biblical vocabulary and motifs, then we may do exactly the same sort of comparative redactional analysis on the Book of Mormon that scholars have been doing on the Bible. Smith's apparent, fundamental source material still survives: the Bible. Like the Gospel writers as understood by Crossan, Brodie, and Helms, Joseph Smith seems to have created new holy fictions by running the old ones through the shredder and reassembling the shreds in wholly new combinations. His method appears to be precisely that of the old rabbis and of the New Testament evangelists. So, not only did Smith do the same sort of thing biblical writers themselves did to produce new Bible text, he even did it the same way, as I hope now to demonstrate by turning to a specific passage of the Book of Mormon.

NEPHITE BODHISATTVAS

Let us choose for closer scrutiny a section of Mormon scripture, 3 Nephi 19 and 28, which tells of Jesus ordaining a Nephite set of twelve disciples, three of whom are granted supernatural longevity in order to continue the work of preaching the gospel until the second advent of Christ. We will compare the episode of the three Nephite apostles with a parallel account glossing John 21:22 that appears in Doctrine and Covenants 7.

In 3 Nephi 19, Jesus names the Nephite Twelve who, on the spot, fulfill the command of Jesus in Matthew's Great Commission, teaching the multitudes what Jesus has taught them, which is to pray to the Father in Jesus' own name. On the same occasion, the Twelve are filled with the descending Holy Spirit: "And behold, they were encircled about as if it were by fire; and it came down from heaven, and the multitude did witness it, and did bear record" (19:14). Obviously, this whole sequence is meant to explicitly recall and replay the New Testament events whereby the original apostles were chosen for their mission and sent forth. Those events are telescoped here as the narrative jumps, so to speak, from Mark 3 to Acts 2, from the calling and numbering of the disciples to their endowment with the Spirit. There are several interesting inferences to be drawn.

First, since this sequence is a cameo of the longer Gospel-Acts sequence, what 3 Nephi does is provide a commentary by Joseph Smith on that original sequence. He has produced what he sees as the gist of the original, which is a legitimization myth for a group of leaders to mind the store in the absence of Jesus (Max Weber's "routinization of charisma"). The whole Mark-Acts sequence is based on the Pentateuchal accounts of Moses heeding Jethro's advice to share the burden with a chosen group of seventy elders. In Exodus 18, these men are barely chosen before they are endowed with the Holy Spirit. This pattern is broadly reproduced in Mark 3 where we can detect an underlying pre-Markan version in vv. 20-21, 31-32, 13-19, exactly paralleling Exodus 18:5-7, 13-27. Acts 2 reflects the alternate account of the same event (Num. 11:16-17, 24-30), in which these seventy assistants receive the spirit of Moses, much as elsewhere the spirit of Elijah rests on Elisha (2 Kgs. 2:9-11).

By chopping all the intervening material in the Gospels between the initial calling of the Twelve and their endowment with the Spirit, Smith has correctly recognized that both stories are functionally equivalent, both of them trying to buttress the ecclesiastical authority of the college of apostles. To say that Jesus chose them *before* his death and resurrection means much the same as saying the Spirit filled them, thus placing his *Imprimatur* on them, *after* the death and resurrection. Of the two, we may guess that the Gospel version is the later of the two, the Acts version being the earlier. As in the comparison between Acts 10 (the Cornelius episode) and Matthew 28 (the Great Commission to preach to the gentiles), we have to assume that the original story of a revelation from the Spirit eventually became suspect as being dangerously subjective, like the visions of Gnostic heretics, and so gave way to a later, more literal, concrete, objective version in which the earthly Jesus had already guaranteed the point at issue. Hard-nosed conservatives denied the validity of dreams and visions to validate some new development and demanded proof that the earthly Jesus had mandated the controversial novelty. (Of course, if he had, we would not have witnessed such a debate!) From then on, it proved irresistible to supply such proof in the form of a newly invented saying of Jesus.

So, if we find one account of the Twelve being consecrated by the endowment with the Spirit after the resurrection of Jesus, we are not surprised to find another in which they are already constituted as the Twelve in the time of Jesus' earthly ministry. This suggests that the actual origin of this group lay in the days of the early church, not in the earlier time of the earthly Jesus, but that it was eventually imaginatively retrojected into that earlier period.[34]

Smith has eliminated all the narrative material separating the two apostolic legitimization stories. Why has he done it? Remember, all that intervening matter in the Gospels is largely devoted, first, to expounding the teachings that Jesus had supposedly chosen these men to spread. As becomes especially clear in Luke,[35] the reason the disciples have been retrojected into the earthly lifetime of Jesus is so that the bishops of Luke's day could appeal to the Twelve as witnesses of what Jesus really did and said in order to cut the ground from under those who would like to fashion their own arbitrary reminiscences.

Once you retroject the post-resurrection group of Twelve back before the crucifixion, you inadvertently produce the anomaly that, though already working with Jesus, the disciples seem completely unprepared for what happens to Jesus. To put the Twelve on the scene with Jesus to have them share his charisma by association is to present the Twelve as already in the role of triumphant, elite authorities, much like a group of local Congressmen posing for pictures with the president. But this stance ill-befits a narrative the whole point of which is to have Jesus inexorably moving towards a tragic martyr death. When Simon Peter dares rebuke the soon-to-be-suffering Son of Man, "God forbid, Lord! This shall never happen to you!" (Matt. 16:22), he is saying no more than Paul says in Romans 5:9: "For we know that Christ, being raised from the dead, will never die again." The difference is that whereas Paul writes *explicitly* after the resurrection of Christ, Peter in Matthew speaks *implicitly* after the resurrection.

As Theodore J. Weeden boldly delineated in his *Mark: Traditions in Conflict*,[36] the clash between arrogant triumphalism on the part of the Twelve and self-abasing servanthood embodied by Jesus reflects an early church debate between those who brag, "I am of Cephas (or Paul, or Apollos)" versus those who say, "I am of Christ!" In 2 Corinthians Paul makes it clear that his own career of apostolic suffering and set-back is *ipso facto* more Christ-like than that of the miracle-mongering "super-apostles" of Corinth simply because the power of God is seen nowhere better than amid the cruciform sufferings of men.[37] Though Joseph Smith himself would finally follow in his master's footsteps to the atoning gallows, his New Christianity as shown in 3 Nephi is a triumphal Christianity without the cross. Keep in mind that once Jesus touches down in ancient America, we are seeing a recap of major Gospel events. We are seeing, so to speak, the American version of the Gospel. The story is being acted out almost like a Hill Cumorah Pageant by multitudes like those of Galilee, by disciples such as Peter and Andrew, and by the Savior himself, and it all eventuates in Jesus appointing the New Twelve and then returning to heaven. All is there, all in place as in the original Gospel narrative, save that the cross is nowhere to be found. This is the Docetic Christology of Gnostics, Encratites, Muslims and others. Christ appears in the world to teach authoritatively, to set up the institution that tells such stories as this one in his name, and then to return to heaven, but by no means to die.

Some may protest this reading since, obviously, the whole business is happening after the crucifixion and resurrection in Jerusalem. Why should Jesus die again? Yes, but then why does he appear in America at all? Why not just have missionaries from Jerusalem make their way to America to announce the momentous tidings that have taken place in the Holy Land? Or, to put it another way, if Jesus himself had to appear to the ancient Americans, why did he not also appear personally to the Corinthians, the Ephesians, the Romans, etc.? To have Jesus appear in person in ancient America and essentially repeat the gospel story is to posit a separate and distinctive incarnation of Jesus Christ for America. To make the pattern complete, we might have expected to see Jesus crucified anew by wicked Lamanites. And that is exactly what we would see except for a different Christology, that of a Christ with a crown rather than a cross.

Here again, Smith's redaction of the Gospel story enables us to look back at the New Testament Gospels and see things in a clearer light. For Smith has recapitulated the Christological evolution underlying the Gospels. At first, we may imagine, the atoning martyrdom of Jesus made sense as a way of rationalizing the shock the disciples felt at God allowing his faithful servant to die. It was to be understood as the wisdom of God made manifest in the foolishness of men. This is the way Paul sees it in 1 Corinthians 1:18-25 where he mentions no miracles, nothing spectacular, only a crucified man. Early Christians expected the imminent return of "this same Jesus" (Acts 1:11) who would make his next appearance as "the Messiah appointed for you" (Acts 3:20). His Messiahship lay in the imminent future, not in the past. But as more time went by and still no second coming materialized, Christians began to reinterpret the past career of Jesus, the only one available to them, in messianic terms, adding the technicolor of miracles and divine self-disclosures.[38] In the Gospels, later than Paul, Jesus becomes a demigod striding the earth. When arrested, he flattens the soldiers like bowling pins with a single utterance (Jn. 18:6) and then condescends to come along quietly anyway.[39]

Paradoxes and historical implausibilities like these reflect the ill fit of the two motifs now forcibly juxtaposed in the Gospels: the tragic martyrdom of a superhuman demigod! The ultimate conclusion to this line of reasoning is to say that since Jesus *could* not be defeated and destroyed by his enemies, then he *wasn't.* As in the *Gospel of Peter,* where the crucified Jesus feels no pain, or in the *Acts of John,* where Jesus appears to John in a cave in the Mount of Olives to tell him that the form on the cross is not really he. Or as in the *Gospel of Barnabas* where Jesus ascends to heaven during the arrest while some other man is taken and crucified. The Book of Mormon has gone the whole way: in its American incarnation of Jesus, a "second first coming," so to speak, the crucifixion is *eliminated altogether.* The tension found in the Gospels between an original account of the Servant Messiah tragically martyred and the later overlay of triumphalism where, in truth, it is the resurrected Jesus who appears throughout from the baptism on,[40] is neatly eliminated in the Book of Mormon in favor of the latter conception. It is *explicitly* the mighty Risen One who appears in America, just as for the canonical Gospels it is *implicitly* the Risen One who is born in Bethlehem and continues on throughout the story. As the Christology of divine triumphalism had already won the day in Corinth (occasioning Paul's polemics, already quoted), it has long reigned unopposed in optimistic, "can-do" American Christianity, no matter the denominational label on the bottle. But Latter-day Saints are the only ones to make it so explicit.

IF IT TARRY, WAIT FOR IT

We ought to note briefly that Joseph Smith was not without precedent when he wrote of a parallel life and ministry of Jesus taking place in his own homeland to supply an independent pedigree for the faith community there. The various British tales of young Jesus visiting the shores of Britain with his uncle Joseph of Arimathea, and of Joseph later returning there carrying the Holy Grail with him, are foundation legends for Celtic Christianity, trying to stake an apostolic claim independent of Rome.[41] Advocates of the British Israel theory[42] and Christian Identity sects still employ these legends for the same reason.[43] And Smith was doing the same sort of thing, inventing a separate origin for his own kind of American Christianity. The idea is summed up well in Galatians 1:11-12, "For I would have you know, brethren, that the gospel that was preached by me is not according to man. For I did not receive it from man, nor was I taught it, but it came through a revelation of Jesus Christ." Paul, in order to protect his own independent authority, denies he is in any way dependent on the earlier apostles or that his Christianity is derivative from theirs or possibly a distortion of it, as someone seems to have been alleging. Rather, he reverses the implied accusation: since his gospel came directly from God, then if that of the Jerusalem apostles is in any important respect at variance, it is the Jerusalem apostles who must be the heretics, the revisionists, just as the USSR and China used to accuse one another of being revisionists distorting the pure Marxist-Leninist gospel. In the same way, Smith, by having Jesus Christ himself found the Nephite church in America, is claiming to have his Christianity direct from the horse's mouth. If the Methodist, Baptist, and Congregationalist ministers choose to remain aloof from his reforms, they are only incriminating themselves as heirs of a corrupt gospel, a degenerate Christianity, "another Jesus, a different Spirit, a different gospel" (2 Cor. 11:4). Smith would say with Paul, "I think that I am not in the least inferior to these superlative apostles" (2 Cor. 11:5).

So, to return to the main point, the story in 3 Nephi collapses the two-fold story of the authorization of the original Twelve into a single continuous story directly linking the choosing of the Nephite Twelve with their Pentecost of the Spirit and fire. In the Gospels and Acts, these events in the lives of the Jerusalem apostles are separated by many chapters because in the Gospels, the original Twelve are used as object lessons or "straight men" during the teaching period of Jesus' ministry, often in order to warn the reader about the seductions and abuses of power in the church hierarchy (cf. Mk. 9:33-35; 10:35-37, 41; 1 Cor. 1:11-12; 12:21-25). This is inevitably the sort of argument made by those who do not currently wield power, aimed at those who do. By eliminating this material, with its frequent embarrassments to the disciples—that is, by having nothing analogous, nothing with Nephite disciples as the butt of the story—Smith gives an unambiguously positive portrait of the New Twelve. On the one hand, he has implicitly removed the gospel's critique of the kind of power that Smith himself would come to wield and, on the other, he has made the New World Twelve appear superior to their Jerusalem predecessors. Mormon Christianity is thus not merely a return to or a restoration of the primitive church: it is an improvement on the original, and we will presently see another sign pointing in the same direction.

If the Spirit-baptism of the Nephite Twelve recalls both the infilling of the seventy elders of Israel with the Spirit Moses had and the anointing of Elisha with the wonder-working spirit of Elijah, then we find ourselves in position to understand the 3 Nephi motif of Jesus asking the New Twelve, just before he ascends for good, what request they would make of him (3 Ne. 28:1). We do not find such a scene in any of the Gospels except, perhaps, for a garbled echo in Mk. 10:35ff, but we do find it in the analogous scene of dialogue between Elijah and Elisha just before the former ascends into heaven: "Ask what I shall do for you before I am taken from you" (2 Kgs. 2:9). What I am suggesting is that Smith was sensitive to the implicit connections between the sources of the Pentecost narrative upon which he bases the Spirit-baptism scene of the Nephite Twelve and that he used the various original motifs in a new combination to construct his own new episode. He based it on the choosing of the Twelve in Galilee and on the Spirit-baptism of the 120 in Jerusalem on Pentecost, seeing that these passages were in turn dependent on the two Pentateuchal accounts of the ordination of the Seventy as well as the story of the ascension of Elijah.

Smith further reinforces the greater spiritual quality of the New Twelve and the new religion over the old by combining the thrice-repeated Gethsemane prayer in the Synoptics with the so-called High Priestly Prayer of John 17. Here (3 Ne. 19:19-35), Jesus prays in serenity, as seems becoming to the Son of God, not in the indecorous tones of an agitated death row convict as he does in the Synoptic Gethsemane. (John likewise rewrote the scene in Jn. 12:27-30.) And yet, as in the Synoptic Gethsemane, Jesus prays at a distance from them and subsequently returns thrice to his waiting disciples. In the Synoptics Jesus finds the disciples asleep each time he returns to them and we are to understand that they have somehow missed an opportunity to aid him, perhaps to save him from an untimely death. But in 3 Nephi, the New Twelve are made of sterner stuff than the old. Jesus finds them fervently watching and praying. Once again, the New American Christians imagine themselves superior in devotion to the original disciples and the religion represented by them. They are Elisha to mainstream American Protestantism's Elijah.

We have noted that the element of tension between the martyr Jesus and the triumphant demigod Jesus in the Gospels arose as a result of early Christians coping with the delay of the Second Advent by essentially retelling the first coming as if it were already the second, already the coming in divine glory. It was that hindsight reinterpretation that provided the basis for the Book of Mormon's triumphalist Christology. But we are not finished with the New Testament writers' attempts to deal with the anxieties of the delayed parousia of Christ. Let us glance briefly at the three most important New Testament attempts to rationalize the failure of the promise of Jesus made in Mark 9:1 (8:44 in Joseph Smith's Inspired Version), "Amen, I say to you, there are some standing here who will not taste death till they have seen the kingdom of God come with power." This was a dangerous statement, one open to clear and embarrassing disconfirmation. What happened when years went by and all those with Jesus were sound asleep in their graves, like Abraham, not having received what was promised, though espying it, as Moses did the Promised Land, from afar (Heb. 11:13)? Quite a bit of jeering, like what the Emmaus disciples no doubt expected from their neighbors once they got home. Scoffers began to mock, saying, "Where is the promise of his coming? For ever since the fathers [first generation] fell asleep, all things continue on as they have since the beginning of time" (2 Pet. [another pseudepigraph, see below] 3:4).

Christians had their answers ready (1 Pet. 3:15), though we might wonder how convincing they sounded to anyone else. 2 Peter's answer is to say that even though there had been a delay, it was a good thing, not a bad one, since it meant God had extended the deadline for repentance (3:9). Such straw-grabbing transformations of necessity into virtue are typical among end-of-the-world movements whose deadlines pass.[44] Mark's own attempt to sidetrack criticism aimed at the failure of the promise in 9:1 was his placement of the Transfiguration story immediately following the prediction (9:2-8). Mark seems to want to lead the reader to accept the Transfiguration where Jesus appears already as we imagine him in heaven, conversing with his Old Testament colleagues Moses and Elijah, as a kind of proleptic, anticipatory coming of the kingdom of God. Yet this can scarcely have been the original point of the troublesome saying in Mark 9:1. Having forgotten the original apocalyptic meaning of the phrase "kingdom of God" as a future *time,* Mark sees the term, as centuries of subsequent Christians have done, as denoting a *place* far removed from us[45] but of which one might have a vision like Moses did atop Sinai. This would explain why Jesus takes with him only Peter, James, and John: Mark had to adjust the Transfiguration scene to accommodate it to Jesus' having said that only "some" of those standing with him would see the vision before they died. Mark's intent was to reinterpret the promise of the Second Coming as referring to something secretly happening in the generation of Jesus. (Thus also: "Lord, how is it that you will manifest yourself to us, and not to the world?" Jn. 14:22.) It was not generally known because, at the time, only a few saw it and were then sworn to secrecy (Mk. 9:9). In passing, it is worth noting that of all the miracles 2 Peter might have attested, he chooses the Transfiguration (1:16-19) and then makes it somehow a confirmation of the prophecy of Jesus in Mk. 9:1.

We find in John 21, a later appendix to that Gospel (see the original conclusion at the end of chapter 20), a related attempt to explain away the albatross promise. It appears that by the time the Gospel of John was written, of all the Twelve, only the unnamed "Beloved Disciple," traditionally identified with John the son of Zebedee,[46] was left alive, but that soon after, he too gave up the ghost. This occasioned a crisis, as that disciple had been the last ray of hope that the second advent might come soon. With him dead, the scoffing began in earnest.

The response of "the community of the Beloved Disciple"[47] was to append a new chapter to their Gospel containing the famous scene where Jesus tells Peter to mind his own business, that for all he needs to know, the Beloved Disciple might as well be granted to live through the Second Coming. (The same point is made to provide for the delay of the Second Coming in Acts 1:6-8). The original promise, as we read it in Mark 9:1, was made to "some," but in John 21 it has shrunk to apply to the only remaining disciple. (Similarly, we might wonder if Mk. 13:30 preserves a still earlier version where the whole generation was expected to behold the Parousia and that Mk. 9:1 is already a later narrowing of scope to accommodate the death of the greater part of Jesus' contemporaries.)

The far-fetched apologetical argument in John 21:23 is that technically Jesus didn't say that the Beloved Disciple *would* live till the Parousia, only that, *hypothetically,* he *might.* Like Matthew's attempt to disarm the scoffing of opponents on another front (Matt. 27:62-66; 28:4, 11-15), we may wonder if this rebuttal produced less skepticism or more. At any rate, we are going to find both Mark's and John's attempts to explain away the failure of the Parousia reflected in our 3 Nephi passage. There Smith has ingeniously utilized both underlying passages in the service of a radically new way of dealing with the problem, one that in the 1820s had become all the more serious.

APOCALYPSE AND APOLOGIA

First, in 3 Nephi 19, we find clear borrowings from the Synoptic Transfiguration narratives (there being none in John's Gospel, since there Jesus is practically transfigured from page one[48]): "And it came to pass that Jesus blessed them as they did pray unto him; and his countenance did smile upon them, and behold they were as white as the countenance and also the garments of Jesus; and behold the whiteness thereof did exceed all the whiteness, yea, even there could be nothing upon earth so white as the whiteness thereof" (3 Ne. 19:25). In verses 31-34, we learn that Jesus went on to pray to the Father in glossolalic utterances beyond the capacity of mere humans to relate or record. It is a moment of epiphany like that of Paul, swept up to the Third Heaven in 2 Corinthians 12:1-10. The same set of elements recur later on in the sequel to this scene in 3 Nephi 28. Jesus, in a last dialogue with the Nephite apostles before his final ascension—the whole scene being strikingly reminiscent of the Nag Hammadi Gnostic text, the *Apocryphon of James,* wherein Jesus has ascended from the Mount of Olives and returned before reascending for good–bids each one make whatever request he wishes. Nine of them make the unspectacular request that when, as old men, their labors in the gospel are over, they may leave the world behind to join their Lord in Heaven. (What had they expected otherwise?) That artificial-sounding request reveals its point only after Jesus asks the same question of the last three disciples. They remain coyly silent until Jesus draws them out, whereupon they admit that, like the compassionate Bodhisattvas of Mahayana Buddhism who defer their own well-earned Nirvana to labor on for the good of others, they would prefer to remain alive in the flesh to spread the gospel till the end of the age. To depart and be with Christ would be good, but to continue on for the sake of the churches is better (Phil. 1:23-25).

Jesus happily grants their request, and to equip them for their long career, he transfigures them so their bodies will neither age and die nor succumb to attempts to martyr them. "Therefore, that they might not taste of death there was a change wrought upon their bodies, that they might not suffer pain nor sorrow save it were for the sins of the world" (28:38). And then the narrator takes the reader on a proleptic survey of the vicissitudes they will endure, thanks to this divine empowerment. Most of these are derived from Paul's catalogue of apostolic sufferings in 2 Corinthians 11:23-33,[49] a passage adjacent to that of Paul's heavenly journey which Smith used in composing the scene in 3 Nephi 19 where Jesus speaks revelations that man may not utter. The same source is used again here in 3 Nephi 28 since the Nephite disciples are made to share the Pauline rapture and to hear the unutterable secrets spoken in the tongues of angels (cf. *The Testament of Job* XLVIII-L where Job's daughters are overcome with heavenly rapture and speak with the tongues of angels. There, too, we are told that the utmost revelations received upon that occasion have been discretely left unrecorded [LI:4]). In short, what happened to Jesus himself in chapter 19 will now happen to them in chapter 28. When one adds the note that they will suffer to atone for sins (!), all becomes clear: the Three Nephites are veritable vicars of Christ on earth. (Again, we are strikingly reminded of the *Apocryphon of James* where Jesus, about to ascend, challenges the disciples to become like him, even to ascend into heaven like him, even to get there before him![50])

Second, the request of the three Nephite Bodhisattvas is also more than a little reminiscent of another revelation vouchsafed to Joseph Smith, that recorded in Doctrine and Covenants 7. Not only is the stylistic similarity to the Book of Mormon revealing, implying that the Book of Mormon originated in the same fashion as the narrative of Doctrine and Covenants 7, the content forms an exact parallel to the story of the Three Nephites in 3 Nephi 28. The Doctrine and Covenants reads:

> And the Lord said unto me: "John, my beloved [note that Smith makes explicit the traditional guess that the Beloved Disciple was John, son of Zebedee], what desirest thou? For if you shall ask what you will, it shall be granted unto you." And I said unto him: "Lord, give unto me power over death, that I may live and bring souls unto thee." And the Lord said unto me: "Verily, verily, I say unto thee, because thou desirest this thou shalt tarry until I come in my glory, and shalt prophesy before nations, kindreds, tongues and people[s]." And for this cause the Lord said unto Peter: "If I will that he tarry till I come, what is that to thee? For he desired of me that he might bring souls unto me, but thou desiredst that thou mightest come speedily unto me in my kingdom. I say unto thee, Peter, this was a good desire; but my beloved has desired that he might do more, or a greater work; therefore I will make him as a flaming fire and a ministering angel; he shall minister for those who shall be heirs of salvation who dwell on the earth. And I will make thee to minister for him and for thy brother James; and unto you three I will give this power and the keys of this ministry until I come" (7:1-6; interestingly, this expansion of John 21 does not occur in Smith's Inspired Version of the Bible).

Here are all the basic elements of 3 Nephi 28: Jesus invites the disciples to make any request of him before he ascends. In verse 4's analepsis (implied flashback), we learn that he had already elicited and granted Peter's request which involved ministering for Christ till he died and then going straight to the heavenly kingdom, precisely as the first nine Nephite disciples asked in 3 Nephi 28:2, "We desire ... that we may speedily come unto thee in thy kingdom." Thus there is exactly the same contrast between Peter (and implicitly James) on the one hand and John on the other as we see in the case of the nine Nephite disciples and the last three, almost word for word.

Again, like the Three Nephites, John is miraculously transfigured to make possible such longevity. This is closely reminiscent of the transfiguration of the patriarch Enoch into the fiery form of the angel Metatron, the Lesser Yahve, in the Hekhaloth apocalypse *3 Enoch.* Enoch, like John, was the especial beloved of God (Gen. 5:24). Thus the same honor is granted to both, just as in early Christian Adoptionist Christology it was Jesus himself, having proved his worth as a servant of God, who was transfigured and taken up to reign alongside of God (see *Shepherd of Hermas,* Similitude 5, 6:1-8).

Incidentally, it seems highly probable that, in view of the mention in the Doctrine and Covenants of the three Pillars (Gal. 2:9), James, Peter, and John,[51] Smith had them in mind already as the model for the Three Nephites in 3 Nephi, making the trio of Nephite Beloved Disciples into the Nephite Pillars in one case and exalting John above the other two in the other case. Note that just as John's Gospel left the identity of the Beloved Disciple a secret, so does 3 Nephi pointedly refuse to disclose the names of the Three Nephites.

I think it no accident that in 3 Nephi 19 and 28 and in Doctrine and Covenants 7, Smith has taken up elements from the Synoptic Transfiguration as well as from the dialogue between Jesus and Peter over the fate of John and worked them together into two parallel narratives in which John in one case and the Three Nephites in the other are transfigured to remain upon the earth till the Second Coming. The effect of the singular juxtaposition and recombination of these various elements is to come up with a completely new explanation of the delay of the Parousia. You will recall that Mark's strategy was to reinterpret "seeing the kingdom of God come with power" as a reference not to the end of the age but rather to the Transfiguration, something *else* that *could* have been seen before the death of the disciples. John's strategy was quite different: he tried to escape the terrible embarrassment by saying that everyone had stupidly misinterpreted not the character of the predicted Eschaton as in Mark, but rather the role of the Beloved Disciple in that scenario. The disappointed Millerites of the nineteenth century used pretty much the Johannine rationalization (William Miller must have misinterpreted Daniel's prophecy of the judgment to occur on 21 March 1844), while Jehovah's Witnesses preferred the Markan strategy when their own date for the Second Advent passed, reinterpreting what it was that had invisibly taken place.

Smith rejected the assumption, common to Mark and John, that the kingdom of God as predicted by Jesus was supposed to come *before the expiration of normal life spans.* John 21:22 would never have created the crisis implied by the narrator's desperate reinterpretation unless the saying, like the promise in Mark 9:1, had been universally taken to presuppose that the disciples would die. When, in Mormon scripture, Jesus grants the requests of the Three Nephites and of John for eternal life in the flesh, he supposes nothing else than the long continuance of the world beyond apostolic times. Smith's bold version may justly be ranked as equally or more desperate than the reinterpretations of Mark 9 and John 21, but it is no less brilliant for that.

Essentially, Smith makes these four characters assume the role of the Wandering Jew.[52] This Passion legend, cut from the same pious cloth as the tales of St. Veronica and of Longinus the blind centurion at the cross, depicts a Jew in the crowd along the Via Dolorosa who reviles Jesus in his lowest moment and is cursed by Jesus to "Tarry till I come again." He walks wearily through the world seeing sorrow upon sorrow, never to be released from this tiresome penance till the trump of Gabriel should sound. Probably intended as an allegory justifying the tribulations of Jews through the centuries, the legend in all of its many forms obviously presupposes that the bitter exchange between Jesus and the Jews occurred in the distant past; thus the motif cannot possibly have been an early one. Even so, Smith's application of the same motif to John and the Three Nephites reveals itself to be no tradition from the era of Jesus but rather a late apologetical attempt to root out a problem that could only be solved by rewriting the story.

And finally, it is perhaps not right to say that Smith's version has the world continue far beyond the limits of the Apostolic Era. It would be closer to the truth to say that, by elongating the lives and apostolic ministries of John and the Three Nephites, Smith is extending the Apostolic Age up to and including our own time. The apostles turn out to be our contemporaries in the literal sense! New chapters continue to be added to the Acts of the Apostles in our own day. And need we add that this was exactly the point of a *new* "ancient" scripture to be added onto the canon.[53] Smith himself was that Nephi unto whom Jesus spoke one day, saying, "Behold, other scriptures I would that ye should write, that ye have not. ... How be it that ye have not written this thing, that many saints did arise and appear unto many and did minister unto them?" (3 Ne. 23:6, 11). "And now it came to pass that Jesus commanded that it should be written; therefore it was written according as he commanded" (3 Ne. 23:13). It was called the Book of Mormon, with none other than Joseph Smith for its inspired author.

NOTES

1. Norman Golb, *Who Wrote the Dead Sea Scrolls? The Search for the Secret of Qumran* (New York: Scribners, 1995), 382-85.

2. Traditionally, scholars have taken for granted that the Dead Sea Scrolls were the product of Essene scribes living in a monastery at Qumran. Though Norman Golb has cast serious, even damning, doubt on this assumption, many scholars continue to cling to the notion. John J. Collins (*The Scepter and the Star: The Messiahs of the Dead Sea Scrolls and Other Ancient Literature* [New York: Doubleday, 1995]) maintains substantially the traditional Essene view, while Robert Eisenman, who identifies the scrolls' Teacher of Righteousness with Jesus' brother James the Just, the Wicked Priest with Ananas, and the Spouter of Lies as Paul, believes that Qumran was a monastery (Eisenman and Michael Wise, trans., *The Dead Sea Scrolls Uncovered* [Rockport: Element, 1992]; Eisenman, *Maccabees, Zadokites, Christians and Qumran: A New Hypothesis of Qumran Origins,* Studia Post-Biblica XXXIV [Leiden: E. J. Brill, 1983]; *James the Just in the Habakkuk Pesher,* Studia Post-Biblica XXXV [Leiden: E. J. Brill, 1986]; Michael Baigent and Richard Leigh, *The Dead Sea Scrolls Deception* [New York: Simon and Schuster, 1993]), as does Barbara Thiering, who identifies the Wicked Priest as Jesus and the Teacher of Righteousness as John the Baptist (*The Gospels and Qumran: A New Hypothesis,* Australian and New Zealand Studies in Theology and Religion [Sydney: Theological Explorations, 1981]; *The Qumran Origins of the Christian Church,* Australian and New Zealand Studies in Theology and Religion [Sydney: Theological Explorations, 1983]; *Jesus and the Riddle of the Dead Sea Scrolls: Unlocking the Secrets of his Life Story* [New York: Harper-Collins, 1992]; *Jesus of the Apocalypse: The Life of Jesus After the Crucifixion* [New York: Doubleday, 1995]).

3. Kurt Rudolf, *Gnosis: The Nature and History of Gnosticism,* trans. Robert McLachlan Wilson (New York: Harper & Row, 1983), 43.

4. Whitney R. Cross, *The Burned-Over District: The Social and Intellectual History of Enthusiastic Religion in Western New York, 1800-1850* (New York: Harper & Row, 1965).

5. Jacques Derrida, *Of Grammatology,* trans. Gayatri Chakravorty Spivak (Baltimore: Johns Hopkins University Press, 1978), Part II, chaps. 1 and 2, 101-64.

6. See Dan Vogel, *Religious Seekers and the Advent of Mormonism* (Salt Lake City: Signature Books, 1988).

7. Lama Anagarika Govinda, "Introductory Foreword" to W. Y. Evans-Wentz, ed., *The Tibetan Book of the Dead; Or the After-Death Experiences on the Bardo Plane, According to Lama Kazi Dawa-Samdup's English Rendering* (New York: Oxford University Press, 1978), liv-lv.

8. William Nelson, *Fact or Fiction: The Dilemma of the Renaissance Storyteller* (Cambridge, MA: Harvard University Press, 1973).

9. Hans Frei, *The Eclipse of Biblical Narrative: A Study in Eighteenth- and Nineteenth-Century Hermeneutics* (New Haven, CT: Yale University Press, 1977); George A. Lindbeck, *The Nature of Doctrine: Religion and Theology in a Postliberal Age* (Philadelphia: Westminster Press, 1984); William C. Placher, *Unapologetic Theology: A Christian Voice in a Pluralistic Conversation* (Louisville, KY: Westminster/John Knox, 1989).

10. Peter L. Berger and Thomas Luckmann, *The Social Construction of Reality: A Treatise in the Sociology of Knowledge* (Garden City, NY: Doubleday Anchor, 1967), 25.

11. Rudolf Bultmann, "New Testament and Mythology," in Hans Werner Bartsch, ed., *Kerygma and Myth,* trans. Reginald H. Fuller (New York: Harper & Row, 1961), 5.

12. Paul D. Hanson, *The Dawn of Apocalyptic: The Historical and Sociological Roots of Jewish Apocalyptic Eschatology* (Philadelphia: Fortress Press, 1975), 252.

13. D. S. Russell, *The Method and Message of Jewish Apocalyptic 200 BC–AD 100* (Philadelphia: Westminster Press, 1964), 127-39; John J. Collins, *The Apocalyptic Imagination: An Introduction to the Jewish Matrix of Christianity* (New York: Crossroad, 1989), 30-31.

14. Frank Kermode, *The Art of Telling: Essays on Fiction* (Cambridge, MA: Harvard University Press, 1983), chap. 8, "Institutional Control of Interpretation," 168-84; James Barr, *The Bible in the Modern World* (New York: Harper & Row, 1973), chap. IX, "Limitation and Selection," 150-67.

15. Walter J. Hollenweger, *The Pentecostals: The Charismatic Movement in the Churches* (Minneapolis: Augsburg, 1973), 31-32: "It was now realized that the recently formed Assemblies of God would have to take action against the innovators ["Jesus Only" or "Oneness" believers], as vigorously as the Methodists, Baptists and Holiness denominations had acted against themselves [the Pentecostals] ten years previously"; David Reed, "Aspects of the Origins of Oneness Pentecostalism," in Vinson Sinan, ed., *Aspects of Pentecostal-Charismatic Origins* (Plainfield, IL: Logos International, 1975), 143-68.

16. See Clark H. Pinnock, *Biblical Revelation: The Foundation of Christian Theology* (Chicago: Moody Press, 1976), 94: "Critical theories which propose deceitful literary forms and historical blunders do indeed manifest belief in the humanity of Scripture, but explicitly repudiate its divine authorship."

17. Gordon H. Fraser, *What Does the Book of Mormon Teach? An Examination*

of the Historical and Scientific Statements of the Book of Mormon (Chicago: Moody Press, 1964).

18. William J. Samarin, *Tongues of Men and Angels: The Religious Language of Pentecostalism* (New York: Macmillan, 1972); Eugene A. Nida, *Glossolalia: A Case of Pseudo-Linguistic Structure,* cited in John P. Kildahl, *The Psychology of Speaking in Tongues* (New York: Harper & Row, 1972), 47; Felitias D. Goodman, *Speaking in Tongues: A Cross-Cultural Study of Glossolalia* (Chicago: University of Chicago Press, 1972), 99-125.

19. Martin Dibelius, *From Tradition to Gospel,* trans. Bertram Lee Woolf (New York: Scribner's, n.d.); Rudolf Bultmann, *History of the Synoptic Tradition,* trans. John Marsh (New York: Harper & Row, 1972); Vincent Taylor, *The Formation of the Gospel Tradition* (London: Macmillan, 1957); Joachim Jeremias, *The Parables of Jesus,* trans. S. H. Hooke (New York: Harper & Row, 1954; 2nd ed. 1972); Reginald H. Fuller, *The Formation of the Resurrection Narratives* (New York: Macmillan, 1971).

20. Charles H. Talbert, *What Is a Gospel? The Genre of the Canonical Gospels* (Philadelphia: Fortress Press, 1977); Philip L. Shuler, *A Genre for the Gospels: The Biographical Character of Matthew* (Philadelphia: Fortress Press, 1982); Richard A. Burridge, *What Are the Gospels? A Comparison with Graeco-Roman Biography,* Society for New Testament Studies Monograph Series, 70 (New York: Cambridge University Press, 1992).

21. Richard I. Pervo, *Profit with Delight: The Literary Genre of the Acts of the Apostles* (Philadelphia: Fortress Press, 1987); Mikeal C. Parsons and Richard I. Pervo, *Rethinking the Unity of Luke and Acts* (Minneapolis: Fortress Press, 1993); Richard I. Pervo, "Romancing an Oft-Neglected Stone: The Pastoral Epistles and the Epistolary Novel," *Journal of Higher Criticism* 1 (Fall 1994): 25-48.

22. J. C. O'Neil, "Gunkel versus Wellhausen: The Unfinished Task of the *Religionsgeschichtliche Schule,*" *Journal of Higher Criticism* 2 (Fall 1995): 115-21.

23. Hans Conzelmann, *The Theology of Saint Luke* (originally "The Middle of Time"), trans. Geoffrey Buswell (New York: Harper & Row, 1961); Willi Marxsen, *Mark the Evangelist: Studies on the Redaction History of the Gospel,* trans. James Boyce, Donald Juel, William Poehlmann, and Roy A. Harrisville (New York: Abingdon Press, 1969); Günter Bornkamm, Gerhard Barth, and Heinz Joachim Held, *Tradition and Interpretation in Matthew,* New Testament Library, trans. Percy Scott (Philadelphia: Westminster, 1969); Joachim Rohde, *Rediscovering the Teaching of the Evangelists,* trans. Dorothea M. Barton, New Testament Library (Philadelphia: Westminster, 1968); Norman Perrin, *What Is Redaction Criticism?* Guides to Biblical Scholarship (Philadelphia: Fortress Press, 1976).

24. Frank Kermode, *The Genesis of Secrecy: On the Interpretation of Narrative* (Cambridge: Harvard University Press, 1979); Robert M. Fowler, *Let the Reader Understand: Reader-Response Criticism and the Gospel of Mark* (Minneapolis: Fortress Press, 1991); Werner H. Kelber, ed., *The Passion in Mark: Studies*

on Mark 14-16 (Philadelphia: Fortress Press, 1976); Frans Neirynck, *Duality in Mark: Contributions to the Study of the Markan Redaction,* Bibliotheca Ephemeridum Theologicarum Lovaniensium XXXI (Leuven: Leuven University Press, 1972); Mark Allan Powell, *What Is Narrative Criticism?* Guides to Biblical Scholarship (Minneapolis: Fortress Press, 1990); Earl Richard, *Acts 6:1-8:4: The Author's Method of Composition,* SBL Dissertation Series 41 (Missoula: Scholars Press, 1978).

25. John Dominic Crossan, *The Cross that Spoke: The Origins of the Passion Narratives* (San Francisco: Harper & Row, 1988); Crossan, *The Historical Jesus: The Life of a Mediterranean Jewish Peasant* (San Francisco: Harper-Collins, 1991), 367-90.

26. Thomas Louis Brodie, "Luke the Literary Interpreter: Luke-Acts as a Systematic Rewriting and Updating of the Elijah-Elisha Narrative in 1 and 2 Kings" (Pontifical University of Saint Thomas Aquinas, 1981), 173-88.

27. Randel Helms, *Gospel Fictions* (Buffalo: Prometheus Books, 1988), 21.

28. "What happens when a mystic encounters the holy scriptures of his tradition is briefly this: the sacred text is smelted down and a new dimension is discovered in it. In other words, the sacred text loses its shape and takes on a new one for the mystic. ... The holiness of the texts resides precisely in their capacity for such metamorphosis" (Gershom Scholem, *On the Kabbalah and Its Symbolism,* trans. Ralph Manheim [New York: Schocken Books, 1974], 11-12).

29. Isaac Beshevis Singer, *Satan in Goray,* trans. Jacob Sloan (New York: Fawcett Crest, 1955), 140.

30. Ibid., 146-47.

31. E.g., Michael D. Goulder, *Midrash and Lection in Matthew* (London: SPCK, 1974).

32. Dennis Ronald MacDonald, *The Legend and the Apostle: The Battle for Paul in Story and Canon* (Philadelphia: Westminster, 1983), 17-33.

33. Ethan Smith, *View of the Hebrews; Or the Tribes of Israel in America* (Poultney, VT, 1823; 2nd ed., 1825).

34. Walter Schmithals, *The Office of Apostle in the Early Church,* trans. John E. Steely (New York: Abingdon Press, 1969), 68-70.

35. Charles H. Talbert, *Luke and the Gnostics: An Examination of the Lucan Purpose* (New York: Abingdon Press, 1966), chap. 1, "The Authentic Witness," 17-32.

36. Theodore J. Weeden, *Mark: Traditions in Conflict* (Philadelphia: Fortress Press, 1971).

37. Dieter Giorgi, *The Opponents of Paul in Second Corinthians,* trans. Harold Attridge, et al., (Philadelphia: Fortress Press, 1986).

38. William Wrede, *The Messianic Secret,* trans. J. C. G. Greig, The Library of Theological Translations (Greenwood: Attic Press, 1971).

39. Ernst Käsemann calls this a "naive docetism" on John's part (see *The Testament of Jesus: A Study of the Gospel of John in Light of Chapter 17,* trans. Gerhard Krodel [Philadelphia: Westminster Press, 1978], 26).

40. James M. Robinson, "On the *Gattung* of Mark (and John)," in Donald G. Miller, ed., *Jesus and Man's Hope* (Pittsburgh: Pittsburgh Theological Seminary, 1970), 99-130. Robinson demonstrates the early Christian tendency to superimpose a later, post-Easter period of plain revelation of Christian doctrines onto the earlier, pre-Easter period of enigmas and parables, resulting in the obscuring of that pre-Easter stage as well as any difference between the two periods.

41. Arthur Edward Waite, *The Hidden Church of the Holy Graal: Its Legends and Symbolism Considered in Their Affinity with Certain Mysteries of Initiation and Other Traces of a Secret Tradition in Christian Times* (London: Rebman Limited, 1909), Book VII, "The Holy Graal in the Light of the Celtic Church," 433-61; Lionel Smithett Lewis, *St. Joseph of Arimathea at Glastonbury: Or the Apostolic Church of Britain* (London: James Clarke & Co. LTD, 1964); R. W. Morgan, *St. Paul in Britain; Or the Origin of British as Opposed to Papal Christianity* (London: Covenant Publishing Co. LTD, 1925).

42. J. H. Allen, *Judah's Sceptre and Joseph's Birthright: An Analysis of the Prophecies of the Scriptures in Regard to the Royal Family of Judah and the Many Nations of Israel, the Ten Lost Tribes* (Merrimac: Destiny Publishers, 1917); H. L. Goudge, *The British Israel Theory* (New York: Morehouse-Gorham Co., 1943).

43. Michael Barkun, *Religion and the Racist Right: The Origins of the Christian Identity Movement* (Chapel Hill: University of North Carolina Press, 1994); "The Identity Movement," in J. Gordon Melton, *Encyclopedic Handbook of Cults in America,* Garland Reference Library of Social Science, vol. 797; Religious Information Systems Series, vol. 7 (Revised and Updated Edition; New York: Garland Publishing, 1992), 68-80; William L. Ingram, "God and Race: British Israelism and Christian Identity," in Timothy Miller, ed., *America's Alternative Religions* (Albany: State University of New York Press, 1995), 119-26.

44. Leon Festinger, Henry W. Rieken, and Stanley Schachter, *When Prophecy Fails: A Social and Psychological Study of a Modern Group that Predicted the Destruction of the World* (New York: Harper & Row, 1964), chap. I, "Unfulfilled Prophecies and Disappointed Messiahs," 3-32.

45. Johannes Weiss, *Jesus' Proclamation of the Kingdom of God,* trans. Richard H. Hiers and D. Larrimore Holland, Lives of Jesus Series (Philadelphia: Fortress Press, 1971); Rudolf Otto, *The Kingdom of God and the Son of Man: A Study in the History of Religion* (Boston: Starr King Press, 1938; 2nd ed., 1943; rpt., 1951).

46. R. Alan Culpepper, *John the Son of Zebedee: The Life of a Legend* (Columbia: University of South Carolina Press, 1994); James H. Charlesworth, *The Beloved Disciple: Whose Witness Validates the Gospel of John?* (Valley Forge: Trinity Press International, 1995).

47. Raymond E. Brown, *The Community of the Beloved Disciple: The Life, Loves, and Hates of an Individual Church in New Testament Times* (New York: Paulist Press, 1979).

48. Käsemann, *Testament of Jesus,* chap. II, "The Glory of Christ," 4-26.

49. Here, too, we find Smith's eagle-eye at work. As Darrell J. Doughty has only recently pointed out, the list of Pauline sufferings, far from contrasting with the depiction of Paul in Acts as a triumphant "divine man" (as Ernst Hänchen and Philipp Vielhauer contend), seems to presuppose precisely such a "Pauline legend." Joseph Smith could see this with no trouble, as is implied when he ascribes the same resume of martyr-sufferings to the Three Nephites who endure it all by virtue of having superhuman transfigured bodies.

50. The frequent parallels between specific Book of Mormon texts and various Jewish and Gnostic Christian pseudepigrapha call for a much more extensive study than is possible to even begin here.

51. Roman Catholic exegetes have traditionally identified James the Just with James the son of Zebedee, while Protestants have identified James the Just as Jesus' brother, distinguishing the other James as another person altogether. On the Protestant reading, the brother of Jesus becomes one of the three Pillars without having been numbered among the disciples of Jesus.

52. George K. Anderson, *The Legend of the Wandering Jew* (Hanover: Brown University Press; University Press of New England, 1965), 101-102, identifies the Three Nephites as variants of the Wandering Jew but says nothing of the application of the same motif to John in the Doctrines and Covenants.

53. 2 Peter is itself a pseudepigraph closely analogous to the Book of Mormon in trying to extend the Apostolic Age into its readers' time, in this case, somewhere in the mid-second century. It invokes Peter to address new problems which have arisen since "the fathers fell asleep," including Peter himself!

CONTRIBUTORS

SCOTT C. DUNN (M.A., applied linguistics, Brigham Young University) is the former production manager of *BYU Studies* and former managing editor of *Sunstone* magazine. He is the author of *Samoan for Missionaries,* a textbook used by the LDS Missionary Training Center, and has published in the *Journal of Mormon History* and elsewhere. He is currently a technical writer in the computer industry–a contributing editor for *PC World* and contributor to *The PC Bible,* 2nd. ed. He lives in Seattle, Washington.

EDWIN FIRMAGE, JR. (M.A., ancient history, University of California, Berkeley) is a contributor to the *Anchor Bible Dictionary* and *Theologishes Wörterbuch zum Alten Testament* and has published in such journals as *Maarav* and *Vetus Testamentum.* He is currently a fine-art photographer and printer in Salt Lake City and the recent publisher of *Simple Gifts: Photographs and Reflections from the Landscape,* with original essays by the Dalai Lama, Thomas Merton Legacy Trust executor Patrick Hart, environmentalist Chip Ward, and others.

THOMAS W. MURPHY (M.A., anthropology, University of Washington) is chair of the Department of Anthropology at Edmonds Community College Lynnwood, Washington, where he is also advisor to the Native American Student Association. He has published in *Ethnohistory, Journal for the Scientific Study of Religion,* and elsewhere, and is the recipient of a Dialogue Foundation Best Article award for "Laban's Ghost: On Writing and Transgression." His dissertation, in progress, is on Mormon representations of American Indians.

ROBERT M. PRICE (Ph.D., New Testament; Ph.D., theology, both from Drew University) is a professor of biblical criticism at the Center for Inquiry Institute in Amherst, New York, and editor of the *Journal of Higher Criticism.* His books include *Deconstructing Jesus, Paul as Text: The Apostle and the Apocrypha,* and *The Widow Traditions in Luke-Acts: A Feminist-Critical Scrutiny*. He has published in *American Rationalist, Deolog, Evangelical Quarterly, Journal of Psychology and Theology, Hervormde Teologiese Studies, Reformed Journal,* and elsewhere.

GEORGE D. SMITH (MBA, New York University) is a founder of Signature Books and president of Smith Research Associates in San Francisco. He is the editor of *An Intimate Chronicle: The Journals of William Clayton, Faithful History: Essays on Writing Mormon History,* and *Religion, Feminism, and Freedom of Conscience: A Mormon/Humanist Dialogue*. He has published on American and Mormon history in *Dialogue: A Journal of Mormon Thought,* the *Journal of the John Whitmer Historical Association, Free Inquiry,* and elsewhere.

SUSAN STAKER (M.A., English, University of Utah) is an editorial director at Adobe Systems in Seattle, Washington, and a former editor at *Sunstone* magazine and Signature Books. She is the co-author of *Sisters and Little Saints: One Hundred Years of Primary,* co-compiler of the index (volume ten) to *Wilford Woodruff's Journal: 1833-1898,* a contributor to *The Prophet Puzzle: Interpretive Essays on Joseph Smith,* and editor of *Waiting for World's End: The Diaries of Wilford Woodruff.* She has published in the *Ensign* and *Utah Historical Quarterly.*

DAN VOGEL (B.A., history, California State University, Long Beach) is a writer living in Westerville, Ohio. His books include *Indian Origins and the Book of Mormon,* the multi-volume *Early Mormon Documents* (Best Documentary Book Award, Mormon History Association), and *Religious Seekers and the Advent of Mormonism.* He has published in *Dialogue: A Journal of Mormon Thought, Journal of the John Whitmer Historical Association, Journal of Mormon History,* and elsewhere, and is currently working on a biography of Joseph Smith.

DAVID P. WRIGHT (Ph.D., Near Eastern studies, University of California, Berkeley) is an associate professor of Judaic studies at Brandeis University in Massachusetts. He is the author of *The Disposal of Impurity: Elimination Rites in the Bible and in Hittite and Mesopotamian Literature* and *Ritual in Narrative: The Dynamics of Feasting, Mourning, and Retaliation Rites in the Ugaritic Tale of Aqhat;* coeditor of *Pomegranates and Golden Bells: Studies in Biblical, Jewish, and Near Eastern Ritual, Law, and Literature;* and a contributor to other volumes.

About the Editors

DAN VOGEL is the author of several books on Mormon history, including the award-winning, five-volume series-in-progress, *Early Mormon Documents*. He is the editor of *The Word of God: Essays on Mormon Scripture* and a contributor to *Differing Visions: Dissenters in Mormon History* and *The Prophet Puzzle: Interpretive Essays on Joseph Smith*, among others. He has delivered papers at the annual Mormon History Association meetings, Sunstone Symposium, and other conferences, and has published in a variety of professional journals. He and his wife live in Westerville, Ohio.

BRENT LEE METCALFE is the editor and host of *Mormon Scripture Studies: An E-Journal of Critical Thought*, editor of *New Approaches to the Book of Mormon: Explorations in Critical Methodology*, and a contributor to other anthologies and journals. He has published on Web site design and engineering at EarthWeb's developer.com and c|net's builder. com, reflecting his career in the computer industry as a developer and technical editor. He is currently employed at an electronic games development studio in Salt Lake City. He and his family live in Draper, Utah.